SEE HOW YOUR COLLEGE EXPERIENCE CAN HELP STUDENTS . . .

1 ▸ SET GOALS

2 ▸ SUCCEED

3 ▸ STAY IN COLLEGE

Written by the leading authorities on ~~first-year seminar~~ and grounded in research, *Your College Experience* by **John Gardner** and **Betsy Barefoot** offers today's diverse students the practical help they need to make the transition to college and get the most out of their time there.

Goal setting has always been central to this text, and the Tenth Edition has been revised with added coverage and activities to strengthen this material throughout. In addition, a new focus on self-assessment of strengths will help students see where they are already succeeding so that they get off to a great start and stay in college.

A full package of instructional support materials—including an Instructor's Annotated Edition, Instructor's Manual, PowerPoint slides, videos, and a Test Bank—provides new and experienced instructors all the tools they will need to engage students in this course and increase student retention.

1 THIS BOOK HELPS STUDENTS SET GOALS

NEW! A new section on goal setting in Chapter 1 gets students thinking about how to succeed right from the start of the course. Then each chapter guides students through a three-step process of assessing their current strengths, setting goals for areas to grow in, and making plans for reaching those goals.

Assessing Your Strengths & Setting Goals boxes in each chapter ask students to identify their strengths and then set goals around their own objectives for the chapter material. This helps students stay engaged throughout the course. ▼

Stay on Track exercises at the end of each chapter ask students to plan how to apply strengths to current and future work in other courses and in their career. ▼

ASSESSING YOUR STRENGTHS

Time management is a challenge for almost all college students. Are you a good time manager? Now that you have read the first section of this chapter, list the strengths you have in this area.

_____

_____

_____

_____

SETTING GOALS

What are your most important objective~~s~~
challenges you have had in the past wit~~h~~
management (e.g., I will keep an hour-b~~y~~

1. _____

_____

2. _____

1 STAY ON TRACK

Successful college students stay focused. They "stay on track." They know what they have to do to be successful, they set goals, and they monitor their progress toward their goals.

Reflect on what you have learned about college success in this chapter and how you are going to apply the chapter information or strategies in college and in your career. List your ideas.

1. _____

_____

_____

_____

2. _____

2 THIS BOOK HELPS STUDENTS SUCCEED

New features throughout the text help students further engage in the course.

NEW! Chapter-opening profiles help students see themselves in the text. Each chapter begins with the true story of a recent first-year student who has used ▶ ▶ ▶ ▶ the strategies in the chapter to succeed in college. Students come from diverse backgrounds and attend all types of colleges around the country.

CHAPTER 3
Understanding Emotional Intelligence

IN THIS CHAPTER YOU WILL EXPLORE

What emotional intelligence is

Why emotional intelligence matters in college and in life

How to assess your emotional intelligence

Specific skills that are connected to emotional intelligence

What you can do to improve your emotional competencies

❝ As an Asian, American culture was totally different for me. People talk, behave, and think in ways that I did not understand. This made me feel insecure about who I was.

Sabeena Maharjan, 21
Journalism and Broadcasting major
Oklahoma City Community College

When Sabeena Maharjan finished high school in 2007, she knew that she wanted to study journalism and broadcasting so that she could use the media to positively effect change in her home country of Nepal. She came to the United States to pursue this dream and opted to enroll at Oklahoma City Community College after speaking with other Nepalese students and with the international student adviser at the college.

Sabeena got involved on campus in the International Students Association. She also partici... ...al activities with fellow ...nts. But, as Sabeena ...her first year in col- ...ging because of the ...r, course load, cul- ...es, and insecurities. ...did not let these chal- ...her determination to ...r ability to understand ...r emotions helped her ...challenging first year. ...ry important to handle

Sabeena Maharjan ▶

Work Together

One way to enhance your memory is through working collaboratively with others. Each of you can share your own memory strategies such as mnemonics or acrostics. You can also check specific facts and details through group consensus.

▲
▲
▲
▲

NEW! Thought-provoking images and exercises in every chapter encourage critical thinking. Features, photos, and exercises include activities to help students master concepts and think critically about the material.

TECH TIP STAY CONNECTED

Whatever your communication MO—smart phone, *Facebook*, or wiki—cyber etiquette is crucial. Just because you're hiding behind a computer screen doesn't mean that you should abandon your classroom manners. Failure to treat your fellow students and instructors with respect will brand you as an ignorant boor. Would you want to share a chat room with someone who writes in all caps (the digital equivalent of shouting) and belittles others' opinions? No one else does either. Emotional intelligence means being aware of your own and others' feelings. Transpose that mantra to your online world and you're good to go.

1 ▶ THE PROBLEM
There's a brave new world of ways to communicate in college, and you feel like you're from another planet.

2 ▶ THE FIX
Learn the nuts and bolts of connecting through cyberspace. If you still have questions, at least you'll have a good idea of what you're talking about.

3 ▶ HOW TO DO IT
1. **E-mail:** The most popular way to communicate online. If you have Internet access, you can send e-mail messages galore, free of charge.

2. **Texting:** Just like passing notes, only it's done between smart phones or other mobile devices. Downside: You have to pay a small fee for the service.

3. **Instant messaging:** Also like passing notes, but via desktop computers and laptops. Upside: Like e-mail, it's free.

4. **Blogs:** Informal Web sites made up of journal entries, articles, and other posts. Note: Blogs can only be modified by their authors, and they can reflect biased or even uninformed viewpoints.

5. **Wikis:** Blogs that invite the world to weigh in on a subject. Visitors can share their knowledge by adding new entries or modifying or deleting old ones. Note: Unlike blogs, wikis often pop up through search engines like Google.

6. **Online social networks:** Web sites that let people share opinions, photos, music, and videos with other registered members of the group.

7. **Chat rooms:** Cybersites people can join to "talk" (i.e., type to one another on keyboards) in real time.

8. **Web conference:** An online meeting between two or more people. Participants often speak to each other via Web-camera (à la *Skype*) and can even work on documents or presentations together.

A FEW WORDS ABOUT TECHNOLOGY OVERLOAD

Apply extreme caution when researching an essay online and simultaneously fielding nonstop phone calls, text messages, e-mails, and *Facebook* updates *and* listening to your iPod: Your brain might explode. Well, not really, but even digital natives need to unplug once in a while.

Excessive multitasking raises your stress levels. It also dulls your powers of concentration, so your work suffers. Experts recommend not trying to do more than two complex tasks at once. And remember: In days of yore, students were happy to go somewhere quiet and read a book, or simply take a walk and think. For a little brain refreshment, why not step away from your gadgets and give one of these old-school, low-tech concepts a whirl?

NEW! Tech Tip features in every ▶ ▶ ▶ ▶ chapter introduce essential skills—such as cyber etiquette in this example—that can span the classroom and real life.

Bedford/St. Martin's is proud to offer a complete package of instructor support materials, including an Instructor's Annotated Edition with strategies and activities to help you teach this course. For more on instructor materials, see the next page.

NEW! The Instructor's Annotated Edition includes clearly marked **Retention Strategies** in every chapter: best practices from John Gardner and Betsy Barefoot for keeping students in school.

■ RETENTION STRATEGY: Introduce the concept of "locus of control," or the extent to which individuals believe they can control events that affect them; then relate the concept to wise choices in time management. Students who learn to take responsibility for their own choices increase their chances of persisting and graduating.

---

22 CHAPTER 2 Managing Your Time

Nine More Minutes

Are you ever tempted to hit the snooze button repeatedly when you shouldn't? In the morning, get up in time to eat breakfast and make it to class without feeling frazzled. Think of your alarm clock as an important tool for college success.

■ RETENTION STRATEGY: Introduce the concept of "locus of control," or the extent to which individuals believe they can control events that affect them; then relate the concept to wise choices in time management. Students who learn to take responsibility for their own choices increase their chances of persisting and graduating.

IN CLASS: Ask students to think about times when they have procrastinated in completing an assignment or a project. Why do they think they procrastinated? Why is procrastination a problem in managing time? Are there psychological reasons why people procrastinate?

IN CLASS: Ask students to share how they dealt with distractions and procrastination. To stimulate discussion, ask students to brainstorm ideas, make a list on the board, and vote on what strategies would work best for them.

internships. If you value learning about many things and postponing a specific decision about your major, you might want to spend your time exploring many different areas of interest and taking as many different types of courses as possible. To take control of your life and your time and to guide your decisions, begin by setting some goals for the future.

OVERCOMING PROCRASTINATION

Procrastination is a serious problem that trips up many otherwise capable people. There are numerous reasons why students procrastinate. In the book *Procrastination: Why You Do It, What to Do About It*, psychologists Jane Burka and Lenora Yuen summarize a number of research studies about procrastination.[1] According to these authors, even students who are highly motivated often fear failure, and some students even fear success (although that might seem counterintuitive). Some students procrastinate because they are perfectionists; not doing a task might be easier than having to live up to your own very high expectations—or those of your parents, teachers, or peers. Others procrastinate because they find an assigned task boring or irrelevant or consider it "busy work," believing that they can learn the material just as effectively without doing the homework.

Simply not enjoying an assignment is not a good reason to put it off; it's an *excuse*, not a valid *reason*. Throughout life you'll be faced with tasks that you don't find interesting, and in many cases you won't have the option not

[1]Jane B. Burka and Lenora M. Yuen, *Procrastination: Why You Do It, What to Do About It* (Reading, MA: Addison-Wesley, 1983).

NEW! This 16-page insert appears at the beginning of the Instructor's Annotated Edition and includes new retention-specific **Active Learning Strategies,** as well as other chapter-specific activities that help with writing, critical thinking, working in groups, planning, reflecting, and taking action.

ACTIVE LEARNING STRATEGIES

FOR INSTRUCTORS ONLY

The following exercises, which do not appear in the student edition, will help your students sharpen their critical skills for college success: writing, critical thinking, learning in groups, planning, reflecting, and taking action. Your students can also further explore the topics of each chapter by completing the exercises on this text's Web site at **bedfordstmartins.com/gardner.**

CHAPTER 1

WORKING TOGETHER The Many Reasons for College

Have your students form small groups to discuss the reasons for attending college, which were covered in this chapter. In the groups, have students share the reasons that seem most relevant to them. Each group should compile a list of the most important reasons and discuss their lists as a class with you as the leader. What did each student learn about himself or herself? What did you learn about each student's priorities?

EXERCISE 1.1 Solving a Problem

Ask your students to respond to the following questions in class or in an e-mail to you: What has been your biggest

chapters that address their most important concerns. Before you assign those chapters, encourage students to read them and try to follow the advice found in the chapters. Take a brief look at the chapters your students have chosen; you will see the topics that concern them most, and you can design your class to appeal to their interests.

RETENTION EXERCISE Smart Goal Setting

Ask students to pick a goal—either short-term or long-term—and ask them to use the SMART template below to make their goal even more attainable. Students who are skilled at setting and attaining goals are more likely to persist in college.

Write a short-term or long-term personal goal that is related to your college experience. Use the

A COMPLETE PACKAGE OF INSTRUCTOR SUPPORT MATERIALS, INCLUDING . . .

The Instructor's Manual with Test Bank
(available in print or online)

Includes everything you need to manage your course:

> Over 300 **NEW** test questions

> Over 800 total multiple-choice, true/false, short answer, and essay questions

> **NEW** midterm and final exams

> **NEW** assessment tests

> **NEW** *Guide to Teaching with YouTube* that helps you select videos for every topic

> Teaching suggestions

> Additional in-class, group, and video exercises

> A list of common concerns of first-year students

> An introduction to the first-year experience course

> A sample lesson plan for each chapter

> Case studies

PowerPoint Slides

Complete lecture outlines for each chapter of the book including images and figures from the text. Use as is or add your own material to make each presentation your own.

French Fries Are Not Vegetables

is a comprehensive instructional DVD featuring three different resources for class and professional use.

> **A 30-minute documentary** follows 5 students through the life-changing transition of the first year of college. Their honest, funny, and intense observations shed light on everything from eating habits to concerns about grades and finances.

> **Conversation Starters** are 16 very brief videos combining student and instructor interviews on the most important topics taught in first-year seminar courses, including money management, diversity, emotional intelligence, and critical thinking.

> **Teaching Ideas and Conversations**, a 45-minute documentary, features 15 expert instructors giving advice on what makes a successful first-year course.

For more information

The following supplements are available: **Instructor's Manual with Test Bank**, the **Computerized Test Bank**, the password-protected **instructor's Web site**, the free **companion Web site**, **VideoCentral**, the *French Fries Are Not Vegetables* DVD, and our **course management solutions**.

> Visit **bedfordstmartins.com/gardner/catalog**.

> Speak with your Bedford/St. Martin's sales rep.

A handy chart on the inside front cover of the **Instructor's Annotated Edition** also shows you where to find each asset.

ACTIVE LEARNING STRATEGIES

The following exercises, which do not appear in the student edition, will help your students sharpen their critical skills for college success: writing, critical thinking, learning in groups, planning, reflecting, and taking action. Your students can also further explore the topics of each chapter by completing the exercises on this text's Web site at **bedfordstmartins.com/gardner**.

CHAPTER 1

WORKING TOGETHER The Many Reasons for College

Have your students form small groups to discuss the reasons for attending college, which were covered in this chapter. In the groups, have students share the reasons that seem most relevant to them. Each group should compile a list of the most important reasons and discuss their lists as a class with you as the leader. What did each student learn about himself or herself? What did you learn about each student's priorities?

EXERCISE 1.1 Solving a Problem

Ask your students to respond to the following questions in class or in an e-mail to you: What has been your biggest unresolved problem in college to date? What steps have you taken to solve it? Respond to students personally, and if they still have questions, invite them to meet with you during office hours.

EXERCISE 1.2 With or Without

This chapter stressed the differences between a high school education and a college education. Ask students to imagine they are still trying to decide whether or not to attend college. Drawing from the material in this chapter as well as from their own ideas, have students make a list of reasons to earn a college degree and a list of reasons not to go to college. For example, pipe fitters earn impressive salaries, while librarians earn much less. How do students justify a college education on those terms?

EXERCISE 1.3 Focusing on Your Concerns

Have students browse the table of contents of this book. Direct them to find one or more chapters that address their most important concerns. Before you assign those chapters, encourage students to read them and try to follow the advice found in the chapters. Take a brief look at the chapters your students have chosen; you will see the topics that concern them most, and you can design your class to appeal to their interests.

RETENTION EXERCISE Smart Goal Setting

Ask students to pick a goal—either short-term or long-term—and ask them to use the SMART template below to make their goal even more attainable. Students who are skilled at setting and attaining goals are more likely to persist in college.

Write a short-term or long-term personal goal that is related to your college experience. Use the SMART method to further develop your goal.

S: How can you make this goal more **S**pecific?

M: How will you **M**easure whether you have attained this goal at a high level?

A: How do you know that there is a reasonable chance you can **A**ttain this goal?

R: How is this goal **R**elevant to your interests and broader sense of life purpose?

T: What is your **T**ime period for achieving this goal?

CHAPTER 2

WORKING TOGETHER Comparing Class Schedules

In small groups, have your students share their current class schedules with each other. Encourage them to exchange ideas on how to handle time-management problems effectively and the challenges they see in each other's schedules. Discuss together how students can arrange their schedules differently for the next term.

EXERCISE 2.1 Goal Setting

Have students complete the following lists:

A. List five goals you would like to set for yourself for the coming decade.
B. List two measurable objectives for achieving each of the goals you set.

EXERCISE 2.2 The Ideal Class Schedule

After students have participated in the Working Together exercise, use the weekly timetable (see Figure 2.2, page 29) to have students create their ideal class schedules. Then direct them to look in their campus's schedule of courses for next term and try to find courses they need that fit their ideal schedule. Have students complete this activity before meeting with advisers to talk about registration for the next term.

EXERCISE 2.3 Your Daily Plan

Have students make a to-do list for the next day. Tell them to list all appointments, noting hours of the day, plus any to-do activities. Tell students to label each item with an A, B, or C, the A's deserving the most attention and the C's deserving the least. Encourage students to check out the different calendar and personal planner formats available at the campus bookstore and buy one they think will work for them.

RETENTION EXERCISE Tracking "Actual Time"

Have students use a weekly timetable (see example in Figure 2.2), a planner, or a calendar on their computer or phone to keep track of how they spend time every hour for an entire week. Tell them to fill in every time slot. At the end of this week, ask students to count how many hours they spent on various activities. How many hours did they spend studying? With family? Socializing? By themselves during personal time? Exercising? Relaxing? Working? Sleeping? Doing household chores such as laundry or dishes? Watching television? Eating? Shopping? Reading for pleasure? Talking on the phone? Texting? What activities merit more time? Which activities should take less time? In what ways did students waste time?

CHAPTER 3

WORKING TOGETHER What Would You Have Done?

Share the following scenario with your students. Download a copy of this scenario at **bedfordstmartins.com/gardner**.

It's late afternoon on a Thursday, and the only thing between Josh and the weekend is a big biology test at 10:00 a.m. on Friday. There's a lot at stake with this test: It will count for one-third of his final grade. His cell phone rings. It's Susie with an invitation. "A group of us are planning to go out tonight. We thought about an early dinner and a movie. We won't be late," she says. The last time Josh went out on a night before a big test, he came home late. This time he is committed to coming home by 9:00 p.m. to review for the test. Josh goes out with Susie and her friends. He is having a wonderful time, and every time he thinks about going home, he says to himself, "Just a little longer and I will go." Before he knows it, it's 2:00 a.m., and the test is only eight hours away. Josh is exhausted and stressed. He has to decide whether he should sleep a few hours or pull an all-nighter to pass the test. He decides to sleep. He sets the alarm for 4:00 a.m., when he wakes up groggy and out of sorts. Josh starts to study, but his roommate's alarm goes off at 6:00 a.m. His roommate keeps hitting the snooze button, so the alarm goes off every 15 minutes after that. Josh is annoyed. He doesn't want to leave the room, but he has to concentrate. He complains, "I'm trying to study. Will you please be quiet!" His stress is getting worse, and now it's 8:30 a.m. His cell phone rings. It's Josh's mother reminding him about his grandmother's birthday. He snaps, "Mom. Please don't bother me now. I am studying." He quickly hangs up; he has had it. This is his worst nightmare. He is stressed, on edge, and exhausted, and he feels a big headache coming on.

Divide the class into groups of four or five. Ask the groups to spend fifteen or twenty minutes discussing the following questions. Then ask each group to report its responses to the entire class for discussion. If you were in Josh's place, what would you have done? How would you evaluate Josh's emotional intelligence? What could he have done differently? What competencies does he need to improve?

RETENTION EXERCISE Matching Behaviors with EI Competencies

Have students match the unsuccessful student behaviors in the first column on the next page

Unsuccessful Student Behavior	Related EI Competency
1. Experience stress and do not handle it well	A. Emotional self-awareness
2. Frequently feel overwhelmed	B. Self-regard
3. Don't get along with others	C. Assertiveness
4. Give up easily	D. Independence
5. Engage in destructive behaviors such as binge drinking and drugs	E. Self-actualization
6. Act very impulsively	F. Reality testing
7. Are not able to solve problems	G. Flexibility
8. Are dependent on others	H. Problem solving
9. Show unethical behavior such as stealing or cheating	I. Stress tolerance
10. Have trouble working in teams	J. Impulse control
11. Have very stereotypical views of others and are unaware of their biases and unwilling to change	K. Empathy
12. Are often sad	L. Social responsibility
13. Are not optimistic	M. Interpersonal relationship
14. Have an "I can't" attitude	
15. Blame others for their problems	
16. Think they will get a 4.0 GPA but have missed many classes	
17. Have a hard time making decisions without input from others	

with the related EI competencies in the second column that would help the student change or overcome the behavior. (Sometimes more than one competency relates to a single behavior.) Download a copy of this table at **bedfordstmartins.com/gardner**.

CHAPTER 4

WORKING TOGETHER Multiple Intelligences

After all students have completed the Multiple Intelligences Inventory, ask them to determine their highest point scores. Then break the class into groups according to those scores. Ask group members to discuss the classes they're now taking, out-of-class activities in which they're involved, and intended majors. Each group should then describe their conversation to the whole class.

EXERCISE 4.1 Myers-Briggs Exploration

For classes using the Myers-Briggs Type Indicator, have all class members learn their own types. Form three groups of three to five students each. All members of group 1 should be extraverted/sensing types, and all members of group 2 should be introverted/intuitive types. In group 3, include as many of the different preferences represented as possible. Ask each group to outline or write a brief recruiting brochure aimed at convincing prospective students to come to your college or university. After the groups have finished, ask all three groups to share their results with the rest of the class. Ask students whether they notice any differences in the groups' approaches. Which group do they think produced the best plan for a brochure? Why?

EXERCISE 4.2 Learning Styles Models

In small groups, have students discuss the four learning styles models that are presented in this chapter. Which was the easiest to understand? Which was the most difficult? Which of the models did group members like best? Why? Each group should report its opinions to the whole class.

EXERCISE 4.3 Learning More about Learning Disabilities

Have students use the library or the Internet to find the names of three famous people not mentioned in this chapter who have learning disabilities and how they have dealt with or overcome those disabilities. Ask students to share with the class what they learned from their research.

RETENTION EXERCISE Multiple Intelligences and Success

After students take the short Multiple Intelligences Inventory, divide them into eight groups (one for each intelligence) and ask each group to think of ways that each intelligence (according to Howard Gardner) supports student success and the likelihood that someone will remain in college and graduate. Conversely, ask them to decide whether and why a specific intelligence makes it difficult for someone to be successful in college.

CHAPTER 5

WORKING TOGETHER Gathering Information for Decision Making

Divide the class into groups of four to six, and have each group choose a major problem on campus, such as binge drinking, cheating, date rape, parking, safety, class size, or lack of student participation in organizations. Between this class and the next, students should seek information about their group's problem and identify possible solutions by interviewing a campus authority on the topic, searching campus library holdings, and/or conducting a survey of other students. During the next class, have students share their findings with other members of their group and cite their sources. Groups should try to reach a consensus on the best way to solve the problem that the group chose. If any members of the group are using emotional rather than logical arguments, point those out to them.

EXERCISE 5.1 Did Lincoln Tell the Truth?

Distribute the following paragraphs from a fictional blog, or project them on a screen. Ask students how they would go about sorting the facts from the opinions in order to discover the truth. Download a copy of this excerpt at **bedfordstmartins .com/gardner**.

On October 3, 1863, as the Civil War was raging between the Nation and the Confederate States, President Abraham Lincoln created a new holiday, Thanksgiving, as a day "to give thanks for the many blessings bestowed on Americans." He lamented that the war had caused much suffering, and asked "the Almighty Hand to heal the wounds of the nation and to restore it . . . to the full enjoyment of peace, harmony, tranquility, and Union."

Yet even today, Lincoln's motives are questioned. According to some, Abraham Lincoln trashed the Declaration of Independence; violated his oath to uphold, protect, and defend the Constitution of the United States; and manipulated the nation into a fratricidal war that cost more than 600,000 lives. His armies were blockading Southern ports, depriving the Southern people of all necessities of life, including medicines. Southern soldiers in Northern prisons were dying from hunger, cold, and disease in the land of plenty. Northern prisoners were also dying at the hands of their Southern captors, who had no food, clothing, or medicines to help themselves or anyone else. "Happy Thanksgiving to all," indeed!

EXERCISE 5.2 Reflecting on Arguments

Review the lists of questions on page 93 of this chapter with students. Are they the kinds of questions that students tend to ask when they read, listen to, or take part in discussions? Have students revisit the list each evening for the next week and think about whether they have asked such questions that day and tried to notice whether people were stating their assumptions or conclusions.

EXERCISE 5.3 The Challenge of Classroom Thinking

Have students think about their experiences in each of their classes so far this term and respond to the following questions:

- Have your instructors pointed out any conflicts or contradictions in the ideas they have presented? Have you noted any contradictions that they have not acknowledged?

- Have your instructors asked questions for which they sometimes don't seem to have the answers?
- Have your instructors challenged you or other members of the class to explain yourself more fully?
- Have your instructors challenged the arguments of other experts? Have they called on students in the class to question or challenge certain ideas?
- How have you reacted to your instructors' words? Do your responses reflect critical thinking?

Ask students to write down their thoughts for possible discussion in class and to consider sharing them with their instructors.

RETENTION EXERCISE Learning about a Liberal Education

Have students choose one of their instructors whose field is in the humanities (art, literature, languages, history, government, etc.), mathematics, or the sciences (social, biological, or physical). Students should make an appointment to interview the instructor about how a liberal education and the instructor's particular field of study contribute to a fuller life, no matter what a student's major is.

CHAPTER 6

WORKING TOGETHER Comparing Notes

Have students pair up and compare class notes for this course. Students should take a few minutes to explain their note-taking systems to each other and agree on what's important. In the next class, they should use a recall column. After that class, have students share notes again and check on how each of them used the recall column. They should compare notes and what each student believed to be important. Discuss the results with the class.

EXERCISE 6.1 Using Your Five Senses to Learn

Have students refer back to pages 103–104 in this chapter and decide which mode or modes of learning seem to work best for them: aural, visual,

interactive, tactile, or kinesthetic. Ask for suggestions on how they can adapt to other styles. For example, if students are not aural learners, how can they use their preferred ways of learning to master information that is presented in lecture-style courses? Have students brainstorm ways to convert lecture material into a format that is a better match for how they best use their five senses in the learning process.

EXERCISE 6.2 What System of Note Taking Works for You?

Have students pick one of their lecture courses and try each of the methods of note taking described in this chapter over the next four or five class periods: Cornell, outline, paragraph, and list formats, or a combination. Ask students to find time within a couple of hours after a lecture to review their notes and decide which method seems to work best for them. Which method will be easiest to review when studying for tests? Are there any advantages to using a combination of methods (such as using an outline in conjunction with the Cornell format for taking notes in class, then using the recall column for testing yourself on the contents of your outline)?

EXERCISE 6.3 Using a Recall Column to Memorize

Have students refer to Figure 6.1 (p. 109) and study the material provided in the right-hand column until they think they know it well enough to take a test on it. Then cover the right-hand column. Using the recall column, ask students to try to recite, in their own words, the main ideas from these sample notes. Allow them to uncover the right-hand column when they need to refer to it. Ask students whether this system seems to work. If not, why not?

RETENTION EXERCISE Engagement

Ask students working in small groups, either during class or out of class, to discuss the term *engagement*. What does *engagement* mean to them? Why do they think college and university educators focus so much on getting students engaged? Why do older students tend to be more engaged in learning than students just out of high school? Ask them to consider whether within their peer group it's cool to be "engaged in learning." Have groups share their ideas with the whole class.

CHAPTER 7

WORKING TOGETHER Thinking Back to High School

Ask students to write down the reading methods that worked best for them in high school. Then ask them to share these methods with others in the class to initiate a discussion about how reading in college differs from reading in high school.

EXERCISE 7.1 Previewing and Creating a Visual Map

Have students preview this chapter and create a visual map, noting the following information: title; introduction; key points from the introduction; any graphics (maps, charts, tables, diagrams); study questions or exercises built into or concluding the chapter; and summary paragraphs. Ask students to create either a wheel or a branching map as shown in Figure 7.1 (p. 128), adding spokes or tiers as necessary. In small groups, have students compare their work. Now ask them to arrange the same information in outline form. Which seems to work better? Why?

EXERCISE 7.2 Doing What It Takes to Understand

How far must students go to understand the material in a textbook? Here is one way to find out. Have them do the following:

1. Read a brief chapter in your textbook as if you were reading for pleasure.
2. Read it a second time, but pause at the end of each section to mentally review what you just read.
3. Read it a third time, pausing at the end of each section for review. Then go back and highlight important words or sentences.
4. Read it a fourth time, and do all of the above. This time, ask a friend to read with you, and discuss each passage in the chapter before going on to the next. Stop and take notes, write in the margins, highlight, and so forth.

EXERCISE 7.3 Preparing to Read, Think, and Mark

Direct students to choose a reading assignment from one of their classes. After they preview the material as described earlier in this chapter, have students begin reading until they reach a major heading or have read at least a page or two. They should then stop and write down what they remember from the material. Next, have them go back to the same material and mark what they believe are the main ideas. Suggest that students list four main ideas from the reading so they don't fall into the trap of marking too much.

RETENTION EXERCISE Plan for Active Reading

Ask students to bring a textbook from another course to your next class. During class, ask them to consider the four-step "Plan for Active Reading" on page 126. Ask them which step is the hardest and which is the easiest. The easiest may be "marking." Ask students to check their textbooks to see if any have too much highlighting, or too many marks. The hardest stage may be "reading with concentration." Ask students to get in small groups and develop a list of ideas for "concentrating while reading." Do any of the steps seem unnecessary to your students? Discuss the importance of each step.

CHAPTER 8

WORKING TOGETHER The Name Game

Have the students sit in a circle. Each student then states his or her first name preceded by a descriptive adjective (for example, Sophisticated Susan, Tall Tom, and Jolly Jennifer). Proceed around the circle, having each student state his or her name and descriptor, followed by the names and descriptors of all preceding students. Students can help each other when someone's memory fails. After all students have had a turn, discuss what the class learned from the exercise.

EXERCISE 8.1 Getting the Big Picture

Select a concept from this book, and have students respond to the four questions under the heading "Improving Your Memory," listed on page 151. Have students share their work in small groups. Then ask one person in the group to share with the entire class.

EXERCISE 8.2 Using Memory Strategies

Have students practice using association, visualization, and flash cards to improve their memories. Ask them to try the following strategies with a week's lessons from one of their courses:

1. Visualization. Close your eyes and "see" your notes or textbook assignments in action. Break your notes into chunks, and create a visual image for each chunk.
2. Association. Associate a chunk of information with something familiar. If you want to remember that the word *always* usually signifies a wrong answer on multiple-choice or true/false quizzes, associate *always* with a concept such as "always wrong."
3. Flash cards. Write a key word from the material on one side of a card, and put the details on the other side. An example might be as follows: Write the words "Ways to Remember" on one side; on the other side, write, "Go over it again. Use all senses. Organize it. Mnemonics. Association. Visualization. Flash cards." Review the cards often, looking at only five to nine cards at a time.

After students have tried all three methods, ask which method worked best for them.

EXERCISE 8.3 How Accurate Is Your Memory?

This exercise demonstrates how difficult it can be to remember things accurately. One student whispers the name of an object (e.g., lamp, bike, hamburger) to another student. The second student then whispers the word to a third student and adds a second word. The third student whispers both words to another student, adding still another word, and so forth. Each student who adds a word should write it down. When the final student recites the list, students whose words were left out or changed should speak up. The class should then discuss what strategies they were using to remember the list and why they forgot certain items.

RETENTION EXERCISE Creating an Acrostic

Divide the class into small groups, and have students select a list of words that someone in the group needs to remember. For instance, a group member might select the original thirteen colonies in the United States or famous composers of the Romantic period. Have each group create a sentence that everyone can remember, using the first letters of each word in the list. For instance, the composers Liszt, Chopin, Berlioz, Weber, Schumann, and Wagner could be remembered by using the sentence "Let's Call Brother While Sister Waits."

CHAPTER 9

WORKING TOGETHER Forming a Study Group

Have students form a study group for a course. Students should think about their strengths and weaknesses in a learning or studying situation. For instance, do they excel at memorizing facts but find it difficult to comprehend theories? Do they learn best by repeatedly reading the information or by applying the knowledge to a real situation? Do they prefer to learn by processing information in their heads or by participating in a hands-on demonstration? Ask students to make some notes about their learning and studying strengths and weaknesses. Then have each study group brainstorm how each strength can help others prepare for tests and exams. What helpful strengths will each student look for in another person? How can they help others? How can others help them? Students should create a study plan for their study groups. They should review the test schedule for the course and set times for future meetings. What will each member of the group do in preparation for the next meeting?

EXERCISE 9.1 Designing an Exam Plan

Use the following guidelines to have students design an exam plan for one of their courses:

1. What type of exam will be used?
2. What material will be covered? Is the exam cumulative?
3. What types of questions will the exam contain?
4. How many questions do you think there will be?

5. What approach will you use to study for the exam?

6. How many study sessions—and how much time—will you need?

Now ask students to list all material to be covered and to create a study schedule for the week before the exam, allowing as many 1-hour blocks as they will need.

EXERCISE 9.2 Create Your Own Peaceful Scene

Have students think about the most peaceful place they can imagine, real or imaginary. It might be a place they remember fondly from childhood, a special family vacation spot, a place where they always feel safe, a place they have always wanted to go, or a place from a favorite book or movie. Now have them think about what they would hear, see, smell, taste, and feel if they were there right now. Do not just have them think about how relaxed they would feel; ask them to be specific about *what* they would experience: the warmth of a fire, a gentle breeze, the sand between their toes, rain on the roof. Have students use all five senses to take themselves to their peaceful places. Practice this technique regularly with students, and they will be able to re-create peaceful scenes with ease when they need to relax.

EXERCISE 9.3 Positive Self-Messages

Some people have a mantra, something they say to themselves to keep focused. Have students adopt a mantra of their own—a phrase or sentence to say to themselves whenever they begin to doubt their ability to succeed academically or when they start to feel anxious about a test. It can be something as simple as "I know I can do it!" or "I will succeed!" They could also quote a favorite song lyric or make the mantra special to fit their personalities.

RETENTION EXERCISE Test Taking

As you approach the midterm, ask your students to think back on the tests they've taken so far. In small groups, ask them to identify their worst and their best grade. Then ask them to discuss with each other what factors might have affected their performance, especially factors they can control (such as amount and timing of preparation, sleep, exercise, diet, self-management of distractions, etc.).

CHAPTER 10

WORKING TOGETHER Write, Pair, Write, Share

Direct your students to do this exercise in small groups of five or six. Use the following instructions:

1. Write. For about 10 minutes use the freewriting technique to write about something that is on your mind. Remember, don't stop to think; just keep writing.

2. Pair. When you are told to stop writing, pair off with another student in your group, and share what you have written by talking about it. Listen to what the other person in your minigroup has to say about what you told her or him. Take notes if you wish.

3. Write. When you are next told to write, reflect on the interaction in your minigroup, but do it individually, on paper. How has the discussion reinforced, modified, or changed your original thoughts on the subject? Write this down.

4. Share. At the given signal, return to your small group of five or six. Appoint a leader, a recorder, and a reporter. Share your thoughts with the entire group. Listen to what group members have to say. Present your report to the group at large. Reflect on what learning has taken place and what the next steps should be. How might you apply this process to one of your other classes?

WORKING TOGETHER Debate

Have students choose a controversial topic that relates to college life. For example, they might decide to debate about whether the campus should build more parking lots, the value of intercollegiate athletics, what constitutes cheating, or student credit card debt. After they decide on a topic, each student should select a side to research, either for or against a proposal about the issue. Give students a week to conduct their research and time in class to prepare for the debate. Decide how many minutes each side or speaker will be allotted, and ask the groups to determine who will speak for the group, who will go first, and so on. After the debate is over, call for a "division of the house," requesting that other students in the class go to one side of the room or the other to indicate whether they agree with the pro or con argument.

EXERCISE 10.1 Engage by Writing

To let students practice private writing, have them write a summary of a reading assignment they recently completed, writing down any questions the reading raised for them. Students should also write down any personal responses they might have to the material. Ask them to share their responses.

EXERCISE 10.2 The Power of Focused Observation

Remember Robert Pirsig's student, who began with the first brick of the opera house and went on to write a 5,000-word paper? Have students find a favorite spot on campus where they can sit comfortably and take a good look at the entire area. Tell them to focus on specific parts of the area. Direct them to choose something—it might be a statue, a building, a tree, or a fence. Have students look carefully at just one portion of the object they selected and start writing about it. Collect their papers, and add your remarks.

EXERCISE 10.3 Parallels

Ask students to respond to these questions: In what ways are speaking and writing similar? In what ways are they different? How do forms of electronic writing, such as e-mail and texting, differ from both speaking and writing?

EXERCISE 10.4 *PowerPoint* Presentation

Have students prepare a three- to five-slide *PowerPoint* presentation to introduce themselves to their classmates. They might create slides about their high school years, their hobbies, their jobs, their families, and so forth. Encourage them to use both visuals and text and be prepared to discuss which features of *PowerPoint* they used to make their presentation as dynamic as possible.

EXERCISE 10.5 Chiseled-in-Stone Speech

Assign students a subject for a 1-minute speech to the class. Tell them they must look like statues during the speech. They should not move their arms, legs, or heads, and they should stare at the back wall of the room without looking at their classmates. Students should note how awkward it feels not to gesture, move, or look at their listeners. Despite having stage fright, a very common reaction to public speaking, it's also natural to want to connect with the audience and get ideas across to them. Have students then give their speeches again, this time connecting with their audience.

RETENTION EXERCISE Getting Involved

Make a list of offices, centers, or activities on your campus in which students can become involved and can practice their writing and speaking skills. (Examples could include the campus radio station, a newspaper or literary magazine, student government or other leadership activity, a Greek organization, a tutoring center, a writing center, etc.) Divide students into pairs or small teams (three or four) and have each group visit one of these offices to learn more about its focus and requirements for student involvement. Have each group make a brief presentation to the class about what group members learned and especially what writing or speaking experience students could gain by becoming involved with these activities.

CHAPTER 11

WORKING TOGETHER Conducting a Group Search at the Library

Have students plan a library visit in groups of three. Before they go, one member of the group should call a librarian and ask for a brief meeting. When they arrive, they should ask the librarian to show them where to find reference books, periodicals, and abstracts. Students should also ask how to use the databases on the library computers to aid their searches. Then decide which database each student will search, and have students search for a topic of their choosing. Students should print their findings and share them with the class. What did they learn?

EXERCISE 11.1 Getting Oriented to Periodicals

To encourage students to get familiar with the periodicals in the library, have them complete the following tasks and questions:

1. Find out how your library arranges periodicals (magazines, journals, newspapers). It probably isn't obvious, so don't hesitate to ask. Why do you think the periodicals are organized in this way?
2. Select an important event that was in the news the year you were born. To find out what was happening then, you might want to consult an almanac or ask a reference librarian to recommend a chronology. Find a contemporary (written at the time of the event) news report as well as a scholarly article that analyzes the event in a journal. Describe the event. Why was it significant? Note some of the differences you found between the news report and the scholarly article.

EXERCISE 11.2 Looking Up a Career in Information Studies

1. Have students go online and find a schedule of courses for people who are getting degrees in library or information studies at a university. Here are a few universities to check out: University of Michigan, University of Pittsburgh, University of North Carolina, University of South Carolina, University of Rhode Island, McGill University, Emporia State University, University of Arizona.
2. Direct students to examine the course titles. Would they like to study those areas and topics? Why or why not?
3. Encourage students to ask a librarian where he or she obtained the master of library science degree.
4. Have students find out whether this librarian would recommend a career in information management to them. Students should ask, "Do you like your job? Why?"

EXERCISE 11.3 Ethics

The last time a certain student and his fifty classmates needed an article from a print journal, he discovered that someone had torn the article from the bound periodical. So he went for his second choice. Somebody had ripped out that article, too. "The next time there's some journal article I need, I'm razoring it out," he told his classmates. Ask students why they think this student feels he must respond in this way. How could instructors help prevent such occurrences? How could librarians help students avoid these incidents?

RETENTION EXERCISE Getting Comfortable in Your Library

To encourage students to get familiar with the library, have them complete the following tasks and questions:

1. Find out where your library displays current newspapers, and discover whether the newspaper from your hometown is available.
2. Make an appointment with a librarian so you can talk about your assignment in some depth.
3. Unobtrusively observe what goes on around the information services or reference area (not the circulation desk where you check out books). Watch at least five transactions. Watch the people who ask questions, and watch the staff people who answer them. Does it appear to you that the "customers" receive friendly, competent help? Do the staff members sit and point, or are they on their feet? Do they sometimes accompany inquirers to stack areas or work with them at the computer stations? How might what you observe influence your strategy for getting help if and when you need it?

CHAPTER 12

WORKING TOGETHER Work-Shadowing

Have students do this exercise with a partner: At the career center, arrange to "work-shadow" a professional in a field that interests you. Spend at least a day, preferably longer, observing this person. Reflect on what you observe. Did the work environment meet your expectations? Are you more or less interested in this occupation? You and your partner should then share your conclusions with the rest of the class.

EXERCISE 12.1 What Are Your Life Goals?

The following list includes some life goals that people set for themselves. This list can help students begin to think about the kinds of goals they might want to set. Ask students to put a check mark next to each of the goals they would like to achieve in their lives. Next, they should review the goals they have checked and circle the five they want most. Finally, students should review their list of five goals and rank them by priority on a 1-to-5 scale: 1 for most important, 5 for least important. Discuss the choices in class. Download a copy of this list at **bedfordstmartins.com/gardner**.

____ The love and admiration of friends

____ Good health

____ Lifetime financial security

____ A lovely home

____ International fame

____ Freedom within my work setting

____ A good love relationship

____ A satisfying religious faith

____ Recognition as an attractive person

____ An understanding of the meaning of life

____ Success in my profession

____ A personal contribution to the elimination of poverty and sickness

____ A chance to direct the destiny of a nation

____ Freedom to do what I want

____ A satisfying and fulfilling marriage

(Adapted from Human Potential Seminar by James D. McHolland, Evanston, IL, 1975. Used by permission of the author.)

EXERCISE 12.2 Finding Your Interests

1. Have students complete an interest inventory at the campus career center or online. One such inventory is the Holland Self-Directed Search, at **www.self-directed-search.com** (there is a fee of around $9.95 for the results). Or they can visit the *Princeton Review* and take the Career Quiz (**http://www.princetonreview.com/careers-after-college.aspx**). Students should list their top five occupational interests based on this instrument.

2. Have students interview a professional in one of these fields. In the interviews, students should find out as much as they can about the education that is required, skills they would need to be successful, typical career opportunities, and outlook for the future. Have them identify five key things that they learned from the interviews.

EXERCISE 12.3 Using Your Career Library

Have students visit the campus career center's library. Many of these libraries have materials organized by the Holland model that students learned about in this chapter. This method of organization enables students to research careers that are compatible with their personality types. Suggest that they talk to a career counselor about some of the jobs that interest them. Have students summarize in writing what they have learned.

EXERCISE 12.4 Investigating an Occupation

Encourage students to learn about a particular occupation in which they have an interest, using the campus career center, the library, or the Internet. Students should find out the following:

1. The U.S. Department of Labor's projections for demand for members of this occupation
2. The minimum entry-level credentials for this occupation
3. The salary level ranges from entry level through advanced experience levels
4. What the work environment is like
5. Two other important characteristics of the occupation

EXERCISE 12.5 Writing a Résumé and Cover Letter

Give students this assignment:

1. Prepare two résumés, using the chronological model for one and the skills model for the other. Then, using either model, write another résumé that projects what you would like your résumé to contain five years from now. This University of Utah Web site provides examples of ways to write and organize chronological and skills résumés: **http://www.usu.edu/career/students/resumes.php**.

2. Using the career center or campus library, find a professional whose career path matches your major or career interests. Write this person a cover letter to go with your résumé, and turn these in to your instructor.

RETENTION EXERCISE My Current Thinking about Career Choice

Ask students to make a list of their personal interests, preferences, characteristics, strengths, and skills. They should match the list to the skills and interests needed by successful people in a field that interests them and note other influences that might be drawing them to that career (such as parents' preferences). Have students share their notes with a career counselor to get some feedback on how well their career interests mesh with their strengths and skills.

CHAPTER 13

WORKING TOGETHER Financial Advice

Divide the class into groups of four or five, and have each group appoint a secretary to take notes on the discussion. Ask members in each group to share any financial advice they have received from friends or family. Have them share who pays the bills in their family and who knows what's going on financially at home. Bring the class together, and ask the secretary from each group to report on what group members shared. Pose such questions as "Is it okay for only one person in the family to know how much money is in the bank and how much money goes out each month just to cover needs?" Ask for recommendations on how to stay healthy financially through honest communication.

EXERCISE 13.1 Calculating Interest Charges

Ask students to select a recent credit card bill and note on a piece of paper the amount spent that month. Then have them assume they charged the same amount in each of the next eleven months and paid only the minimum payment each month. Now have them calculate the balance they will have in one year, including interest charges. To help them complete this

assignment, refer them to online interest rate calculators, such as the one at **http://www .bankrate.com/brm/calc/minpayment.asp**. If they're not sure of some amounts, have them use 15.99 percent as their APR and 31.99 percent as the APR default rate.

EXERCISE 13.2 Debit or Credit?

By a show of hands, ask how many students have at least one credit card. Then ask how many have debit cards. Ask students who have at least one of each which they use the most and why. Ask students who have credit cards but no debit card to explain why they don't feel they need the latter. Underscore the difference between debit cards and credit cards.

EXERCISE 13.3 Ten Years from Today

Assign an essay in which students use their critical-thinking skills to imagine their financial situation in ten years, basing their forecasts on how they currently handle money. Ask them to include what changes they would make in their current financial habits in order to be assured of a stable income for themselves and their families.

RETENTION EXERCISE Being Financially True to Yourself

Assign a paper asking students to share any concerns they have about their current financial situation. Have them include any improvements they have made in keeping track of their money as well as any areas they feel are getting out of hand. After reading the papers, share the positives and negatives with the class without identifying student contributors. Ask for recommendations or further questions.

CHAPTER 14

WORKING TOGETHER Roommate Gripes

Residence hall authorities report that the most common areas of conflict between roommates are those listed on the next page. Have students check the ones that are true for them. Download a copy of this list at **bedfordstmartins.com/gardner**.

____ One roommate needs quiet to study; the other needs music or sound.

____ One roommate is neat; the other is messy.

____ One roommate smokes; the other hates smoking.

____ One roommate brings in lots of guests; the other finds them obnoxious.

____ One roommate wants privacy with romantic partners or has sex in front of the other roommate, who is uncomfortable and feels "sexiled."

____ One roommate likes the room warm; the other likes it cool.

____ One roommate considers the room a place to have fun; the other considers it a place to study.

____ One roommate likes to borrow; the other isn't comfortable lending.

____ One roommate is a morning person; the other is a night owl.

____ One roommate follows all the residence hall rules; the other breaks them.

Have students form groups of four to six people and discuss what they checked and how they can attempt to resolve any conflicts. Ask groups to share with the class their opinions about which conflicts are the most difficult to resolve.

EXERCISE 14.1 Thinking about Your Friends

Have students take an inventory of the people they hang out with. Ask them to create a chart, using letters to identify the individuals they are describing in a column on the left and the following headings along the top.

Friend	Basis for friendship
Things you have in common	Negatives about friendship
Ways you are different	

Have students review the list. If the negatives tend to outweigh the positives, what should the student do about his or her friendship with this person?

EXERCISE 14.2 Looking for Love

Have students read the *Facebook* profiles and blogs of students from your campus. Ask them to respond to the following questions in writing: What questions, issues, or themes do people seem to be writing about most? What does this tell you about people's needs in relationships? In class, discuss what students found.

EXERCISE 14.3 Balancing Relationships and College

1. Have students respond to the following questions in writing and subsequent group discussion: If you are in a relationship, what are your greatest concerns about balancing your education with your responsibilities to your partner? What can you do to improve the situation? If the balance poses a serious problem for you, is there someone on campus from whom you can seek counseling? If a student needs counseling but isn't sure where to turn, provide help to find a counselor.

2. If students are married and have children, have them write one letter to their spouse and another to their children explaining why they must often devote time to studies instead of family.

RETENTION EXERCISE Interviewing an Instructor

Assign students to select one of their course instructors and schedule an interview. Provide guidelines for students, such as the following:

- How to schedule an interview appointment
- The importance of being on time for the interview
- Appropriate questions to ask, such as how and when the instructor developed an interest in teaching, where the instructor went to undergraduate and graduate school, and what the instructor likes most or least about teaching

Ask students to give a short (5- to 10-minute) oral presentation in class or write a short report about their interviews. Send a brief e-mail or written "thank you" to instructors whom your students interviewed. Let them know that you designed this assignment to help your first-year students learn more about instructors and become more comfortable with them out of class.

CHAPTER 15

WORKING TOGETHER Reflections on Identity

1. Have students form groups of four to six people. Have them identify areas in which they all share similarities, and keep a written record of those areas. Group members must all agree with an item before it can be added to the list. Next, ask students to create a list of differences.

2. Have students respond to the following questions: How easy or difficult was it to come up with similarities and to agree on them? To what level of depth do the group similarities go? (For example, "We all have hair" versus "We are all religious people.") Was it easy or hard to identify differences? Which list was longer?

EXERCISE 15.1 Examining the Curriculum

At this point, students might have identified some majors that interest them. Have students use your campus's course catalog to identify courses in majors that focus on the topics of multiculturalism and diversity. Why do they think academic departments have included these subjects in the curriculum? How would studying diversity and multiculturalism help students to prepare for the fields of their choice?

EXERCISE 15.2 Diversity on Your Campus

Have students identify the steps your college or university takes to ensure that students feel welcome. Enrollment statistics are typically available from the campus's Office of Institutional Research and might be accessible online. From looking at the data, students should determine which groups are well represented on your campus. Which groups are not? What efforts does the college make to increase diversity?

EXERCISE 15.3 Appreciating Your Gender

Have students read the following four questions pertaining to gender and create a list of answers:

- What aspects do you like about being your gender?
- What are the best things that have happened to you because you are that gender?
- What are some things that have happened because of your gender that you do not want to experience again?
- What would you like other people to know about your gender?

RETENTION EXERCISE Diversity

Ask your students to take the perspective of someone different from them and write a short essay on whether or in what ways the institutional environment is supportive of that individual. Examples would be white men or women, students of color, students of different religions, students with different sexual orientations, students of different ages.

CHAPTER 16

WORKING TOGETHER Recommendations for Stress Management

If students could make only three recommendations to an incoming first-year college student about managing college stress, what would they be? Have students use their experience as well as what they have learned in this chapter to make recommendations. In groups of four, have students compare their lists with those of other students and try to come to a consensus on the three most important recommendations.

EXERCISE 16.1 Monitoring Your Stress

Following is a list of physical and emotional conditions that people can feel when stressed. Have students check the ones that best describe them. Then have students review the ones they have checked and write a paragraph describing how they feel when they are under stress, how they manage the symptoms of stress, and how they attempt to deal with expected and unexpected stressors. Download a copy of this list at **bedfordstmartins .com/gardner**.

_____ My breathing is rapid and shallow.

_____ I have trouble solving problems.

_____ I feel tightness in my chest.

_____ I feel irritable.

_____ I feel jittery.

_____ I have trouble concentrating.

_____ My pulse races.

_____ My muscles feel tense, especially around my shoulders, chest, forehead, and back of neck.

_____ My hands are cold or sweaty.

_____ I have butterflies in my stomach.

_____ I experience diarrhea or constipation.

_____ I have to urinate more frequently.

_____ My mouth is dry.

_____ I tremble or feel shaky.

_____ I have a quiver in my voice.

_____ Things easily confuse me.

_____ I have trouble remembering things.

_____ I feel overwhelmed.

_____ I am anxious about things I have to do.

_____ I feel depressed.

_____ I feel frustrated.

_____ I have insomnia.

_____ I wake up far too early and can't go back to sleep.

_____ I have noticed changes in my eating habits.

_____ I feel fatigued a good bit of the time.

EXERCISE 16.2 Changing Perceptions

Many people get overly stressed because of their negative thought patterns. The old saying "Every negative has a positive" is very true and plays a large role in stress management. Have students use the following steps to practice managing stress by changing their thoughts and perceptions:

1. Identify a stressor for which perceptions can be altered.
2. Recognize the negative thoughts you are having in regard to this situation.
3. Create two or three positive thoughts that you will use to deal with the stressor in the future.
4. Write down the positive thoughts, and keep them with you.
5. Practice saying the positive thoughts to yourself.
6. Use the new positive thoughts when you encounter the stressors.
7. Practice, practice, practice. Change takes time.

EXERCISE 16.3 Doing a Weekly Check

Have students keep a food, physical activity, and sleep journal for three days. The goal is to write down everything they eat and drink, as well as the amount of sleep and physical activity they get each day. After the three days, have students evaluate their food journals.

- Did they have an even distribution among the categories?
- Have they met the recommendation of five fruits and/or vegetables per day?
- Did their grains consist of complex carbohydrates, such as whole wheat?
- Did their liquids consist of high-calorie options, such as soda and beer?

Have students review their physical activity journal at the end of the three days.

- Did they get 30 minutes of physical activity most days? Did they stretch after exercising?
- Did they work all the major muscle groups during their activity?

Have students analyze their sleep during the period.

- Did they get the recommended 7 to 9 hours of sleep per night?
- Did they follow the tips listed in this chapter regarding sleep?
- Did they notice a pattern between the amount of sleep they got in a given night and how well they ate?
- Were they as physically active on days when they did not get a good night's sleep?

At the end of the week, have students write about their experiences.

- Did they feel better or worse during this experiment?
- What will they do about their diet, sleep, and physical activity once this experiment is over?

EXERCISE 16.4 What's Your Decision?

Although students might know about the strategies to keep themselves from contracting an STI, knowledge doesn't always translate into behavior. Ask students to brainstorm a list of all the reasons they can think of why people wouldn't practice the prevention strategies of abstinence, monogamy, or condom use. Then go back over the list and ask students to consider whether each barrier would apply to themselves (yes, no, or maybe). In this way, students can better evaluate where they stand on the issue of safer sex and determine what areas they might need to work on to ensure that they protect themselves—always!

EXERCISE 16.5 Quality of Life

Have students list five ways in which the drinking or substance abuse of others has influenced their quality of life or that of a friend. In small groups, have students share these experiences. What did they find out when they compared their experiences with those of others? Did they handle the situation in a healthy manner? What, if anything, would they do differently in the future?

RETENTION EXERCISE Finding a Balance

Ask students to list all the components of their college experience—for instance, studying, going to classes, taking tests, living in a residence hall, relating to family, working on or off campus, hanging out with friends, exercising, playing a sport—and to rate each as "increases my stress level" or "reduces my stress level." Ask students whether they are in balance—that is, whether they are engaged in as many stress-reducing activities as stress-increasing activities. Make a list of those activities that create the most stress for students, and discuss stress-reducing techniques in class.

TENTH EDITION

YOUR COLLEGE EXPERIENCE

Strategies for Success

Instructor's Annotated Edition

John N. Gardner

President, John N. Gardner Institute for Excellence in Undergraduate Education
Brevard, North Carolina

Distinguished Professor Emeritus, Library and Information Science
Senior Fellow, National Resource Center for
   The First-Year Experience and Students in Transition
University of South Carolina, Columbia

Betsy O. Barefoot

Vice President and Senior Scholar
John N. Gardner Institute for Excellence in Undergraduate Education
Brevard, North Carolina

Bedford/St. Martin's
Boston ▪ New York

For Bedford/St. Martin's

Executive Editor: Edwin Hill
Developmental Editor: Julie Kelly
Senior Production Editor: Christina Horn
Senior Production Supervisor: Nancy Myers
Senior Marketing Manager: Christina Shea
Editorial Assistant: Charlotte Christy
Production Assistants: Elise Keller and Victoria Royal
Copy Editor: Susan Zorn
Indexer: Jake Kawatski
Photo Researcher: Sue McDermott Barlow
Permissions Manager: Kalina K. Ingham
Senior Art Director: Anna Palchik
Text Design: Jerilyn Bockorick
Cover Design: Billy Boardman
Composition: Cenveo Publisher Services/Nesbitt Graphics, Inc.
Printing and Binding: RR Donnelley and Sons

President: Joan E. Feinberg
Editorial Director: Denise B. Wydra
Editor in Chief: Karen S. Henry
Director of Marketing: Karen R. Soeltz
Director of Production: Susan W. Brown
Associate Director, Editorial Production: Elise S. Kaiser
Managing Editor: Elizabeth M. Schaaf

Library of Congress Control Number: 2011937466

Manufactured in the United States of America.

6 5 4 3 2 1
f e d c b a

For information, write: Bedford/St. Martin's, 75 Arlington Street, Boston, MA 02116 (617-399-4000)

ISBN: 978-0-312-60254-3   (Student Edition)
ISBN: 978-1-4576-0382-2   (Instructor's Annotated Edition)

Acknowledgments

Acknowledgments and copyrights appear at the back of the book on page 346, which constitutes an extension of the copyright page.

At the time of publication all Internet URLs published in this text were found to accurately link to their intended Web site. If you do find a broken link, please forward the information to collegesuccess@bedfordstmartins.com so that it can be corrected for the next printing.

Dear Student,

When we were in our first year of college, college success courses were, by and large, nonexistent. Colleges and universities just allowed new students to "sink or swim." As a result, some students made it through their first year successfully, some barely survived, and some dropped out or flunked out.

Today, most colleges and universities offer college success courses to provide essential help to students in navigating their way through the first year. You are likely reading *Your College Experience* because you are enrolled in a college success course. Although this book might seem different from your other textbooks, we believe that it could be the most important book you read this term because it's all about improving your chances for success in college and beyond. This book will help you identify your own strengths as well as your needs for improvement. But before you start reading, you probably have some questions about the book and the course. Here are some of the most common questions we hear from students across the country.

- **Why should I take this course?** Research conducted by colleges and universities has found that first-year students are far more likely to be successful if they participate in courses and programs designed to teach them how to succeed in college. This course is designed to help you avoid some of the pitfalls—both academic and personal—that trip up many beginning students.

- **Aren't all the topics in this book common sense?** In college, issues such as relationships and personal health become even more important when you're living away from home. Even if you're living with your family or have a family of your own, college will challenge you to manage your time, feel comfortable interacting with professors, and study effectively. So while some of this may be common sense, this book will provide new insights and information to help you make decisions that will lead to success.

- **Hasn't this all been covered already in high school?** No. We find that many college success strategies cannot be properly presented or understood until students are actually in college and have an immediate "need to know."

- **What am I going to get out of this course?** This course will provide a supportive environment in which you can share your successes and your frustrations, get to know others who are beginning college, develop a lasting relationship with your instructor and some other students, and begin thinking about your plans for life after college.

As college professors, researchers, and administrators with many years of experience working with first-year students, we're well aware that starting college can be challenging. But we also know that if you apply the ideas in this book to your everyday life, you are more likely to enjoy your time in college, graduate, and achieve your life goals. Welcome to college!

John N. Gardner
Betsy O. Barefoot

John N. Gardner brings unparalleled experience to this authoritative text for first-year seminar courses. He is the recipient of the University of South Carolina's highest award for teaching excellence. He has twenty-five years of experience directing and teaching in the most respected and most widely emulated first-year seminar in the country, the University 101 course at the University of South Carolina. He is recognized as one of the country's leading educators for his role in initiating and orchestrating an international reform movement to improve the beginning college experience. He is also the founding leader of two influential higher education centers that support campuses in their efforts to improve the learning and retention of beginning college students: the National Resource Center for The First-Year Experience and Students in Transition at the University of South Carolina (**www.sc.edu/fye**) and the John N. Gardner Institute for Excellence in Undergraduate Education (**www.jngi.org**) based in Brevard, North Carolina. The experiential basis for all of John Gardner's work is his own miserable first year of college on academic probation, an experience that he hopes to prevent for this book's readers.

Betsy O. Barefoot is a writer, researcher, and teacher whose special area of scholarship is the first year of college. During her tenure at the University of South Carolina from 1988 to 1999, she served as codirector for research and publications at the National Resource Center for The First-Year Experience and Students in Transition. She taught University 101, in addition to special-topics graduate courses on the first-year experience and the principles of college teaching. She conducts first-year seminar faculty training workshops around the United States and in other countries, and she is frequently called on to evaluate first-year seminar outcomes. She currently serves as Vice President and Senior Scholar in the Gardner Institute for Excellence in Undergraduate Education. In her Institute role she led a major national research project to identify institutions of excellence in the first college year. She currently works with both two- and four-year campuses in evaluating all components of the first year.

PREFACE

Anyone who teaches beginning college students knows how much they have changed in recent years. Today's students are increasingly job-focused, technologically adept, and concerned about the future. We are seeing diverse students of all ages and backgrounds enrolling in both two- and four-year institutions, bringing with them the hopes and dreams that a college education can help fulfill. This textbook is designed specifically to give all students the practical help they need to set goals, succeed, and stay in college so that those hopes and dreams can become realities.

We have approached the tenth edition by revisiting a central theme that has always driven *Your College Experience*: goal setting. We wanted to be sure that students were thinking about long- and short-term goals and had the tools they needed to succeed in this course, in their other courses, and in their careers. We began by adding a new section to Chapter 1 called Setting Goals for Your College Experience and Beyond, which explores the importance of setting goals that are specific, measurable, attainable, relevant, and anchored to a time period. We then added activities in every chapter that take students through a three-step process of assessing their current strengths, setting goals for areas in which to grow, and making plans for reaching those goals.

Engaging and retaining today's students are also challenges we know many of you face. To help you meet this challenge, we have created a complete package of support materials, including an Instructor's Annotated Edition and an Instructor's Manual. In the Instructor's Annotated Edition, you will find clearly marked retention strategies and activities to help you engage and retain students. These activities, and all of the instructor support materials, will help both new and experienced instructors as they prepare to teach the course.

What has remained the same in the forty years since the inception of the college success course is our level of commitment and deep understanding of our students. Although this edition of *Your College Experience* has been significantly revised, it is still based on our collective knowledge and experience in teaching first-year students, as well as on feedback from generations of users. It is grounded in the growing body of research on student success and retention and includes many valuable contributions from leading experts in the field. Our contributors were chosen for their knowledge and currency in their fields as well as their own deep commitments to their students and to the discipline. Most of all, it is a text born from our devotion to students and to their success. Simply put, we do not like to see students fail. We are confident that if students both read and heed the information herein, they will become engaged in the college experience, learn, and persist to graduation.

We have written this text for students of any age in both two- and four-year residential and commuter institutions. Our writing style is intended to convey respect and admiration for students while recognizing their continued need for challenge and support. We have addressed every topic that our experience, our research, and our reviewers tell us is a concern for students at any type of school with any kind of educational background.

Your College Experience uses a simple and logical organization. Part One, Preparing for Success, sets the stage by challenging students to explore their purpose for attending college and by helping them learn how to apply that purpose to both short- and long-term goal setting. The chapters in this section also introduce readers to the fundamental elements of a college education. Part Two, Preparing to Study, enumerates essential study skills and guides students in communicating and finding information. Part Three, Preparing for Life, emphasizes practical considerations that all students must face, such as choosing a major and money management, while also addressing the importance of learning about human and intellectual differences and the relationship between a healthy body and an eager mind.

Whether you are considering this textbook for use in your first-year seminar or have already made a decision to adopt it, we thank you for your interest, and we trust that you will find it to be a valuable teaching aid. We also hope that this book will guide you and your campus in understanding the broad range of issues that can affect student success.

A REVISION FOCUSED ON HELPING ALL STUDENTS WITH GOAL SETTING, SUCCESS, AND STAYING IN COLLEGE

We have added a number of substantive new features to further increase the probability of your students' success in college.

Coverage on goal setting in Chapter 1. A new section on goal setting gets students thinking about how to succeed right from the start of the course.

A new three-step process that guides students through assessing their current strengths, setting goals for areas to grow in, and setting goals for improvement. Assessing Your Strengths and Setting Goals boxes in each chapter ask students to identify their strengths and then to set goals based on their own objectives for the chapter material. This helps students engage in the course material. Stay on Track exercises at the end of each chapter ask students to plan how to apply strengths to current and future work in other courses and in their career.

Chapter-opening profiles that help students see themselves in the text. Each chapter of the text opens with a true story of a recent first-year student who has used the strategies in the chapter to succeed in college. The profiled students come from diverse backgrounds and attend all kinds of colleges around the country.

Thought-provoking images and exercises in every chapter that encourage critical thinking. Features, photos, and exercises include activities to help students master concepts and think critically about the material.

An increased focus on technology and learning. Tech Tip features in every chapter introduce critical technology skills—such as using a digital planner, practicing online etiquette, and creating community in an online course—that can span the classroom and real life.

Clearly marked Retention Strategies in every chapter of the Instructor's Annotated Edition. These best practices from John Gardner and Betsy Barefoot help students persist in the first year.

Retention-specific exercises and activities. A 16-page insert at the beginning of the Instructor's Annotated Edition includes chapter-specific activities that help with writing, critical thinking, working in groups, planning, reflecting, and taking action.

EXTENSIVE RESOURCES FOR INSTRUCTORS

- **Instructor's Annotated Edition.** A valuable tool for new and experienced instructors alike, the Instructor's Annotated Edition includes the full text of the student edition with abundant marginal annotations, chapter-specific exercises, and helpful suggestions for teaching, fully updated and revised by the authors. New to this edition are numerous Retention Strategy tips and exercises to help you help your students succeed and stay in school.

- **Instructor's Manual and Test Bank.** The Instructor's Manual and Test Bank includes chapter objectives, teaching suggestions, a list of common concerns of first-year students, an introduction to the first-year experience course, a sample lesson plan for each chapter, and various case studies that are relevant to the topics covered. Available in print and online. ISBN: 978-1-4576-0400-3. Look for the following:

  - **New!** Over 300 new questions added to the tenth edition Test Bank.
  - **New!** A midterm and final exam.
  - **New!** *Guide to Teaching with YouTube* by Chris Gurrie (University of Tampa) provides tips and tricks on easily finding videos to supplement each topic in the course.

- **Computerized Test Bank.** The number of multiple-choice and true/false questions has been doubled from the prior edition. The Test Bank contains more than 800 multiple-choice, true/false, short-answer, and essay questions designed to assess students' understanding of key concepts. An answer key is included. ISBN: 978-1-4576-0418-8.

- *French Fries Are Not Vegetables.* This comprehensive instructional DVD features multiple resources for class and professional use. Also available online. ISBN: 978-0-312-65073-5.

- **Custom with Care program.** Bedford/St. Martin's Custom Publishing offers the highest-quality books and media, created in consultation with publishing professionals who are committed to the discipline. Make *Your College Experience* more closely fit your course and goals by integrating your own materials, including only the parts of the text you intend to use in your course, or both. Contact your local Bedford/ St. Martin's sales representative for more information.

- **TradeUp.** Bring more value and choice to your students' first-year experience by packaging *Your College Experience*, Tenth Edition, with one of a thousand titles from Macmillan publishers at a 50 percent discount from the regular price. Contact your local Bedford/ St. Martin's sales representative for more information.

STUDENT RESOURCES

- **Free book companion site for *Your College Experience:* bedfordstmartins .com/gardner.** You and your students *need* value and *want* powerful online content that you can use anywhere, anytime. The companion site for *Your College Experience* gives you both, with free and open resources for you to use. These resources include the following:

  - **Student Life videos** illustrate important concepts, skills, and situations that students will need to understand and master to become successful at college. Each video ends with questions to encourage further contemplation and discussion.
  - **New! Self-Tests** help students master concepts.
  - **Downloadable podcasts** offer quick advice on note taking, money management, succeeding on tests, and many more topics
  - **"Where to Go for Help" library of links** directs students to further online resources for support and much more. From the companion Web site, you can also access instructor materials whenever you need them.

- *VideoCentral: College Success* is a premiere collection of videos for the college success classroom. The site features the 30-minute documentary *French Fries Are Not Vegetables and Other College Lessons: A Documentary of the First Year of College,* which follows five students through the life-changing transition of the first year of college. Learn more at **bedfordstmartins.com/collegesuccess/catalog.** *VideoCentral* also includes access to the following:

  - 16 brief *Conversation Starters* that combine student and instructor interviews on the most important topics taught in first-year seminar courses.
  - 16 accompanying video glossary definitions with questions that bring these topics to life.

- **Interactive e-book.** With extra multimedia content and tools, the *Your College Experience e-Book* lets students easily search, annotate, and share notes. Instructors can customize and rearrange chapters, add and share notes, and link to quizzes and activities. *Your College Experience e-Book* can be purchased standalone or packaged with a print book. To order the e-book packaged with the print book, use

ISBN 978-1-4576-2042-3. To order the e-book standalone, use ISBN 978-1-4576-1892-5.

- *CourseSmart e-Book for Your College Experience.* We've partnered with CourseSmart to offer a downloadable version of *Your College Experience*, Tenth Edition, at about half the price of the print book. To learn more about this low-cost alternative, go to **coursesmart .com**. ISBN: 978-1-4576-0415-7.

  - **Let students choose their e-book format.** Students can purchase *Your College Experience* in popular e-book formats for computers, tablets, and e-readers. For more details, visit **bedfordstmartins .com/ebooks.**

- *The Bedford/St. Martin's Planner* includes everything that students need to plan and use their time effectively, with advice on preparing schedules and to-do lists, along with blank schedules and calendars (monthly and weekly) for planning. Integrated into the planner are tips and advice on fixing common grammar errors, taking notes, and succeeding on tests; an address book; and an annotated list of useful Web sites. The planner fits easily into a backpack or purse, so students can take it anywhere. To order *The Bedford/St. Martin's Planner* packaged **free** with the text, use ISBN 978-1-4576-1441-5. To order the planner standalone, use ISBN 978-0-312-57447-5.

- *Bedford/St. Martin's Insider's Guides.* These concise and student-friendly booklets on topics that are critical to college success are a perfect complement to your textbook and course. Bundle one with *any* Bedford/St. Martin's textbook at no additional cost. Topics include:

  - **New!** *Insider's Guide to Academic Planning*
  - *Insider's Guide to Beating Test Anxiety*
  - **New!** *Insider's Guide to Career Services*
  - *Insider's Guide to College Ethics and Personal Responsibility*
  - *Insider's Guide to College Etiquette*
  - *Insider's Guide to Community College*
  - **New!** *Insider's Guide to Confidence*
  - *Insider's Guide to Credit Cards*
  - *Insider's Guide to Getting Involved on Campus*
  - *Insider's Guide to Global Citizenship*
  - *Insider's Guide to Time Management*

  For more information on ordering one of these guides **free** with the text, go to **bedfordstmartins.com/gardner/catalog.**

- *Journal Writing: A Beginning.* Designed to give students an opportunity to use writing as a way to explore their thoughts and feelings, this writing journal includes a generous supply of inspirational quotes placed throughout the pages, tips for journaling, and suggested journal topics. To order *Journal Writing: A Beginning* packaged **free** with the text, use ISBN 978-1-4576-1429-3. To order the journal standalone, use ISBN 978-0-312-59027-7.

ACKNOWLEDGMENTS

Special thanks to the reviewers of this edition, whose wisdom and suggestions guided the creation of the tenth edition of the text:

Laurie Adamson, Olympic College

Jim Archer, South Plains College

Jennifer L. Guerriero, Valencia Community College

Kevin Johnson, Middle Georgia College

Joseph Kaye, Edison State College

Elizabeth Kennedy, Florida Atlantic University

Kimberly Koledoye, Houston Community College

Joseph Kornoski, Montgomery County Community College

Audra Leverton, Hinds Community College

Rhonda Lee Meadows, West Virginia University

Pamela Moss, Midwestern State University

Marissa Santos, Navarro College

Ysabel M. Sarte, Texas A&M University

Melanie Steeves, Dean College

Susannah Waldrop, University of South Carolina Upstate

Shoshana Zeisman, Portland State University

We also thank those who reviewed the Instructor's Manual and Test Bank so thoroughly: Margaret Garroway, Howard Community College; Greta Henglein, Martin Methodist College; Patti Richter, Northwestern State University of Louisiana; Mary Kay Skrabalak, University of Alabama; Brenda Tuberville, Rogers State University.

We would also like to continue to thank our reviewers from the eighth and ninth editions, as they helped to shape the text you see today. **Ninth Edition:** Josie Adamo, Buffalo State College; Leigh A. Adams, Missouri State University–West Plains; Andrés Armijo, University of New Mexico; Camille J. Belolan, Bloomsburg University of Pennsylvania; Richard Conway, Nassau Community College; Matthew Gainous, Ogeechee Technical College; Wendy Grace, Holmes Community College; Janis M. Hausmann, Mount Marty College; Darby Johnsen, Oklahoma City Community College; Tamara Kuzmenkov, Tacoma Community College; Wendy McNeeley, Howard Payne University; Gail Malone Platt, South Plains College; Amy Reese, Baton Rouge Community College; Cristina C. Rodriguez, Los Angeles Pierce College; Rebecca Rogge, Louisiana State University; Janice Waltz, Harrisburg Area Community College; Jodi E. Webb, Bowling Green State University.

Eighth Edition: Eunie Alsaker, Winona State University; Marianne Auten, Paradise Valley Community College; Joanne Baird Giordano, University of Wisconsin–Marathon County; Julia Brown, Northern Virginia Community College; Kara Craig, University of Southern Mississippi; Anne Dawson, Eastern Connecticut State University; Rosie DuBose, Century College; Melissa Gomez, Austin Peay State University; Laurene M. Grimes, Lorain County Community College; Kathleen Hangac, State University of New York at Oswego; Elizabeth H. Hicks, Central Connecticut State University; Claudette Jackson, Baylor University; Rebecca Jordan, University of Kentucky; Elizabeth Kennedy, Florida Atlantic University; Mary P. Lovelidge, Blinn College; Karen Mitchell, Northern Essex Community College; Kate Pandolpho, Ocean

County College; Margaret Puckett, North Central State College; Christel Taylor, University of Wisconsin–Waukesha; Janice Waltz, Harrisburg Area Community College; Jodi E. Webb, Bowling Green State University; Nicole Weir, Montclair State University; Erika Wimby May, Dillard University; Michael B. Wood, Missouri State University; Janice E. Woods, Mohave Community College.

As we look to the future, we are excited about the numerous improvements to this text that our creative Bedford/St. Martin's team has made and will continue to make. Special thanks to Joan Feinberg, President of Bedford/St. Martin's; Denise Wydra, Editorial Director; Karen Henry, Editor in Chief; Edwin Hill, Executive Editor; Julie Kelly, Developmental Editor; Charlotte Christy, Editorial Assistant; Christina Shea, Senior Marketing Manager; Elise Kaiser, Assistant Director of Editorial Production; and Christina Horn, Senior Production Editor.

Most of all, we thank you, the users of our book, for you are the true inspirations for our work.

CONTRIBUTORS

Although this text speaks with the voices of its two authors, it represents contributions from many other people. We gratefully acknowledge those contributions and thank these individuals, whose special expertise has made it possible to introduce new students to their college experience through the holistic approach we deeply believe in.

Chris Gurrie is Assistant Professor of Speech at the University of Tampa. Dr. Gurrie is an active public speaker and participates in invited lectures, workshops, and conferences in the areas of faculty development, first-year life and leadership, communicating effectively with *PowerPoint*, and communication and immediacy. Recent research in communication education, immediacy, and technology has resulted in articles published in communication and first-year outlets. Gurrie is an advocate of experiential learning and has participated in first-year activities at the University of Tampa as the chairman of the First Year Committee and as a faculty adviser. He contributed to the Tech Tip feature in each chapter of this book and wrote the *Guide to Teaching with YouTube,* available online and as part of the Instructor's Manual.

We would also like to acknowledge and thank the numerous colleagues who have contributed to this book in its previous editions:

Chapters 2, 6, 7, 8, 9: Jeanne L. Higbee, University of Minnesota, Twin Cities

Chapter 3: Catherine Andersen, Gallaudet University

Chapters 4, 14: Tom Carskadon, Mississippi State University

Chapter 7: Mary Ellen O'Leary, University of South Carolina at Columbia

Chapter 9: Christel Taylor, University of Wisconsin at Waukesha

Chapter 10: Constance Staley, University of Colorado at Colorado Springs

Chapter 10: R. Stephen Staley, Colorado Technical University

Chapter 11: Charles Curran, University of South Carolina at Columbia

Chapter 11: Rose Parkman Marshall, University of South Carolina at Columbia

Chapter 11: Margit Watts, University of Hawaii, Manoa

Chapter 12: Philip Gardner, Michigan State University

Chapter 13: Natala Kleather (Tally) Hart, founding head of the Economic Access Initiative at Ohio State University

Chapter 13: Kate Trombitas, Ohio State University

Chapter 15: Juan J. Flores, Folsom Lake College

Chapter 16: Michelle Murphy Burcin, University of South Carolina at Columbia

End-of-chapter materials: Julie Alexander-Hamilton

BRIEF CONTENTS

PART 1 **PREPARING FOR SUCCESS** 1

1 Exploring Your Purpose for Attending College 3

2 Managing Your Time 19

3 Understanding Emotional Intelligence 41

4 Discovering How You Learn 59

PART 2 **PREPARING TO STUDY** 81

5 Thinking Critically: The Basis of a College Education 83

6 Being Engaged in Learning: Listening, Taking Notes, and Participating in Class 101

7 Reading to Learn from College Textbooks 125

8 Learning to Study, Comprehend, and Remember 143

9 Improving Your Performance on Exams and Tests 159

10 Writing and Speaking Effectively 183

11 Developing Library, Research, and Information Literacy Skills 207

PART 3 **PREPARING FOR LIFE** 229

12 Making the Right Choice for Majors and Careers 231

13 Managing Your Money 255

14 Establishing and Maintaining Relationships in College 273

15 Appreciating Diversity 289

16 Maintaining Wellness 307

CONTENTS

Letter to Students   iii

About the Authors   iv

Preface   v

Brief Contents   xiii

PART 1 ▶ PREPARING FOR SUCCESS   1

1 Exploring Your Purpose for Attending College   3

STUDENT PROFILE: Denzel Gantt   3

The College Experience   4

Why College Is Important to Our Society   5

Why College Is Important for You   6

Setting Goals for Your College Experience and Beyond   7

TECH TIP: Expand Your Skills   8

Outcomes of College   9

Making the Transition   11

Challenges and Opportunities for Adult and Returning Students   12

First-Year Motivation and Commitment   13

What Is Your Purpose in College?   13

BUILD YOUR EXPERIENCE   16

WHERE TO GO FOR HELP   18

2 Managing Your Time   19

STUDENT PROFILE: Emma Kay   19

Taking Control of Your Time   20

Overcoming Procrastination   22

Setting Priorities   24

Staying Focused   25

Getting Organized   26

Use a Planner   26

Chart a Weekly Timetable   28

Maintain a To-Do List   28

Making Sure Your Schedule Works for You 30

Create a Workable Class Schedule 31
Don't Overextend Yourself 33
Reduce Distractions 33
TECH TIP: Get Organized 35

Respecting Others' Time 36

BUILD YOUR **EXPERIENCE** 38

WHERE TO GO FOR HELP 40

3 Understanding Emotional Intelligence 41

STUDENT PROFILE: Sabeena Maharjan 41

What Is Emotional Intelligence? 43

Assessing Your Emotional Intelligence 45

Identifying Competencies 46

Intrapersonal Skills 47
Interpersonal Skills 47
Adaptability 48
Stress Management 49
General Mood and Effective Performance 49
TECH TIP: Stay Connected 50

How Emotions Affect Success 51

How to Improve Your Emotional Intelligence 54

BUILD YOUR **EXPERIENCE** 56

WHERE TO GO FOR HELP 58

4 Discovering How You Learn 59

STUDENT PROFILE: Robert Schein 59

The VARK Learning Styles Inventory 61

Scoring the VARK 63
Scoring Chart 64
Using VARK Results to Study More Effectively 65

The Kolb Inventory of Learning Styles 66

The Myers-Briggs Type Indicator 67

Extraversion (E) versus Introversion (I):
  The Inner or Outer World 68
Sensing (S) versus Intuition (N): Facts or Ideas 69
Thinking (T) versus Feeling (F): Logic or Values 69

Judging (J) versus Perceiving (P): Organization or Adaptability 70
How to Use Your Strongest—and Weakest—Preferences 70

Multiple Intelligences 71

When Learning Styles and Teaching Styles Conflict 73

TECH TIP: Branch Out 74

Learning with a Disability 75

Attention Disorders 76
Cognitive Learning Disabilities 76

BUILD YOUR EXPERIENCE 78

WHERE TO GO FOR HELP 80

PART 2 ▶ PREPARING TO STUDY 81

5 Thinking Critically: The Basis of a College Education 83

STUDENT PROFILE: Kelsey McManus 83

What Is Critical Thinking, and Why Is It Important? 85

Becoming a Critical Thinker 86

Ask Questions 87
Consider Multiple Points of View 87
Draw Conclusions 88

How Collaboration Fosters Critical Thinking 88

Thinking Critically about Arguments 90

Challenge Assumptions 90
Examine the Evidence 91
TECH TIP: Research Wisely 93
Beware of Logical Fallacies 94

Critical Thinking in College and Everyday Life 96

BUILD YOUR EXPERIENCE 98

WHERE TO GO FOR HELP 100

6 Being Engaged in Learning: Listening, Taking Notes, and Participating in Class 101

STUDENT PROFILE: Jordan Hardy 101

Using Your Senses in the Learning Process 103

Preparing for Class 104

Participating in Class 104

Listening Critically and with an Open Mind 105

Speaking Up 106

Taking Effective Notes 108

Note-Taking Formats 108

Cornell Format 108

Outline Format 108

Paragraph Format 108

List Format 109

Note-Taking Techniques 110

Taking Notes in Nonlecture Courses 114

Taking Notes in Science and Mathematics Courses 115

Using Technology to Take Notes 115

TECH TIP: Take Notes Like a Rock Star 116

Reviewing Your Notes 117

Comparing Notes 118

Class Notes and Homework 119

Becoming Engaged in Learning 120

BUILD YOUR EXPERIENCE 122

WHERE TO GO FOR HELP 124

7 Reading to Learn from College Textbooks 125

STUDENT PROFILE: Kameron Fehrmann 125

A Plan for Active Reading 126

Previewing 126

Mapping 127

Alternatives to Mapping 127

Marking Your Textbook 129

Reading with Concentration 131

Reviewing 131

Strategies for Reading Textbooks 132

Math Texts 133

Science Texts 133

Social Science and Humanities Texts 135

TECH TIP: Embrace the E-Book 136

Supplementary Material 137

Monitoring Your Reading 137

Improving Your Reading 137

Developing Your Vocabulary 138
If English Is Not Your First Language 138

BUILD YOUR EXPERIENCE 140

WHERE TO GO FOR HELP 142

8 Learning to Study, Comprehend, and Remember 143

STUDENT PROFILE: Noelle Green 143

Studying to Understand and Remember 144

TECH TIP: Don't Be a Virtual Wallflower 147

How Memory Works 147

Connecting Memory to Deep Learning 148
Myths about Memory 149

Improving Your Memory 150

Mnemonics 151
Using Review Sheets, Mind Maps, and Other Tools 152
Summaries 154

BUILD YOUR EXPERIENCE 156

WHERE TO GO FOR HELP 158

9 Improving Your Performance on Exams and Tests 159

STUDENT PROFILE: Kenzie Snyderman 159

Getting Prepared for Tests and Exams 160

Prepare Physically 162
Prepare Emotionally 163
Prepare for Test Taking 163
Prepare for Math and Science Exams 164

Taking Tests and Exams 164

Essay Questions 165
Multiple-Choice Questions 166
Fill-in-the-Blank Questions 168
True/False Questions 168
Matching Questions 168

Types of Tests 169

Problem-Solving Tests 169
Machine-Scored Tests 170
Computerized Tests 170
Laboratory Tests 170

Open-Book and Open-Note Tests   171
Take-Home Tests   171
TECH TIP: Fear Not the Online Test   172

Overcoming Test Anxiety   173

Types of Test Anxiety   174
Symptoms of Test Anxiety   174
Strategies for Combating Test Anxiety   175
Getting the Test Back   176

Academic Honesty and Misconduct   176

Cheating   176
Plagiarism   177
Consequences of Cheating and Plagiarism   177
Reducing the Likelihood of Academic Dishonesty   178

BUILD YOUR EXPERIENCE   180

WHERE TO GO FOR HELP   182

10   Writing and Speaking Effectively   183

STUDENT PROFILE: Jason Hardtke   183

WRITING   186

Using Freewriting to Discover What You Want to Say   186

Narrowing Your Topic   187
Exploratory Writing   187
TECH TIP: Blog for Brilliance   188

The Writing Process   189

Prewriting: The Idea Stage   189
Writing: The Beginning of Organization   189
Rewriting: The Polishing Stage   190
Allocating Time   190

Choosing the Best Way to Communicate with Your Audience   193

SPEAKING   194

Preparing a Speech   194

Step 1. Clarify Your Objective   194
Step 2. Analyze Your Audience   195
Step 3. Collect and Organize Your Information   195
Step 4. Choose Your Visual Aids   195
Step 5. Prepare Your Notes   197
Step 6. Practice Your Delivery   197

Using Your Voice and Body Language 197

The GUIDE Checklist 198

G: Get Your Audience's Attention 199

U: "You"—Don't Forget Yourself 199

I: Ideas, Ideas, Ideas! 200

D: Develop an Organizational Structure 201

E: Exit Gracefully and Memorably 201

Speaking on the Spot 202

BUILD YOUR EXPERIENCE 204

WHERE TO GO FOR HELP 206

11 Developing Library, Research, and Information Literacy Skills 207

STUDENT PROFILE: Paul Govoni 207

Information Literacy 208

Learning to Be Information Literate 210

What's Research—and What's Not? 211

Employing Information Literacy Skills 211

Choosing, Narrowing, and Researching a Topic 212

Using the Library 213

Taking Advantage of Everything Your Library Has to Offer 214

TECH TIP: Check Your Engine 215

Asking a Librarian 216

Electronic Resources 217

Library Catalogs 217

Periodical Databases 217

The World Wide Web 218

Guidelines for Effective Searches 219

Evaluating Sources 220

Relevance 220

Authority 221

Bias 222

A Note on Internet Sources 222

Making Use of What You Find 223

Synthesizing Information and Ideas 223

Citing Your Sources 223

About Plagiarism 224

BUILD YOUR EXPERIENCE 226

WHERE TO GO FOR HELP 228

PART 3 PREPARING FOR LIFE 229

12 Making the Right Choice for Majors and Careers 231

STUDENT PROFILE: Megan Henley 231

Careers and the New Economy 232

Aligning Your Sense of Purpose and Your Career 235

Connecting Your Major and Your Interests with Your Career 236

Exploring Your Interests 237

Factors That Affect Career Choices 239

Planning for Your Career 240

Planning for Two-Year Students 242

Getting Experience 243

Skills Employers Look For 245

Content Skills 245

Transferable Skills 245

Key Competencies 246

Working in College 247

On-Campus Jobs 247

Off-Campus Jobs 248

Building a Résumé 248

TECH TIP: Job Search Wisely 249

Writing a Cover Letter 250

Interviewing 250

BUILD YOUR EXPERIENCE 252

WHERE TO GO FOR HELP 254

13 Managing Your Money 255

STUDENT PROFILE: Cindy Kuriakose 255

Living on a Budget 256

Creating a Budget 257

Cutting Costs 259

Getting Financial Aid 260

Types of Aid 260

Qualifying for Aid 262

How to Avoid Losing Your Funding 263

Achieving a Balance between Working and Borrowing 264

Advantages and Disadvantages of Working 264

Student Loans 265

Managing Credit Wisely 265

Understanding Credit 266

Frequently Asked Questions about Credit Cards 267

TECH TIP: Create Wealth and Security 268

Debit Cards 269

Planning for the Future 269

BUILD YOUR EXPERIENCE 270

WHERE TO GO FOR HELP 272

 14 Establishing and Maintaining Relationships in College 273

STUDENT PROFILE: Benjamin Smock 273

Building Relationships with College Instructors 275

What Your Instructors Expect from You 275

What You Can Expect from Your Instructors 276

Making the Most of the Learning Relationship 276

Understanding Academic Freedom 277

When Things Go Wrong between You and an Instructor 277

Friendships in and beyond College 278

Roommates 278

Social Networking 278

TECH TIP: Maintain Some Mystery 279

Getting Serious with Relationships 280

Breaking Up 280

Relationships You Should Avoid 281

Family Connections 281

Marriage and Parenting during College 281

Relationships with Your Parents 282

Getting Involved 283

To Greek or Not to Greek? 284

Working 284

Community Service 285

BUILD YOUR EXPERIENCE 286

WHERE TO GO FOR HELP 288

 **15 Appreciating Diversity** 289

STUDENT PROFILE: Students of Gallaudet
University 289

**Understanding Diversity and the Source of
Our Beliefs** 291

Forms of Diversity 293

    Ethnicity, Culture, Race, and Religion 293

    Age 294

    Learning and Physical Abilities 295

    Gender 295

    Sexual Orientation 295

Seeking Diversity on Campus 296

    The Curriculum 296

    Student-Run Organizations 297

    Fraternities and Sororities 298

    Career/Major Groups 298

    Political/Activist Organizations 298

    Special-Interest Groups 299

**Discrimination, Prejudice, and Insensitivity
on College Campuses** 299

    Raising Awareness 299

    What You Can Do to Fight Hate on Campus 300

Challenge Yourself to Experience Diversity 301

    TECH TIP: The Case for Volunteering 302

BUILD YOUR EXPERIENCE 304

WHERE TO GO FOR HELP 306

 16 Maintaining Wellness 307

STUDENT PROFILE: Dalton Eidem 307

Managing Stress 309

    Diet and Exercise 310

    Sleep 313

    Taking Control 314

    Other Ways to Relieve Stress 315

Mental Health 315

    Depression 315

    Suicide 316

Nutrition and Weight Management 316

Healthy Eating 316

Obesity 319

Eating Disorders 319

Sexual Health 319

TECH TIP: Surf for Health 320

Sexually Transmitted Infections 321

Negotiating for Safer Sex 321

Birth Control 323

Substance Abuse 325

Making Decisions about Alcohol 325

Tobacco—The Other Legal Drug 329

Prescription Drug Abuse and Addiction 331

Illegal Drugs 332

BUILD YOUR EXPERIENCE 336

WHERE TO GO FOR HELP 338

Epilogue: Taking the Next Steps to Success 339

Glossary 343

Credits 346

Index 347

Preparing for Success

PART 1

Preparing to Study

PART 2

Preparing for Life

PART 3

CHAPTER 1

Exploring Your Purpose for Attending College

IN THIS CHAPTER YOU WILL EXPLORE

What college is all about

The importance of thinking about your own purpose in attending college

How college "levels the playing field" for students from different backgrounds

The many differences between high school and college

The challenges of being an adult or returning student

The benefits of a college education

How to make sensible choices for college success

Setting goals for your college experience and beyond

> **Ask for help! There are so many resources available on campus, but you will never know until you ask.**
>
> Denzel Gantt, 18
> Biology major
> Florida Atlantic University

Denzel Gantt always knew he wanted to go to college. He was born and raised in southern Florida, and when it came time to choose a college, Florida Atlantic University was an easy choice: "Not going to college was never an option. I decided to go to FAU because it got me out of the nest but was close enough to home so that I can still help my mother out."

Now that his first year is under way, Denzel has learned there are some key differences between high school and college, specifically the amount of time he spends studying. "In high school I studied maybe five hours a week." Now he finds himself studying many more hours, something he learned was important right away in his first-year experience course. He also quickly learned the importance of organizing, managing his time, and staying on top of his assignments. "In my first-year experience course I learned

Denzel Gantt ▶

the value and importance of a planner because life can get pretty hectic. To keep it all in your brain, you have to write some of it down."

Setting goals and finding a purpose for being in college have also led to his success. After using the multitude of resources on campus—including his adviser, the career center, and his first-year experience course—Denzel has decided his ultimate goal is to attend pharmacy school. Now he is able to work with his adviser and instructors to make sure he achieves that goal.

Since begining at FAU, Denzel's perception of college has changed immensely. "College is one of those things in life that you have to experience. You have to find out for yourself; it can't be told to you." When asked the one piece of advice he would give to other first-year students, Denzel says, "Ask for help! There are so many resources available, but you will never know until you ask."

The fact that you are reading this textbook probably means that, like Denzel, you are enrolled in a first-year seminar or "college success" course designed to introduce you to college and help you make the most of it. In this chapter, we'll discuss how you fit into the whole idea of college. We'll consider why the United States has more colleges and universities than any other country in the world. We'll also help you explore the purposes of college—many that your college might define for you—and set goals for your college experience. But even more important, we'll help you define your purposes for being here and offer many strategies to help you succeed.

The College Experience

> ### YOUR TURN
> So far, is life at your college or university what you expected or hoped for? Why or why not?

So what is the college experience? Depending on who you are, your life circumstances, and why you decided to enroll, college can mean different things. College is often portrayed in books and films as a place where young people live away from home in ivy-covered residence halls. We frequently see college depicted as a place with a major focus on big-time sports, heavy drinking, and partying. And, yes, there is some of that at some colleges. But most students today don't move away from home, don't live on campus, and don't see much ivy. College is really far more than any single image you might carry around in your head.

There are many ways to define college. For starters, college is an established process designed to further formal education so that students who attend and graduate will be prepared for certain roles in society. Today, those roles are found especially in what has become known as "the information economy." This means most college graduates are going to be earning their living by creating, managing, and using information. Because the amount of available information expands all the time, your college classes can't possibly teach you all you need to know for the future. The most important skill you will need to learn in college is how to keep learning throughout your life.

ASSESSING YOUR STRENGTHS

Think about the topic of this chapter. Do you already have a good understanding of the benefits of college and some experience in setting and reaching goals? Now that you have read the first section of this chapter, list the strengths you have in this area.

_____

_____

_____

_____

SETTING GOALS

What are *your* most important objectives in learning the material in this chapter? Think about challenges you have had in the past with understanding what college is all about or setting personal goals. List three goals that relate to chapter material (e.g., I will be able to list reasons why college is important for me).

1. _____

_____

2. _____

_____

3. _____

_____

WHY COLLEGE IS IMPORTANT TO OUR SOCIETY

American society values higher education, which explains why the United States has so many colleges and universities—more than 4,400. College is the primary way in which people achieve upward social mobility, or the ability to attain a higher standard of living. In earlier centuries, a high standard of living was almost always a function of family background. Either you were born into power and money or you spent your life working for others who had power and money. But in most countries today, receiving a college degree helps to level the playing field for everyone. A college degree can minimize or eliminate differences due to background, race, ethnicity, family income level, national origin, immigration status, family lineage, and personal connections. Simply put, college participation is about ensuring that more

■ RETENTION STRATEGY: Make a positive prediction of your students' success as a result of taking this course by briefly explaining to them the pervasive research finding that students who participate in college success courses are more likely to persist in and graduate from college.

DID YOU KNOW?

When asked the reasons they are in college, 83% of first-year students say, "to learn more about what interests me"; 65% say, "to get training for a better job"; and 60% say, "to prepare for graduate or professional school."

people have the opportunity to be evaluated on the basis of merit rather than family status, money, or other forms of privilege. It makes achieving the American dream possible.

College is also important because it is society's primary means of preparing citizens for leadership roles. Without a college degree, a person will find it difficult to be a leader in a community, company, profession, or the military.

Another purpose of a four-year college degree is to prepare students for continuing their education in a graduate or professional school. If you want to become a medical doctor, dentist, lawyer, or college professor, a four-year college degree is just the beginning.

Consider staying in touch with your students electronically either by setting up a class e-mail list or by having some kind of Web presence through which students can network with their peers outside of class. Most first-year students can comfortably communicate online. At some institutions, college success classes are linked electronically with similar classes in other parts of the country. This kind of communication gives students the opportunity to develop new perspectives on beginning college successfully.

WHY COLLEGE IS IMPORTANT FOR YOU

College is about thinking, and it will help you understand how to become a "critical thinker"—someone who doesn't believe everything he or she hears or reads but instead looks for evidence before forming an opinion. Developing critical-thinking skills will empower you to make sound decisions throughout your life.

Although college is often thought of as a time when traditional-age students become young adults, we realize that many of you are already adults. Whatever your age, college can be a time when you take some risks, learn new things, and meet new and different people—all in a relatively safe environment. It's OK to experiment in college, within limits, because that's what college is designed for.

College will provide you with numerous opportunities for developing a variety of social networks, both formal and informal. These networks will help you make friends and develop alliances with faculty members and fellow students who share your interests and goals. Social networking Web sites (such as *Facebook* and *Twitter*) provide a way to enrich your real-life social networks in college.

College definitely can and should be fun, and we hope it will be for you. You will meet new people, go to athletic events and parties, build camaraderie with new friends, and feel a sense of school spirit. Many college graduates relive memories of college days throughout their lives, fanatically root for their institution's athletic teams, return for homecoming and class reunions, and encourage their own children to attend their alma mater. In fact, you might be a legacy student—someone whose parents or grandparents attended the same institution.

In addition to being fun, college is a lot of work. Being a college student means spending hours studying each week, staying up late at night, taking high-stakes exams, and possibly working harder than you ever have. For many students, college becomes much like a job, with defined duties, expectations, and obligations.

But most important, college will be a set of experiences that will help you to further define and achieve your own purpose. You might feel that you know exactly what you want to do with your life—where you want to go from here. Or, like many students, you might be struggling to find where you fit in life and work. It is possible that as you discover more about yourself and your abilities, your purpose for coming to college will change. In fact, the vast majority of college students change their academic major at least once during the college years, and some students find they need to transfer to another institution to meet their academic goals.

How would you describe your reasons for being in college and at this particular college? Perhaps you, like the vast majority of college students, see college as the pathway to a good job. Maybe you are in college to train or retrain for an occupation, or maybe you have recently experienced an upheaval in your life. Perhaps you are here to fulfill a lifelong dream of getting an education. Or maybe you are bored or in a rut and see college as a way out of it. As it happens, many students enter college without a purpose that has been clearly thought out. They have just been swept along by life's events, and now here they are.

Your college or university might require you to select a major during or before your first year, even before you have figured out your own purpose for college. Some institutions will allow you to be "undecided" or to select "no preference" for a year or two. Even if you are ready to select a major, it's a good idea to keep an open mind. There are so many avenues to pursue while you're in college—many that you might not have even considered. Or you might come to learn that the career you always dreamed of isn't what you thought it would be at all. You will learn more about choosing a major and a career later in this book, but you ought to use your first year to explore and think about your purpose for college and how that might connect with the rest of your life.

> Take a poll to determine how many students are "undecided" versus "have already picked a major." Assure the students that both are perfectly acceptable places to be when they first come to college. Explain that it is important for students to keep an open mind in their studies and use this time to explore their options.

> ■ RETENTION STRATEGY: While being undecided can have a negative correlation with retention, this is not always the case. Make sure you do not reinforce any stigma for students who are "undecided." Instead, urge them to think of themselves more positively as "exploratory." It is very important to get such students to use your career center early in the first year to influence their direction and commitment. Tell them this course will deal with major, career, and course selection.

YOUR TURN

How would you describe your reasons for coming to college at this time in your life? Do you think your reasons will change during your college career? Why or why not?

Setting Goals for Your College Experience and Beyond

In order to achieve your purpose(s) for being in college, an important first step will be to establish goals—goals for today, this week, this year, and beyond. While some students prefer to "go with the flow" and let life happen to them, those students are less likely to achieve success in college or in a career. So instead of "going with the flow" and simply reacting to what college and life present, think instead about how you can take more control over the decisions and choices you make now that lay the foundation for the achievement of future life goals. Many of us find it easy to make vague plans for the future, but we need to determine which short-term steps are necessary if those plans are to become a reality. Researchers who study the importance of goal setting believe that you are more likely to reach goals if you have plans that are SMART: Specific, Measurable, Attainable, Relevant, and anchored to a Time period.[1]

[1]G. T. Doran, "There's a S.M.A.R.T. Way to Write Management's Goals and Objectives," *Management Review* 70, no. 11 (1981): 35–36.

TECH TIP EXPAND YOUR SKILLS

These days, if you want to become a successful student—and, ultimately, move yourself to the top of the job heap—some computer know-how beyond *Facebook* and *Xbox* is crucial. Chances are, it's time for your tech skills to grow up.

1 ▶ THE PROBLEM

You've entered college with limited computer skills.

2 ▶ THE FIX

Assess your ability to use basic software (like *Word*, *Excel*, and *PowerPoint*). Once you've determined your most pressing needs, fill in the gaps.

3 ▶ HOW TO DO IT

PROGRAM	ESSENTIAL SKILLS	GOOD TO KNOW
Microsoft *Word* Word processing program that helps you create polished documents. You'll use this for most of your written assignments.	How to . . . • Open and save documents • Cut, copy, and paste • Adjust font and page layout • Undo changes • Bold text • E-mail documents	How to . . . • Use page numbers • Insert page breaks • Create bullet points • Merge documents • Run a word count • Add footnotes and endnotes
Microsoft *Excel* A spreadsheet application that's great for constructing charts and lists and for analyzing data.	How to . . . • Build basic spreadsheets • Save files • Enter and move data • Make calculations • Create charts and graphs • Copy or merge cells	How to . . . • Format cells, rows, and columns • Use the VLOOKUP function • Freeze panes • Write macros • Use absolute and relative cell references
Microsoft *PowerPoint* Presentation software that lets you craft first-rate digital slide shows with text, graphics, and multimedia elements.	How to . . . • Create and delete slides • Insert images or graphs • Select a design template • Animate or edit slides • Create a slideshow • Switch background colors	How to . . . • Print slides and handouts • Merge or reorder slides • Add hyperlinks • Control slide transitions and timing • Copy to CD or USB drive

CALLING IN THE EXPERTS

Some campuses offer a one-stop shop—a learning-based computer lab—that can get you up to speed. Not available on your campus? Try some other proven strategies:

- Beg a techie friend to take you on as a project.
- Consult your professor or teaching assistant.
- Take a course in basic computer skills, either online or on campus.
- Spend some time on your own figuring out the programs through trial and error.
- Read a beginner's manual or ask questions on online computer forums.
- Look into workshops at your college library or student success center.
- Join a computer club to surround yourself with software prodigies.

PERSONAL BEST

List your tech goals here, along with the steps you need to take to hone your skills:

_____

_____

_____

STEPS TO PAINLESS ONLINE ENROLLMENT

1. Consult your academic adviser in advance, to make sure you're taking the courses you need for your major and in the right sequence.
2. Write down three different game plans, in case some of the classes you want are already filled or closed.
3. Register on time. While you're at it, find out your school's drop/add policy. That way, you can avoid paying a penalty if you decide to switch out of a course or into a new one.

EQUALLY IMPORTANT

- The ability to log into course-management systems like *Blackboard* or *Moodle*. These let you track your grades, check assignments, submit projects online, access outside reading for classes, and so on.
- Access to (and scrupulous monitoring of) your school e-mail account. Professors and administrators use school e-mail to communicate critical messages about everything from class cancellations to tuition bills.

For instance, let's assume that after you graduate you think you might want to work in an underdeveloped country, perhaps spending some time in the Peace Corps. What are some short-term goals that would help you reach this long-term objective? One goal might be to take courses focused on different countries or cultures. But that goal isn't very specific, nor does it state a particular time period. A much more specific goal would be to take one course each year that would help you build a body of knowledge about other countries and cultures. An even more specific goal would be to review the course catalog and identify the courses you wanted to take and list them on a personal time line. You could also look for courses that give you the opportunity to engage in **service learning**. Course-based service activities will give you a taste of the kind of work you might be doing later in an underdeveloped country.

You might also want to gain some actual experience before making a final decision about working in other countries. Another intermediate goal could be traveling to other countries or combining the earning of college credits with performing service abroad through an international organization such as the Partnership for Service Learning. Your goal for this week could be doing an Internet search or visiting your campus study-abroad office to research your options for international travel or service work.

Before working toward any long-term goal, it's important for you to be realistic and honest with yourself. Is this your goal—one that you value and desire to pursue—or is this a goal that a parent or friend argued was "right" for you? Given your abilities and interests, is the goal realistic? Remember that dreaming up long-term goals is the easy part. You need to be very specific and systematic about the steps you will take today, this week, and throughout your college experience to reach your goals.

service learning Unpaid volunteer service that is embedded in courses across the curriculum.

Outcomes of College

Although a college degree clearly will make you more professionally marketable, the college experience can enrich your life in many other ways. We hope you will take advantage of the many opportunities you'll have to learn the skills of leadership, experience diversity, explore other countries and cultures, clarify your beliefs and values, and make decisions about the rest of your life—not just what you want to do but also, more important, how you want to live.

When you made the decision to come to college, you probably didn't think about all of the positive ways in which college could affect the rest of your life. Your reasons for coming might have been more personal and more immediate. There are all sorts of reasons, circumstances, events, and pressures that bring students to college; and when you put different people with different motivations and purposes together, it creates an interesting environment for learning.

Many college graduates report that higher education changed them for the better. Read the information in the following box to learn how completing a college degree will make a positive difference for you.

Ask your students whether they have thought about where they would like to be in the next five years. Ten years? What skills and values drive these goals? Challenge your students to write down a five- or ten-year plan and refer to the plan throughout their college years as a motivational reminder.

Ask your students which is more important: education for its own sake or education for the sake of earning more money? This might lead to a lively debate.

OUTCOMES OF THE COLLEGE EXPERIENCE

> You will learn how to accumulate knowledge.

> You will be more likely to seek appropriate information before making a decision. Such information will also help you to realize how our lives are shaped by global, local, political, social, psychological, economic, environmental, and physical forces.

> You will grow intellectually through interactions with cultures, languages, ethnic groups, religions, nationalities, and socioeconomic groups other than your own.

> You will gain self-esteem and self-confidence, which will help you realize how you might make a difference in the world.

> You will tend to be more flexible in your views, more future-oriented, more willing to appreciate differences of opinion, and more interested in political and public affairs.

> If you have children, they will be more likely to have greater learning potential, which in turn will help them to achieve more in life.

> You will be an efficient consumer, save more money, make better investments, and be more likely to spend money on your home and on intellectual and cultural interests as well as on your children.

> You will be better able to deal with bureaucracies, the legal system, tax laws, and advertising claims.

> You will be more involved in education, hobbies, and civic and community affairs.

> You will be more concerned with wellness and preventive health care. Through diet, exercise, stress management, a positive attitude, and other factors, you will live longer and suffer fewer disabilities.

■ RETENTION STRATEGY: Try to get students to understand the significance of these outcomes. This will aid motivation, commitment, and retention.

We know that college will make your life different from the one you would have had if you had never been a college student. Consider the following list. You will note that the first item is that college graduates earn more money. (Look at Figure 1.1 to see exactly how much more.) However, note that these differences go far beyond making more money. When compared to non-college graduates, those who graduate from college are more likely to:

- earn more money
- have a less erratic job history
- achieve more promotions
- have fewer children
- be more involved in their children's school lives
- have more discretionary time and money
- become leaders in their communities and employment settings
- stay married longer to the same person
- be elected to public office
- participate in and enjoy the arts

When compared to nongraduates, college graduates are less likely to:

- be imprisoned
- become dependent on alcohol or drugs
- be duped, conned, or swindled
- be involuntarily unemployed
- use tobacco products

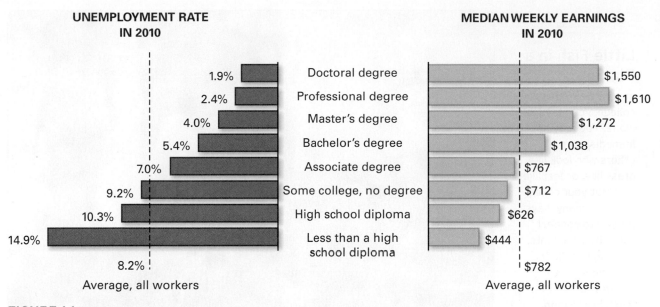

UNEMPLOYMENT RATE IN 2010

		MEDIAN WEEKLY EARNINGS IN 2010
1.9%	Doctoral degree	$1,550
2.4%	Professional degree	$1,610
4.0%	Master's degree	$1,272
5.4%	Bachelor's degree	$1,038
7.0%	Associate degree	$767
9.2%	Some college, no degree	$712
10.3%	High school diploma	$626
14.9%	Less than a high school diploma	$444
8.2%		$782
Average, all workers		Average, all workers

FIGURE 1.1

Education Pays

Source: U.S. Department of Labor, Bureau of Labor Statistics, Current Population Survey, 2010.

Making the Transition

If you just graduated from high school, you will find some distinct differences between high school and college. For instance, you will probably be part of a more diverse student body, not just in terms of race but also in terms of age, religion, political opinions, and life experiences. If you attend a large college or university, you might feel like a number—not as special as you felt in high school. You will have more potential friends to choose from, but familiar assumptions about people based on where they live, where they go to church, or what high school they attend might not apply to the new people you're meeting.

You will be able to choose from many more types of courses, but managing your time is sure to be more complex because your classes will meet on various days and times, and you will have additional commitments, including work, family, activities, and sports. Your college classes might have many more students in them and meet for longer class periods. Tests are given less frequently in college—sometimes only twice a term—and you will most likely be required to do more writing in college. You will be encouraged to do original research and to investigate differing points of view on a topic. You will be expected to study outside of class, prepare assignments, do assigned reading, and be ready for in-class discussions. Your instructors might rely far less on textbooks and far more on lectures than your high school teachers did. Your instructors will rarely monitor your progress; you're on your own. But you will have more freedom to express views that are different from those of your instructors. They will usually have private offices and keep regular office hours in order to be available for you.

> **YOUR TURN**
>
> In what ways are you already finding that college is different from high school? Did you anticipate these differences? Why or why not?

Little Fish in a Big Sea

In your first weeks in college, you may feel alone. You may not immediately meet others who look like, dress like, or feel like you. But your college will offer many ways for you to connect with other students, and soon you'll find new friends with whom you'll share much in common.

If you have both returning students and traditional students in class, consider a discussion in which representatives from each group share their concerns. For example, some returning students might believe they will not be able to keep up with "those kids," while the younger students might feel the class will be more difficult because of the presence of older students.

CHALLENGES AND OPPORTUNITIES FOR ADULT AND RETURNING STUDENTS

If you're a "returning" student—someone who might have experienced some college before—or if you are an adult living and working off campus, you might also find that college presents new challenges and opportunities. For instance, college might feel liberating, like a new beginning or a stimulating challenge or like a path to a career. However, working full-time and attending college at night, on weekends, or both can mean extra stress, especially with a family at home.

Adult students often experience a daunting lack of freedom because of many important conflicting responsibilities. Working, caring for a family, and meeting your other commitments will compete for the time and attention it takes to do your best or even to simply stay in college. You might wonder how you will ever get through college and still manage to care for your family. You might worry that they won't understand why you have to spend time in class and studying.

In spite of your concerns, you should know that many college professors value working with adult students because, unlike eighteen-year-olds, your life

YOUR TURN

As an adult or returning student, what challenges in college have you already faced? To whom can you turn for help? How might you avoid such challenges in the future?

experiences have shown you how important an education can be. Adult students tend to have intrinsic motivation that comes with maturity and experience, and that motivation will compensate for any initial difficulties you might have. You will bring a unique and rich perspective to what you're learning in your classes, a perspective that most eighteen-year-olds lack.

FIRST-YEAR MOTIVATION AND COMMITMENT

What attitudes and behaviors will help you to achieve your goals and be successful in college? If you are fresh out of high school, it will be important for you to learn to deal with newfound freedom. Your college professors are not going to tell you what, how, or when to study. If you live on campus, your parents won't be able to wake you in the morning, see that you eat properly and get enough sleep, monitor whether or how well you do your homework, or remind you to allow enough time to get to class. In almost every aspect of your life, you will have to assume primary responsibility for your own attitudes and behaviors.

If you are an adult student, you might find yourself with less freedom: You might have a difficult daily commute and have to arrange and pay for child care. You might have to juggle work and school responsibilities and still find time for family and other duties. As you walk around campus, you might feel uncertain about your ability to keep up with academic work. You also might find it difficult to relate to younger students, some of whom don't seem to take academic work seriously.

Whatever challenges you are facing, what will motivate you to be successful? And what about the enormous investment of time and money that getting a college degree requires? Are you convinced that the investment will pay off? Have you selected a major, or is this on your list of things to do after you arrive? Do you know where to go when you need help with a personal or financial problem? If you are a minority student on your campus, are you concerned about how you will be treated?

Thoughts like these are very common. Although your classmates might not say it out loud, many of them share your concerns, doubts, and fears. This course will be a safe place for you to talk about all of these issues with people who care about you and your success in college.

> **YOUR TURN**
>
> On a scale of 1 to 5, with 5 being high, rate your own level of motivation for college. What do you think accounts for your current motivation level? If you don't think you are motivated, what strategies can you think of that would help motivate you?

Ask students to name the different freedoms they have in college. Then divide the class into small groups and reach a consensus on the freedoms that pose the greatest challenges for college students. Be sure the students understand the difference between achieving group consensus by resolving their differences, and simply taking a vote, which often ignores the concerns of the minority in favor of the majority.

■ RETENTION STRATEGY: The ways that students use their collegiate freedoms will often determine whether they persist or drop out. Discuss with students the twin concepts of freedom and responsibility and how these connect with the likelihood of success in college.

What Is Your Purpose in College?

Consider these differences in the way a student might feel about college:
I belong in college. . . . . versus . . . . .What on earth am I doing here? Where would you fall between these opposite attitudes? You might find that your exact position shifts depending on what's going on in your academic and personal life at any given time. But no matter how you

Grand Opening

Students attend college for many reasons, and it's a good idea to be open to all kinds of possibilities. Some students dream about opening a small business, and the future for small businesses looks bright in the current economy.

feel on a particular day, as you begin college you will need to spend time sorting out your own sense of purpose and level of motivation. The clearer you are about why you're in college, the easier it will be to stay motivated, even when times are tough.

To build a clearer sense of purpose, look around you and get to know other students who work hard to be successful. Identify students who have the same major or the same career interests, and learn about the courses they have taken, work experiences they have had, and their plans for the future. Look for courses that are relevant to your interests—but don't stop there. Seek relevance in those required general education courses that at first might seem to be a waste of time or energy. Remember that general education courses are designed to give you the kinds of knowledge and skills you need for the rest of your life. Visit your career center, your library, and the Internet to investigate your interests and learn how to develop and apply them in college and beyond. A great Web site to help you research your career interests is the U.S. Department of Labor's Bureau of Labor Statistics (**http://www.bls.gov**), which includes information about average wages for each career by region, job growth statistics, and unemployment rates.

Talk to your residence hall advisers as well as your professors, academic advisers, and campus chaplains. College is designed to give you all the tools you need to find and achieve your purpose. It's all at your fingertips—but the rest is up to you.

Assign a campus scavenger hunt. Have the class divide into small teams, and direct each team to visit one office on campus that provides services and academic support to students. Each team is to report back to the class with information on the name, location, and services offered. Students could also bring written material to distribute in class. Another scavenger hunt might involve students visiting as many offices as possible and taking photos of themselves at each office while gathering some information. Most students have digital cameras or camera phones. It could be fun for the students to share the pictures in class or upload them to a secure Web site.

■ RETENTION STRATEGY: Retention and degree attainment are more likely with students who have a strongly developed sense of purpose and the ability to set short-term and long-term goals.

CHECKLIST FOR SUCCESS

GETTING OFF TO THE RIGHT START

☐ **Keep up with your weekly schedule and do your work on time.** Get a paper calendar or an electronic one, and use it consistently to keep track of assignments and appointments.

☐ **Be on time for class.** If you are frequently late, you give your instructors and fellow students the unspoken message that you don't think the class is important.

☐ **If you are a full-time student, limit the hours you work. If you must work, look for a job on campus.** Students who work a reasonable number of hours per week (about fifteen) and especially those who work on campus are more likely to do well in college.

☐ **Improve your study habits.** Find the most effective methods for reading textbooks, listening, taking notes, studying, and using information resources.

☐ **Use the academic skills center, library, and campus career center.** These essential services are there to help you be a better student and plan for your future.

☐ **Learn to think critically.** If you don't carefully examine and evaluate what you see, read, and hear, you're not really learning.

☐ **Strive to improve your writing and speaking.** The more you write and speak in public, the easier these skills will become now and in the future.

☐ **Speak up in class.** Research indicates that you will usually remember more about what goes on in class when you get involved.

☐ **Learn from criticism.** Criticism can be helpful to your learning. If you get a low grade, meet with your instructor to discuss how you can improve.

☐ **Study with a group.** Research shows that students who study in groups often earn the highest grades and have the fewest academic problems.

☐ **Become engaged in campus activities.** Visit the student activities office; join a club or organization that interests you; participate in community service.

☐ **Meet with your instructors out of class.** Instructors generally have office hours; successful students use them.

☐ **Find a competent and caring academic adviser or counselor.** If your personality and that of your adviser clash, ask the department office to find another adviser for you.

☐ **Take your health seriously.** How much you sleep, what you eat, whether you exercise, and how well you deal with stress will affect your college success.

☐ **Have realistic expectations.** If you are disappointed in your grades, remember that college is a new experience and your grades will probably improve if you continue to apply yourself.

BUILD YOUR EXPERIENCE

1 STAY ON TRACK

Successful college students stay focused. They "stay on track." They know what they have to do to be successful, they set goals, and they monitor their progress toward their goals.

Reflect on what you have learned about college success in this chapter and how you are going to apply the chapter information or strategies in college and in your career. List your ideas.

1. _____
   _____
   _____

2. _____
   _____
   _____

3. _____
   _____
   _____

2 ONE-MINUTE PAPER

Chapter 1 explores how deciding to go to college, experiencing college life, and finding your own path can be a unique journey. Sometimes things that seem simple are more complex and interesting if they are given some thought. Take a minute (or several) to think about and note what you found most useful or meaningful during this class. Did anything that was covered in this chapter leave you with more questions than answers?

No matter how well prepared you are in your teaching, what a student hears and understands might not always be what you think you have said. The one-minute paper is a quick and easy assessment tool that will help alert you when students don't understand what was said or discussed in class. The one-minute paper will also give timid students an opportunity to ask questions and seek clarification. Ideally, you should ask for such a paper several minutes before the end of a class. The paper will also help you begin your next class, by clarifying points your students seem to be unsure of.

3 APPLYING WHAT YOU'VE LEARNED

Now that you have read and discussed this chapter, consider how you can apply what you have learned to your academic and personal life. The following prompts will help you reflect on chapter material and its relevance to you both now and in the future.

1. Review the Outcomes of College section of this chapter. While landing a lucrative career is probably high on your list of goals after college, take a look at the other possible outcomes of obtaining a college degree. List five outcomes from this section that are most relevant to you. If you think of an outcome that is not noted in the chapter, add it to your top five. Why are these outcomes important to you?

2. College students often feel the stress of trying to balance their personal and academic lives. The ups and downs of life are inevitable, but we can control our choices and attitudes. As a first-year student, you will want to begin developing a personal strategy for bouncing back after a particularly difficult time. Your strategy should include at least three steps you can take to get back on track and move forward.

4 BUILDING YOUR PORTFOLIO

What's in It for Me? Skills Matrix   How might the courses in which you are enrolled right now affect your future? Although it might be hard to imagine that there is a direct connection to your career or lifestyle after college, the classes and experiences you are now engaged in can play an important role in your future.

Developing a skills matrix will help you reflect on your college experiences and track the skills that will eventually help you land a great summer job, the hard-to-get internship, a scholarship, and, one day, a career.

1. Using Microsoft *Excel* or another spreadsheet software, develop a skills matrix to identify courses and out-of-class experiences that enhance the following skills: communications, creativity, critical thinking, leadership, research, social responsibility, and teamwork. View an example at the book Web site **bedfordstmartins.com/gardner**.

2. Add any additional skills categories or courses you would like to track.

3. Indicate what you did in your courses or activities that helped you learn one of these skills. Be specific about the assignment, project, or activity that helped you learn.

4. Save your skills matrix on your computer, flash drive, or external hard drive.

5. Update your matrix often. Add new skills categories, courses, and activities. Change the title to indicate the appropriate time period (e.g., Skills Learned in My First Two Years of College).

6. Start an electronic collection of your college work. Save papers, projects, and other relevant material in one location on your computer or on an external storage device. Be sure to back up your work to avoid digital disasters!

For more on this topic watch
French Fries Are Not Vegetables and Other College Lessons

WHERE TO GO FOR HELP. . .

ON CAMPUS

To find the college support services you need, ask your academic adviser or counselor or consult your college catalog, phone book, and college Web site. Or call or visit student services (or student affairs) offices. Most of these services are free. In subsequent chapters, we will include a Where to Go for Help feature that is specific to the chapter topic.

> **Academic Advisement Center** Help in choosing courses; information on degree requirements; help in finding a major.

> **Academic Skills Center** Tutoring; help in study and memory skills; help in studying for exams.

> **Adult Reentry Center** Programs for returning students; supportive contacts with other adult students; information about services such as child care.

> **Career Center** Career library; interest assessments; counseling; help in finding a major; job and internship listings; co-op listings; interviews with prospective employers; help with résumés and interview skills.

> **Chaplains** Worship services; fellowship; personal counseling.

> **Commuter Services** List of off-campus housing, roommate lists, orientation to community, maps, public transportation guides, child-care listings.

> **Computer Center** Minicourses; handouts on campus computer resources.

> **Counseling Center** Confidential counseling for personal concerns; stress management programs.

> **Disabled Student Services** Assistance in overcoming physical barriers or learning disabilities.

> **Financial Aid and Scholarship Office** Information on financial aid programs, scholarships, and grants.

> **Fitness Center** Facilities and equipment for exercise and recreational sports.

> **Health Center** Help in personal nutrition, weight control, exercise, and sexuality; information on substance abuse programs and other health issues; often includes a pharmacy.

> **Housing Office** Help in locating on- or off-campus housing.

> **Legal Services** Legal aid for students; if your campus has a law school, possible assistance by senior law students.

> **Math Center** Help with math skills.

> **Writing Center** Help with writing assignments.

MY INSTITUTION'S RESOURCES

_____

_____

_____

_____

_____

_____

_____

_____

CHAPTER 2
Managing Your Time

**IN THIS CHAPTER
YOU WILL EXPLORE**

How to take control of your
time and your life

How to use goals and objectives
to guide your planning

How to prioritize your use
of time

How to combat procrastination

How to use a planner and
other tools

How to organize your day,
your week, your school term

The value of a to-do list

How to avoid distractions

> It is difficult balancing school, volunteer
work, and a job, but as long as you have
everything scheduled and planned it is easily
achievable and very rewarding.

Emma Kay, 19
Business Management major
California State University, Chico

When Emma Kay started college, she had already begun to build
a solid foundation in time-management skills. She was born in
London, England, and moved to Chico, Calif., when she was
three years old. During her senior year of high school she participated in a "college connections" program, which meant taking
all of her classes at a local college for transferable credit. Part of
the curriculum was geared toward learning how to manage time
and set priorities. She credits that course with helping her
learn how to manage time in her first year
of college and beyond. But even with a
solid foundation, Emma didn't make
it through her first year of college
without a few time-management
roadblocks. "Sometimes I just got
overwhelmed with school and just
wanted to work or hang out with my
friends and would put my schoolwork
on the back burner. This had some
bad side effects. Once I saw the drop
in my grades I knew that I had to
reprioritize and get back on track."

Emma Kay ▶

One of the keys to Emma's success with time management is organization. "I use both paper and electronic organizational tools. If my computer ever goes down, I still have all of my information, plans, and due dates in my planner, and vice versa—if I lose my planner, I still have everything on my computer."

Emma recognizes that prioritizing is key to maintaining her busy schedule and her sanity. "My first priority is school, second comes work, and then everything else (volunteering, exercising, friends, and family). I find places in my schedule to fit them in every week. All of these things are important and essential for me to be successful and happy. It's like each piece of my life is a puzzle piece. If I don't keep making sure that each piece fits, or if there is any piece missing, the puzzle doesn't work and breaks apart."

Emma recently changed her major from Interior Design to Business Management. She just returned from a semester abroad in France and is planning to transfer to a school more geared toward her new major and minors. After college she hopes to go to a big city and find a job with an accounting firm and work toward getting her certified public accountant (CPA) license. Her advice to other first-year students: "Take a class on time management and balancing all of your priorities. It definitely helped me ease into college life and balance my life."

How do you approach time? You might find that you view this important resource differently from Emma or your classmates. Some of these differences might have to do with your personality and background. And often, these differences are so automatic and ingrained that you don't even think about them. For example, if you're a natural organizer, you probably enter all due dates for assignments on your calendar, cell phone, or computer as soon as you receive each syllabus. If you take a more laid-back approach to life, you might prefer to be more flexible and go with the flow rather than following a daily or weekly schedule. You might be good at dealing with the unexpected, but you also might be a procrastinator.

Most fundamentally, how you manage time reflects what you value—what is most important to you and what consequences you are willing to accept when you make certain choices. For instance, when you value friendships above everything else, your academic work can take a back seat to social activities. What you value most and how that relates to the way you spend your time often change in college. How you manage this resource corresponds to how successful you will be in college and throughout life.

Time management involves:

Knowing your goals	Taking control of your time
Setting priorities to meet your goals	Making a commitment to punctuality
Anticipating the unexpected	Carrying out your plans

Guide students to understand that the demands of college require practical time-management plans, regardless of their previous habits, diverse backgrounds, and different personal styles.

Taking Control of Your Time

The first step to effective time management is recognizing that you can be in control. How often do you find yourself saying, "I don't have time"? Once a week? Once a day? Several times a day? The next time you find yourself saying this, stop and ask yourself whether it is really true. Do you really not have time, or have you made a choice, consciously or unconsciously, not to make time for that particular task or activity?

◼ ASSESSING YOUR STRENGTHS ◼

Time management is a challenge for almost all college students. Are you a good time manager? Now that you have read the first section of this chapter, list the strengths you have in this area.

_____

_____

_____

_____

◼ SETTING GOALS ◼

What are your most important objectives in learning the material in this chapter? Think about challenges you have had in the past with managing your time. List three goals that relate to time management (e.g., I will keep an hour-by-hour record this week of how I spend my time).

1. _____

_____

2. _____

_____

3. _____

_____

When we say that we don't have time, we imply that we don't have a choice. But we do have a choice. We have control over how we use our time. We have control over many of the commitments we choose to make. And we also have control over many small decisions that affect our time-management success, such as what time we get up in the morning, how much sleep we get, what we eat, how much time we spend studying, and whether we get exercise. All of these small decisions have a big impact on our success in college and in life.

Being in control means that you make your own decisions. Two of the most often cited differences between high school and college are increased **autonomy**, or independence, and greater responsibility. If you are not a recent high school graduate, you have most likely already experienced a higher level of independence, but returning to school creates responsibilities above and beyond those you already have, whether those include employment, family, community service, or other activities.

Whether you are beginning college immediately after high school or are continuing your education after a break, make sure that the way you spend your time aligns with your most important values. For instance, if you value becoming an expert in a particular academic area, you'll want to learn everything you can in that field by taking related classes and participating in

◼ **RETENTION STRATEGY:** Ask students to discuss times when they have succeeded or struggled with time management. Successful students often report that their number one success strategy is time management, and conversely students who leave college often do so because they could not manage their time.

autonomy Self-direction or independence. College students usually have more autonomy than they did in high school.

IN CLASS: Assign students to groups of three to six, and have them compare high school and college in terms of recognizing the need for a better time-management plan. For groups of students who are not recent high school graduates, modify the activity to explore differences between being in college and the world of work or the responsibilities of being a homemaker or parent.

■ RETENTION STRATEGY: Introduce the concept of "locus of control," or the extent to which individuals believe they can control events that affect them; then relate the concept to wise choices in time management. Students who learn to take responsibility for their own choices increase their chances of persisting and graduating.

IN CLASS: Ask students to think about times when they have procrastinated in completing an assignment or a project. Why do they think they procrastinated? Why is procrastination a problem in managing time? Are there psychological reasons why people procrastinate?

IN CLASS: Ask students to share how they deal with distractions and procrastination. To stimulate discussion, ask students to brainstorm ideas, make a list on the board, and vote on what strategies would work best for them.

internships. If you value learning about many things and postponing a specific decision about your major, you might want to spend your time exploring many different areas of interest and taking as many different types of courses as possible. To take control of your life and your time and to guide your decisions, begin by setting some goals for the future.

OVERCOMING PROCRASTINATION

Procrastination is a serious problem that trips up many otherwise capable people. There are numerous reasons why students procrastinate. In the book *Procrastination: Why You Do It, What to Do About It*, psychologists Jane Burka and Lenora Yuen summarize a number of research studies about procrastination.[1] According to these authors, even students who are highly motivated often fear failure, and some students even fear success (although that might seem counterintuitive). Some students procrastinate because they are perfectionists; not doing a task might be easier than having to live up to your own very high expectations—or those of your parents, teachers, or peers. Others procrastinate because they find an assigned task boring or irrelevant or consider it "busy work," believing that they can learn the material just as effectively without doing the homework.

Simply not enjoying an assignment is not a good reason to put it off; it's an *excuse*, not a valid *reason*. Throughout life you'll be faced with tasks that you don't find interesting, and in many cases you won't have the option not

[1]Jane B. Burka and Lenora M. Yuen, *Procrastination: Why You Do It, What to Do About It* (Reading, MA: Addison-Wesley, 1983).

to do them. For instance, when you work in an entry-level job, you might find that you are assigned tedious tasks that are generally reserved for new employees. On a more personal level, you might occasionally put off cleaning your house or your room until the day comes when you can't find an important file or document. At that point, cleaning your personal space becomes an essential task, not an optional one.

When you're in college, procrastinating can signal that it's time to reassess your goals and objectives; maybe you are not ready to make a commitment to academic priorities at this point in your life. Only you can decide, but a counselor or academic adviser can help you sort it out.

Here are some strategies for beating procrastination:

■ Remind yourself of the possible consequences if you do not get down to work, and then get started.

■ Create a to-do list. Check off things as you get them done. Use the list to focus on the things that aren't getting done. Move them to the top of the next day's list, and make up your mind to do them. Working from a list will give you a feeling of accomplishment.

■ Break big jobs into smaller steps. Tackle short, easy-to-accomplish tasks first.

■ Promise yourself a reward for finishing the task, such as watching your favorite TV show or going out with friends. For more substantial tasks, give yourself bigger and better rewards.

■ Find a place to study that's comfortable and doesn't allow for distractions and interruptions. Say "no" to friends and family members who want your attention; agree to spend time with them later.

■ Don't talk on the phone, send e-mail or text messages, or surf the Web during planned study sessions. If you study in your room, close your door.

If these ideas don't sufficiently motivate you to get to work, you might want to reexamine your purposes, values, and priorities. Keep coming back to some basic questions: Why am I in college here and now? Why am I in this course? What is really important to me? Are these values important enough to forgo some short-term fun or laziness in order to get down to work? Are my academic goals really my own, or were they imposed on me by family members, my employer, or societal expectations? If you are not willing to stop procrastinating and get to work on the tasks at hand, perhaps you should reconsider why you are in college and if this is the right time to pursue higher education.

Researchers at Carleton University in Canada have found that college students who procrastinate in their studies also avoid confronting other tasks and problems and are more likely to develop unhealthy habits, such as higher levels of alcohol consumption, smoking, insomnia, a poor diet, or lack of exercise.[2] If you cannot get procrastination under control, it is in your best interest to seek help at your campus counseling service before you begin to feel as though you are also losing control over other aspects of your life.

OUTSIDE CLASS: Assign a short paper on how students experience the results of procrastination. They should describe the situation, revealing the cause of procrastination and the consequences. The paper should also explain how the student could have handled the situation better.

IN CLASS: Discuss ways to avoid procrastination. What works for you? Give examples from your experience.

■ RETENTION STRATEGY: Procrastination can be related to poor academic performance and hence attrition.

[2]Timothy A. Pychyl and Fuschia M. Sirois, "Procrastination: Costs to Health and Well-being" (presentation at the APA Convention, August 22, 2002, Chicago).

Work Study

Did you know that the majority of college students have jobs? If you need to work, try to find a job that is flexible and allows you to study during your off-time. Use every available minute to stay up to date with your classwork.

SETTING PRIORITIES

To help combat the urge to procrastinate, you should think about how to prioritize your tasks, goals, and values. Which goals and objectives are most important to you and most consistent with your values? Which are the most urgent? For example, studying in order to get a good grade on tomorrow's test might have to take priority over attending a job fair today. However, don't ignore long-term goals in order to meet short-term goals. With good time management you can study during the week prior to the test so that you can attend the job fair the day before. Skilled time managers often establish priorities by maintaining a to-do list (discussed in more detail later in this chapter), ranking the items on the list to determine schedules and deadlines for each task.

Another aspect of setting priorities while in college is finding an appropriate way to balance your academic schedule with the rest of your life. Social activities are an important part of the college experience. Time alone and time to think are also essential to your overall well-being.

For many students, the greatest challenge of prioritizing will be balancing school with work and family obligations that are equally important and are not optional. Good advance planning will help you meet these challenges. But you will also need to talk with your family members and your employer to make sure that they understand your academic responsibilities. Most professors will work with you when conflicts arise, but if you

YOUR TURN

What are your most pressing obligations, other than your studies, that will have to fit into your time-management plan? Are any of them more important to you than doing well in college? Why or why not?

have problems that can't be resolved easily, be sure to seek support from the professionals in your college's counseling center. They will understand your challenges and help you manage and prioritize your many responsibilities.

STAYING FOCUSED

Many of the decisions you make today are reversible. You can change your major, your career, and even your life goals. But it is important to take control of your life by establishing your own goals for the future, setting your priorities, and managing your time accordingly. Many first-year students, especially recent high school graduates, might temporarily forget their primary purposes for coming to college, lose sight of their goals, and spend their first term of college engaging in a wide array of new experiences. This is okay to do within limits, but some students spend the next four or five years trying to make up for poor decisions they made early in their college careers, such as skipping class and not taking their assignments seriously. Such decisions can lead to plummeting grade point averages (GPAs) and the threat of academic probation or, worse, academic dismissal. Staying focused means always keeping your eyes on your most important purposes for being in college. Ask yourself whether what you are doing at any moment contributes to, or detracts from, those purposes.

> **DID YOU KNOW?**
> --------------------------------
> 35% of first-year students find it difficult to adjust to the academic demands of college.

Many students of all ages question their decision to attend college and might sometimes feel overwhelmed by the additional responsibilities it brings. Prioritizing, rethinking some commitments, letting some things go, and weighing the advantages and disadvantages of attending school part-time versus full-time can help you work through this adjustment period. Again, keep your long-term goals in mind and find ways to manage your stress rather than reacting to it. While this book is full of suggestions for enhancing academic success, the bottom line is to stay focused and take control of your time and your life. Make a plan that begins with your priorities: attending classes, studying, working, and spending time with the people who are important to you. Then think about the necessities of life: sleeping, eating, exercising, and relaxing. Leave time for fun things such as talking with friends, checking out *Facebook*, watching TV, and going out. But finish what *needs* to be done before you move from work to pleasure. And don't forget about personal time. If you live in a residence hall or share an apartment with other students, talk with your roommates about how you can coordinate your class schedules so that each of you has some privacy. If you live with your family, particularly if you are a parent, work together to create special family times as well as quiet study times.

IN CLASS: Time management often requires the use of the word *no*. Ask students to discuss how saying *no* relates to the way they manage their time.

IN CLASS: Have pairs of students discuss their "perfect life" ten years from now. What goals do they need to set now to achieve their dreams?

IN CLASS: Brainstorm skills and experiences that students might like to have on their résumés when they complete their education that will make them stand out from the pack and impress future employers. Encourage students to write down ideas they could set for themselves as short-term goals.

> **YOUR TURN**
>
> List your current priorities in order of importance. What does your list suggest about why you consider some things more important? Less important? Have you put any items in the wrong place? What should you change, and why?

Getting Organized

In college, as in life, you will quickly learn that managing time is important to success. Almost all successful people use some sort of calendar or planner, either paper or electronic, to help them keep up with their appointments, assignments or tasks, and other important activities and commitments.

USE A PLANNER

Your college might design and sell a calendar in the campus bookstore designed specifically for your school, with important dates and deadlines already provided. Or you might prefer to use an online calendar or the calendar that comes on your computer or cell phone. Regardless of the format you prefer (electronic or hard copy), it's a good idea to begin the term by completing a term assignment preview (Figure 2.1). This is a template you can use to map your schedule for an entire term.

DID YOU KNOW?

48% of first-year students find it difficult to manage their time effectively.

To create a term assignment preview, begin by entering all of your commitments for each week: classes, assignment due dates, work hours, family commitments, and so on. Examine your toughest weeks during the term. If paper deadlines and test dates fall during the same week, find time to finish some assignments early to free up study and writing time. Note this on your cell phone or calendar. If you use an electronic calendar, set a reminder for these important deadlines and dates. Break large assignments (term papers, for example) into smaller steps, such as choosing a topic, doing research, creating an outline, learning necessary computer skills, writing a first draft, and so on. Add deadlines in your term assignment preview for each of the smaller portions of the project. Breaking a large project into smaller steps is something you will probably have to do for yourself. Most professors won't provide this level of detailed assistance.

After you complete your term assignment preview, enter important dates and notes from the preview sheets into your calendar or planner and continue to enter all due dates as soon as you know them. Write down meeting times and locations, scheduled social events (including phone numbers in case you need to cancel), study time for each class you're taking, and so forth. It's best not to rely solely on an electronic calendar. Keep a backup copy on paper in case you lose your phone, you can't access the Internet, or your computer crashes. It's also a good idea to carry your calendar or planner with you in a place where you're not likely to lose it. Your first term of college is the time to get into the habit of using a planner to help you keep track of commitments and maintain control of your schedule. This practice will become invaluable to you in your career. Check your notes daily at the same time of day for the current week as well as the coming week. It takes just a moment to be certain that you aren't forgetting something important, and it helps to relieve stress.

YOUR TURN

What kind of planner do you currently use, if any? Does your method of planning work for you? Why or why not?

	Monday	Tuesday	Wednesday	Thursday	Friday
Week 1	✕	✕	First day of <u>Classes!</u>	Read Ch. 1–2 English	Discuss Ch. 1–2 History in Class Work 2–5
Week 2	English Quiz Ch. 1–2 Work 4–7	Psych Quiz Ch. 1	English Essay #1 Due Work 4–7	History Quiz Ch. 1–2	English Quiz Ch. 1–2 Work 2–5
Week 3	English Quiz Ch. 3–4 Work 4–7	Psych Quiz Ch. 2 Read Bio Ch. 1–2	English Essay Due Work 4–7	Be Ready for Bio Lab Experiment	Discuss English pp. 151–214 Work 2–5
Week 4	Work 4–7	Read English pp. 214–275	English Essay Due Work 4–7 Discuss pp. 214–275	Read English pp. 276–311	Discuss English pp. 276–311 Work 2–5

	Monday	Tuesday	Wednesday	Thursday	Friday
Week 5	Work 4–7	Psych Quiz Ch. 3–4	English Essay Due Work 4–7	Bio Lab Experiment	Prepare Psych Experiment Work 2–5
Week 6	Work 4–7	Present Psych Experiment	English Essay Due Work 4–7	Bio Lab Experiment	Work 2–5
Week 7	Work 4–7	Study for English Mid-Term	English Mid-Term!! Work 4–7	Bio Lab Experiment	Study Psych Mid-Term Work 2–5
Week 8	Study for Psych Mid-Term Work 4–7	Psych Mid-Term!!	Study for History Mid-Term Work 4–7	Bio Lab Experiment Study for History Mid-Term	History Mid-Term!! Work 2–5

FIGURE 2.1

Term Assignment Preview

Using the course syllabi provided by your instructors, create your own term calendar. You can find blank templates on the book's Web site at **bedfordstmartins.com/gardner**. Remember, for longer assignments, such as term papers, divide the task into smaller parts and establish your own deadline for each part of the assignment, such as deadlines for choosing a topic, completing your library research, developing an outline of the paper, writing a first draft, and so on.

CHART A WEEKLY TIMETABLE

Now that you have created a term preview, the weekly timetable model in Figure 2.2 can help you tentatively plan how to spend your hours in a typical week. Here are some tips for creating a weekly schedule:

- As you create your schedule, try to reserve at least 2 hours of study time for each hour spent in class. This universally accepted "2-for-1" rule reflects faculty members' expectations for how much work you should be doing to earn a good grade in their classes. This means that if you take a typical full-time class load of fifteen credits, for example, you should plan to study an additional 30 hours per week. Think of this 45-hour-per-week commitment as comparable to a full-time job. If you are also working, reconsider how many hours per week it will be reasonable for you to be employed above and beyond this commitment, or consider reducing your credit load.

biorhythms The internal mechanisms that drive our daily patterns of physical, emotional, and mental activity.

- Depending on your **biorhythms**, obligations, and potential distractions, decide whether you study more effectively in the day or in the evening, or a combination of both. Determine whether you are capable of getting up very early in the morning to study or how late you can stay up at night and still wake up for morning classes.

- Not all assignments are equal. Estimate how much time you will need for each one, and begin your work early. A good time manager frequently finishes assignments before actual due dates to allow for emergencies.

YOUR TURN

What are the best and worst times for you to study? Why? Have you found a particular time when it's easier for you to concentrate or be creative?

Keep track of how much time it takes you to complete different kinds of tasks. For example, depending on your skills and interests, it might take longer to read a chapter in a biology text than to read one in a literature text. Keeping track of your time will help you estimate how much time to allocate for similar tasks in the future. How long does it really take you to solve a set of twenty math problems or to write up a chemistry lab? Use your weekly timetable to track how you actually spend your time for an entire week.

MAINTAIN A TO-DO LIST

Once you have plotted your future commitments with a term planner and decided how your time will be spent each week, you can stay on top of your obligations with a to-do list, which is especially handy for last-minute reminders. It can help you keep track of errands you need to run, appointments you need to make, e-mail messages you need to send, and so on—anything you're prone to forget. You can keep this list on your cell phone or in your notebook, or you can post it on your bulletin board. Some people start a new list every day or once a week. Others keep a running list, and throw a page away only when everything on the list is done. Whichever method you prefer, use your to-do list to keep track of all the tasks you need to remember, not just academics. You might want to develop a system for prioritizing the items on

	Sunday	Monday	Tuesday	Wednesday	Thursday	Friday	Saturday
6:00							
7:00							
8:00			BREAKFAST	⟶			
9:00	SLEEP IN!	Review English	PSYCH 101	Review English	PSYCH 101	Review English	
10:00		English 101	Review PSYCH	English 101	Review PSYCH	English 101	ENJOY!
11:00		LUNCH		LUNCH			
12:00		HISTORY 101	LUNCH	HISTORY 101	LUNCH	HISTORY 101	
1:00							
2:00		BIO 101		BIO 101	BIO 101 LAB	WORK	
3:00					↓		BE LAZY!
4:00		WORK		WORK		↓	
5:00							GO
6:00	STUDY ENGLISH	DINNER	DINNER	DINNER	DINNER	DINNER	OUT
7:00	STUDY HISTORY	↓	STUDY ENGLISH		STUDY ENGLISH		WITH
8:00			STUDY HISTORY		STUDY HISTORY		FRIENDS
9:00		STUDY PSYCH	STUDY BIO	STUDY PSYCH			
10:00							
11:00							

FIGURE 2.2

Weekly Timetable

Using your term calendar, create your own weekly timetable. You can find blank templates on the book's Web site at **bedfordstmartins.com/gardner**. As you complete your timetable, keep in mind the suggestions in this chapter. Do you want your classes back to back or with breaks in between? How early in the morning are you willing to start classes? Do you prefer—or do work or family commitments require you—to take evening classes? Are there times of day when you are more alert? Less alert? How many days per week do you want to attend classes? At some institutions you can go to school full-time by attending classes exclusively on Saturday. Plan how you will spend your time for the coming week. Track all of your activities for a full week by entering into your schedule everything you do and how much time each task requires. Use this record to help you estimate the time you will need for similar activities in the future.

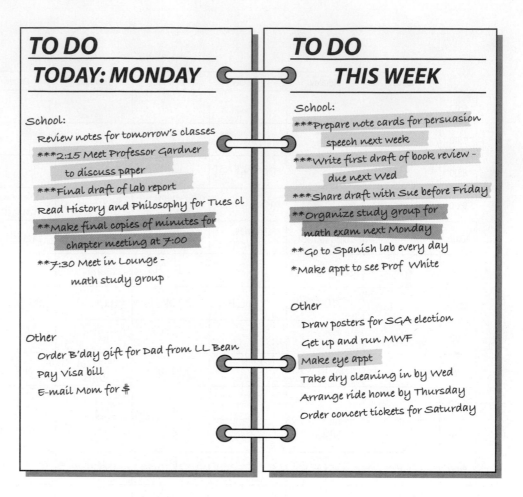

TO DO
TODAY: MONDAY

School:

Review notes for tomorrow's classes
***2:15 Meet Professor Gardner
   to discuss paper
***Final draft of lab report
Read History and Philosophy for Tues cl
**Make final copies of minutes for
   chapter meeting at 7:00
**7:30 Meet in Lounge –
   math study group

Other

Order B'day gift for Dad from LL Bean
Pay Visa bill
E-mail Mom for $

TO DO
THIS WEEK

School:

***Prepare note cards for persuasion
   speech next week
***Write first draft of book review –
   due next Wed
***Share draft with Sue before Friday
**Organize study group for
   math exam next Monday
**Go to Spanish lab every day
*Make appt to see Prof White

Other

Draw posters for SGA election
Get up and run MWF
Make eye appt
Take dry cleaning in by Wed
Arrange ride home by Thursday
Order concert tickets for Saturday

your list: highlight; different colors of ink; one, two, or three stars; or lettered tasks with A, B, C (see Figure 2.3). As you complete each task, cross it off your list. You might be surprised by how much you have accomplished—and how good you feel about it.

Making Sure Your Schedule Works for You

As a first-year student, you might not have had much flexibility in determining your course schedule; by the time you were allowed to register for classes, some sections of the courses you needed might already have been closed. You also might not have known whether you would prefer taking classes back to back or giving yourself a break between classes.

How might you wisely use time between classes? This might have been your first opportunity to take classes that do not meet five days a week. Do you prefer spreading your classes over five or six days of the week, or would you like to go to class just two or three days a week or even once a week for a longer class period? Your attention span and other commitments should

ORGANIZE YOUR DAYS

Being a good student does not necessarily mean studying day and night and doing little else. Notice that the Daily Planner (Figure 2.4) includes time for classes and studying as well as time for other activities. Keep the following points in mind as you organize your day:

> **Set realistic goals for your study time.** Assess how long it takes to read a chapter in different types of textbooks and how long it takes you to review your notes from different instructors, and schedule your time accordingly. Give yourself adequate time to review and then test your knowledge when preparing for exams.

> **Use waiting time to review** (on the bus, before class, before appointments). Prevent forgetting what you have learned by allowing time to review as soon as is reasonable after class. (Reviewing immediately after class might be possible but not reasonable if you are too burned out to concentrate!)

> **Know your best times of day to study.** Schedule other activities, such as laundry, e-mail, or spending time with friends, for times when it will be difficult to concentrate.

> **Restrict repetitive, distracting, and time-consuming tasks** such as checking your e-mail, *Facebook*, or text messages to a certain time, not every hour.

> **Avoid multitasking.** Even though you might actually be quite good at it, or at least think that you are, the reality is (and research shows) that you will be able to study most effectively and retain the most information if you concentrate on one task at a time.

> **Be flexible.** You cannot anticipate every disruption to your plans. Build extra time into your schedule so that unexpected interruptions do not prevent you from meeting your goals.

OUTSIDE CLASS: Ask students to read this box, and assign a short paper on three points they find most valuable and why. Students can meet in groups to discuss their answers. Each group can present their most valuable points and defend their choices. Make a summary of the points the students find most valuable when organizing their days.

influence your decision. In the future, you might have more control over how you schedule your classes. Before you register, think about how to make your class schedule work for you—in other words, how you can create a schedule that allows you to use your time more efficiently. Also consider your own biorhythms and recognize the part of the day or evening in which you are most alert and engaged.

CREATE A WORKABLE CLASS SCHEDULE

If you live on campus, you might want to create a schedule that situates you near a dining hall at mealtimes or allows you to spend breaks between classes at the library. Or you might need breaks in your schedule for relaxation, catching up with friends, or spending time in a student lounge, college union, or campus center. You might want to avoid returning to your residence hall room to take a nap between classes if the result is you feel lethargic or over-sleep and miss later classes. Also, if you attend a large university, be sure that you allow adequate time to get from one class to another.

If you're a commuter student or if you must carry a heavy workload to afford going to school, you might prefer to schedule your classes in blocks without breaks. However, while taking back-to-back classes allows you to cut travel time by attending school one or two days a week and might pro-vide for more flexible scheduling of a job or family commitments, it can also have significant drawbacks.

IN CLASS: Ask students to discuss how much time they spend on the Internet each day. How much on social networking sites? Is this a time-management problem?

IN CLASS: A student's schedule controls how each day (and the total week) is structured. Discuss how a class schedule is a factor in time management.

Month(s) October

Monday the _____ 3 _____

7 AM		2	Review for stats Quiz—Wed!
8		3	Do English reading assignment
9		4	
10	Stats	5	
11	English 101	6	Gym
NOON		7	
1 PM	Lunch w/Jenn	8	

Tuesday the _____ 4 _____

7 AM		2	
8		3	History (3:30)
9	Gym	4	
10		5	Review for stats Quiz
11	Volunteer @ MSPCA	6	Work 6–11
NOON		7	
1 PM	Biology (1:30)	8	

Wednesday the _____ 5 _____

7 AM		2	Do English Reading Assignment
8	Review for stats Quiz	3	
9		4	
10	Stats (Quiz Today!)	5	Meet w/Bio Study Group
11	English 101	6	
NOON		7	
1 PM		8	Volleyball

FIGURE 2.4
Daily Planner

On your daily planner, be sure to enter times for exercise, obligations, and classes. Also add your personal activities, and block out time to study.

When all your classes are scheduled in a block of time, you run several risks. If you become ill on a class day, you could fall behind in all of your classes. You might also become fatigued from sitting in class after class. When one class immediately follows another, it will be difficult for you to have a last-minute study period immediately before a test because you will be attending another class and are likely to have no more than a 15-minute break. Finally, remember that for back-to-back classes, several exams might be held on the same day. Scheduling classes in blocks might work better if you have the option of attending lectures at alternative times in case you are absent, if you alternate classes with free periods, and if you seek out instructors who are flexible with due dates for assignments.

YOUR TURN

Knowing what you know now about your schedule, what will you do differently next term? Will you try to schedule classes close together or spread them apart? Why?

DON'T OVEREXTEND YOURSELF

Being overextended is a primary source of stress for college students. Determine what a realistic workload is for you, but note that this can vary significantly from one person to another. Although being involved in campus life is very important, don't allow your academic work to take a backseat to extracurricular activities or other time commitments. Do not take on more than you can handle. Learn to say "no." Do not feel obligated to provide a reason; you have the right to decline requests that will prevent you from getting your own work done.

IN CLASS: Ask students to discuss how they know when they are overextended and stressed out. What can they do if they feel stressed?

Even with the best intentions, some students who use a time-management plan overextend themselves. If there is not enough time to carry your course load and meet your commitments, drop a course before the drop deadline so that you won't have a low grade on your permanent record. If you receive financial aid, keep in mind that you must be registered for a minimum number of credit hours to be considered a full-time student and thereby maintain your current level of financial aid.

If dropping a course is not feasible or if other activities are lower on your list of priorities, which is likely for most college students, assess your other time commitments and let go of one or more. Doing so can be very difficult, especially if you think that you are letting other people down. However, it is far preferable to excuse yourself from an activity in a way that is respectful to others than to fail to come through at the last minute because you have committed to more than you can possibly achieve.

REDUCE DISTRACTIONS

IN CLASS: Ask students to think about distractions and report the kinds of distractions they have in their environments. How are distractions a problem?

Where should you study? Some students find that it's best not to study in places associated with leisure, such as the kitchen table, the living room, or in front of the TV, because these places lend themselves to interruptions and other distractions. Similarly, it might be unwise to study on your bed because you might drift off to sleep when you need to study or learn to associate your bed with studying and not be able to go to sleep when you

Better Late Than Never?

Be on time to class, but if you have an emergency situation that causes you to run late, talk to your instructor. He or she will understand a real emergency and help you make up work you missed.

need to. Instead, find quiet places, both on campus and at home, where you can concentrate and develop a study mind-set each time you sit down to do your work.

Try to stick to a routine as you study. The more firmly you have established a specific time and a quiet place to study, the more effective you will be in keeping up with your schedule. If you have larger blocks of time available on the weekend, for example, take advantage of that time to review or catch up on major projects, such as term papers, that can't be completed effectively in 50-minute blocks. Break down large tasks and take one thing at a time; you will make more progress toward your ultimate academic goals.

Here are some more tips to help you deal with distractions:

- Turn off the computer, TV, CD or DVD player, iPod, or radio unless the background noise or music really helps you concentrate on your studies or drowns out more distracting noises (people laughing or talking in other rooms or hallways, for instance). Consider silencing your cell phone so that you aren't distracted by incoming calls or text messages.

TECH TIP GET ORGANIZED

Mapping out your schedule needn't be a chore. Think of a well-appointed calendar as a compass for a college student. It's a guide for navigating your current semester and will also keep you pointed toward your long-term goals.

1 ▶ THE PROBLEM

You haven't planned the semester on your calendar yet.

2 ▶ THE FIX

Map out this term's assignments and make a running to-do list on paper. Then take it digital.

3 ▶ HOW TO DO IT

- **Find out if your college sells a special planner** in the campus bookstore with important dates or deadlines already marked. If not, grab a sheet of paper or download a blank calendar page from the Internet.

- **Draw up a semester plan,** entering your commitments for each week: classes, work hours, assignment deadlines, study groups (including contact numbers), and exam and vacation dates.

- **Transfer all the information** into *Outlook*, *iCal*, or a similar *ShareWare* program. When you open *Outlook* or *iCal*, you can view by day, week, or month. Simply click on a date or time slot, follow instructions on the toolbar to create a new entry, and start typing.

- **A useful trick** is to highlight the most important items. As you type in each new entry, you'll have the option to set color-code items by category (e.g., school, work, family). Set reminder alarms to keep yourself on track.

- **Use the to-do list** on the side of the screen to jot down and prioritize tasks. Start a new to-do list every day or once a week. Every time you complete a task, cross it off the list.

- **Sync your calendar and to-do list** to your computer, phone, or BlackBerry. If you need help, visit your college's computer lab or IT department. Alternately, turn to a hyperorganized friend for advice, or click to an *Outlook* tutorial on the Internet.

- **Back up everything,** and file your original paper calendar away for safekeeping in case you experience technical difficulties down the road.

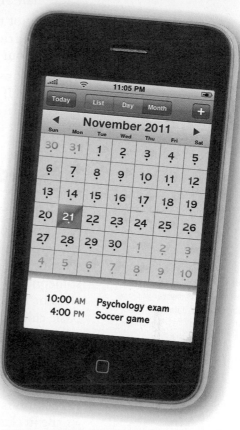

DON'T HAVE OUTLOOK?

No problem. You'll find lots of free time-management tools online, like *Google Calendar* (**www.google.com**), *Yahoo Calendar* (**www.calendar.yahoo.com**), or the calendar in *Windows Live Hotmail* (**www.explore.live.com/windows-live-calendar**).

PERSONAL BEST

Set up a calendar with all of your classes for the semester, and create specific to-do lists for your first three assignments.

EXTRA CREDIT

While you're at it, write up a tentative four-year plan, including required classes in your major and the types of internships or volunteer work you'll need to build your résumé. The exercise will help to demystify the college process—even if you change your major many times down the road.

- Stay away from the computer if you're going to be tempted to check e-mail or *Facebook*.
- Try not to let personal concerns interfere with studying. If necessary, call a friend or write in a journal before you start to study, and then put your worries away.
- Develop an agreement with your roommate(s) or family about quiet hours. If that's not possible, find a quiet place where you can go to concentrate.

IN CLASS: Facilitate a discussion of behaviors that students consider rude or disrespectful. What role can students play in enhancing respect for others in the classroom?

IN CLASS: Discuss how time management relates to respect. Why might a faculty member and other students be irritated if a student arrives late to class? What might tardy students miss?

Respecting Others' Time

How does time management relate to respect? Think of the last time you made an appointment with someone who either forgot the appointment entirely or was very late. Were you upset or disappointed by the person for wasting your time? Most of us have experienced the frustration of having someone else disrespect our time. In college, if you repeatedly arrive late for class or leave before class periods have officially ended, you are breaking the basic rules of politeness, and you are intentionally or unintentionally showing a lack of respect for your instructors and your classmates.

At times, instructors might perceive certain behaviors to be inappropriate or disrespectful. In college, punctuality is a virtue. This might be a difficult adjustment for some students, but you need to be aware of faculty members' expectations at your college or university.

Be in class on time. Arrive early enough to shed your coat, shuffle through your backpack, and have your assignments, notebooks, and writing utensils ready to go. Likewise, be on time for scheduled appointments. Avoid behaviors that show a lack of respect for both the instructor and other students, such as leaving class to feed a parking meter or answer your cell phone, returning 5 or 10 minutes later, thus disrupting class twice. Similarly, text messaging, sending instant messages, doing homework for another class, falling asleep, or talking (even whispering) disrupts the class. Make adequate transportation plans in advance, get enough sleep at night, wake up early enough to be on time for class, and complete assignments prior to class.

Time management is a lifelong skill. Securing a good job after college will likely mean managing your own time and possibly that of other people you supervise. If you decide to go to graduate or professional school, time management will continue to be essential to your success. But not only is time management important for you, it is also a way in which you show respect for others: your friends, family, and your college instructors.

CHECKLIST FOR SUCCESS

TIME MANAGEMENT

☐ **Make sure the way you use your time supports your goals for being in college.** All your time doesn't have to be spent studying, but remember the "2 hours out of class for each hour in class" rule.

☐ **Work to overcome procrastination in your academic work and your life.** If procrastination is a serious problem, seek help from your campus counseling center.

☐ **Get organized by using a planner.** Choose either an electronic format or a paper calendar. Your campus bookstore will have a campus-specific version.

☐ **Devise a weekly timetable of activities, and then stick to it.** Be sure to include special events or responsibilities in addition to recurring activities such as classes, athletic practice, or work hours.

☐ **Create and use day-by-day paper or electronic to-do lists.** Crossing off those tasks you have completed will give you a real sense of satisfaction.

☐ **Identify the things that distract you, and work on reducing those distractions.** Distractions can include people who want your time and attention, loud music, or the chirp of your cell phone letting you know that you have a text message.

☐ **Practice punctuality so you don't miss important activities and unintentionally offend others who are expecting you to be on time.** When you are unavoidably late, apologize to others who were expecting you to be on time.

BUILD YOUR EXPERIENCE

1 STAY ON TRACK

Successful college students stay focused. They "stay on track." They know what they have to do to be successful, they set goals, and they monitor their progress toward their goals.

Reflect on what you have learned about college success in this chapter and how you are going to apply the chapter information or strategies in college and in your career. List your ideas.

1. _____

   _____

   _____

2. _____

   _____

   _____

3. _____

   _____

   _____

2 ONE-MINUTE PAPER

Chapter 2 gives you a lot of tips for managing your time. It can be frustrating to realize that you have to spend time organizing yourself in order to manage your time effectively. Did any of the time-management tips in this chapter really appeal to you? If so, which ones and why? Did anything in this chapter leave you with more questions than answers? If so, what are your questions?

No matter how well prepared you are in your teaching, what a student hears and understands might not always be what you think you have said. The one-minute paper is a quick and easy assessment tool that will help alert you when students don't understand what was said or discussed in class. The one-minute paper will also give timid students an opportunity to ask questions and seek clarification. Ideally, you should ask for such a paper several minutes before the end of a class. The paper will also help you begin your next class by clarifying points your students seem to be unsure of.

 APPLYING WHAT YOU'VE LEARNED

Now that you have read and discussed this chapter, consider how you can apply what you have learned to your academic and personal life. The following prompts will help you to reflect on chapter material and its relevance to you both now and in the future.

1. Review the Overcoming Procrastination section of this chapter. Think of one upcoming assignment in any of your current classes and describe how you can avoid waiting until the last minute to get it done. Break down the assignment, and list each step that you will take to complete the assignment. Give yourself a due date for each step and one for completing the assignment.

2. After reading about effective time-management strategies, consider the way in which you manage your own time. If you were grading your current set of time-management skills, what grade (A, B, C, or lower) would you give yourself? Why? What is your biggest challenge to becoming a more effective time manager?

BUILDING YOUR PORTFOLIO

Time Is of the Essence   This chapter includes many great tips for effectively managing your time. Those skills are necessary for reducing the stress of everyday life, but have you thought about managing your time over the long term? What are your long-term goals? Preparing yourself for a particular career is probably high on your list, and it's not too early to begin thinking about what kind of preparation is necessary for the career (or careers) you are considering.

First, to help you determine the careers you're most interested in pursuing, schedule an appointment with the career center on your campus and ask for information on career assessments to help you identify your preferences and interests. This portfolio assignment will help you realize that it is important to plan ahead and consider what implications your long-term goals have for managing your time right now.

1. In a *Word* document or *Excel* spreadsheet, create a table. See an example on the book's Web site at **bedfordstmartins.com/gardner**.

2. Choose a career or careers in which you're most interested. In the example on the Web site, a student needs to plan ahead for activities that will help to prepare for a future as a certified public accountant. It is okay if you have not decided on just one major or career; this is a process that you can repeat as your interests change. An "action step" is something that you need to do within a certain time frame.

3. Talk with someone in the career center, a professor, an upperclass student in your desired major, or a professional in your chosen career to get an idea of what you need to be considering, even now.

4. Fill in the action steps, to-dos, time line, and notes sections of your own chart, and update the chart as you learn more about the career you are exploring.

5. Save your work in your portfolio.

For more on this topic watch
French Fries Are Not Vegetables and Other College Lessons

WHERE TO GO FOR HELP...

ON CAMPUS

> **Academic Skills Center** Along with assistance in studying for exams, reading textbooks, and taking notes, your campus academic skills center has specialists in time management who can offer advice for your specific problems.

> **Counseling Center** If your problems with time management involve emotional issues you are unable to resolve, consider visiting your school's counseling office.

> **Your Academic Adviser/Counselor** If you have a good relationship with this person, he or she might be able to offer advice or to refer you to another person on campus, including those in the offices mentioned above.

> **A Fellow Student** A friend who is a good student and willing to help you with time management can be one of your most valuable resources.

MY INSTITUTION'S RESOURCES

_____

_____

_____

_____

_____

_____

_____

CHAPTER 3
Understanding Emotional Intelligence

IN THIS CHAPTER YOU WILL EXPLORE

What emotional intelligence is

Why emotional intelligence matters in college and in life

How to assess your emotional intelligence

Specific skills that are connected to emotional intelligence

What you can do to improve your emotional competencies

> 66 **As an Asian, American culture was totally different for me. People talk, behave, and think in ways that I did not understand. This made me feel insecure about who I was.**
>
> Sabeena Maharjan, 21
> Journalism and Broadcasting major
> Oklahoma City Community College

When Sabeena Maharjan finished high school in 2007, she knew that she wanted to study journalism and broadcasting so that she could use the media to positively effect change in her home country of Nepal. She came to the United States to pursue this dream and opted to enroll at Oklahoma City Community College after speaking with other Nepalese students and with the international student adviser at the college.

Sabeena got involved on campus in the International Students Association. She also participated in cultural activities with fellow Nepalese students. But, as Sabeena readily admits, her first year in college was challenging because of the language barrier, course load, cultural differences, and insecurities. However, she did not let these challenges sidetrack her determination to succeed, and her ability to understand and manage her emotions helped her through her challenging first year. "For me it is very important to handle

Sabeena Maharjan ▶

emotions productively. The first year of college is always full of stress because you have so many things to do. I found it stressful when I had to study multiple numbers of subjects in limited time. Exams are the greatest source of stress for me. I even developed a 100-degree fever when I had two tests to take in a day."

The first step Sabeena took in overcoming these challenges was to talk with her professors. "I missed quizzes and deadlines because I didn't know to look at the syllabus. I talked to my professors, and by communicating regularly I understood better how to deal with academics and what the expectations were." She also tackled time management and organization to help her deal with stress. She kept an updated calendar and to-do list with her every day to help her prioritize and complete assignments on time. Sabeena also made time to run in the wellness center to help relieve stress. She adds, "Yet another important thing is to perceive things positively and control our thoughts from being negative."

Now, Sabeena is looking forward to finding an internship in public relations or mass communication and then completing a four-year degree at the University of Central Oklahoma. Her advice to other first-year students? "The first year of college can bring unexpected realities. We cannot change the events, but we can change our thoughts to make us feel better. If you are confused, remember that confusion is the first step toward knowledge. Always talk about your problems to a professor, friend, or counselor. Communication is the key to success."

The ability to understand and get along with people is vital for success in school, work, and life. Another element of success is the ability to manage time well and get things done. Why do some individuals handle stressful situations with ease while others, like Sabeena, struggle? Although we tend to think of these abilities as inborn personality traits that can't be changed, the fact is that social skills and stress-management skills can be learned and improved.

Particularly in the first year of college, many students who are intellectually capable of succeeding have difficulty establishing positive relationships with others, dealing with pressure, or making wise decisions. Other students exude optimism and happiness and seem to adapt to their new environment without any trouble. The difference lies not in academic talent but in emotional intelligence (EI), or the ability to recognize and manage moods, feelings, and attitudes. A growing body of evidence shows a clear connection between students' EI and whether or not they stay in college.

As you read this chapter, you will develop an understanding of emotional intelligence, and you will learn how to use it to become a more successful student and person. You will begin to look at yourself and others through an EI lens, observe the behaviors that help people do well, get to know yourself better, and take the time to examine why you are feeling the way that you do before you act. Then, as you read each subsequent chapter in this book, try to apply what you have learned about EI and think about how it might relate to the behaviors of successful college students. You can't always control the challenges and frustrations of life, but with practice you *can* control how you respond to them.

There are many competing theories and assessment tools for EI—just look online. Four basic models are the most widely used because of their reliability and validity: the MSCEIT (Mayer-Salovey-Caruso Emotional Intelligence Test) developed by John Mayer, Peter Salovey, and David Caruso; Daniel Goleman and Richard Boyatzis's Emotional Competence Inventory; Esther Orioli and Robert Cooper's EQ Map; and the EQ-i (Emotional Quotient Inventory) and the EQ 360, developed by Reuven Bar-On. Because the EQ-i was the first validated tool for college-age students and because most of the research in college has been done using this instrument, this is the tool and model we use as the focus of this chapter.

DID YOU KNOW?

40% of college students feel overwhelmed by all they have to do in their first year of college.

◾ ASSESSING YOUR STRENGTHS ◾

How well you understand and manage your emotions will affect your success in college. Now that you have read the first section of this chapter, list what you believe are your current strengths in the area of emotional intelligence.

_____

_____

_____

_____

◾ SETTING GOALS ◾

What are your most important objectives in learning the material in this chapter? Think about challenges you have had in the past with understanding your emotions and managing your reactions to frustrating circumstances. List three goals that relate to emotional intelligence (e.g., This week I will keep a list of interactions with other people that frustrate me and how I react).

1. _____

_____

2. _____

_____

3. _____

_____

What Is Emotional Intelligence?

Emotional intelligence is the ability to identify, use, understand, and manage emotions. Emotions are a big part of who you are; you should not ignore them. The better the emotional read you have on a situation, the more appropriately you can respond to it. Being aware of your own and others' feelings helps you to gather accurate information about the world around you and allows you to respond in appropriate ways.

There are many competing theories about EI, some of them very complex. While experts vary in their definitions and models, all agree that emotions are real, can be changed for the better, and have a profound impact on whether or not a person is successful.

> **YOUR TURN**
>
> Do you know anybody (including yourself) who is "book smart" but not very good with people? Do you know anyone who has serious problems managing time? What kinds of challenges do these people face? How would improving emotional awareness help?

emotional intelligence
The ability to recognize, understand, use, and manage moods, feelings, and attitudes.

◾ RETENTION STRATEGY: Emotions can be distractions and disruptions or they can be supporters and enablers of college success and retention. Ask students to discuss how their emotions help them engage in their coursework.

Anger Management

Since the 1960s, college students have used their anger about political, social, and campus-specific issues (like tuition increases) in positive ways through organized demonstrations. Such demonstrations have influenced major actions in American history, such as the decision of a former U.S. president to resign and the end of the Vietnam War. Are there any issues that would "bring students to the barricades" today?

Emotional intelligence is not a new concept, although it was made popular by Daniel Goleman's best-selling book *Emotional Intelligence: Why It Can Matter More Than IQ* (1995). The concept of intelligence having more than the cognitive or academic component has been discussed for decades. As early as the 1970s, experts who studied intelligence began to believe that looking only at the cognitive part did not give a full picture of individuals' potential. In the next chapter of this book, students will learn about Howard Gardner's theory of multiple intelligences, learning styles (Kolb and VARK), and the Myers-Briggs Type Indicator as tools they can use to help define their strengths and challenges.

In the simplest terms, emotional intelligence consists of two general abilities:[1]

- **Understanding emotions** involves the capacity to monitor and label feelings accurately (nervous, happy, angry, relieved, and so forth) and to determine why you feel the way you do. It also involves predicting how others might feel in a given situation. Emotions contain information, and the ability to understand and think about that information plays an important role in behavior.

- **Managing emotions** builds on the belief that feelings can be modified, even improved. At times, you need to stay open to your feelings, learn from them, and use them to take appropriate action. Other times, it is better to disengage from an emotion and return to it later. Anger, for example, can blind you and lead you to act in negative or antisocial ways; used positively, however, the same emotion can help you overcome adversity, bias, and injustice.

Identifying and using emotions can help you know which moods are best for different situations and learn how to put yourself in the "right" mood. Developing an awareness of emotions allows you to use your feelings to enhance your thinking. If you are feeling sad, for instance, you might view the

[1]Adapted from *BarON EQ-i Technical Manual*. Copyright © 1997, 1999, 2000 by Multi-Health Systems, Toronto, Canada. Reproduced by permission of Multi-Health Systems.

world in a certain way, while if you feel happy, you are likely to interpret the same events differently. Once you start paying attention to emotions, you can learn not only how to cope with life's pressures and demands, but also how to harness your knowledge of the way you feel for more effective problem solving, reasoning, decision making, and creative endeavors.

Assessing Your Emotional Intelligence

A number of sophisticated tools can be used to assess emotional intelligence. Some first-year seminars and many campus counseling centers offer the opportunity to complete a professionally administered questionnaire, such as the Emotional Quotient Inventory (EQ-i), which provides a detailed assessment of your

> ### YOUR TURN
>
> After you complete the EI questionnaire below, are there any areas that you would like to work on? If so, why do you identify these as areas for improvement? Give specifics. What could you do to improve in these areas?

EMOTIONAL INTELLIGENCE QUESTIONNAIRE

Your daily life gives you many opportunities to take a hard look at how you handle emotions. Here are some questions that can help you begin thinking about your own EI.

1. What do you do when you are under stress?

☐ a. I tend to deal with it calmly and rationally.

☐ b. I get upset, but it usually blows over quickly.

☐ c. I get upset but keep it to myself.

2. My friends would say that:

☐ a. I will play, but only after I get my work done.

☐ b. I am ready for fun anytime.

☐ c. I hardly ever go out.

3. When something changes at the last minute:

☐ a. I easily adapt.

☐ b. I get frustrated.

☐ c. It doesn't matter, since I don't really expect things to happen as I plan.

4. My friends would say that:

☐ a. I am sensitive to their concerns.

☐ b. I spend too much time worrying about other people's needs.

☐ c. I don't like to deal with other people's petty problems.

5. When I have a problem to solve, such as too many things due at the end of the week:

☐ a. I write down a list of the tasks I must complete, come up with a plan indicating specifically what I can accomplish and what I cannot, and follow my plan.

☐ b. I am very optimistic about getting things done and just dig right in and get to work.

☐ c. I get a little frazzled. Usually I get a number of things done and then push aside the things that I can't do.

Review your responses. A responses indicate that you probably have a good basis for strong emotional intelligence. **B** responses indicate you may have some strengths and some challenges in your EI. **C** responses indicate that your success in life and school could be negatively affected by your EI.

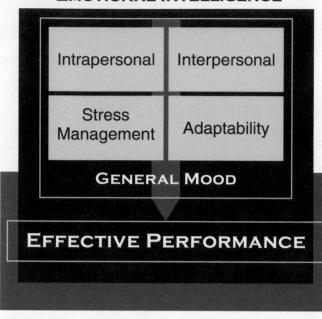

FIGURE 3.1

Bar-On Model of Emotional Intelligence

emotional skills and a graphic representation of where you stand in comparison with other students. But even without a formal test, you can take a number of steps to get in touch with your own EI (see the box on page 45). You'll have to dig deep inside yourself and be willing to be honest about how you really think and how you really behave. This can take time, and that's fine. Think of your EI as a work in progress.

This chapter lays out EI "competencies" and describes them on the next several pages. Ask the students to think about the contexts within the college experience, as they are coming to know it, in which they could practice developing these competencies. The basic idea is for the students to see how college is an environment that can develop them more fully. For example, one of the competencies describes "interpersonal skills." In what kinds of college activities, settings, and circumstances could students hope to develop these skills?

Identifying Competencies

Emotional intelligence includes many capabilities and skills that influence a person's ability to cope with life's pressures and demands. Reuven Bar-On, a professor at the University of Texas, Austin, and world-renowned EI expert, developed a model that demonstrates how these categories of emotional intelligence directly affect general mood and lead to effective performance (see Figure 3.1).

Let's take a closer look at the specific skills and competencies that Bar-On has identified as the pieces that make up a person's emotional intelligence.[2] It's something like a jigsaw puzzle, and when you have put all of the pieces together, you will begin to see yourself and others more clearly.

[2]Adapted from R. Bar-On, "The Bar-On Model of Emotional-Social Intelligence (ESI)," *Psicothema,* 2006, 18 (suppl. 13-25): 21, http://www.eiconsortium.org/pdf/baron_model_of_emotional_social_intelligence.pdf.

Help Yourself

Do you depend on other people to raise your own level of self-esteem? It is easy to allow comments from others to affect how we feel about ourselves. If you have a strong level of emotional intelligence, you will be less vulnerable to insult or empty flattery.

INTRAPERSONAL SKILLS

The first category, intrapersonal, relates to how well you know and like yourself, as well as how effectively you can do the things you need to do to stay happy. This category is made up of five specific competencies:

- **Emotional self-awareness.** Knowing how and why you feel the way you do.
- **Assertiveness.** Standing up for yourself when you need to without being too aggressive.
- **Independence.** Making important decisions on your own without having to get everyone's opinion.
- **Self-regard.** Liking yourself in spite of your flaws (and we all have them).
- **Self-actualization.** Being satisfied and comfortable with what you have achieved in school, work, and your personal life.

Understanding yourself and why you think and act as you do is the glue that holds all of the EI competencies together. Knowledge of self is strongly connected to respect for others and their way of life. If you don't understand yourself and why you do the things you do, it can be difficult for you to understand others. What's more, if you don't like yourself, you can hardly expect others to like you.

IN CLASS: At the beginning of class, ask your students to review the fifteen EI competencies, select their strongest and their weakest competency, and write those anonymously on slips of paper, identifying each as a strength or a weakness. Ask another student or a peer leader to tally the results to see which weaknesses and strengths are most common in your class. Facilitate a class discussion to generate ideas for addressing the most common weaknesses students identify.

INTERPERSONAL SKILLS

Recent studies have shown that people with extensive support networks are generally happier and tend to enjoy longer, healthier lives. Forging relationships and

Think Outside the Bowl

Good problem solvers sometimes have to work alone and be persistent. Help is not always readily available. Harness your own creativity to solve your problems in college. That way you won't feel like a fish out of water.

getting along with other people depend on the competencies that form the basis for the interpersonal category:

- **Empathy.** Making an effort to understand another person's situation or point of view.
- **Social responsibility.** Establishing a personal link with a group or community and cooperating with other members in working toward shared goals.
- **Interpersonal relationships.** Seeking out healthy and mutually beneficial relationships—such as friendships, professional networks, family connections, mentoring, and romantic partnerships—and making a persistent effort to maintain them.

ADAPTABILITY

Things change. Adaptability, the ability to adjust your thinking and behavior when faced with new or unexpected situations, helps you cope and ensures that you'll do well in life, no matter what the challenges. This category includes three key competencies:

- **Reality testing.** Ensuring that your feelings are appropriate by checking them against external, objective criteria.
- **Flexibility.** Adapting and adjusting your emotions, viewpoints, and actions as situations change.
- **Problem solving.** Approaching challenges step by step and not giving up in the face of obstacles.

"The key to stress management is knowing how to vent your frustration."

Don't Blow Your Top

There are good ways and bad ways to vent frustration. Having it out with another person and eating a gallon of ice cream are poor strategies. But going for a walk or a run, doing yoga, or "talking it out" with someone you trust will help you deal with the frustrations that are common to college life without making things worse.

STRESS MANAGEMENT

In college, at work, and at home, now and in the future, you'll be faced with what can seem like never-ending pressures and demands. Managing the inevitable resulting stress depends on two skills:

- **Stress tolerance.** Recognizing the causes of stress and responding in appropriate ways; staying strong under pressure.
- **Impulse control.** Thinking carefully about potential consequences before you act and delaying gratification for the sake of achieving long-term goals.

IN CLASS: Point students to Chapter 16, Maintaining Wellness, for an overview of specific stress-management techniques.

GENERAL MOOD AND EFFECTIVE PERFORMANCE

It might sound sappy, but having a positive attitude really does improve your chances of doing well. Bar-On emphasizes the importance of two emotions in particular:

- **Optimism.** Looking for the "bright side" of any problem or difficulty and being confident that things will work out for the best.
- **Happiness.** Being satisfied with yourself, with others, and with your situation in general.

It makes sense: If you feel good about yourself and manage your emotions, you can expect to get along with others and enjoy a happy, successful life.

IN CLASS: Ask students to role-play stressful or difficult situations in college. You can use, for example, the two case studies in Chapter 3 of the Instructor's Manual or you can create your own scenario. Ask students to react to and discuss the situations.

YOUR TURN

On the basis of what you have learned so far about EI and the competencies that are involved, choose three competencies you lack or need to improve. How can you improve in those areas?

TECH TIP STAY CONNECTED

Whatever your communication MO—smart phone, *Facebook*, or wiki—cyber etiquette is crucial. Just because you're hiding behind a computer screen doesn't mean that you should abandon your classroom manners. Failure to treat your fellow students and instructors with respect will brand you as an ignorant boor. Would you want to share a chat room with someone who writes in all caps (the digital equivalent of shouting) and belittles others' opinions? No one else does either. Emotional intelligence means being aware of your own and others' feelings. Transpose that mantra to your online world and you're good to go.

---

1 ▶ THE PROBLEM

There's a brave new world of ways to communicate in college, and you feel like you're from another planet.

2 ▶ THE FIX

Learn the nuts and bolts of connecting through cyberspace. If you still have questions, at least you'll have a good idea of what you're talking about.

3 ▶ HOW TO DO IT

1. E-mail: The most popular way to communicate online. If you have Internet access, you can send e-mail messages galore, free of charge.

2. Texting: Just like passing notes, only it's done between smart phones or other mobile devices. Downside: You have to pay a small fee for the service.

3. Instant messaging: Also like passing notes, but via desktop computers and laptops. Upside: Like e-mail, it's free.

4. Blogs: Informal Web sites made up of journal entries, articles, and other posts. Note: Blogs can only be modified by their authors, and they can reflect biased or even uninformed viewpoints.

5. Wikis: Blogs that invite the world to weigh in on a subject. Visitors can share their knowledge by adding new entries or modifying or deleting old ones. Note: Unlike blogs, wikis often pop up through search engines like Google.

6. Online social networks: Web sites that let people share opinions, photos, music, and videos with other registered members of the group.

7. Chat rooms: Cybersites people can join to "talk" (i.e., type to one another on keyboards) in real time.

8. Web conference: An online meeting between two or more people. Participants often speak to each other via Web-camera (à la *Skype*) and can even work on documents or presentations together.

A FEW WORDS ABOUT TECHNOLOGY OVERLOAD

Apply extreme caution when researching an essay online and simultaneously fielding nonstop phone calls, text messages, e-mails, and *Facebook* updates *and* listening to your iPod: Your brain might explode. Well, not really, but even digital natives need to unplug once in a while.

Excessive multitasking raises your stress levels. It also dulls your powers of concentration, so your work suffers. Experts recommend not trying to do more than two complex tasks at once. And remember: In days of yore, students were happy to go somewhere quiet and read a book, or simply take a walk and think. For a little brain refreshment, why not step away from your gadgets and give one of these old-school, low-tech concepts a whirl?

Accentuate the Positive

You probably know people who always find the negative in any situation. Constantly focusing on what's missing or what's not perfect will likely make you the kind of person whom others avoid. Practice looking on the bright side.

How Emotions Affect Success

Emotions are strongly tied to physical and psychological well-being. For example, some studies have suggested that cancer patients who have strong EI live longer. People who are aware of the needs of others tend to be happier than people who are not. A large study done at the University of Pennsylvania found that the best athletes do well in part because they're extremely optimistic. In light of tremendous obstacles and with the odds stacked against them, emotionally intelligent people nonetheless go on to succeed.

A number of studies link strong EI skills to college success in particular. Here are a few highlights:

- **Emotionally intelligent students get higher grades.** Researchers looked at students' grade point averages at the end of the first year of college. Students who had tested high for intrapersonal skills, stress tolerance, and adaptability when they entered in the fall did better academically than those who had lower overall EI test scores.

- **Students who can't manage their emotions struggle academically.** Some students have experienced full-blown panic attacks before tests. Others who are depressed can't concentrate on coursework. And far too many turn to risky behaviors (drug and alcohol abuse, eating disorders, and worse) in an effort to cope. Dr. Richard Kadison, chief of Mental Health

YOUR TURN

Describe yourself as a successful person ten years after college. What kinds of skills will you have? Don't just focus on your degree or a job description; include the EI competencies that help explain why you have become successful.

Ask the students to keep a chart or notes and record how frequently they notice fellow students who strike them as being "together" emotionally and who are also doing well in college academically. Ask them to consider what at least might be the correlation, if not some elements of causation.

Patience Is a Virtue

Delaying gratification when you really want something is tough for people of all ages. But sometimes postponing your desires is the right thing to do. Delaying things you can't afford or don't have time for will help you reach your long-term goals.

Service at Harvard University, notes that "the emotional well-being of students goes hand-in-hand with their academic development. If they're not doing well emotionally, they are not going to reach their academic potential."[3] Even students who manage to succeed academically in spite of emotional difficulties can be at risk if unhealthy behavior patterns follow them after college.

- **Students who can delay gratification tend to do better overall.** Impulse control leads to achievement. In the famous "Marshmallow Study" performed at Stanford University, researchers examined the long-term behaviors of individuals who, as four-year-olds, did or did not practice delayed gratification. The children were given one marshmallow and told that if they didn't eat it right away, they could have another. Fourteen years later, the children who ate their marshmallow immediately were more likely to experience significant stress, irritability, and inability to focus on goals. The children who waited scored an average of 210 points higher on the SAT; had better confidence, concentration, and reliability; held better-paying jobs; and reported being more satisfied with life. The following chart details the differences between the two groups of students after fourteen years.

DID YOU KNOW?

11% of first-year students feel depressed.

IN CLASS: A component of "impulse control" is "delaying gratification." Divide the class into small groups and ask them to discuss this concept and how it relates to today's society—children, college students, and adults. When is it okay for us to get what we want immediately, and when are we better off practicing delayed gratification?

[3]Richard Kadison and Theresa Foy DiGeronimo, *College of the Overwhelmed: The Campus Mental Health Crisis and What to Do About It* (San Francisco: Jossey-Bass, 2004), p. 156.

THE STANFORD MARSHMALLOW STUDY

Impulse Controlled	**Impulsive**
> Assertive	> Indecisive
> Cope with frustration	> Overreact to frustration
> Work better under pressure	> Overwhelmed by stress
> Self-reliant, confident	> Lower self-image
> Trustworthy	> Stubborn
> Dependable	> Impulsive
> Delay gratification	> Don't delay gratification
> Academically competent	> Poorer students
> Respond to reason	> Prone to jealousy and envy
> Concentrate	> Provoke arguments
> Eager to learn	> Sharp temper
> Follow through on plans	> Give up in face of failure
> SAT: 610 verbal, 652 math	> SAT: 524 verbal, 528 math

Source: Y. Shoda, W. Mischel, and P. K. Peake, "Predicting Adolescent Cognitive and Self-Regulatory Competencies from Preschool Delay of Gratification," *Developmental Psychology*, 26(6) (1990): 978-86.

■ **EI skills can be enhanced in a first-year seminar.** In two separate studies, one conducted in Australia and another conducted in the United States, researchers found that college students enrolled in a first-year seminar who demonstrated good EI skills were more likely to do better in college than students who did not exhibit those behaviors. A follow-up study indicated that the students who had good EI skills also raised their scores on a measure of EI.

Without strong EI in college, it is possible to do well enough to get by, but you might miss out on the full range and depth of competencies and skills that can help you to succeed in your chosen field and have a fulfilling and meaningful life.

IN CLASS: Ask students to describe the behaviors of a really successful student and one who is not successful. Keep a running tally in two columns on a blackboard or projection screen. Encourage the students to be as specific as they can be when describing each behavior, and ask them to consider behaviors both in and out of the classroom. When the list is complete, ask the class as a group to develop a list of the top eight behaviors of a successful student and those of a not-so-successful student. How do those behaviors relate to the EI competencies described on pp. 47–49?

■ IN CLASS: Ask the students to think about this course, its content, and its in-class activities. What have they been doing in this class—or could do more of—that might help them develop their EI skills?

■ RETENTION STRATEGY: Students who are easily frustrated and make impulsive decisions may give up on college. Encourage any student who expresses the wish to drop out or transfer to have a one-to-one discussion with you or a counselor before taking that step.

How to Improve Your Emotional Intelligence

Developing your EI is an important step toward getting the full benefit of a college education. Think about it. Do you often give up because something is just too hard or you can't figure it out? Do you take responsibility for what you do, or do you blame others if you fail? Can you really be successful in life if you don't handle change well or if you are not open to diverse groups and their opinions? How can you communicate effectively if you are not assertive or if you are overly aggressive? If you're inflexible, how can you solve problems, get along with co-workers and family members, or learn from other people's points of view?

The good news is you can improve your EI. It might not be easy—old habits are hard to change—but it can definitely be done. Here are some suggestions:

1. **Identify your strengths and weaknesses.** Take a hard look at yourself, and consider how you respond to situations. Most people have trouble assessing their own behaviors realistically, so ask someone you trust and respect for insight. And if you have an opportunity to take a formal emotional intelligence test or to meet with a behavioral counselor, by all means, do.

2. **Set realistic goals.** As you identify areas of emotional intelligence that you would like to improve, be as specific as possible. Instead of deciding to be more assertive, for example, focus on a particular issue that is giving you trouble, such as nagging resentment toward a friend who always orders the most expensive thing on the menu and then expects to split the whole check evenly.

3. **Formulate a plan.** With a particular goal in mind, identify a series of steps you could take to achieve the goal, and define the results that would indicate success. As you contemplate your plan, consider all of the emotional competencies discussed on pages 47–49 of this chapter: You might find that to be more assertive with your friend about the restaurant situation, for instance, you need to figure out why you're frustrated (emotional self-awareness), identify possible causes for your friend's behavior (empathy), and consider what you might be doing to encourage it (reality testing).

4. **Check your progress on a regular basis.** Continually reassess whether or not you have met your goals, and adjust your strategy as needed.

Suppose you know that you don't handle stress well. When things get tough—too many things are due at once, your roommate leaves clothes and leftover food all over the place, and your significant other seems a bit distant—you begin to fall apart. Here is a model you might use for improving the way you handle stress.

EI competency: Stress tolerance

Specific goal: To get control of the things that are causing stress this week

Plan: Identify each stressor, and select a strategy for addressing it

- List everything that needs to be done this week. Allot time for each item on the list, and stick to a schedule. Reassess the schedule many times during the week.

- Ask yourself whether your roommate is bothering you only because you are stressed. Do you do some of the same things your roommate does? Ask yourself what the next step should be: Talking to your roommate? Looking for another place to study?

- Ask yourself whether your significant other is acting differently for any reason. Is he or she under stress? Are you overreacting because you feel insecure in the relationship? After answering these questions, decide what the next step will be: Talking to your significant other and sharing your feelings with him or her? Reassessing the situation in another week when things calm down?

- Identify what reduces stress for you and still allows you to stay on target to get things done. Exercising? Working in small chunks with rewards when you finish something? Playing a musical instrument?

  Success indicator: You are feeling less stressed, and you have accomplished many of the things on your list. You are working out three times a week. Your significant other seems just fine, and your place is still a mess but it's not bothering you. You leave your room and decide to study in the library.

It's important not to try to improve everything at once. Instead, identify specific EI competencies that you can define, describe, and identify, and then set measurable goals for change. Don't expect success overnight. Remember that it took you a while to develop your specific approach to life, and it will take commitment and practice to change it.

IN CLASS: Now that your students have been thinking and talking about EI, ask them to write their own personal definition of EI. Have them share it with another student and receive feedback.

YOUR TURN

Using this example as a model, select an EI competency that you would like to improve, choose a specific goal, and formulate a plan for accomplishing it. What kinds of results do you hope to achieve? How will improving your EI in this area help you become a happier, more confident person?

CHECKLIST FOR SUCCESS

EVALUATING YOUR EMOTIONAL INTELLIGENCE

☐ **Using the questionnaire in this chapter, assess your emotional intelligence.** Note areas in which your EI is strong and areas that need improvement.

☐ **Be aware of how your emotions affect the way you react to difficult or frustrating situations.** Use your awareness ahead of time to try to control your negative reactions.

☐ **Learn and then practice EI improvement strategies such as:**

- Identifying your strengths and weaknesses
- Setting realistic goals
- Formulating a plan
- Checking your progress on a regular basis

☐ **If you aren't satisfied with your emotional reactions, make an appointment in the campus counseling center to discuss your feelings and get help.** Counselors can help you monitor and understand your emotional responses in a confidential setting.

BUILD YOUR EXPERIENCE

1 STAY ON TRACK

Successful college students stay focused. They "stay on track." They know what they have to do to be successful, they set goals, and they monitor their progress toward their goals.

Reflect on what you have learned about college success in this chapter and how you are going to apply the chapter information or strategies in college and in your career. List your ideas.

1. _____

_____

_____

2. _____

_____

_____

3. _____

_____

_____

2 ONE-MINUTE PAPER

Emotional intelligence might be a term that you were not familiar with before reading this chapter. What did you find to be the most interesting information in this chapter? Make a note of any information that was hard to understand or apply to your own life. What kinds of questions do you still have for your instructor?

No matter how well prepared you are in your teaching, what a student hears and understands might not always be what you think you have said. The one-minute paper is a quick and easy assessment tool that will help alert you when students don't understand what was said or discussed in class. The one-minute paper will also give timid students an opportunity to ask questions and seek clarification. Ideally, you should ask for such a paper several minutes before the end of a class. The paper will also help you begin your next class by clarifying points your students seem to be unsure of.

3 | APPLYING WHAT YOU'VE LEARNED

Now that you have read and discussed this chapter, consider how you can apply what you have learned to your academic and personal life. The following prompts will help you reflect on the chapter material and its relevance to you both now and in the future.

1. Managing stress is an important skill in college. Take a look through your course syllabi, and make a list of assignments, exams, and the dates. Do any of your assignments or exams seem to cluster around the same time in the term? Can you anticipate times when you might be especially likely to get stressed? What can you do in advance to avoid becoming overwhelmed and overstressed?

2. College life offers many opportunities to meet new people and to develop a new support network. But finding friends and mentors you can trust is not always easy. What steps have you taken so far to meet new people and build a network of support in college?

4 | BUILDING YOUR PORTFOLIO

Know Thyself   Understanding your own behavior can sometimes be more difficult than understanding someone else's. Review the questionnaire on page 45 of this chapter. Were you honest in your assessment of yourself?

1. In a *Word* document, list the questions from page 45 that you answered with a B or a C. For example, did you rate yourself with a B or a C on a question such as "I am okay when things change at the last minute"?

2. Next, note the EI competencies that relate to each question. For the example above, the key competency is adaptability, as evidenced in reality testing, flexibility, and problem solving.

3. For each question that you have listed, describe your strategy for improving your response to certain situations. For example, when things change suddenly, you might say, "I am going to take a few minutes to think about what I need to do next. I will remind myself that I am still in control of my actions."

4. Save your responses in your portfolio. Revisit your responses to the questions listed above as you experience similar situations.

Pay special attention to how your emotional intelligence affects your daily life. As you become more aware of your emotions and actions, you will begin to see how you can improve in the areas that are most difficult for you.

For more on this topic watch
French Fries Are Not Vegetables and Other College Lessons

WHERE TO GO FOR HELP. . .

If you think that you might need some help developing some of these EI skills, especially if you feel that you are not happy or optimistic or you're not handling stress well, do something about it. Although you can look online and get some tips about being an optimistic person, for example, there is nothing like getting some help from a professional. Consider visiting your academic adviser or a wellness or counseling center on campus. Look for any related workshops that are offered on campus or nearby. Remember that the good news about EI is that with persistence it can be improved.

MY INSTITUTION'S RESOURCES

_____

_____

_____

_____

_____

_____

CHAPTER 4

Discovering How You Learn

IN THIS CHAPTER YOU WILL EXPLORE

Many approaches to understanding your learning styles or preferences

How learning styles and teaching styles often differ

How to optimize your learning style in any classroom setting

How to understand and recognize a learning disability

> **Apply your learning style to your everyday life. Eventually you will learn in a different, smarter, and more efficient way.**
>
> Robert Schein, 23
> Undeclared major
> Truman College

"I didn't have much knowledge of learning styles before I started college," Robert Schein from Truman College in Chicago tells us. But in his first semester, he enrolled in the College Success Seminar. There, he took the VARK and learned that he's both a kinesthetic learner—meaning he learns by doing—and a read/write learner—meaning he learns by reading and writing down material from class. Since then he has been able to employ numerous strategies that apply specifically to his form of multimodal learning to help him succeed in class. He does things like rewriting terms and concepts in his own words so that he better understands what they mean and using note cards to help him memorize. "[Knowing my learning style] has improved my performance. When I take notes, I read them silently on note cards and continue to return to them so I can memorize the meaning."

It's not surprising that Robert is a kinesthetic learner too, since he spends 10 to 15 hours a week working in his family car business. "A hands-on approach has my name written all over it," he says. "I like being able to use my

Robert Schein ▶

hands and express myself, and I like being able to figure things out just by playing with them for a bit." He translates this hands-on approach to learning as well, by doing things like taking practice exams until he feels ready for the real exam.

Robert chose Truman College because it was close to home and because he felt that he would receive more one-on-one attention from instructors by going to a community college for his associate's degree. When Robert enrolled, he took advantage of the TRIO program, which helps prepare students for a successful transfer to a four-year institution through advising, tutoring, and transfer assistance. And it looks like all that work is paying off: In the fall, Robert will be transferring to Northeastern Illinois University to pursue a B.S. in Computer Information Systems. Robert plans to finish his degree and then explore job opportunities as well as master's programs. In ten years, he hopes to be working in computer science or finance, and he plans to continue to rely on his learning styles: "Apply your learning style to your everyday life. Eventually you will learn in a different, smarter, and more efficient way."

Have you ever thought about how you learn, or are you like Robert and never thought about learning styles before coming to college? People learn differently. This is hardly a novel idea, but if you are to do well in college, it is important that you become aware of your preferred way, or style, of learning. Experts agree that there is no one best way to learn.

Maybe you have trouble paying attention to a long lecture, or maybe listening is the way you learn best. You might love classroom discussion, or you might consider hearing what other students have to say in class a big waste of time.

Perhaps you have not thought about how college instructors, and even particular courses, have their own inherent styles, which can be different from your preferred style of learning. Many instructors rely almost solely on lecturing; others use lots of visual aids, such as *PowerPoint* outlines, charts, graphs, and pictures. In science courses, you will conduct experiments or go on field trips where you can observe or touch what you are studying. In dance, theater, or physical education courses, learning takes place in both your body and your mind. And in almost all courses, you'll learn by reading both textbooks and other materials. Some instructors are friendly and warm; others seem to want little interaction with students. It's safe to say that in at least some of your college courses, you won't find a close match between the way you learn most effectively and the way you're being taught. This chapter will help you first to understand how you learn best and then to think of ways in which you can create a link between your style of learning and the expectations of each course and instructor.

There are many ways of thinking about and describing **learning styles**. Some of these will make a lot of sense to you; others might initially seem confusing or counterintuitive. Some learning style theories are very simple, and some are complex. You will notice some overlap between the different theories, but using several of them might help you do a more precise job of discovering your learning style. If you are interested in reading more about learning styles, the library and campus learning center will have many resources.

In addition to its focus on learning styles, this chapter will also explore **learning disabilities**, which are very common among college students. You might know

learning styles
Particular ways of learning, unique to each individual. For example, one person prefers reading to understand how something works, whereas another prefers using a "hands-on" approach.

learning disabilities
Disorders, such as dyslexia, that affect people's ability to either interpret what they see and hear or connect information across different areas of the brain.

YOUR TURN

Which of your current classes would you describe as your favorite? Do you think that your choice has anything to do with the instructor's teaching style? Why or why not?

◢▰▰ ASSESSING YOUR STRENGTHS ▰▰◣

Understanding your own preferred style of learning will help you study and earn good grades. Do you know how you learn best? Now that you have read the first section of this chapter, list your insights about your own learning styles.

_____

_____

_____

_____

◢▰▰ SETTING GOALS ▰▰◣

What are your most important objectives in learning the material in this chapter? Think about challenges you have had with relating to the way some instructors teach and expect you to learn. List three goals that relate to understanding learning styles (e.g., I will make a list of my favorite and least favorite classes and think about how my preferences might relate to my preferred style of learning).

1. _____

_____

2. _____

_____

3. _____

_____

someone who has been diagnosed with a learning disability, such as dyslexia or attention deficit disorder. It is also possible that you have a special learning need and are not aware of it. This chapter seeks to increase your self-awareness and your knowledge about such challenges to learning. In reading this chapter, you will learn more about common types of learning disabilities, how to recognize them, and what to do if you or someone you know has a learning disability.

■ RETENTION STRATEGY: One aspect of retention is giving students the tools they will need for successful academic learning. At the beginning of the chapter, ask students to brainstorm ways that each style supports student success.

The VARK Learning Styles Inventory

The VARK Inventory focuses on how learners prefer to use their senses (hearing, seeing, writing, reading, or experiencing) to learn. The acronym VARK stands for "Visual," "Aural," "Read/Write," and "Kinesthetic." Visual learners prefer to learn information through charts, graphs, symbols, and other visual means. Aural learners prefer to hear information. Read/Write learners prefer to learn information that is displayed as words. Kinesthetic learners prefer to learn through experience and practice, whether simulated or real. To determine your learning style according to the VARK Inventory, respond to the following questionnaire.

THE VARK QUESTIONNAIRE, VERSION 7.0

This questionnaire is designed to tell you something about your preferences for the way you work with information. Choose answers that explain your preference. Check the box next to those items. Please select as many boxes as apply to you. If none of the response options apply to you, leave the item blank.

1. You are helping someone who wants to go to your airport, town center, or railway station. You would:
   - ☐ a. go with her.
   - ☐ b. tell her the directions.
   - ☐ c. write down the directions (without a map).
   - ☐ d. draw, or give her a map.

2. You are not sure whether a word should be spelled "dependent" or "dependant." You would:
   - ☐ a. see the words in your mind and choose by the way they look.
   - ☐ b. think about how each word sounds and choose one.
   - ☐ c. find it in a dictionary.
   - ☐ d. write both words on paper and choose one.

3. You are planning a holiday for a group. You want some feedback from them about the plan. You would:
   - ☐ a. describe some of the highlights.
   - ☐ b. use a map or Web site to show them the places.
   - ☐ c. give them a copy of the printed itinerary.
   - ☐ d. phone, text, or e-mail them.

4. You are going to cook something as a special treat for your family. You would:
   - ☐ a. cook something you know without the need for instructions.
   - ☐ b. ask friends for suggestions.
   - ☐ c. look through the cookbook for ideas from the pictures.
   - ☐ d. use a cookbook where you know there is a good recipe.

5. A group of tourists want to learn about the parks or wildlife reserves in your area. You would:
   - ☐ a. talk about, or arrange a talk for them, about parks or wildlife reserves.
   - ☐ b. show them Internet pictures, photographs, or picture books.
   - ☐ c. take them to a park or wildlife reserve and walk with them.
   - ☐ d. give them a book or pamphlets about the parks or wildlife reserves.

6. You are about to purchase a digital camera or mobile phone. Other than price, what would most influence your decision?
   - ☐ a. Trying or testing it.
   - ☐ b. Reading the details about its features.
   - ☐ c. It is a modern design and looks good.
   - ☐ d. The salesperson telling me about its features.

7. Remember a time when you learned how to do something new. Try to avoid choosing a physical skill (e.g., riding a bike). You learned best by:
   - ☐ a. watching a demonstration.
   - ☐ b. listening to somebody explaining it and asking questions.
   - ☐ c. diagrams and charts—visual clues.
   - ☐ d. written instructions—e.g., a manual or textbook.

8. You have a problem with your knee. You would prefer that the doctor:
   - ☐ a. give you a Web address or something to read about it.
   - ☐ b. use a plastic model of a knee to show what was wrong.
   - ☐ c. describe what was wrong.
   - ☐ d. show you a diagram of what was wrong.

9. You want to learn a new program, skill, or game on a computer. You would:
   - ☐ a. read the written instructions that came with the program.
   - ☐ b. talk with people who know about the program.
   - ☐ c. use the controls or keyboard.
   - ☐ d. follow the diagrams in the book that came with it.

10. You like Web sites that have:
    - ☐ a. things you can click on, shift, or try.
    - ☐ b. interesting design and visual features.
    - ☐ c. interesting written descriptions, lists, and explanations.
    - ☐ d. audio channels where you can hear music, radio programs, or interviews.

11. Other than price, what would most influence your decision to buy a new nonfiction book?
    - ☐ a. The way it looks is appealing.
    - ☐ b. Quickly reading parts of it.
    - ☐ c. A friend talks about it and recommends it.
    - ☐ d. It has real-life stories, experiences, and examples.

12. You are using a book, CD, or Web site to learn how to take photos with your new digital camera. You would like to have:
    - ☐ a. a chance to ask questions and talk about the camera and its features.
    - ☐ b. clear written instructions with lists and bullet points about what to do.
    - ☐ c. diagrams showing the camera and what each part does.
    - ☐ d. many examples of good and poor photos and how to improve them.

13. You prefer a teacher or a presenter who uses:
    - ☐ a. demonstrations, models, or practical sessions.
    - ☐ b. question and answer, talk, group discussion, or guest speakers.
    - ☐ c. handouts, books, or readings.
    - ☐ d. diagrams, charts, or graphs.

14. You have finished a competition or test and would like some feedback. You would like to have feedback:
    - ☐ a. using examples from what you have done.
    - ☐ b. using a written description of your results.
    - ☐ c. from somebody who talks it through with you.
    - ☐ d. using graphs showing what you had achieved.

15. You are going to choose food at a restaurant or café. You would:
    - ☐ a. choose something that you have had there before.
    - ☐ b. listen to the waiter or ask friends to recommend choices.
    - ☐ c. choose from the descriptions in the menu.
    - ☐ d. look at what others are eating or look at pictures of each dish.

16. You have to make an important speech at a conference or special occasion. You would:
    - ☐ a. make diagrams or get graphs to help explain things.
    - ☐ b. write a few key words and practice saying your speech over and over.
    - ☐ c. write out your speech and learn from reading it over several times.
    - ☐ d. gather many examples and stories to make the talk real and practical.

SCORING THE VARK

Use the following scoring chart to find the VARK category to which each of your answers belongs. Circle the letters that correspond to your answers. For example, if you answered b and c for question 3, circle V and R in the 3 row.

Question	A Category	B Category	C Category	D Category
3	K	(V)	(R)	A

Count the number of each of the VARK letters you have circled to get your score for each VARK category.

SCORING CHART

Question	A Category	B Category	C Category	D Category
1	K	A	R	V
2	V	A	R	K
3	K	V	R	A
4	K	A	V	R
5	A	V	K	R
6	K	R	V	A
7	K	A	V	R
8	R.	K	A	V
9	R	A	K	V
10	K	V	R	A
11	V	R	A	K
12	A	R	V	K
13	K	A	R	V
14	K	R	A	V
15	K	A	R	V
16	V	A	R	K

Total number of **V**s circled = _____

Total number of **A**s circled = _____

Total number of **R**s circled = _____

Total number of **K**s circled = _____

Because you could choose more than one answer for each question, the scoring is not just a simple matter of counting. It is like four stepping stones across some water. Enter your scores **from highest to lowest** on the stones in the figure, with their V, A, R, and K labels.

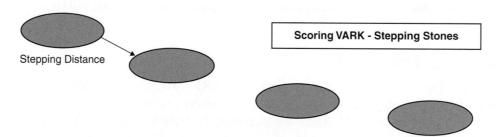

Stepping Distance

Scoring VARK - Stepping Stones

Your stepping distance comes from this table:

The total of my four VARK scores is	My stepping distance is
16-21	1
22-27	2
28-32	3
More than 32	4

Follow these steps to establish your preferences.

1. Your first preference is always your highest score. Check that first stone as one of your preferences.

2. Now subtract your second highest score from your first. If that figure is larger than your stepping distance, you have a single preference. Otherwise, check this stone as another preference and continue with step 3.

3. Subtract your third score from your second one. If that figure is larger than your stepping distance, you have a bimodal preference. If not, check your third stone as a preference and continue with step 4.

4. Last, subtract your fourth score from your third one. If that figure is larger than your stepping distance, you have a trimodal preference. Otherwise, check your fourth stone as a preference, and you have all four modes as your preferences!

Note: If you are bimodal or trimodal or you have checked all four modes as your preferences, you can be described as *multimodal* in your VARK preferences.

> **YOUR TURN**
>
> Did your VARK score surprise you at all? Did you know what type of learner you were before taking the test? If so, when did you discover this? How do you use your modality to your benefit?

IN CLASS: After the students have completed the inventory, discuss the model. Take a poll to determine the variety of learning styles among the class. What does this mean for the dynamics of the class?

OUTSIDE CLASS: Ask students to write a short paper on what they learned after completing and scoring the VARK.

USING VARK RESULTS TO STUDY MORE EFFECTIVELY

How can knowing your VARK score help you do better in your college classes? The following table offers suggestions for using learning styles to develop your own study strategies.

Study Strategies by Learning Style

Visual	Aural	Read/Write	Kinesthetic
Underline or highlight your notes.	Talk with others to verify the accuracy of your lecture notes.	Write and rewrite your notes.	Use all your senses in learning: sight, touch, taste, smell, and hearing.
Use symbols, charts, or graphs to display your notes.	Put your notes on tape and listen or tape class lectures.	Read your notes silently.	Supplement your notes with real-world examples.
Use different arrangements of words on the page.	Read your notes out loud; ask yourself questions and speak your answers.	Organize diagrams or flow charts into statements.	Move and gesture while you are reading or speaking your notes.
Redraw your pages from memory.		Write imaginary exam questions and respond in writing.	

The Kolb Inventory of Learning Styles

A learning model that is more complex than the VARK Inventory is the widely used and referenced Kolb Inventory of Learning Styles. While the VARK Inventory investigates how learners prefer to use their senses in learning, the Kolb Inventory focuses on abilities we need to develop in order to learn. This inventory, developed in the 1980s by David Kolb, is based on a four-stage cycle of learning (see Figure 4.1).

According to Kolb, effective learners need four kinds of abilities:

- *Concrete experience* abilities, which allow them to be receptive to others and open to other people's feelings and specific experiences. An example of this type of ability is learning from and empathizing with others.

- *Reflective observation* abilities, which help learners to reflect on their experiences from many perspectives. An example of this type of ability is remaining impartial while considering a situation from a number of different points of view.

- *Abstract conceptualization* abilities, which help learners to integrate observations into logically sound theories. An example of this type of ability is analyzing ideas intellectually and systematically.

- *Active experimentation* abilities, which enable learners to make decisions, solve problems, and test what they have learned in new situations. An example of this type of ability is being ready to move quickly from thinking to action.

IN CLASS: After a short explanation of the Experiential Learning Model, group the students to discuss their understandings of this model. What questions do they have? Do they consider this model useful? Why or why not?

If you are interested in using the Kolb Inventory of Learning Styles, the twelve-item questionnaire and workbook are available online. For information about costs of single or multiple copies, go to http://www.haygroup.com/tl/Questionnaires_Workbooks/Kolb_Learning_Style_Inventory.aspx.

Kolb's Inventory of Learning Styles measures differences along two basic dimensions that represent opposite styles of learning. The first dimension is *abstract-concrete*; the second is *active-reflective*. See Figure 4.1 to visualize how these polar-opposite characteristics link together to create four discrete groups of learners: *divergers*, *assimilators*, *convergers*, and *accommodators*.

Doing well in college will require you to adopt some behaviors that are characteristic of each of these four learning styles. Some of them might be uncomfortable for you, but that discomfort will indicate that you're growing, stretching, and not relying on the learning style that might be easiest or most natural.

If you are a diverger, you are adept at reflecting on situations from many viewpoints. You excel at brainstorming, and you're imaginative, people oriented, and sometimes emotional. On the downside, you sometimes have difficulty making decisions. Divergers tend to major in the humanities or social sciences.

FIGURE 4.1
Kolb's Four-Stage Cycle of Learning

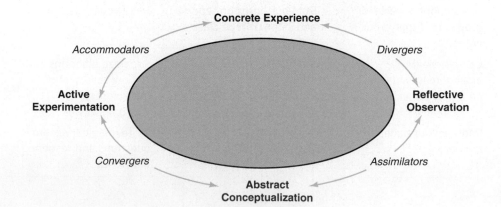

If you are an assimilator, you like to think about abstract concepts. You are comfortable in classes where the instructor lectures about theoretical ideas without relating the lectures to real-world situations. Assimilators often major in math, physics, or chemistry.

If you are a converger, you like the world of ideas and theories, but you also are good at thinking about how to apply those theories to real-world, practical situations. You differ from divergers in your preference for tasks and problems rather than social and interpersonal issues. Convergers tend to choose health-related and engineering majors.

If you are an accommodator, you prefer hands-on learning. You are skilled at making things happen, and you rely on your intuition. You like people, but you can be pushy and impatient at times, and you might use trial and error, rather than logic, to solve problems. Accommodators often major in business, especially in marketing or sales.[1]

In all your classes, but especially in liberal arts and social science courses, you will need to develop the strengths of divergers: imagination, brainstorming, and listening with an open mind. The abilities that are characteristic of assimilators, developing theories and concepts, are valuable for all students, especially those in the sciences. If you major in the health sciences or in engineering, you will routinely practice the skills of convergers: experimenting with new ideas and choosing the best solution. Finally, whatever your major and ultimate career, you'll need to get things done, take some risks, and become a leader—skills that are characteristic of accommodators.

IN CLASS: Ask students to discuss the following statement: "Doing well in college will require you to adopt some behaviors that are characteristic of each of the four styles."

YOUR TURN

On the basis of the descriptions we have provided here, where do you see yourself in the Kolb Inventory? Are you more like a diverger, assimilator, converger, or accommodator? How can you use this knowledge in your courses?

The Myers-Briggs Type Indicator

One of the best-known and most widely used personality inventories that can also be used to describe learning styles is the Myers-Briggs Type Indicator, or MBTI.[2] While the VARK measures your preferences for using your senses to learn and the Kolb Inventory focuses on learning abilities, the MBTI investigates basic personality characteristics and how those relate to human interaction and learning. The MBTI was created by Isabel Briggs Myers and her mother, Katharine Cook Briggs. The inventory identifies and measures psychological type as developed in the personality theory of Carl Gustav Jung, the great twentieth-century psychoanalyst. The MBTI is given to several million people around the world each year. Employers often use this test to give employees insight into how they perceive the world, go about making decisions, and get along with other people. Many first-year seminar or college success courses also include a focus on the MBTI because it provides a good way to begin a dialogue about human interaction and how personality type affects learning.

An online bibliography listing almost 8,000 known studies on the MBTI is available at www.capt.org. Volume 60 of the *Journal of Psychological Type* contains abstracts of over 400 studies that have appeared in that publication, available through the Mississippi State University Psychology Department.

[1]Adapted from David A. Kolb, "Learning Styles and Disciplinary Differences," in *The Modern American College*, ed. Arthur W. Chickering (San Francisco: Jossey Bass, 1981), pp. 232–35.

[2]Isabel Briggs Myers, *Introduction to Type*, 6th ed. (Palo Alto, CA: CPP, 1998).

All the psychological types described by the MBTI are normal and healthy; there is no good or bad or right or wrong—people are simply different. When you complete the Myers-Briggs survey instrument, your score represents your "psychological type"—the combination of your preferences on four different scales. These scales measure how you take in information and how you then make decisions or come to conclusions about that information. Each preference has a one-letter abbreviation. The four letters together make up your type. Although this book doesn't include the actual survey, you will find a description of the basic MBTI types below. Which one sounds most like you?

EXTRAVERSION (E) VERSUS INTROVERSION (I): THE INNER OR OUTER WORLD

The E-I preference indicates whether you direct your energy and attention primarily toward the outer world of people, events, and things or the inner world of thoughts, feelings, and reflections.

Extraverts tend to be outgoing, gregarious, and talkative. They often think "with the volume on," saying out loud what is going through their minds. They are energized by people and activity, and they seek this in both work and play. They are people of action; they like to spend more time doing things than thinking about them. At their best, they are good communicators who are quick to act and lead. However, they might seem to talk too much and too loudly, drowning others out or acting before they think. (Note that when the term is being used in the context of psychological type and the MBTI, "extravert" is spelled with an "a" and not an "o," even though "extrovert" is the more common spelling.)

Introverts prefer to reflect carefully and think things through before taking action. They think a lot, but if you want to know what's on their minds, you might have to ask them. They are refreshed by quiet and privacy. At their

For instructors in any academic specialty, workshops (including online workshops) to train and qualify you to give the MBTI are available from several reputable organizations listed on the Myers & Briggs Foundation Web site (www.myersbriggs.org).

Take a Time-out

Do you find that you need some occasional time by yourself? Although introverts are more likely to enjoy time alone, even extraverts can benefit from private time to relax or escape from the hustle and bustle of daily life.

best, introverts are good, careful listeners whose thoughts are deep and whose actions are well considered. On the other hand, they might seem too shy and not aware enough of the people and situations around them, or they can think about things so long that they neglect to actually start doing anything.

SENSING (S) VERSUS INTUITION (N): FACTS OR IDEAS

YOUR TURN

After reading this description, do you consider yourself an extravert or an introvert? Why? Do you ever wish you were like the other? If so, when and why?

The S-N preference indicates how you perceive the world and take in information: directly, through your five senses, or indirectly, by using your intuition.

Sensing types are interested above all in the facts, what is known and what they can be sure of. Typically sensing types are practical, factual, realistic, and down-to-earth. They can be very accurate, steady, precise, patient, and effective with routine and details. They are often relatively traditional and conventional. They dislike unnecessary complication, and they prefer to practice skills they already know. At their best, sensing types can be counted on to do things right, taking care of every last detail. However, they can plod along while missing the point of why they are doing what they do, not seeing the forest (the whole picture) for the trees (the details).

Intuitive types are fascinated by possibilities—not so much the facts themselves, but what those facts mean, what concepts might describe those facts, how those might relate to other concepts, and what the implications of the facts would be. Intuitive types are less tied to the here and now and tend to look farther into the future and the past. They need inspiration and meaning for what they do, and they tend to work in bursts of energy and enthusiasm. Often, they are original, creative, and nontraditional. They can have trouble with routine and details, however, and they would rather learn a new skill than keep practicing one they have already mastered. They can exaggerate facts sometimes without realizing it. At their best, intuitive types are bright, innovative people who thrive in academic settings and the world of invention and ideas, although they can also be impractical dreamers whose visions fall short because of inattention to detail.

IN CLASS: Ask students their thoughts about an inventory that claims to measure types. Ask for student volunteers to do an Internet search on the Myers-Briggs Type Inventory and share their findings in class.

THINKING (T) VERSUS FEELING (F): LOGIC OR VALUES

IN CLASS: Develop a lesson on the Myers-Briggs types. Explain how the letters are used and make up a type. Ask someone on campus who has experience with the Myers-Briggs to assist you or to come to class. Usually career counselors and student development staff have worked with the Myers-Briggs.

The T-F preference indicates how you prefer to make your decisions: through logical, rational analysis or through your subjective values, likes, and dislikes. *Thinking* types are usually logical, rational, analytical, and critical. They pride themselves on reasoning their way to the best possible decisions. They tend to decide things relatively impersonally and objectively, and they are less swayed by feelings and emotions—both their own and other people's. In fact, other people's feelings sometimes puzzle or surprise them. They can deal with interpersonal disharmony and can be firm and assertive when they need to be. In all of their dealings, they need and value fairness. At their best, thinking types are firm, fair, logical, and just. On the other hand, they can seem cold, insensitive to other people's feelings, and overly blunt and hurtful in their criticisms.

There is fierce academic debate as to whether the four MBTI preferences are simply additive or truly interactive. Type theory posits that feeling, for instance, will be manifested differently in an ISFP than, say, in an ENFP. This matter is too complicated for a brief introduction to students, but in the exercises and resources they will find more detailed descriptions of their complete four-letter types than they can get by simply compiling the descriptions of the four scales.

Estimates of the relative frequencies of each four-letter psychological type for men and women in the general population can be found in the 1998 edition of the *MBTI® Manual* and in Volume 37 of the *Journal of Psychological Type*.

Feeling types are typically warm, empathic, sympathetic, and interested in the happiness of others as well as themselves. They need and value harmony, and they can become distressed and distracted by argument and conflict. They sometimes have trouble being assertive when it would be appropriate to do so. Above all, they need and value kindness. At their best, feeling types are warm and affirming, and they facilitate cooperation and goodwill among those around them while pursuing the best human values. However, feeling types can be illogical, emotionally demanding, reluctant to tackle unpleasant tasks, and unaffected by objective reason and evidence.

JUDGING (J) VERSUS PERCEIVING (P): ORGANIZATION OR ADAPTABILITY

The J-P preference indicates how you characteristically approach the outside world: by making decisions and judgments or by observing and perceiving instead.

Judging types approach the world in a planned, orderly, organized way; they try to order and control their part of it as much as possible. They make their decisions relatively quickly and easily because they like to make and follow plans. They are usually punctual and tidy, and they appreciate those traits in others. At their best, judging types are natural organizers who get things done and get them done on time. However, judging types might jump to conclusions prematurely, be too judgmental of people, make decisions too hastily without enough information, and have trouble changing their plans even when those plans are not working.

Perceiving types don't try to control their world as much as adapt to it. Theirs is a flexible, wait-and-see approach. They deal comfortably and well with changes, unexpected developments, and emergencies, adjusting their plans and behaviors as needed. They tend to delay decisions so that they can keep their options open and gather more information. They might procrastinate to a serious degree, however, and they can try to juggle too many things at once without finishing any of them. At their best, perceiving types are spontaneous, flexible individuals who roll with the punches and find ways to take the proverbial lemons in life and turn them into lemonade. On the other hand, perceiving types can be messy, disorganized procrastinators.

It is inappropriate, unethical, and illegal to use the MBTI as a screening device to decide whether or not to hire an applicant for a job (or admit someone to an educational program). The proper use of the MBTI is to help people identify satisfying career specialties for themselves.

HOW TO USE YOUR STRONGEST— AND WEAKEST—PREFERENCES

Because there are two possible choices for each of four different preferences, there are sixteen possible psychological types. No matter what your Myers-Briggs type, all components of personality have value in the learning process. The key to success in college, therefore, is to use all of the attitudes and functions (E, I, S, N, T, F, J, and P) in their most positive sense. As you go about your studies, here is a system we recommend:

1. *Sensing:* Get the facts. Use sensing to find and learn the facts. How do we know facts when we see them? What is the evidence for what is being said?

2. *Intuition:* Get the ideas. Now use intuition to consider what those facts mean. Why are those facts being presented? What concepts and ideas are being supported by those facts? What are the implications? What is the big picture?

3. *Thinking:* Critically analyze. Use thinking to analyze the pros and cons of what is being presented. Are there gaps in the evidence? What more do we need to know? Do the facts really support the conclusions? Are there alternative explanations? How well does what is presented hang together logically? How could our knowledge of it be improved?

4. *Feeling:* Make informed value judgments. Why is this material important? What does it contribute to people's good? Why might it be important to you personally? What is your personal opinion about it?

5. *Introversion:* Think it through. Before you take any action, carefully review everything you have encountered so far.

6. *Judging:* Organize and plan. Don't just dive in! Now is the time to organize and plan your studying so you will learn and remember everything you need to. Don't just plan in your head either; write your plan down, in detail.

7. *Extraversion:* Take action. Now that you have a plan, act on it. Do whatever it takes. Create note cards, study outlines, study groups, and so on. If you are working on a paper, now is the time to start writing.

8. *Perceiving:* Change your plan as needed. Be flexible enough to change something that isn't working. Expect the unexpected, and deal with the unforeseen. Don't give up the whole effort the minute your original plan stops working. Figure out what's wrong, and come up with another, better plan and start following that.

> IN CLASS: If your students have taken the MBTI, try this: Arrange the chairs or desks in a circle or square, beginning with the most sensing students and progressing to the most intuitive students as you circuit around the group. Arrange students by MBTI type, as much as possible so that students are next to people with whom they feel naturally comfortable and can quickly make friends. Note that they are sitting opposite, and are thus most likely to speak and listen to, people whose viewpoints are quite different from theirs. It might sound odd, but it really works!

> Myers's *Introduction to Type* (see note 2) is the only full-length book on psychological type. It is richly informative and requires no prior training in psychology. Our favorite brief discussion is *Introduction to Type in Organizations* by Sandra Hirsh, Consulting Psychologists Press, 1998.

Multiple Intelligences

Another way of measuring how we learn is the theory of *multiple intelligences*, developed in 1983 by Dr. Howard Gardner, a professor of education at Harvard University. Gardner's theory is based on the premise that the traditional notion of human intelligence is very limited. He proposes eight different intelligences to describe how humans learn.

As you might imagine, Gardner's work is controversial because it questions our long-standing definitions of intelligence. Gardner argues that students should be encouraged to develop the abilities they have and that evaluation should measure all forms of intelligence, not just linguistic and logical-mathematical intelligence.

As you think of yourself and your friends, what kinds of intelligences do you have? Do college courses measure all the ways in which you are intelligent? Here is a short inventory that will help you recognize your multiple intelligences.

> IN CLASS: Ask students to discuss the meaning of the term *intelligence*. Why is Howard Gardner's work controversial?

> **YOUR TURN**
>
> Do you agree with Howard Gardner that there are eight styles of learning? Why or why not?

MULTIPLE INTELLIGENCES INVENTORY

According to Gardner, all human beings have at least eight different types of intelligence. Depending on your background and age, some intelligences are likely to be more developed than others. This activity will help you find out what your intelligences are. Knowing this, you can work to strengthen the other intelligences that you do not use as often. Put a check mark next to the items that apply to you.

Verbal/Linguistic Intelligence

_____ I enjoy telling stories and jokes.

_____ I enjoy word games (for example, Scrabble and puzzles).

_____ I am a good speller (most of the time).

_____ I like talking and writing about my ideas.

_____ If something breaks and won't work, I read the instruction book before I try to fix it.

_____ When I work with others in a group presentation, I prefer to do the writing and library research.

Logical/Mathematical Intelligence

_____ I really enjoy my math class.

_____ I like to find out how things work.

_____ I enjoy computer and math games.

_____ I love playing chess, checkers, or Monopoly.

_____ If something breaks and won't work, I look at the pieces and try to figure out how it works.

Visual/Spatial Intelligence

_____ I prefer a map to written directions.

_____ I enjoy hobbies such as photography.

_____ I like to doodle on paper whenever I can.

_____ In a magazine, I prefer looking at the pictures rather than reading the text.

_____ If something breaks and won't work, I tend to study the diagram of how it works.

Bodily/Kinesthetic Intelligence

_____ My favorite class is gym because I like sports.

_____ When looking at things, I like touching them.

_____ I use a lot of body movements when talking.

_____ I tend to tap my fingers or play with my pencil during class.

_____ If something breaks and won't work, I tend to play with the pieces to try to fit them together.

Musical/Rhythmic Intelligence

_____ I enjoy listening to CDs and the radio.

_____ I like to sing.

_____ I like to have music playing when doing homework or studying.

_____ I can remember the melodies of many songs.

_____ If something breaks and won't work, I tend to tap my fingers to a beat while I figure it out.

Interpersonal Intelligence

_____ I get along well with others.

_____ I have several very close friends.

_____ I like working with others in groups.

_____ Friends ask my advice because I seem to be a natural leader.

_____ If something breaks and won't work, I try to find someone who can help me.

Intrapersonal Intelligence

_____ I like to work alone without anyone bothering me.

_____ I don't like crowds.

_____ I know my own strengths and weaknesses.

_____ I find that I am strong-willed, independent, and don't follow the crowd.

_____ If something breaks and won't work, I wonder whether it's worth fixing.

Naturalist Intelligence

_____ I am keenly aware of my surroundings and of what goes on around me.

_____ I like to collect things like rocks, sports cards, and stamps.

_____ I like to get away from the city and enjoy nature.

_____ I enjoy learning the names of living things in the environment, such as flowers and trees.

_____ If something breaks down, I look around me to try and see what I can find to fix the problem.

A **verbal/linguistic learner** likes to read, write, and tell stories and is good at memorizing information. A **logical/mathematical** learner likes to work with numbers and is good at problem-solving and logical processes. A **visual/ spatial** learner likes to draw and play with machines and is good at puzzles and reading maps and charts. A **bodily/ kinesthetic** learner likes to move around and is good at sports, dance, and acting. A **musical/ rhythmic** learner likes to sing and play an instrument and is good at remembering melodies and noticing pitches and rhythms. An **interpersonal** learner likes to have many friends and is good at understanding people, leading others, and mediating conflicts. **Intrapersonal** learners like to work alone, understand themselves well, and are original thinkers. A **naturalistic** learner likes to be outside and is good at preservation, conservation, and organizing a living area. You can use your intelligences to help you make decisions about a major, choose activities, and investigate career options. Which of these eight intelligences best describes you?

TOTAL SCORE

_____ Verbal/Linguistic

_____ Musical/Rhythmic

_____ Logical/Mathematical

_____ Interpersonal

_____ Visual/Spatial

_____ Intrapersonal

_____ Bodily/Kinesthetic

_____ Naturalist

Add the number of check marks you made in each section. Your score for each intelligence will be a number between 1 and 6. Your high scores of 3 or more will help you to get a sense of your own multiple intelligences.

Source: Greg Gay and Gary Hams, "Multiple Intelligences Inventory." Copyright © Learning Disabilities Resource Community, www.ldrc.ca. Reprinted by permission of the authors.

When Learning Styles and Teaching Styles Conflict

Educators who study learning styles maintain that instructors tend to teach in ways that conform to their own particular styles of learning. So an introverted instructor who prefers abstract concepts and reflection (an assimilator, according to Kolb) and learns best in a read/write mode or aural mode will probably structure the course in a lecture format with little opportunity for either interaction or visual and kinesthetic learning. Conversely, an instructor who needs a more interactive, hands-on environment will likely involve students in discussion and learning through experience.

Do you enjoy listening to lectures, or do you find yourself gazing out the window or dozing? When your instructor assigns a group discussion, what is your immediate reaction? Do you dislike talking with other students, or is that the way you learn best? How do you react to lab sessions when you have to conduct an actual experiment? Is this an activity you look forward to or one that you dread? Each of these learning situations appeals to some students more than others, but each is inevitably going to be part of your college experience. Your college or university has intentionally designed courses for you to have the opportunity to listen to professors who are experts in their field, interact with other students in structured groups, and learn through doing. Because these are all important components of your college education, it's important for you to make the most of each situation.

When you recognize a mismatch between how you best learn and how you are being taught, it is important that you take control of your learning process. Don't depend on the instructor or the classroom environment to give you everything you need to maximize your learning. Employ your own preferences, talents, and abilities to develop many different ways to study and

■ RETENTION STRATEGY: Retention is connected to how well students can engage with faculty. A good predictor of first-year persistence is out-of-class interaction between students and faculty.

IN CLASS: Ask the students to share the learning styles that they discovered in this chapter and how they plan to apply them to be successful in any class.

TECH TIP BRANCH OUT

If the thought of a 2-hour lecture in an auditorium crammed with two hundred students fills you with a warm glow, chances are you're an auditory learner. But what if you're a visual learner who needs charts, graphs, and videos? Or a hands-on, group type who thrives best when immersed in a project?

1 ▸ THE PROBLEM

Course-management systems (CMSs) require that you learn material in a whole new way.

2 ▸ THE FIX

Figure out your learning style (by taking an online survey or test like Myers-Briggs), and look for classes that complement your strengths. At the same time, find ways to adapt to teaching techniques that lie outside your comfort zone.

3 ▸ HOW TO DO IT

The basic ingredients of a CMS—video, audio, and text—appeal to different learning styles.

1. If you're an auditory learner, you'll love audio recordings.

To get the most from text, read your notes and textbook passages aloud as you study. (You can even record them to play back to yourself.) While you're at it, listen to books on tape and join a study group for discussions.

To get the most from video clips, listen to them once, and then play them back with your eyes closed.

2. If you're a visual learner, you'll love videos, pictures, maps, and graphs.

To get the most from audio recordings and text, take notes and illustrate them, playing up key points with colored highlighters, pictures, or symbols. Or create a graph or chart to display important concepts.

3. If you're a hands-on learner, you'll love labs, group projects, and any kind of fieldwork.

To get the most from audio, video, and text, sit in the front row of your classroom, take notes, and read things aloud as you study. Build models or spreadsheets. Take fieldtrips to gather experience. In other words, get creative.

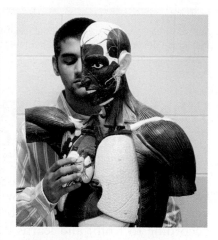

KNOW THIS

A CMS offers lots of other ways to help you connect with your instructors, your classmates, and the material. Not only can you tune in to helpful video or audio recordings, but you can also submit assignments online, keep track of your grades, sketch ideas on whiteboards that other students can view, or even collaborate on written assignments in real time.

PERSONAL BEST

Need help navigating your course or school's CMS? Turn to your favorite type-A classmate, your instructor or TA, or the campus computer lab or student success center.

"As we start a new school year, Mr. Smith, I just want you to know that I'm an Abstract-Sequential learner and trust that you'll conduct yourself accordingly!"

Learn to Adapt

Do you know your personal learning style? In college you will find that some instructors may have teaching styles that are challenging for you. Seek out the kinds of classes that conform to the way you like to learn, but also develop your adaptive strategies to make the most of any classroom setting.

retain information. Look back through this chapter to remind yourself of the ways in which you can use your own learning styles to be more successful in any class you take.

Learning with a Disability

While everyone has a learning style, a portion of the population has what is characterized as a learning disability. Learning disabilities are usually recognized and diagnosed in grade school, but some students can successfully compensate for a learning problem, perhaps without realizing that's what it is, and reach college without having been properly diagnosed or assisted.

Learning disabilities affect people's ability to interpret what they see and hear or to link information across different parts of the brain. These limitations can show up as specific difficulties with spoken and written language, coordination, self-control, or attention. Such difficulties can impede learning to read, write, or do math. The term *learning disability* covers a broad range of possible causes, symptoms, treatments, and outcomes. Because of this, it is difficult to diagnose a learning disability or pinpoint the causes. The types of learning disabilities that most commonly affect college students are attention disorders and disorders that affect the development of academic skills, including reading, writing, and mathematics.

IN CLASS: Ask students to discuss what, if any, direct experience they have had with learning disabilities.

DID YOU KNOW?

3.3% of first-year students report suffering from a learning disability.

ATTENTION DISORDERS

Attention disorders are common in children, adolescents, and adults. Some students who have attention disorders appear to daydream excessively, and once you get their attention, they can be easily distracted. Individuals with attention deficit disorder (ADD) or attention deficit hyperactivity disorder (ADHD) often have trouble organizing tasks or completing their work. They don't seem to listen to or follow directions, and their work might be messy or appear careless. Although they are not strictly classified as learning disabilities, ADD and ADHD can seriously interfere with academic performance, leading some educators to classify them along with other learning disabilities.

If you have trouble paying attention or getting organized, you won't really know whether you have ADD or ADHD until you are evaluated. Check out resources on campus or in the community. After you have been evaluated, follow the advice you get, which might or might not mean taking medication. If you do receive a prescription for medication, be sure to take it according to the physician's directions. In the meantime, if you're having trouble getting and staying organized, whether or not you have an attention disorder, you can improve your focus through your own behavioral choices. The National Institutes of Mental Health offer the following suggestions (found on their Web site) for adults with attention disorders:

> Adults with ADD or ADHD can learn how to organize their lives by using "props," such as a large calendar posted where it will be seen in the morning, date books, lists, and reminder notes. They can have a special place for keys, bills, and the paperwork of everyday life. Tasks can be organized into sections so that completion of each part can give a sense of accomplishment. Above all, adults who have ADD or ADHD should learn as much as they can about their disorder (**http://www.nimh.nih.gov/health/publications/ attention-deficit-hyperactivity-disorder/can-adults-have-adhd.shtml**).

COGNITIVE LEARNING DISABILITIES

Other learning disabilities are related to cognitive skills. Dyslexia, for example, is a common developmental reading disorder. A person can have problems with any of the tasks involved in reading. However, scientists have found that a significant number of people with dyslexia share an inability to distinguish or separate the sounds in spoken words. For instance, dyslexic individuals sometimes have difficulty assigning the appropriate sounds to letters, either individually or when letters combine to form words. However, there is more to reading than recognizing words. If the brain is unable to form images or relate new ideas to those stored in memory, the reader can't understand or remember the new concepts. So other types of reading disabilities can appear when the focus of reading shifts from word identification to comprehension.

Writing, too, involves several brain areas and functions. The brain networks for vocabulary, grammar, hand movement, and memory must all be in good working order. So a developmental writing disorder might result from problems in any of these areas. Someone who can't distinguish the sequence

IN CLASS: Share information on where students should go for help on campus if they think they might have a learning disability.

of sounds in a word will often have problems with spelling. People with writing disabilities, particularly expressive language disorders (the inability to express oneself using accurate language or sentence structure), are often unable to compose complete, grammatical sentences.

A student with a developmental arithmetic disorder will have difficulty recognizing numbers and symbols, memorizing facts such as the multiplication table, aligning numbers, and understanding abstract concepts such as place value and fractions.

Anyone who is diagnosed with a learning disability is in good company. The pop star Jewel; Michael Phelps, the Olympic gold medal swimmer; and actors Keira Knightley, Orlando Bloom, Patrick Dempsey, and Vince Vaughn are just a few of the famous and successful people who have diagnosed learning disabilities. A final important message: A learning disability is a learning difference but is in no way related to intelligence. Having a learning disability is not a sign that you are stupid. In fact, some of the most intelligent individuals in human history have had a learning disability.

The following questions may help you determine whether you or someone you know should seek further screening for a possible learning disability:

- Do you perform poorly on tests even when you feel you have studied and are capable of performing better?
- Do you have trouble spelling words?
- Do you work harder than your classmates at basic reading and writing?
- Do your instructors tell you that your performance in class is inconsistent, such as answering questions correctly in class but incorrectly on a written test?
- Do you have a really short attention span, or do your family members or instructors say that you do things without thinking?

Although responding "yes" to any of these questions does not mean that you have a disability, the resources of your campus learning center or the office for student disability services can help you address any potential problems and devise ways to learn more effectively.

CHECKLIST FOR SUCCESS

USE YOUR LEARNING STYLE TO HELP YOU SUCCEED

☐ **Take a learning styles inventory, either in this chapter or at your campus learning or counseling center(s).** See if the results might explain, at least in part, your level of performance in each class you are taking this term.

☐ **Learn about and accept your unique learning preferences.** Especially make note of your strengths in terms of those things you learn well and easily. See if those skills could be applied to other learning situations.

☐ **Adapt your learning style to the teaching styles of your professors.** Consider talking to your professors about how you might best be able to adapt to their teaching strategies.

☐ **Use your learning style to develop study strategies that work best for you.** You can walk, talk, read, listen, or even dance while you are learning.

☐ **If you need help with making the best use of your learning style, visit your learning center.** Consider taking some courses in the social and behavioral sciences that would help you better understand how humans learn.

☐ **If you think you might have a learning disability, go to your campus learning center and ask for a diagnostic assessment so you can develop successful coping strategies.** Make sure you ask for a personal interpretation and follow-up counseling or tutoring.

BUILD YOUR EXPERIENCE 1 3 2 4

1 STAY ON TRACK

Successful college students stay focused. They "stay on track." They know what they have to do to be successful, they set goals, and they monitor their progress toward their goals.

Reflect on what you have learned about college success in this chapter and how you are going to apply the chapter information or strategies in college and in your career. List your ideas.

1. _____

   _____

   _____

2. _____

   _____

   _____

3. _____

   _____

   _____

2 ONE-MINUTE PAPER

Recognizing that people have different ways of learning can be a relief. After reading this chapter, do you have a better understanding of your own learning style? What did you find to be the most interesting point in this chapter? What would you like to learn more about?

No matter how well prepared you are in your teaching, what a student hears and understands might not always be what you think you have said. The one-minute paper is a quick and easy assessment tool that will help alert you when students don't understand what was said or discussed in class. The one-minute paper will also give timid students an opportunity to ask questions and seek clarification. Ideally, you should ask for such a paper several minutes before the end of a class. The paper will also help you begin your next class by clarifying points your students seem to be unsure of.

3 APPLYING WHAT YOU'VE LEARNED

1. It is almost certain that you will find yourself in a class where your learning style conflicts with your instructor's preferred style of teaching. After reading this chapter, describe what you can do to take control and make the most of your strongest learning preferences.

2. It is important to understand various learning styles in the context of education, but it is also important to understand how learning preferences affect career choices. Considering your own learning styles, what might be the best careers for you? Why?

4 BUILDING YOUR PORTFOLIO

Are We on the Same Page? After reading about the Myers-Briggs Type Indicator in this chapter, can you guess what type you are?

1. Create a *Word* document, and note each type that you think best fits your personality.

   - Extravert or Introvert

   - Sensing or Intuition

   - Thinking or Feeling

   - Judging or Perceiving

2. Note what you think your four MBTI letters would be (for example, ESTP).

3. Using your favorite Internet search engine, search for "suggested careers for MBTI types." You will find several Web sites that suggest specific careers based on specific personality types.

4. Visit one site, and list at least two careers that are recommended for the MBTI type that you identify. Have you thought about these careers before? Do you think they would be a good fit for you? Why or why not?

   (Example: Careers recommended for ESTP: Sales representatives, marketers, police, detectives, paramedics, medical technicians, computer technicians, computer technical support, entrepreneurs. Suggestions found at **http://www.geocities.com/lifexplore/ mbcareer.htm**.)

5. Save your findings in your portfolio. Revisit this document as you continue to explore different majors and careers.

For more on this topic watch
French Fries Are Not Vegetables and Other College Lessons

WHERE TO GO FOR HELP. . .

ON CAMPUS

To learn more about learning styles and learning disabilities, talk to your first-year seminar instructor about campus resources. Most campuses have a learning center or a center for students with disabilities. You might also find that instructors in the areas of education or psychology have a strong interest in the processes of learning. Finally, don't forget your library or the Internet. A great deal of published information is available to describe how we learn.

BOOKS

> **Learning Outside the Lines** Edward M. Hallowell (Foreword), Jonathan Mooney, and David Cole, *Two Ivy League Students with Learning Disabilities and ADHD Give You the Tools for Academic Success and Educational Revolution* (New York: Fireside, 2000).

> Kathleen G. Nadeau, *Survival Guide for College Students with ADD or LD* (Washington, DC: Magination Press, 1994).

> **ADD and the College Student** Patricia O. Quinn, MD (ed.), *A Guide for High School and College Students with Attention Deficit Disorder* (Washington, DC: Magination Press, 2001).

ONLINE

> **LD Pride** **www.ldpride.net/learningstyles .MI.htm.** This site was developed in 1998 by Liz Bogod, an adult with learning disabilities. It provides general information about learning styles and learning disabilities and offers an interactive diagnostic tool to determine your learning style.

> **National Center for Learning Disabilities** **www .ncld.org.** This is the official Web site of the National Center for Learning Disabilities. The site provides a variety of resources on diagnosing and understanding learning disabilities.

> *Facebook* **www.facebook.com.** There are groups on *Facebook* that were created by students who have learning disabilities or ADHD. These groups are a great way to connect with other students with learning disabilities at your college or university or at other institutions. If you have been diagnosed with a disability, the members of these groups can offer support and help you seek out appropriate resources in order to be successful in college.

MY INSTITUTION'S RESOURCES

_____

_____

_____

_____

_____

_____

_____

_____

_____

_____

Preparing for
Success

PART 1

Preparing to
Study

PART 2

Preparing for
Life

PART 3

CHAPTER 5

Thinking Critically: The Basis of a College Education

IN THIS CHAPTER YOU WILL EXPLORE

Why critical thinking is essential for success

The meaning and value of a liberal education

Why there are no "absolutely right" or "positively wrong" answers to important questions

How to sharpen your critical-thinking skills

How logical reasoning can help you make sense of conflicting ideas

> ❝ **Thinking for ourselves and coming up with new conclusions will be really helpful when we enter the workforce.**
>
> Kelsey McManus, 18
> Nursing major
> University of North Carolina–Wilmington

As a nursing student at the University of North Carolina–Wilmington, Kelsey McManus understands the importance of critical-thinking skills both inside and outside the classroom. When Kelsey arrived on campus last fall, she learned that she would be living in the international residence hall with students from all over the world. She quickly learned that interacting with people who don't know anyone else in the United States and who have different customs, study habits, and food, among other things, presents some welcome challenges and tested her critical-thinking skills. "Some of the questions the international students ask about America make me think in a different way because I never think about my own country in that way." One way she has been able to reach out to the students she lives with is by joining the International Student Organization, which helps bring new international students to campus and get them settled into campus life.

Kelsey grew up in Baltimore and decided to attend UNCW because she knew nursing interested her and because the school had recently built a new nursing school (the laid-back atmosphere and location near North

Kelsey McManus ▶

Carolina's beaches didn't hurt either!). So far, her favorite class has been Introduction to Psychology. She has found critical-thinking skills essential to succeeding in all of her classes. "Professors will give you a lot of facts and general information, but they expect you to be able to relate all the information and come up with your own conclusions. Thinking for ourselves and coming up with new conclusions will be really helpful when we enter the workforce."

After Kelsey graduates, she's open to new experiences and opportunities, but she hopes to continue on to graduate school. As a future nurse, she knows that "critical-thinking skills will help a lot when dealing with cases and needing to figure out what symptoms lead to which diagnoses. They will also be helpful in clinical settings." If she had one thing to tell other first-year students, she'd tell them to look for ways to recognize problems and come up with their own unique solution.

Critical thinking is one of the most important concepts in this book. Point out the relationship between this concept and your institution's mission statement in the campus bulletin or catalog. Discuss the campus mission statement to help your students understand your institution's educational goals; tie in the meaning of a liberal education as appropriate. You might want to point out that most employers value critical-thinking skills above the particular information or knowledge students may have gleaned from their classes.

> **YOUR TURN**
>
> In your own words, define *liberal education*. Why would a "free" mind be an asset for you now and in the future?

As Kelsey mentioned, arguably the most important skill you'll acquire in college is the ability and confidence to think for yourself. Courses in every discipline will encourage you to ask questions, to sort through competing information and ideas, to form well-reasoned opinions, and to defend them. A liberal college education teaches you to investigate all sides of an issue and all possible solutions to a problem before you reach a conclusion or decide on a plan of action. Indeed, the word *liberal* (from the Latin *libero*, meaning "to free") has no political connotation in this context but represents the purpose of a college education: to liberate your mind from biases, superstitions, prejudices, and lack of knowledge so that you'll be in a better position to seek answers to difficult questions.

If you have just completed high school, you might be experiencing an awakening as you adjust to college. If you're an older returning student, discovering that your instructors trust you to find valid answers could be both surprising and stressful. If a high school teacher asked, "What are the three branches of the U.S. government?" there was only one acceptable answer: "legislative, executive, and judicial." A college instructor, on the other hand, might ask, "Under what circumstances might conflicts arise among the three branches of government, and what does this reveal about the democratic process?" There is no simple—or single—answer, and that's the point of higher education. Questions that suggest complex answers engage you in the process of critical thinking.

Most important questions don't have simple answers, and satisfying answers can be elusive. To reach them, you will have to discover numerous ways to view important issues. You will need to become comfortable with uncertainty. And you must be willing to challenge assumptions and conclusions, even those presented by so-called experts. It is natural to find critical thinking difficult and to feel frustrated by answers that are seldom entirely wrong or right. Yet the complicated questions are usually the ones that are most worthy of study, and working out the answers can be both intellectually exciting and personally rewarding. In this chapter, we will explain how developing and applying your critical-thinking skills can make the search for truth a worthwhile and stimulating adventure.

◤ ASSESSING YOUR STRENGTHS

Critical thinking is one of the most valuable skills you can practice for success in college and in the workplace. Are you a good critical thinker? Now that you have read the first section of this chapter, list specific examples of your strengths in critical thinking.

_____

_____

_____

_____

◤ SETTING GOALS

What are your most important objectives in learning the material in this chapter? Do you know the difference between critical thinking and "being critical"? List three goals that relate to developing and practicing critical-thinking skills (e.g., This week I will watch one TV news show, such as *Meet the Press*, *The O'Reilly Factor*, or *The Daily Show*, and make a list of "facts" I question and why).

1. _____

_____

2. _____

_____

3. _____

_____

What Is Critical Thinking, and Why Is It Important?

Let's start with what critical thinking is *not*. By "critical," we do not mean "negative" or "harsh." Rather, the term refers to thoughtful consideration of the information, ideas, and arguments that you encounter. Critical thinking is the ability to think for yourself and to reliably and responsibly make the decisions that affect your life.

As Richard Paul and Linda Elder of the National Council for Excellence in Critical Thinking explain it, "critical thinking is that mode of thinking about any subject, content, or problem in which the thinker improves the quality of his or her thinking by skillfully . . . imposing intellectual standards upon [his or her thoughts]."[1] They believe that much of our thinking, left to itself, is biased, distorted, partial, uninformed, or downright prejudiced. Yet

[1] Richard Paul and Linda Elder, *The Miniature Guide to Critical Thinking Concepts and Tools* (Dillon Beach, CA: Foundation for Critical Thinking Press, 2008).

■ RETENTION STRATEGY: Critical thinking is one of the most difficult concepts to teach and learn in college, yet it is the foundation for college success and retention. Have your students interview one of their instructors about how critical thinking and a liberal education contribute to a fuller life. This exercise will also help them become more engaged in the campus.

IN CLASS: Ask students for their definition of critical thinking. As each student responds, ask the next student to refine what the previous student said.

the quality of our life and the quality of what we produce, make, or build depend precisely on the quality of our thoughts.

Paul and Elder also caution that shoddy thinking is costly. How so? You probably know people who simply follow authority. They do not question, are not curious, and do not challenge people or groups who claim special knowledge or insight. These people do not usually think for themselves but rely on others to think for them. They might indulge in wishful, hopeful, and emotional thinking, assuming that what they believe is true simply because they wish it, hope it, or feel it to be true. As you might have noticed, such people tend not to have much control over their circumstances or to possess any real power in business or society.

Critical thinkers, in contrast, investigate problems, ask questions, pose new answers that challenge the status quo, discover new information, question authorities and traditional beliefs, challenge received dogmas and doctrines, make independent judgments, and develop creative solutions. When employers say they want workers who can find reliable information, analyze it, organize it, draw conclusions from it, and present it convincingly to others, they are seeking individuals who are critical thinkers.

> ### YOUR TURN
>
> On the basis of the explanation above, how would you rate yourself as a critical thinker?

Whatever else you do in college, make it a point to develop and sharpen your critical-thinking skills. You won't become an accomplished critical thinker overnight. But with practice, you can learn how to tell whether information is truthful and accurate. You can make better decisions, come up with fresh solutions to difficult problems, and communicate your ideas strategically and persuasively.[2]

Becoming a Critical Thinker

In essence, critical thinking is a search for truth. In college and in life, you'll be confronted by a mass of information and ideas. Much of what you read and hear will seem suspect, and a lot of it will be contradictory. (If you have ever talked back to a television commercial or doubted a politician's campaign promises, you know this already.) How do you decide what to believe?

> ### YOUR TURN
>
> Think of a problem you had to solve in the past. How did you do it? How can you draw on that experience to improve your ability to solve academic problems?

Paul and Elder remind us that there may be more than one right answer to any given question. The task is to determine which of the "truths" you read or hear are the most plausible and then draw on them to develop ideas of your own. Difficult problems practically demand that you weigh options and think through consequences before you can reach an informed decision. Critical thinking also involves improving the way you think about a subject, statement, or idea. To do that, you'll need to ask questions, consider several different points of view, and draw your own conclusions.

[2]Liz Brown, *Critical Thinking* (New York: Weigl Publishers, 2008), p. 4.

ASK QUESTIONS

The first step of thinking critically is to engage your curiosity. Instead of accepting statements and assertions at face value, question them. When you come across an idea or a "fact" that strikes you as interesting, confusing, or suspicious, ask yourself first what it means. Do you fully understand what is being said, or do you need to pause and think to make sense of the idea? Do you agree with the statement? Why or why not? Can the material be interpreted in more than one way?

Don't stop there. Ask whether you can trust the person or institution making a particular claim, and ask whether they have provided enough evidence to back up an assertion (more on this later). Ask who might be likely to agree or disagree and why. Ask how a new concept relates to what you already know, where you might find more information about the subject, and what you could do with what you learn. Finally, ask yourself about the implications and consequences of accepting something as truth. Will you have to change your perspective or give up a long-held belief? Will it require you to do something differently? Will it be necessary to investigate the issue further? Do you anticipate having to try to bring other people around to a new way of thinking?

> ### DID YOU KNOW?
>
> 54% of first-year students say they "frequently evaluate the quality or reliability of information they receive."

> ### YOUR TURN
>
> Imagine that your state has just approved a license plate design incorporating a cross and the slogan "I Believe." Almost immediately, a number of organizations begin protesting that this is a violation of the First Amendment of the U.S. Constitution. What kinds of questions will you ask to get at the truth?

CONSIDER MULTIPLE POINTS OF VIEW

Once you start asking questions, you'll typically discover a slew of different possible answers competing for your attention. Don't be too quick to latch onto one and move on. To be a critical thinker, you need to be fair and open-minded, even if you don't agree with certain ideas at first. Give them all a fair hearing, because your goal is to find the truth or the best action, not to confirm what you already believe.

Often, you will recognize the existence of competing points of view on your own, perhaps because they're held by people you know personally. You might discover them in what you read, watch, or listen to for pleasure. Reading assignments might deliberately expose you to conflicting arguments and theories about a subject, or you might encounter differences of opinion as you do research for a project.

In class discussions, also, your instructors might often insist that more than one valid point of view exists: "So, for some types of students, you agree that bilingual education might be best? What types of students might not benefit?" Your instructors will expect you to explain in concrete terms any point you reject: "You think this essay is flawed. Well, what are your reasons?" They might challenge the authority of experts: "Dr. Fleming's theory sounds impressive. But here are some facts he doesn't account for. . . ." Your

IN CLASS: Critical thinking and information literacy are related concepts. If students have difficulty knowing what to do with information they read or find, consider incorporating the goals of information literacy (see pages 211–12 of Chapter 11, Developing Library, Research, and Information Literacy Skills) into your discussion of critical thinking.

IN CLASS: Ask whether students have been told that once they make up their minds, they have to stick with their decisions. If so, who told them that? Under what circumstances? Why does it make more sense to be able to change your mind if you believe you have a better solution?

instructors will also sometimes reinforce your personal views and experiences: "So something like this happened to you once, and you felt exactly the same way. Can you tell us why?"

The more ideas you entertain, the more sophisticated your own thinking will become. Ultimately, you will discover not only that it is okay to change your mind, but that a willingness to do so is the mark of a reasonable, educated person.

DRAW CONCLUSIONS

Once you have considered different points of view, it's up to you to reach your own conclusions, to craft a new idea based on what you've learned, or to make a decision about what you'll do with the information you have.

This process isn't necessarily a matter of figuring out the best idea. Depending on the goals of the activity, it might be simply the one that you think is the most fun or the most practical, or it might be a new idea of your own creation. For a business decision, it might involve additional cost-benefit analysis to decide which computer equipment to purchase for your office. In a chemistry lab, it might be a matter of interpreting the results of an experiment. In a creative writing workshop, students might collaborate to select the most workable plot for a classmate's short story. Or a social worker might conduct multiple interviews before recommending a counseling plan for a struggling family.

Drawing conclusions involves looking at the outcome of your inquiry in a more demanding, critical way. If you are looking for solutions to a problem, which ones really seem most promising after you have conducted an exhaustive search for materials? Do some answers conflict with others? Which ones can be achieved? If you have found new evidence, what does that new evidence show? Do your original beliefs hold up? Do they need to be modified? Which notions should be abandoned? Most important, consider what you would need to do or say to persuade someone else that your ideas are valid. Thoughtful conclusions aren't very useful if you can't share them with others.

IN CLASS: Discuss the value of collaborative thinking as it applies to critical thinking, especially in the area of creative brainstorming.

YOUR TURN

If you never have worked with a study group, now is the time to try it and discover how much more learning can take place in a shorter period of time. How do you think you could benefit from joining a study group? What reasons might you give for not joining one?

How Collaboration Fosters Critical Thinking

A 1995 study by Professor Anuradha A. Gokhale at Western Illinois University, published in the *Journal of Technology Education*, found that students who participated in collaborative learning performed significantly better on a test requiring critical thinking than did students who studied individually. The study also found that the two groups did equally well on a test that required only memorization.[3]

Having more than one student involved in the learning process generates a greater number of ideas. People think more clearly when they are talking as

[3]Anuradha Gokhale, "Collaborative Learning Enhances Critical Thinking," *Journal of Technology Education* 7, no. 1 (1995).

Get a Second Opinion

One way to become a better critical thinker is to practice with other people. By getting feedback from another person, you can see the possible flaws in your own position. You will also learn that there are few black-and-white answers to any question.

well as listening (a very good reason to participate actively in your classes). Creative brainstorming and group discussion encourage original thought. These habits also teach participants to consider alternative points of view carefully and to express and defend their own ideas clearly. As a group negotiates ideas and learns to agree on the most reliable thoughts, it moves closer to a surer solution.

Collaboration occurs not only face to face, but also over the Internet. Christopher P. Sessums, creator of an award-winning blog, writes:

> Weblogs offer several key features that I believe can support a constructive, collaborative, reflective environment. For one, it's convenient. The medium supports self-expression and "voice." Collaboration and connectivity can be conducted efficiently, especially in terms of participants' time or place. Publishing your thoughts online forces you to concretize your thoughts.

"Collaborative weblogs," Sessums concludes, "promote the idea of learners as creators of knowledge, not merely consumers of information."[4] So do online discussion groups, wikis (which allow users to add, update, and otherwise improve material that others have posted), and, of course, face-to-face collaboration.

Whether in person or through electronic communication, teamwork improves your ability to think critically. As you leave college and enter the world of work, you will find that collaboration is essential in almost any career you pursue, not only with people in your work setting, but also with others around the globe.

[4]Christopher Sessums, Eduspaces Web log, November 9, 2005. Available at: http://eduspaces .net/csessums/weblog/archive/2005/11.

Thinking Critically about Arguments

What does the word *argument* mean to you? If you're like most people, the first image it conjures up might be an ugly fight you had with a friend, a yelling match you witnessed on the street, or a heated disagreement between family members. True, such unpleasant confrontations are arguments. But the word also refers to a calm, reasoned effort to persuade someone of the value of an idea.

When you think of it this way, you'll quickly recognize that arguments are central to academic study, work, and life in general. Scholarly articles, business memos, and requests for spending money all have something in common: The effective ones make a general claim, provide reasons to support it, and back up those reasons with evidence. That's what argument is.

As we have already seen, it's important to consider multiple points of view, or arguments, in tackling new ideas and complex questions. But arguments are not all equally valid. Good critical thinking involves thinking creatively about the assumptions that might have been left out and scrutinizing the quality of the evidence that is used to support a claim. Whether examining an argument or communicating one, a good critical thinker is careful to ensure that ideas are presented in an understandable, logical way.

CHALLENGE ASSUMPTIONS

■ RETENTION STRATEGY: You may find that some students believe that the "grass is greener" somewhere else and may be tempted to transfer to a different institution. Help them challenge these assumptions before making a snap decision to transfer.

All too often, our beliefs are based on gut feelings or on blind acceptance of something we've heard or read. To some extent, that's unavoidable. If we made a habit of questioning absolutely everything, we would have trouble making it through the day. Yet some assumptions should be examined more thoughtfully, especially if they will influence an important decision or serve as the foundation for an argument.

For an example, imagine that the mayor of the city where your school is located has announced that he wants to make a bid to host the Olympic Games. Many people on campus are excited at the prospect, but your friend Richard is less than thrilled.

IN CLASS: Ask what is the importance of seeking the truth and how this relates to Richard's opening remarks.

"The Olympic Games just about ruined my hometown," Richard tells you. "Road signs all over Atlanta had to be changed so that visitors could find the game sites easily. Because the city couldn't supply enough workers to complete the task on time, the organizers brought thousands of immigrants to town to help with the task, and some of them were illegal aliens.

YOUR TURN

So far, what unstated assumptions do you see in Richard's argument? Explain why you might question some of his claims.

"The Games are intended to foster national and international pride, but these immigrants could care less about that. They were there to earn money for their families. The Hispanic population nearly doubled once the Games were over. And if people understood how much political corruption went on behind the scenes, they would understand why the Olympic Games are not healthy for a host city."

Another friend, Sally, overhears your conversation, and she's not buying Richard's conclusions. "How do you know all of that is accurate?" she asks. "I just know it," says Richard.

Eager to get at the truth of the matter, Sally decides to look into other points of view. She does a quick Web search and finds an article about the Atlanta Olympics in the *American Historical Review*, the journal of record for the history profession in the United States. Its author notes that "the Games provided an enormous engine for growth" and comments that the city's "surging population is the most obvious marker of Atlanta's post-Olympic transformation." The article continues: "By the 1996 Games the metro population had reached three million, and today [is] 4,458,253. Winning the Olympic bid marked a turning point that put Atlanta on the world's radar screen."[5]

Although Sally has found good information from a reputable source, you should be uncomfortable with the totally upbeat tone of the article. If you and Sally dig a little further, you might land on the Web site of the Utah Office of Tourism, which includes a report that was prepared when that state was investigating the potential impacts of hosting the 2002 Winter Games in Salt Lake City. According to the report, "Among the key legacies of the Atlanta Olympics was the regeneration of certain downtown districts that had fallen into urban decay." The authors also note that "the Olympic-spurred development in [Atlanta] has provided a much-needed stimulus for revitalization."[6]

Finding a second positive analysis would give you a compelling reason to believe that the Olympic Games are good for a city, but Richard might easily discover a report from the European Tour Operators Association, which concludes that visitors are likely to stay away from host countries during and following the Games, causing a significant long-term decline in revenue for hotels and other businesses that depend on tourism.[7]

Unfortunately, simply learning more about the benefits and costs of hosting the Olympics doesn't yield any concrete answers. Even so, you, Richard, and Sally have uncovered assumptions and have developed a better understanding of the issue. That's an important first step.

> **YOUR TURN**
>
> What's the difference between Richard's approach to the truth and Sally's? Which is more sensible? Why?

> **YOUR TURN**
>
> In your opinion, is hosting the Olympics good or bad for a city? Why? How can you reconcile Richard's views on the subject with Sally's findings? If you think the truth lies in between, how would you go about discovering it?

IN CLASS: How many of your students have justified the accuracy of what they have said by giving an answer like Richard's ("I just know it")? Encourage them to tell you what they mean by such an answer.

IN CLASS: Point out that Sally's research contains specifics—numbers, facts, and so forth—that Richard had ignored. Without specifics, truth can be very elusive!

IN CLASS: Ask your students why they should be uncomfortable with the upbeat tone of the material Sally found, even though it comes from a scholarly source. They might need some prodding to understand that an overly positive spin on a subject can suggest bias or, in the case of this piece (taken from the schedule for the American Historical Association's 2006 conference in Atlanta), a purpose that is out of sync with the reader's inquiry.

EXAMINE THE EVIDENCE

The evidence that is offered as support for an argument can vary in quality. While Richard started with no proof other than his convictions ("I just know

---

[5]Mary G. Rolinson, visiting lecturer in the Georgia State University History Department, "Atlanta Before and After the Olympics." Copyright © American Historical Association. Available at: http://www.historians.org/perspectives/issues/2006/0611/0611ann6.cfm.

[6]Utah Office of Tourism, *Observations from Past Olympic Host Communities: Executive Summary*. Available at: http://travel.utah.gov/research_and_planning/2002_olympics.

[7]"Olympics Have Negative Effect on Tourism," July 10, 2008. Available at: http://www.travelbite.co.uk.

it"), Sally looked to expert opinion and research studies for answers to her question. Even so, one of her sources sounded overly positive, prompting a need to confirm the author's claims with additional evidence from other sources.

Like Sally, critical thinkers are careful to check that the evidence supporting an argument—whether someone else's or their own—is of the highest possible quality. To do that, simply ask a few questions about the arguments as you consider them:

- What general idea am I being asked to accept?
- Are good and sufficient reasons given to support the overall claim?
- Are those reasons backed up with evidence in the form of facts, statistics, and quotations?
- Does the evidence support the conclusions?
- Is the argument based on logical reasoning, or does it appeal mainly to the emotions?
- Do I recognize any questionable assumptions?
- Can I think of any counterarguments? What facts can I muster as proof?
- What do I know about the person or organization making the argument?

IN CLASS: Ask why emotional decisions sometimes stray from the truth. When might an emotional decision be appropriate (falling in love, praising a movie, etc.)? When might it be inappropriate?

> **YOUR TURN**
>
> What, if anything, is wrong with making decisions purely on the basis of your emotions?

If, after you have evaluated the evidence used in support of a claim, you're still not certain of its quality, it's best to keep looking. Drawing on questionable evidence for an argument has a tendency to backfire. In most cases, a little persistence will help you find something better. (You can find tips on how to find and evaluate sources in Chapter 11, Developing Library, Research, and Information Literacy Skills.)

Facebook Causes Lung Cancer

Do you believe everything you read? The Internet and other forms of media are filled with outlandish claims that are often totally false. Use your own critical-thinking abilities to practice healthy skepticism about anything you see in print that seems far-fetched. Check it out by using other credible sources.

TECH TIP RESEARCH WISELY

Don't assume that any information you find on the Internet is accurate or unbiased. Thanks to the First Amendment, people can publish whatever they want to online. It's up to you to filter out what's valuable, objective, and up-to-date.

1▶ THE PROBLEM

You're not sure how to evaluate the types of information found on the Web.

2▶ THE FIX

Get some context.

3▶ HOW TO DO IT

- **Portals:** One-stop shops that serve up a full range of cyber services. Expect to find search engines; news, weather, and news updates; stock quotes; reference tools; even movie reviews. (Bonus: Most services are free.) Prime examples: **Google.com** and **Yahoo.com.**

- **News:** Sites that offer news and analysis of current events, politics, business trends, sports, entertainment, and so on. They're often sponsored by magazines, newspapers, and radio stations and include special online extras. Prime examples: **NYTimes.com**, Harvard Business Review (**hbr.org**), and **CNN.com.**

- **Corporate and marketing:** Promotional sites for businesses. Some company Web sites let you order their products or services online; others even list job openings. Prime examples: **Ford.com** and **BenJerry.com.**

- **Informational:** Fact-based sites, often created by government agencies. Click to these for information on everything from passports to city bus schedules to census data. Prime examples: **NYCsubway.org** and **Travel.State.gov.**

- **Blogs:** Informal Web sites where people can air their views and opinions. Some businesses create blogs to connect with their customers; other blogs are strictly personal, designed to share with family and friends. Prime examples: **Gawker.com** and **TheLawsonsSpillTheirGuts.blogspot.com.**

- **Wikis:** Informational Web sites that allow for open editing by registered users or, in some cases, by the general public. Prime examples: **Wikipedia.com** and **TechCrunch.com.**

Keep in mind that there's a big difference between the *Journal of the American Medical Association* and a journal written by Fred from Pomona. And no, you can't use an ad for Shake Weight as a source for a fitness article: It's an ad. Be discerning. To make sure that the research you use is unbiased and current, look for tip-offs. Most reputable Web sites are easy to navigate, contain little advertising, and list author names and credentials.

PERSONAL BEST

Should you trust the information on a wiki? In a word, no. Wikis are useful, but not academically viable research sources. (Do not list **Wikipedia.com** in the bibliography of a college essay. Ever.) *Wiki-wiki* means "quick" in Hawaiian, and different people can manipulate Wikipedia that fast.

BEWARE OF LOGICAL FALLACIES

A critical thinker has an attitude—an attitude of wanting to avoid nonsense, to find the truth and to discover the best action. It's an attitude that rejects intuiting what is right in favor of requiring reasons. Instead of being defensive or emotional, critical thinkers aim to be logical.

Although logical reasoning is essential to solving any problem, whether simple or complex, you need to go one step further to make sure that an argument hasn't been compromised by faulty reasoning. Here are some of the most common missteps people make in their use of logic:

- **Attacking the person.** It's perfectly acceptable to argue against other people's positions or to attack their arguments. It is not okay, however, to go after their personalities. Any argument that resorts to personal attack ("Why should we believe a cheater?") is unworthy of consideration.

- **Begging.** "Please, officer, don't give me a ticket because if you do, I'll lose my license, and I have five little children to feed and won't be able to feed them if I can't drive my truck." None of the driver's statements offer any evidence, in any legal sense, as to why she shouldn't be given a ticket. Pleading *might* work, if the officer is feeling generous, but an appeal to facts and reason would be more effective: "I fed the meter, but it didn't register the coins. Since the machine is broken, I'm sure you'll agree that I don't deserve a ticket."

False Advertising

Advertisers know that the public can be easily influenced to buy a product if a famous actor, musician, or sports star promotes it. But good critical thinkers will evaluate the product on its own merits. Don't fall victim to false claims, even if they come out of the mouth of a star.

LUSTRE-CREME is the favorite beauty shampoo of 4 out of 5 top Hollywood stars... and you'll love it in its new Lotion Form, too!

Marilyn Monroe
starring in
"GENTLEMEN PREFER BLONDES"
A 20th Century-Fox Production
Color by Technicolor

- **Appealing to false authority.** Citing authorities, such as experts in a field or the opinions of qualified researchers, can offer valuable support for an argument. But a claim based on the authority of someone whose expertise is questionable relies on the appearance of authority rather than real evidence. We see this all the time in advertising: Sports stars who are not doctors, dieticians, or nutritionists urge us to eat a certain brand of food, or famous actors and singers who are not dermatologists extol the medical benefits of a pricey remedy for acne.

- **Jumping on a bandwagon.** Sometimes we are more likely to believe something if a lot of other people believe it. Even the most widely accepted truths, however, can turn out to be wrong. There was a time when nearly everyone believed that the world was flat—until someone came up with evidence to the contrary.

- **Assuming that something is true because it hasn't been proven false.** Go to a bookstore, and you'll find dozens of books detailing close encounters with flying saucers and extraterrestrial beings. These books describe the person who had the close encounter as beyond reproach in integrity and sanity. Because critics could not disprove the claims of the witnesses, the events are said to have really occurred. Even in science, few things are ever proved completely false, but evidence can be discredited.

- **Falling victim to false cause.** Frequently, we make the assumption that just because one event followed another, the first event must have caused the second. This reasoning is the basis for many superstitions. The ancient Chinese once believed that they could make the sun reappear after an eclipse by striking a large gong, because they knew that the sun reappeared after a large gong had been struck on one such occasion. Most effects, however, are usually the result of a complex web of causes. Don't be satisfied with easy before-and-after claims; they are rarely correct.

- **Making hasty generalizations.** If someone selected one green marble from a barrel containing a hundred marbles, you wouldn't assume that the next marble would be green. After all, there are still ninety-nine marbles in the barrel, and you know nothing about the colors of those marbles. However, given fifty draws from the barrel, each of which produced a green marble after the barrel had been shaken thoroughly, you would be more willing to conclude that the next marble drawn would be green, too. Reaching a conclusion based on the opinion of one source is like figuring that all the marbles in the barrel are green after pulling out only one.

Fallacies like these can slip into even the most careful reasoning. One false claim can derail an entire argument, so be on the lookout for weak logic in what you read and write. Never forget that accurate reasoning is a key factor for success in college and in life.

YOUR TURN

Have you ever used any of these fallacies to justify a decision? Why was it wrong to do so? Can you think of other errors of logic that might push you farther from the truth?

Critical Thinking in College and Everyday Life

As you practice the skills of critical thinking in college, they start to become a natural part of your life. Eventually, you will be able to think your way through many everyday situations, such as these:

- You try to reach a classmate on the phone to ask a question about tomorrow's quiz. When you can't reach her, you become so anxious that you can't study or sleep.
- On the day an important paper is due, a heavy snowstorm rolls in. You brave the cold to get to class. When you arrive, no one—including the teacher—is there. You take a seat and wait.

Now let's transform you into a critical thinker and examine the possible outcomes:

- When you can't reach a classmate on the phone to ask a question about tomorrow's quiz, you review the material once more, then call one or more other classmates. Then you consider their views and those of your textbook and class. Instead of deciding on one point of view for each important topic, you decide to keep in mind all of those that make sense, leaving your final decision until you have the quiz in your hand.
- Before heading out to class in a big snowstorm, you check the college Web site and discover that classes have been canceled. You stay at home.

> **YOUR TURN**
>
> Suppose you're shopping for a surround-sound system. One good friend urges you to buy the top of the line. Another well-meaning friend steers you to a different brand, claiming it's just as good as the more expensive brand leader. Now all you know is that two of your good friends have offered information that might or might not be true. How do you think critically about which system to choose?

If you hang on to the guidelines in this chapter, we can't promise your classes will be easier, but they will certainly be more interesting. You will now know how to use critical thinking to figure things out instead of depending purely on how you feel or what you've heard. As you listen to a lecture, try to predict where it is heading and why. When other students raise issues, ask yourself whether they have enough information to justify what they have said. And when you raise your hand, remember that asking a sensible question can be more important than trying to find the elusive—and often nonexistent—"right answer."

Imagine a world in which physicians tried a new procedure on a patient before it had been tested, your history course was taught by someone who never studied history, and you put your total faith in a hair restorer just because the advertising said it would grow hair in two weeks.

As a critical thinker, you would know better.

IN CLASS: Now that your students have reviewed the entire chapter, ask for their thoughts on the meaning and significance of critical thinking.

CHECKLIST FOR SUCCESS

CRITICAL THINKING

☐ **Make sure you understand what *critical thinking* means.** If you are not clear about this term, discuss it with another student, the instructor of this course, or a staff member in the learning center.

☐ **Find ways to express your imagination and curiosity; practice asking questions.** If you have the impulse to raise a question, don't stifle yourself. College is for self-expression and exploration.

☐ **Challenge your own and others' assumptions that are not supported by evidence.** Practice asking politely, calmly, and not in a rejecting manner for additional information to help you better understand the position the individual may be taking.

☐ **During class lectures, presentations, and discussions, practice thinking about the subjects being discussed from multiple points of view.** Start with the view you would most naturally take toward the matter at hand. Then force yourself to imagine what questions might be raised by someone who didn't see the issue the same way you do.

☐ **Draw your own conclusions, and explain to others what evidence you considered that led you to these positions.** Don't assume that anyone automatically understands why you reached your conclusions.

☐ **Join study groups or class project teams, and work as a team member with other students.** When you are a member of a team, volunteer for roles that stretch you. This is how you will really experience significant gains in learning and development.

☐ **Learn to identify false claims in commercials and in political arguments.** Then look for the same faulty reasoning in people you encounter each day.

☐ **Practice critical thinking not only in your academic work but also in your everyday interactions with friends and family.** Your environment both in and out of college will give you lots of opportunities to become a better critical thinker.

BUILD YOUR EXPERIENCE 1 3 2 4

1 STAY ON TRACK

Successful college students stay focused. They "stay on track." They know what they have to do to be successful, they set goals, and they monitor their progress toward their goals.

Reflect on what you have learned about college success in this chapter and how you are going to apply the chapter information or strategies in college and in your career. List your ideas.

1. _____

_____

_____

2. _____

_____

_____

3. _____

_____

_____

2 ONE-MINUTE PAPER

One major shift from being a high school student to being a college student involves the level of critical thinking your college instructors expect of you. After reading this chapter, how would you describe critical thinking to a high school student?

No matter how well prepared you are in your teaching, what a student hears and understands might not always be what you think you have said. The one-minute paper is a quick and easy assessment tool that will help alert you when students don't understand what was said or discussed in class. The one-minute paper will also give timid students an opportunity to ask questions and seek clarification. Ideally, you should ask for such a paper several minutes before the end of a class. The paper will also help you begin your next class by clarifying points your students seem to be unsure of.

3 APPLYING WHAT YOU HAVE LEARNED

Now that you have read and discussed this chapter, consider how you can apply what you have learned to your academic and personal life. The following prompts will help you reflect on chapter material and its relevance to you both now and in the future.

1. After reading this chapter, think of professions (for example, physicians, engineers, marketing professionals) for whom problem solving and thinking "outside of the box" are necessary. Choose one career, and describe why you think critical thinking is a necessary and valuable skill.

2. In your opinion, is it harder to think critically than to base your arguments on how you feel about a topic? Why or why not? What are the advantages of finding answers based on your feelings? Based on critical thinking? How might you use both approaches in seeking answers?

4 BUILDING YOUR PORTFOLIO

My Influences   Our past experiences have shaped the way in which we think and perceive the world around us. Sometimes it is easy to interpret things without stopping to think about why we feel the way we do. How have other people shaped the way you see the world today?

1. In your personal portfolio, create a *Word* document and

   - Describe at least three people (such as family, friends, celebrities, national leaders) who you feel have most influenced the way you think.

   - Describe how these individuals' values, actions, expectations, and words have shaped the way you think about yourself and the world.

2. Describe an experience you have had since coming to college that has challenged you to think about an issue in a new and different way.

3. Save your work in your portfolio.

For more on this topic watch
French Fries Are Not Vegetables and Other College Lessons

WHERE TO GO FOR HELP...

ON CAMPUS

> **Logic Courses** Check out your philosophy department's introductory course in logic. This might be the single best course designed to teach you critical-thinking skills. Nearly every college offers such a course.

> **Argument Courses and Critical-Thinking Courses** These are usually offered in the English department. They will help you develop the ability to formulate logical arguments and avoid such pitfalls as logical fallacies.

> **Debating Skills** Some of the very best critical thinkers developed debating skills during college. Go to either your student activities office or your department of speech/drama, and find out whether your campus has a debate club or team. Debating can be fun, and chances are you will meet some interesting student thinkers that way.

LITERATURE

> *12 Angry Men* **by Reginald Rose (New York: Penguin Classics, 2006)** This is a reprint of the original teleplay, which was written in 1954 and made into a film in 1958. It is also available on DVD. The stirring courtroom drama pits twelve jurors against one another as they argue the outcome of a murder trial in which the defendant is a teenage boy. While critical thinking is needed to arrive at the truth, all the jurors except one use noncritical arguments to arrive at a guilty verdict. However, the analysis of that one holdout produces a remarkable change in their attitudes.

ONLINE

> Check the following Web site for a critical review of *The Encyclopedia of Stupidity:* **http://arts .independent.co.uk/books/reviews/article112328 .ece.**

> A Guide to Critical Thinking About What You See on the Web: **http://www.ithaca.edu/library/ training/think.html.**

MY INSTITUTION'S RESOURCES

_____

_____

_____

_____

_____

_____

_____

_____

Being Engaged in Learning: Listening, Taking Notes, and Participating in Class

IN THIS CHAPTER YOU WILL EXPLORE

How to use your senses in learning and remembering

How to prepare before class

Why you should participate in class by speaking up

How to listen critically

How to assess and improve your note-taking skills

Why it is important to review your notes and textbook materials soon after class

How being engaged in the classroom improves your learning

> " Taking notes should never be a substitute for paying attention and understanding the deeper elements of lectures and verbal discourse.

Jordan Hardy, 19
Political Science major
Santa Monica City College

Jordan Hardy grew up in the Culver City section of Los Angeles. He left high school after his junior year and obtained his GED. The benefits of participating in class and being engaged in learning are obvious to Jordan. "Most of the time the questions you have are questions that will help the whole class. Everyone in the class benefits from an instructor's answer." He points out, however, that no one appreciates a student asking questions just for the participation points

Jordan Hardy ▶

or to show off. "I try to be direct and simple when asking questions so the class can get direct and simple answers."

This same no-nonsense attitude is also present in the way he prepares for class. "I just make sure to be there on time, every time, and to try to stay until the class is over. I'm not a meticulous note-taker. I find myself zoning out as much as the next guy. But as long as I make an effort to pay attention and write down key points and the chapter sections in books I'm supposed to read, I find it pretty easy to maintain good grades.

"In a class with lots of information, I take notes really well. It makes it harder to actually pay attention to concepts, but it certainly pays off for tests and such. In less formal classes such as speech or ethics, which are very idea heavy, I tend to not take notes that much, or even at all. Taking notes should never be a substitute for paying attention and understanding the deeper elements of lectures and verbal discourse."

Jordan plans to transfer to Stanford, Berkeley, or another four-year California school. In ten years he hopes to be an author and analyst on issues of political philosophy and sociobiology. He also hopes to put his class participation skills to good use. "It is my dream to take part in debates and public speeches." His advice to other first-year students: "Take it easy and go with the flow. Try to get as much as you can out of your classes, and try to do your best, whether or not you feel like it. It always pays off in the end."

Jordan's advice is sound when you consider that in virtually every college class you take, you'll need to master certain skills to earn high grades, such as listening, taking notes, and being engaged in learning. Engagement in learning means that you take an active role in your classes by listening critically, asking questions, contributing to discussions, and providing answers. These active learning behaviors will enhance your ability to understand abstract ideas, find new possibilities, organize those ideas, and recall the material once the class is over.

Your academic success relies on practicing the habits of active engagement both in and out of class. In the classroom, engagement starts with the basics: listening, taking notes, and participating in class discussions. Many of the questions on college exams will be drawn from class lectures and discussions. Therefore you need to attend each class and be actively involved. In addition to taking notes, you might consider recording the lecture and discussion if you have the instructor's permission. If there are points you don't understand, take the time to meet with the instructor after class or during office hours. Another strategy to increase your engagement and your learning is to meet with a study group to compare your understanding of course material with that of your classmates.

This chapter reviews several note-taking methods. Choose the one that works best for you. Because writing down everything the instructor says is probably not possible and you might not be sure what is most important, ask questions in class. This will ensure that you clearly understand your notes. Reviewing your notes with a tutor, someone from your campus learning center, or a friend from class can also help you clarify your understanding of the most important points.

Most of all, be sure to speak up. When you have a question to ask or a comment to share, don't let embarrassment or shyness stop you. You will

IN CLASS: This chapter is one of many that contains information critical to success in the classroom. Emphasize the importance of effective listening, note taking, and engagement in class. Let students know that many test questions on college exams are drawn from class lectures, not textbooks. Ask how many of their current courses are lecture-based and how many are discussion-based.

YOUR TURN

What kind of notes did you take in high school? Do you think you learned how to take good notes? Is the same method working for you now? Why or why not?

◼ ASSESSING YOUR STRENGTHS ◼

Students who are engaged in college life practice the behaviors that are reviewed in this chapter. What about you—how would you rate your level of engagement? Now that you have read the first section of this chapter, list specific examples of your strengths in the area of engagement.

_____

_____

_____

_____

◼ SETTING GOALS ◼

What are _your_ most important objectives in learning the material in this chapter? Do you have a good method of note taking? Do you devote time and energy to academic work by attending class and studying out of class? List three goals that relate to engagement in learning (e.g., I will schedule a visit with one of my professors to show him or her my notes from the last class to make sure I'm writing down the most important points).

1. _____

_____

2. _____

_____

3. _____

_____

be more likely to remember what happens in class if you are an active participant.

Using Your Senses in the Learning Process

You can enhance your memory by using as many of your senses as possible while learning. How do you believe you learn most effectively?

1. **Aural:** Are you an auditory learner? Do you learn by listening to other people talk, or does your mind begin to wander when you listen passively for more than a few minutes?

2. **Visual:** Do you like reading? Do you learn best when you can see the words on the printed page? During a test, can you actually visualize where the information appears in your text? Can you remember data best when it's presented in the form of a picture, graph, chart, map, or video?

◼ RETENTION STRATEGY: This chapter contains a number of strategies for different types of learners. Be sure students identify the strategies that work best for them and help them stay engaged. Research finds that students who exhibit high levels of engagement are retained at a higher level than unengaged students.

IN CLASS: Ask students to try to determine which of their senses they use most when they are trying to sort and remember material for class. You might have them form groups by preferred sense. If some individuals are standing alone, put them in another group and have them explain their method and listen to other students explain theirs.

IN CLASS: Review with your students how the VARK Learning Styles Inventory (Chapter 4) focuses on learners' sensory preferences for learning. Visual learners prefer to learn information through charts, graphs, symbols, and other visual means. Aural learners prefer to hear information. Read/Write learners prefer to learn information displayed as words. Kinesthetic learners prefer to learn through experience and practice.

3. **Interactive:** Do you enjoy discussing coursework with friends, class-mates, or the instructor? Does talking about information from the lec-ture or the text help you remember it?

4. **Tactile:** Do you learn through your sense of touch? Does typing your notes help you remember them?

5. **Kinesthetic:** Can you learn better when your body is in motion? When you are participating in sports, dancing, or working out, do you know immediately if a movement feels right? Do you learn more effectively by doing something than by listening or reading about it?

6. **Olfactory:** Does your sense of taste or smell contribute to your learning process? Do you cook using a recipe or by tasting and adding ingredients? Are you sensitive to odors?

Two or three of these modes probably describe your preferred ways of learning better than the others. At the college level, faculty members tend to share information primarily via lecture and the textbook. However, many students like to learn through visual and interactive means. This creates a mismatch between learning and teaching styles. Is this a problem? Not neces-sarily. It is a problem only if you do not learn how to adapt lecture material and the text to your preferred modes of learning.

Preparing for Class

OUTSIDE CLASS: Give students a reading assignment either on the topic of college success or from your own discipline.

IN CLASS: Follow up with a related lecture in class. Then give students a quiz the next day, drawing about half of the questions from the reading and the rest from your lecture. Lead a discussion on the questions that students missed most, asking them to consider why they missed these questions.

Have you ever noticed how easy it is to learn the words of a song? We remember songs more easily than other kinds of information because songs follow a tune and have a beat and because they often have a personal mean-ing for us: We often relate songs to something in our everyday lives. We remember prose less easily unless we make an effort to relate it to what we already know. In your first-year classes, you'll be listening to and reading material that might seem hard to understand. Beginning on the first day of class, you will be more likely to remember what you hear and read if you try to link it to something you have already learned or experienced.

Because some lectures are hard to follow and understand, you need to be prepared before class begins. You would not want to be unprepared to give a speech, interview for a job, plead a case in court, or compete in a sport. For each of these situations, you would prepare in some way. For the same reasons, you should begin listening, learning, and remembering before the lecture.

Even if lectures don't allow for active participation, you can do a number of things to become more engaged and to make your listening and note taking more efficient. You will then learn and remember more, understand what the instructor considers important, and ultimately earn better grades.

Participating in Class

active learning Learning by participation, such as listening critically, discussing what you are learning, and writing about it.

Learning is not a spectator sport. To really learn, you must listen critically, talk about what you are learning, write about it, relate it to past experi-ences, and make what you learn part of yourself. Participation is the heart of **active learning**. When we say something in class, we are more likely to remember it than we will when someone else says something. So when a teacher tosses a question your way or you have a question to ask, you're actually making it easier to remember the day's lesson.

LISTENING CRITICALLY AND WITH AN OPEN MIND

Listening in class is not like listening to a TV show, listening to a friend, or even listening to a speaker at a meeting. Knowing how to listen in class can help you get more out of what you hear, understand better what you have heard, and save time.

Here are some suggestions:

1. **Be ready for the message.** Prepare yourself to hear, to listen, and to receive the message. If you have done the assigned reading, you will already know details from the text, so you can focus your notes on key concepts during the lecture. You will also be able to notice information that the text does not cover, and you will be prepared to pay closer attention when the instructor is presenting unfamiliar material.

2. **Listen to the main concepts and central ideas, not just to fragmented facts and figures.** Although facts are important, they will be easier to remember and will make more sense when you can place them in a context of concepts, themes, and ideas.

syllabus A formal statement of course requirements and procedures or a course outline provided by instructors to all students on the first day of class.

annotate To add critical or explanatory margin notes on a page as you read.

IN CLASS: Before you start class, remind students to do the warm-up. Ask them to identify the main points covered in the last session. Do they know what topic is being covered today? Do they feel prepared? If not, what could they have done to become more prepared?

BEFORE-CLASS TIPS

1. Do the assigned reading. Otherwise, you might find the lecturer's comments disjointed, and you might not understand some terms that your instructor will use. Some instructors refer to assigned readings for each class session; others might distribute a **syllabus** (course outline) and assume you are keeping up with the assigned readings. Completing assigned reading on time will help you listen better and pick out the most important information when taking notes in class. As you read, take good notes. In books that you own, **annotate** (add critical or explanatory margin notes), highlight, or underline the text. In books that you do not own, such as library books, make a photocopy of the pages and then annotate or highlight.

2. Pay careful attention to your course syllabus. Syllabi are formal statements of course expectations, requirements, and procedures. Instructors assume that students will understand and follow course requirements with few or no reminders once they have received a syllabus.

3. Make use of additional materials provided by the instructors. Many instructors post lecture outlines or notes on a Web site before class. Download and print these materials for easy reference during class. They often provide hints about the topics that the instructor considers most important; they also can create an organizational structure for taking notes.

4. Warm up for class by reviewing chapter introductions and summaries, referring to related sections in your text, and scanning your notes from the previous class period. This prepares you to pay attention, understand, and remember.

5. Get organized. Decide what type of notebook will work best for you. Many study skills experts suggest using three-ring binders because you can punch holes in syllabi and other course handouts and keep them with class notes. You might want to buy notebook paper with a larger left-hand margin (sometimes called "legal-ruled"), which will help you to easily annotate your lecture notes. If you take notes on your laptop, keep your files organized in separate folders for each of your classes, and make sure that the file name of each document reflects the date and topic of the class.

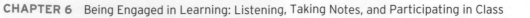

3. **Listen for new ideas.** Even if you are an expert on a topic, you can still learn something new. Do not assume that college instructors will present the same information you learned in a similar course in high school. Even if you're listening to the lecture again (perhaps because you recorded your lectures), you will pick out and learn new information. As a critical thinker, make a note of questions that arise in your mind as you listen, but save the judgments for later.

4. **Repeat mentally.** Words can go in one ear and out the other unless you make an effort to retain them. Think about what you hear, and restate it silently in your own words. If you cannot translate the information into your own words, ask the instructor for further clarification.

5. **Decide whether what you have heard is not important, somewhat important, or very important.** If it's really not important, let it go. If it's very important, make it a major point in your notes by highlighting or underscoring it, or use it as a major topic in your outline if that's the method you use for taking notes. If it's somewhat important, try to relate it to a very important topic by writing it down as a subset of that topic.

6. **Keep an open mind.** Every class holds the promise of letting you discover new ideas and uncover different perspectives. Some teachers might intentionally present information that challenges your value system. One of the purposes of college is to teach you to think in new and different ways and to learn to provide support for your own beliefs. Instructors want you to think for yourself; they don't necessarily expect you to agree with everything they or your classmates say. However, if you want people to respect your values and ideas, you must show respect for theirs as well by listening to what they have to say with an open mind.

7. **Ask questions.** Early in the term, determine whether the instructor is open to responding to questions during the lecture. Some teachers prefer to save questions for the end or want students to ask questions during separate discussion sections or office hours. To some extent, this might depend on the nature and size of the class, such as a large lecture versus a small seminar. If your teacher answers questions as they arise, do not hesitate to ask if you did not hear or understand what was said. It is best to clarify things immediately, if possible, and other students are likely to have the same questions. If you can't hear another student's question or response, ask that it be repeated.

8. **Sort, organize, and categorize.** When you listen, try to match what you are hearing with what you already know. Take an active role in deciding how best to recall what you are learning.

DID YOU KNOW?

42% of first-year students say they frequently contribute to class discussions.

SPEAKING UP

Naturally, you will be more likely to participate in a class in which the teacher emphasizes interactive discussion, calls on students by name, shows signs of approval and interest, and avoids criticizing students for an incorrect answer. Often, answers you and others offer that are not quite correct can lead to new perspectives on a topic.

In large classes instructors often use the lecture method, and large classes can be intimidating. If you ask a question in a class of 100 and think you have made a fool of yourself, you also believe that 99 other people already know the answer. That's somewhat unrealistic, since you have probably asked a question that others were too timid to ask, and they'll silently thank you for doing so. If you're lucky, you might even find that the instructor takes time out to ask or answer questions. To take full advantage of these opportunities, try using the following techniques:

1. **Take a seat as close to the front as possible.** If students are seated by name and your name begins with Z, visit your instructor during office hours and request to be moved up front.

2. **Keep your eyes trained on the instructor.** Sitting up front will make this easier to do.

3. **Focus on the lecture.** Do not let yourself be distracted. It might be wise not to sit near friends who can distract you.

4. **Raise your hand when you don't understand something.** The instructor might answer you immediately, ask you to wait until later in the class, or throw your question to the rest of the class. In each case, you benefit in several ways. The instructor will get to know you, other students will get to know you, and you will learn from both the instructor and your classmates. But don't overdo it. The instructor and your peers will tire of too many questions that disrupt the flow of the class.

5. **Speak up in class.** Ask a question or volunteer to answer a question or make a comment. This becomes easier every time you do it.

6. **Never feel that you're asking a stupid question.** If you don't understand something, you have a right to ask for an explanation.

7. **When the instructor calls on you to answer a question, don't bluff.** If you know the answer, give it. If you're not certain, begin with, "I think . . . , but I'm not sure I have it all correct." If you don't know, just say so.

8. **If you have recently read a book or article that is relevant to the class topic, bring it in.** Use it either to ask questions about the topic or to provide information that was not covered in class.

Speak Up

Participating in class not only helps you learn but also shows your instructor that you're interested and engaged. Like anything else, the first time you raise your hand might make you anxious. But after that first time, you'll likely find that contributing to class raises your interest and enjoyment.

YOUR TURN

Is it hard or easy for you to raise your hand and ask questions in most of your classes? Why? How can you become more involved?

IN CLASS: Take time in class to ask and answer questions. Discuss how to take notes in question-and-answer sessions. Point out the value to the entire class of students' questions. Try putting up overhead transparencies or *PowerPoint* slides that show only part of the material at a time, in comparison to showing the entire message in advance. Discuss how this affects students' attention to the topic.

Taking Effective Notes

What are "effective notes"? They are notes that cover all the important points of the lecture or reading material without being too detailed or too limited. Most important, effective notes prepare you to do well on quizzes or exams. Becoming an effective note-taker takes time and practice, but this skill will help you improve your learning and your grades in the first year and beyond.

NOTE-TAKING FORMATS

■ RETENTION STRATEGY: Although there is no direct research linking note taking and retention, this is one of the critical skills that can determine academic success and therefore the likelihood that students will persist. Note taking is a skill that few students learn in high school because there is less lecturing in high school classes.

You can make class time more productive by using your listening skills to take effective lecture notes, but first you have to decide on a system. Any system can work as long as you use it consistently.

Cornell Format. Using the Cornell format, one of the best-known methods for organizing notes, you create a "recall" column on each page of your notebook by drawing a vertical line about two to three inches from the left border (see Figure 6.1). As you take notes during lecture—whether writing down ideas, making lists, or using an outline or paragraph format— write only in the wider column on the right; leave the recall column on the left blank. (If you have large handwriting and this method seems unwieldy, consider using the back of the previous notebook page for your recall column.) The recall column is the place where you write down the main ideas and important details for tests and examinations as you sift through your notes as soon after class as is feasible, preferably within an hour or two. Many students have found the recall column to be a critical part of effective note taking, one that becomes an important study device for tests and exams.

IN CLASS: Discuss the kinds of courses and topics that might be difficult to outline. Ask students how they might supplement regular note taking in these situations.

IN CLASS: With students taking notes, lecture for about 20 minutes. Assign different students to use the Cornell format, outline format, paragraph format, and list format. Have students work in groups to compare the formats. Discuss the strengths of each.

Outline Format. Some students find that an outline is the best way for them to organize their notes. You probably already know what a formal outline looks like, with key ideas represented by Roman numerals and other ideas relating to each key idea represented in order by uppercase letters, numbers, and lowercase letters. If you use this approach, try to determine the instructor's outline and recreate it in your notes. Add details, definitions, examples, applications, and explanations (see Figures 6.2 and 6.5).

Paragraph Format. You might decide to write summary paragraphs when you are taking notes on what you are reading. This method might not work as well for class notes because it's difficult to summarize a topic until your instructor has covered it completely. By the end of the lecture, you might have forgotten critical information (see Figures 6.3 and 6.5).

YOUR TURN

Which of these four note-taking methods (Cornell, outline, paragraph, list) is most like the one you use? How well does your current system work for you? Explain your answer. What changes will you make in how you take notes now that you have read this portion of the chapter?

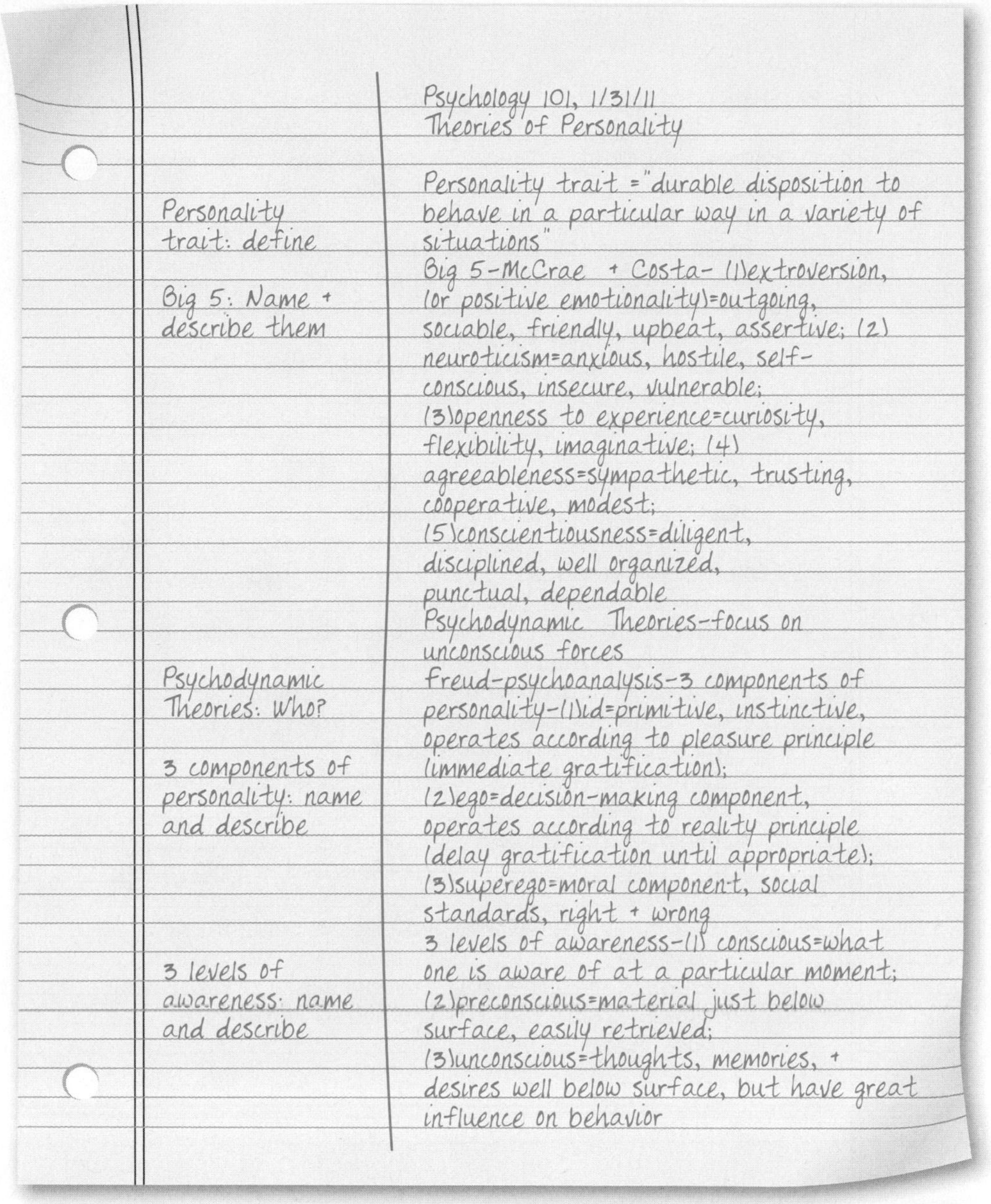

> Psychology 101, 1/31/11
> Theories of Personality
>
> | | |
> |---|---|
> | Personality trait: define | Personality trait = "durable disposition to behave in a particular way in a variety of situations" |
> | Big 5: Name + describe them | Big 5-McCrae + Costa- (1)extroversion, (or positive emotionality)=outgoing, sociable, friendly, upbeat, assertive; (2) neuroticism=anxious, hostile, self-conscious, insecure, vulnerable; (3)openness to experience=curiosity, flexibility, imaginative; (4) agreeableness=sympathetic, trusting, cooperative, modest; (5)conscientiousness=diligent, disciplined, well organized, punctual, dependable |
> | Psychodynamic Theories: Who? | Psychodynamic Theories-focus on unconscious forces freud-psychoanalysis-3 components of personality-(1)id=primitive, instinctive, operates according to pleasure principle (immediate gratification); |
> | 3 components of personality: name and describe | (2)ego=decision-making component, operates according to reality principle (delay gratification until appropriate); (3)superego=moral component, social standards, right + wrong |
> | 3 levels of awareness: name and describe | 3 levels of awareness-(1) conscious=what one is aware of at a particular moment; (2)preconscious=material just below surface, easily retrieved; (3)unconscious=thoughts, memories, + desires well below surface, but have great influence on behavior |

FIGURE 6.1
Note Taking in the Cornell Format

List Format.   This format can be effective in taking notes on lists of terms and definitions, facts, or sequences, such as the body's pulmonary system. It is easy to use lists in combination with the Cornell format, with key terms on the left and their definitions and explanations on the right (see Figure 6.4).

Once you have decided on a format for taking notes, you might also want to develop your own system of abbreviations. For example, you might write "inst" instead of "institution" or "eval" instead of "evaluation." Just make sure you will be able to understand your abbreviations when it's time to review.

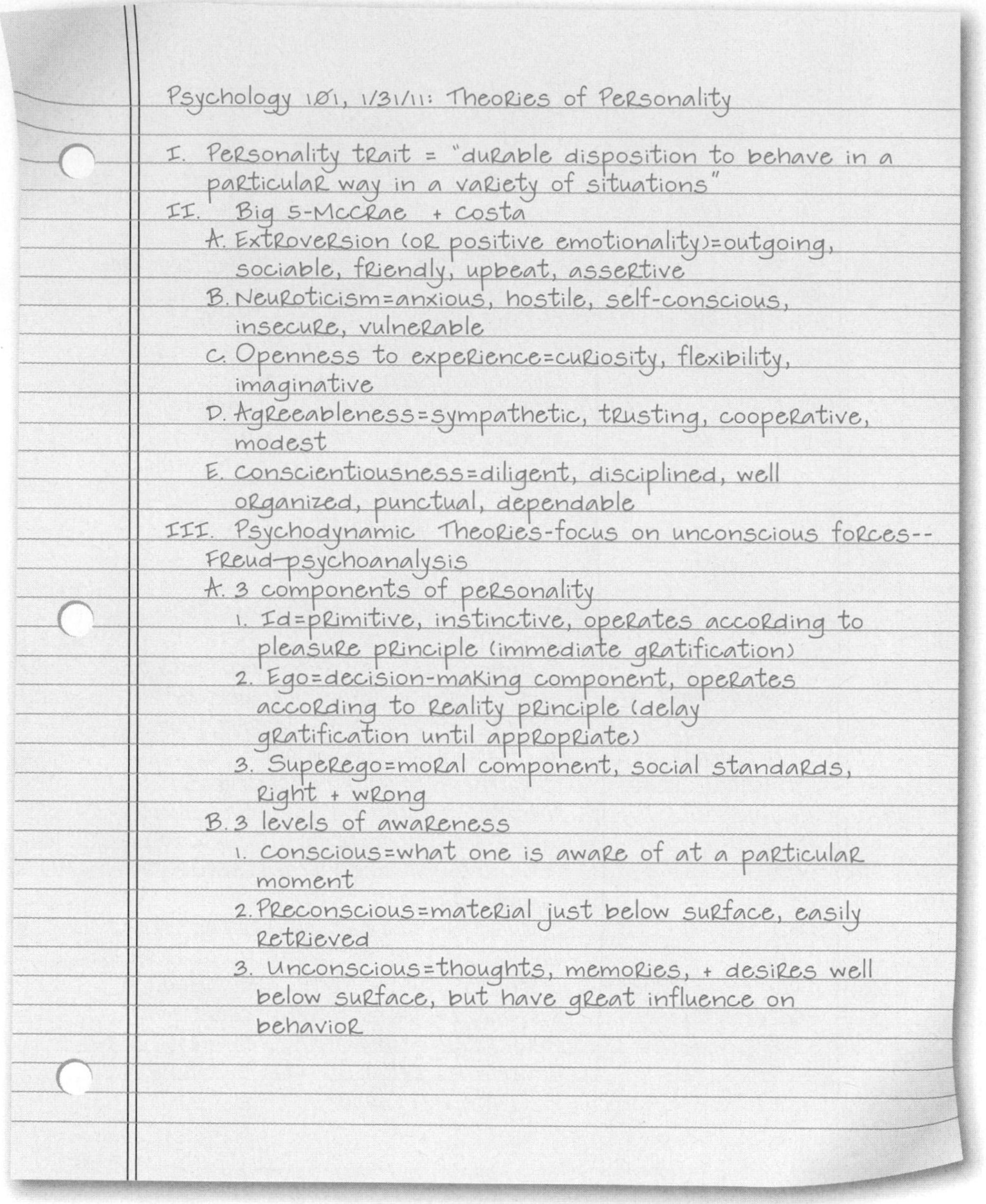

> Psychology 101, 1/31/11: Theories of Personality
>
> I. Personality trait = "durable disposition to behave in a particular way in a variety of situations"
> II. Big 5-McCrae + Costa
>   A. Extroversion (or positive emotionality)=outgoing, sociable, friendly, upbeat, assertive
>   B. Neuroticism=anxious, hostile, self-conscious, insecure, vulnerable
>   C. Openness to experience=curiosity, flexibility, imaginative
>   D. Agreeableness=sympathetic, trusting, cooperative, modest
>   E. Conscientiousness=diligent, disciplined, well organized, punctual, dependable
> III. Psychodynamic Theories-focus on unconscious forces-- Freud-psychoanalysis
>   A. 3 components of personality
>   1. Id=primitive, instinctive, operates according to pleasure principle (immediate gratification)
>   2. Ego=decision-making component, operates according to reality principle (delay gratification until appropriate)
>   3. Superego=moral component, social standards, right + wrong
>   B. 3 levels of awareness
>   1. Conscious=what one is aware of at a particular moment
>   2. Preconscious=material just below surface, easily retrieved
>   3. Unconscious=thoughts, memories, + desires well below surface, but have great influence on behavior

FIGURE 6.2

Note Taking in the Outline Format

IN CLASS: Lecture to the class, and ask students to take notes. Give them an additional 5 minutes to revise and complete their notes. Collect and review their notes, or prepare a handout in which you have taken notes and used a recall column. Discuss the differences and similarities between their notes and yours. You might use overhead transparencies or *PowerPoint* slides to show how you made notes in the assigned reading materials.

NOTE-TAKING TECHNIQUES

Whatever note-taking system you choose, follow these important steps:

1. **Identify the main ideas.** Well-organized lectures always contain key points. The first principle of effective note taking is to identify and write down the most important ideas around which the lecture is built. Although supporting details are important as well, focus your note taking on the main ideas. Such ideas can be buried in details, statistics, anecdotes, or problems, but you will need to identify and record them for further study.

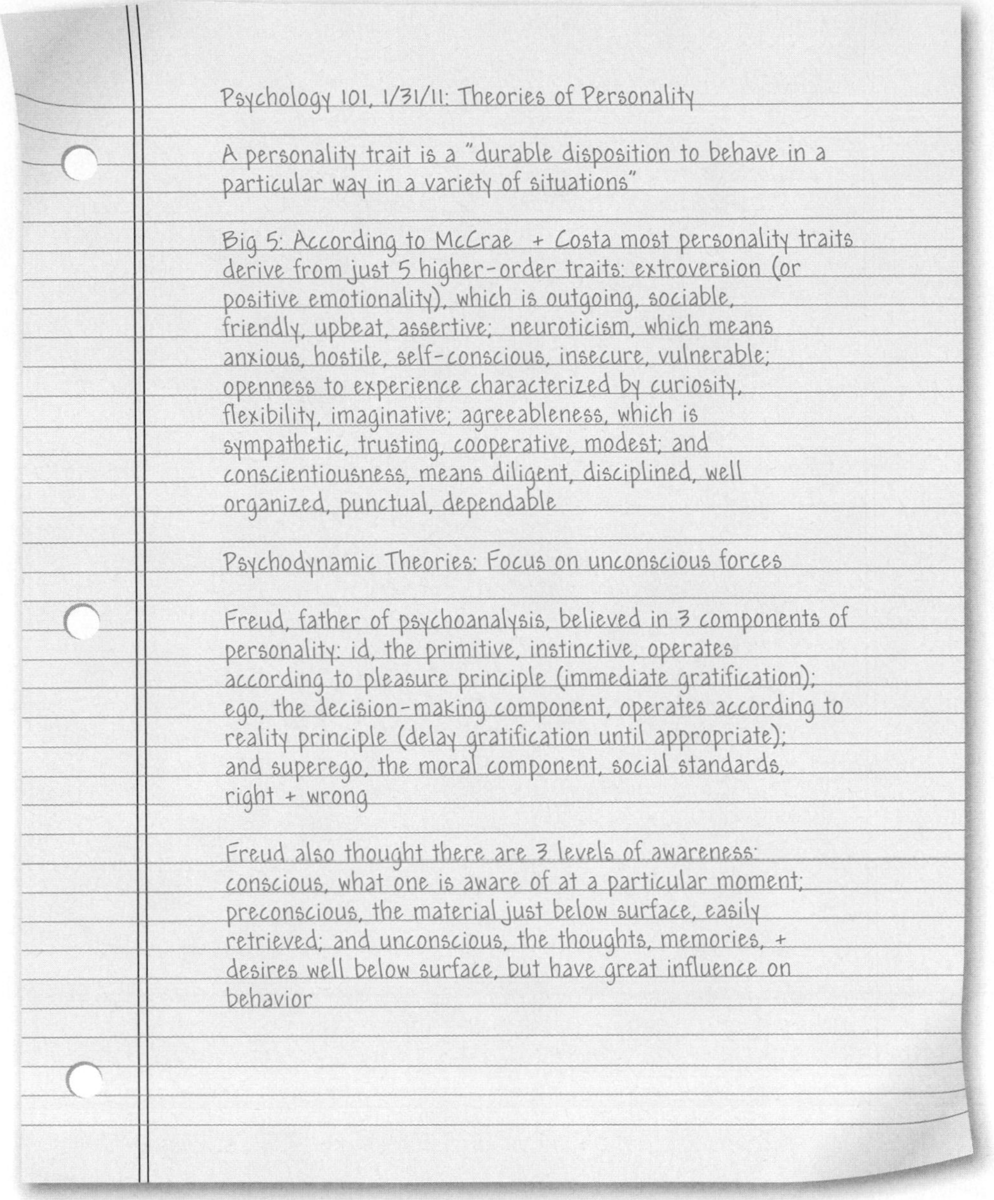

Psychology 101, 1/31/11: Theories of Personality

A personality trait is a "durable disposition to behave in a particular way in a variety of situations"

Big 5: According to McCrae + Costa most personality traits derive from just 5 higher-order traits: extroversion (or positive emotionality), which is outgoing, sociable, friendly, upbeat, assertive; neuroticism, which means anxious, hostile, self-conscious, insecure, vulnerable; openness to experience characterized by curiosity, flexibility, imaginative; agreeableness, which is sympathetic, trusting, cooperative, modest; and conscientiousness, means diligent, disciplined, well organized, punctual, dependable

Psychodynamic Theories: Focus on unconscious forces

Freud, father of psychoanalysis, believed in 3 components of personality: id, the primitive, instinctive, operates according to pleasure principle (immediate gratification); ego, the decision-making component, operates according to reality principle (delay gratification until appropriate); and superego, the moral component, social standards, right + wrong

Freud also thought there are 3 levels of awareness: conscious, what one is aware of at a particular moment; preconscious, the material just below surface, easily retrieved; and unconscious, the thoughts, memories, + desires well below surface, but have great influence on behavior

FIGURE 6.3
Note Taking in the Paragraph Format

Some instructors announce the purpose of a lecture or offer an outline, thus providing you with the skeleton of main ideas, followed by the details. Other instructors develop *PowerPoint* presentations. If they make these materials available on a class Web site before the lecture, you can print them and take notes on the teacher's outline or next to the *PowerPoint* slides.

Some lecturers change their tone of voice or repeat themselves for each key idea. Some ask questions or promote discussion. If a lecturer says something more than once, chances are it is important. Ask yourself, "What does my instructor want me to know at the end of today's class?"

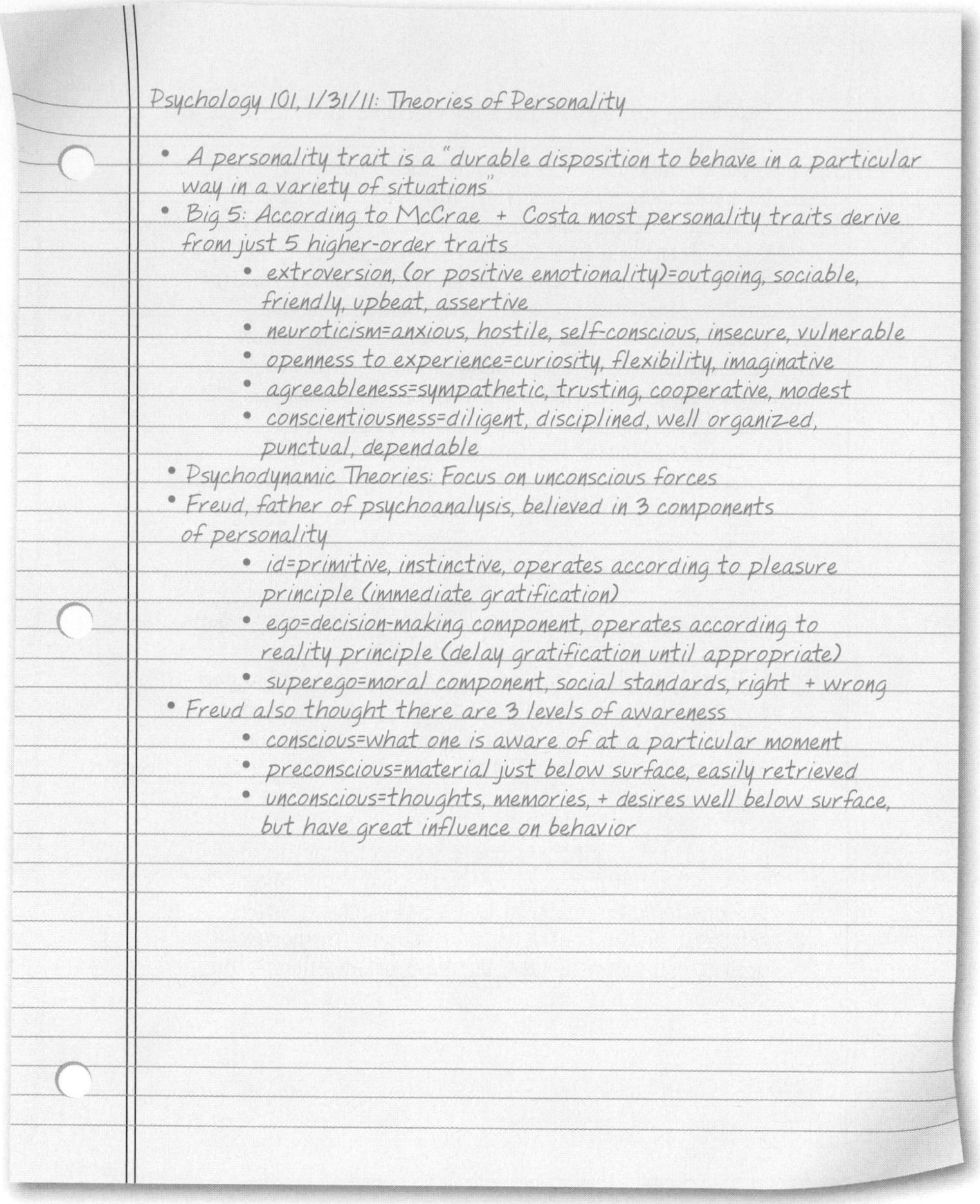

> Psychology 101, 1/31/11: Theories of Personality
>
> - A personality trait is a "durable disposition to behave in a particular way in a variety of situations"
> - Big 5: According to McCrae + Costa most personality traits derive from just 5 higher-order traits
>   - extroversion, (or positive emotionality)=outgoing, sociable, friendly, upbeat, assertive
>   - neuroticism=anxious, hostile, self-conscious, insecure, vulnerable
>   - openness to experience=curiosity, flexibility, imaginative
>   - agreeableness=sympathetic, trusting, cooperative, modest
>   - conscientiousness=diligent, disciplined, well organized, punctual, dependable
> - Psychodynamic Theories: Focus on unconscious forces
> - Freud, father of psychoanalysis, believed in 3 components of personality
>   - id=primitive, instinctive, operates according to pleasure principle (immediate gratification)
>   - ego=decision-making component, operates according to reality principle (delay gratification until appropriate)
>   - superego=moral component, social standards, right + wrong
> - Freud also thought there are 3 levels of awareness
>   - conscious=what one is aware of at a particular moment
>   - preconscious=material just below surface, easily retrieved
>   - unconscious=thoughts, memories, + desires well below surface, but have great influence on behavior

FIGURE 6.4

Note Taking in the List Format

2. **Don't try to write down everything.** Some first-year students try to do just that. They stop being thinkers and become stenographers. As you take notes, leave spaces so that you can fill in additional details that you might have missed during class but remember later. Take the time to review and complete your notes as soon after class as possible.

3. **Don't be thrown by a disorganized lecturer.** When a lecture is disorganized, it's your job to try to organize what is said into general and specific frameworks. When the order is not apparent, you will need to indicate in your notes where the gaps lie. After the lecture, consult the

Personality trait	I. Personality trait = "durable disposition to behave in a particular way in a variety of situations"
	II. Big 5-McCrae + Costa
Big 5: Who?	A. Extroversion (or positive emotionality)=outgoing,
Name +	sociable, friendly, upbeat, assertive
describe them	B. Neuroticism=anxious, hostile, self-conscious,
	insecure, vulnerable
	C. Openness to experience=curiosity, flexibility,
	imaginative
	D. Agreeableness=sympathetic, trusting, cooperative,
	modest
	E. Conscientiousness=diligent, disciplined, well
	organized, punctual, dependable
	III. Psychodynamic Theories-focus on unconscious forces--
	Freud-psychoanalysis
Psychodynamic	A. 3 components of personality
Theories: Who?	1. Id=primitive, instinctive, operates according
3 components.	to pleasure principle (immediate gratification)
Name, define,	2. Ego=decision-making component, operates
relate each to a	according to reality principle (delay
principle	gratification until appropriate)
	3. Superego=moral component, social standards,
	right + wrong
	B. 3 levels of awareness
	1. conscious=what one is aware of at a particular
3 levels of	moment
awareness: name	2. preconscious=material just below surface, easily
and describe	retrieved
	3. unconscious=thoughts, memories, + desires well
	below surface, but have great influence on behavior

FIGURE 6.5

Cornell Format Combined with Outline Format

reading material or classmates to fill in these gaps, or ask your instructor. Most instructors have regular office hours for student appointments, yet it is amazing how few students use these opportunities for one-on-one instruction. Asking questions can help your instructor find out which parts of the lecture need more attention and clarification.

4. **Keep your notes and supplementary materials for each course in a separate three-ring binder.** Label the binder with the course number and name. If the binders are too bulky to carry in your backpack, create a separate folder for each class, stocked with loose-leaf notebook paper. Before class, label and date the paper you will be using for taking notes.

Then, as soon after class as possible, move your notes from the folder to the binder.

5. **Download any notes, outlines, or diagrams, charts, graphs, and other visuals** from the instructor's Web site before class and bring them with you. You might be able to save yourself considerable time during the lecture if you do not have to try to copy complicated graphs and diagrams while the instructor is talking. Instead, you can focus on the ideas being presented while adding your own labels and notes to the visual images.

6. **Organize your notes chronologically in your binder.** Then create separate tabbed sections for homework, lab assignments, returned tests, and other materials.

7. **If handouts are distributed in class, label them and place them in your binder** near the notes for that day. Buy a portable three-ring hole-punch that can be kept in your binder. Do not let handouts accumulate in your folders; add any handouts to your binders as you review your notes each day.

Supplemental Instruction (SI) Classes that provide further opportunity to discuss the information presented in lectures.

Taking Notes in Nonlecture Courses.

Always be ready to adapt your note-taking methods to match the situation. Group discussion is becoming a popular way to teach in college because it engages students in active participation. On your campus you might also have **Supplemental Instruction (SI)** classes that provide further opportunity to discuss the information presented in lectures. How do you keep a record of what's happening in such classes? Assume you are taking notes in a problem-solving group assignment. You would begin your notes by asking yourself, "What is the problem?" and writing down the answer. As the discussion progresses, you would list the solutions that are offered. These would be your main ideas. The important details might include the positive and negative aspects of each view or solution. The important thing to remember when taking notes in nonlecture courses is that you need to record the information presented by your classmates as well as by the instructor and to consider all reasonable ideas, even though they might differ from your own.

When a course has separate lecture and discussion sessions, you will need to understand how the discussion sessions relate to and augment the lectures. If different material is covered in lecture or discussion, you might need to ask for guidance in organizing your notes. When similar topics are covered, you can combine your notes so that you have comprehensive, unified coverage of each topic.

How to organize the notes you take in a class discussion depends on the purpose or form of the discussion. It usually makes good sense to begin with the list of issues or topics that the discussion leader announces. Another approach is to list the questions that participants raise for discussion. If the discussion explores reasons for and against a particular argument, divide your notes into columns or sections for pros and cons. When conflicting views are presented in discussion, record different perspectives and the rationales behind them. Your teacher might ask you to defend your own opinions in comparison to those of other students.

Taking Notes in Science and Mathematics Courses. Many mathematics and science courses build on each other from term to term and from year to year. When you take notes in these courses, you will likely need to refer to them in the future. For example, when taking organic chemistry, you might need to refer to notes taken in earlier chemistry courses. This can be particularly important when time has passed since your last related course, such as after a summer break. Taking notes in math and science courses can be different from taking notes in other types of classes. The box below offers tips to keep in mind specifically when taking notes in quantitative and science classes.

Using Technology to Take Notes. While some students use laptops for note taking, others prefer taking notes by hand so they can easily circle important items or copy complex equations or diagrams while these are

TIPS FOR NOTE TAKING IN QUANTITATIVE AND SCIENCE CLASSES

> Write down any equations, formulas, diagrams, charts, graphs, and definitions that the instructor puts on the board or screen.

> Quote the instructor's words as precisely as possible. Technical terms often have exact meanings and cannot be paraphrased.

> Use standard symbols, abbreviations, and scientific notation.

> Write down all worked problems and examples, step by step. They often provide the template for exam questions. Actively engage in solving the problem yourself as it is being solved at the front of the class. Be sure that you can follow the logic and understand the sequence of steps. If you have questions you cannot ask during lecture, write them down in your notes so that you can ask them in discussion, in the lab, or during the instructor's office hours.

> Consider taking your notes in pencil or erasable pen. You might need to make changes if you are copying long equations while also trying to pay attention to the instructor. You want to keep your notes as neat as possible. Later, you can use colored ink to add other details.

> Listen carefully to other students' questions and the instructor's answers. Take notes on the discussion and during question-and-answer periods.

> Use asterisks, exclamation points, question marks, or symbols of your own to highlight important points in your notes or questions that you need to come back to when you review.

> Refer back to the textbook after class; the text might contain more accurate diagrams and other visual representations than you can draw while taking notes in class. If they are not provided in handouts or on the instructor's Web site, you might even want to scan or photocopy diagrams from the text and include them with your notes in your binder.

> Keep your binders for math and science courses until you graduate (or even longer if there is any chance that you will attend graduate school at some point in the future). They will serve as beneficial review materials for later classes in math and science and for preparing for standardized tests such as the Graduate Record Exam (GRE) or Medical College Admission Test (MCAT). In some cases, these notes can also prove helpful in the workplace.

TECH TIP TAKE NOTES LIKE A ROCK STAR

Studies have shown that people remember only half of what they hear, which is a major reason you need to take lecture notes. Solid note taking will also help you distill key concepts and make it easier to study for tests. So why not take your note-taking skills up a notch?

1 ▶ THE PROBLEM

You don't know how to make your digital lecture notes leap off the screen and engrave themselves on your brain.

2 ▶ THE FIX

Clue into the many ways you can use basic programs like *Word*, *Excel*, and *PowerPoint* to sharpen your note-taking skill set.

3 ▶ HOW TO DO IT

1. ***Word*** is great for taking notes in most classes. To highlight main ideas, you can bold or underline text. You can change the font size and color, highlight whole swaths of text, or insert text boxes or charts. You can make bullet points or properly formatted outlines and insert comment bubbles for emphasis. You can cut and paste material as you review your notes to make things more coherent. You can also create different folders for each of your classes so you can find everything you need with one click. (Note: It's worth playing around on the toolbar until you get it all down pat.)

2. ***Excel*** is especially good for economics and accounting courses, or any class that involves making scientific calculations or financial statements. You can embed messages inside the cells of a spreadsheet to explain calculations. The notes will magically appear whenever you use your cursor to hover over that cell.

3. ***PowerPoint*** can be an invaluable tool for visual learners. Instead of keeping your notes in one giant, potentially confusing *Word* document, you can open up a *PowerPoint* slideshow and type right into it. That way, every time your professor changes gears, you can open a new slide. It's a nice way to break up the material. *Good to know:* Some instructors post the *PowerPoint* slides that they plan to use in class a few hours in advance. Print them out and take them with you as note-taking tools; you can even write notes on the slides themselves.

CLEVER TRICKS

Date your notes. Focus on writing down the main points (the material your professor emphasizes or repeats), using phrases or key words instead of long sentences. Keep all of your notes in order and in one place. Back up *everything*. If you're not a tech whiz, keep a pen and paper handy for sketching graphs and diagrams. Label your notes clearly to make it easy to look things up. And if you find yourself struggling to keep up, practice your listening and typing skills.

PERSONAL BEST

What concrete steps could you take to create an organized note-taking system for the semester? Start by picking a note-taking style that appeals to you. If you love a chart or spreadsheet, *Excel* is your kind of program. If you're an old-school type who loves nothing better than a spiral notebook and a ballpoint pen, that's okay, too.

being presented. If you handwrite your notes, entering them on a computer after class for review purposes might be helpful, especially if you are a kinesthetic learner. After class you can also cut and paste diagrams and other visual representations into your notes and print a copy that might be easier to read than notes you wrote by hand.

Some students, especially aural learners, find it is advantageous to record lectures. But if you record, resist the temptation to become passive in class instead of actively listening. Students with specific types of disabilities might be urged to record lectures or use the services of note-takers who type on a laptop while the student views the notes on a separate screen.

Reviewing Your Notes

Most forgetting takes place within the first 24 hours of encountering the information, a phenomenon known as "the forgetting curve." So if you do not review your notes almost immediately after class, it can be difficult to retrieve the material later. In two weeks, you will have forgotten up to 70 percent of it! Forgetting can be a serious problem when you are expected to learn and remember many different facts, figures, concepts, and relationships for a number of classes. Once you understand how to improve your ability to remember, you will retain information more easily and completely. Retaining information will help your overall understanding as well as your ability to recall important details during exams.

Don't let the forgetting curve take its toll on you. As soon after class as possible, review your notes and fill in the details you still remember but missed writing down. One way to remember is to recite important data to yourself every few minutes. If you are an aural learner, you might want to repeat your notes out loud. Another idea is to tie one idea to another idea, concept, or name so that thinking of one will prompt recall of the other. Or you might want to create your own poem, song, or slogan using the information.

For interactive learners, the best way to learn something might be to teach it to someone else. You will understand something better and remember it longer if you try to explain it. This helps you discover your own reactions and uncover gaps in your comprehension of the material. (Asking and answering questions in class can also provide you with the feedback you need to make certain your understanding is accurate.) Now you're ready to embed the major points from your notes in your memory. Use the three important steps on the next page for remembering the key points from the lecture. These three ways to engage with the material will pay off later, when you begin to study for your exams.

What if you have three classes in a row and no time for studying between them? Recall and recite as soon after class as possible. Review the most recent class first. Never delay recall and recitation longer than one day; if you do, it will take you longer to review, select main ideas, and recite. With practice, you can complete the review of your main ideas from your notes quickly, perhaps between classes, during lunch, or while riding the bus.

IN CLASS: Ask how many students take class notes on laptops. Have these students discuss the advantages and drawbacks of taking notes this way. Ask how they use their notes to study for exams.

IN CLASS: To demonstrate how easy it is to forget information, ask students to think back to a lecture from the previous day and write down as many main ideas and supporting details as they can remember.

OUTSIDE CLASS: For homework, ask students to compare these lists to the notes they took while the class was in session.

KEYS TO REMEMBERING

1. Write down the main ideas. For 5 or 10 minutes, quickly review your notes and select key words or phrases that will act as labels or tags for main ideas and key information in your notes.

2. Recite your ideas out loud. Recite a brief version of what you understand from the class. If you don't have a few minutes after class when you can concentrate on reviewing your notes, find some other time during that same day to review what you have written. You might also want to ask your instructor to glance at your notes to determine whether you have identified the major ideas.

3. Review your notes from the previous class just before the next class session. As you sit in class the next time it meets, waiting for the lecture to begin, use the time to quickly review your notes from the previous class session. This will put you in tune with the lecture that is about to begin and prompt you to ask questions about material from the previous lecture that might not have been clear to you.

COMPARING NOTES

IN CLASS: Talk about comparing notes for the purpose of learning versus plagiarism and cheating. Show how sharing notes can be a good practice to compare what each person thought was important. Show how sharing notes can be counterproductive when students use someone else's notes because they missed class or failed to take good notes themselves.

You might be able to improve your notes by comparing notes with another student or in a study group, Supplemental Instruction session, or a learning community, if one is available to you. Knowing that your notes will be seen by someone else will prompt you to make your notes well organized, clear, and accurate. Compare your notes: Are they as clear and concise as those of other students? Do you agree on the most important points? Share with each other how you take and organize your notes. You might get new ideas for using abbreviations. Take turns testing each other on what you have learned. This will help you predict exam questions and determine whether you can answer them. Comparing notes is not the same as copying another student's notes. You simply cannot learn as well from someone else's notes, no matter how good they are, if you have not attended class.

If your campus has a note-taking service, check with your instructor about making use of this for-pay service, but keep in mind that such notes are intended to supplement the ones you take, not to substitute for them. Some students choose to copy their own notes as a means of review or because they think their notes are messy and that they will not be able to understand them later. Unless you are a tactile learner, copying or typing your notes might not help you learn the material. A more profitable approach might be to summarize your notes in your own words.

Finally, have a backup plan in case you need to be absent because of illness or a family emergency. Exchange phone numbers and e-mail addresses with other students so that you can contact one of them to learn what you missed and get a copy of his or her notes. Also contact your instructor to explain your absence and set up an appointment during office hours to make sure you understand the work you missed.

CLASS NOTES AND HOMEWORK

Good class notes can help you complete homework assignments. Follow these steps:

OUTSIDE CLASS: After students read the suggestions under "Class Notes and Homework," ask them to practice these steps and report the results.

1. **Take 10 minutes to review your notes.** Skim the notes, and put a question mark next to anything you do not understand at first reading. Draw stars next to topics that warrant special emphasis. Try to place the material in context: What has been going on in the course for the past few weeks? How does today's class fit in?

2. **Do a warm-up for your homework.** Before doing the assignment, look through your notes again. Use a separate sheet of paper to rework examples, problems, or exercises. If there is related assigned material in the textbook, review it. Go back to the examples. Cover the solution, and attempt to answer each question or complete each problem. Look at the author's work only after you have made a serious effort to remember it. Keep in mind that it can help to go back through your course notes, reorganize them, highlight the essential items, and thus create new notes that let you connect with the material one more time and could be better than the originals.

3. **Do any assigned problems, and answer any assigned questions.** When you start doing your homework, read each question or problem and ask: What am I supposed to find or find out? What is essential and what is extraneous? Read each problem several times, and state it in your own words. Work the problem without referring to your notes or the text, as though you were taking a test. In this way, you will test your knowledge and know when you are prepared for exams.

4. **Persevere.** Don't give up too soon. When you encounter a problem or question that you cannot readily handle, move on only after a reasonable effort. After you have completed the entire assignment, come back to any items that stumped you. Try once more, and then take a break. You might need to mull over a particularly difficult problem for several days. Let your unconscious mind have a chance. Inspiration might come when you are waiting at a stoplight or just before you fall asleep.

5. **Complete your work.** When you finish an assignment, talk to yourself about what you learned from it. Think about how the problems and questions were different from one another, which strategies were successful, and what form the answers took. Be sure to review any material you have not mastered. Seek assistance from the instructor, a classmate, a study group, the campus learning center, or a tutor to learn how to answer questions that stumped you.

YOUR TURN

What is your reaction to these suggestions about taking notes and studying for class? Which ideas will you implement in your note-taking strategies? Why? Do you think they have the potential to help you earn better grades? If so, in what way?

OUTSIDE CLASS: The literature on the advantages of active learning is extensive. Consider asking students to do a search on the topic, using library and Internet resources. Ask each student to bring in just one benefit of active learning from their search.

Becoming Engaged in Learning

No matter how good your listening and note-taking techniques are, you will not get the most out of college unless you become an engaged learner. Engaged students devote the time and the energy necessary to develop a real love of learning, both in and out of class.

Although you might acquire knowledge by listening to a lecture, you might not be motivated to think about what that knowledge means to you. When you are actively engaged in learning, you will learn not only the material in your notes and textbooks, but also how to:

- Work with others
- Improve your critical thinking, listening, writing, and speaking skills
- Function independently and teach yourself
- Manage your time
- Gain sensitivity to cultural differences

Engagement in learning requires that you be a full and active participant in the learning process. Your instructors will set the stage and provide valuable information, but it's up to you to do the rest. Your college experience will be most rewarding if you take advantage of the resources your college offers, including the library, cultural events, the faculty, and other students. This approach to learning has the potential to make you well rounded in all aspects of life.

Listen Up

Your posture and eye contact will let your instructors know whether or not you are interested in what they are saying. Listen to your instructors and other students; be attentive and try not to let your mind wander during class.

IN CLASS: In the Hawaiian language, the words for *teaching* and *learning* are the same. Ask students how they would explain this. How can one be teaching and learning at the same time? Why is it okay to collaborate with another student? What makes that different from cheating?

OTHER TIPS FOR ENGAGEMENT

> Before choosing a class, ask friends which instructors encourage active learning.

> Go beyond the required reading. Investigate other information sources in the library or on the Internet.

> If you disagree with what your instructor says, politely offer your opinion. Most instructors will listen. They might still disagree with you, but they might also think more of you for showing you can think independently.

> Interact with professors, staff members, and other students. One easy way is through e-mail. Some professors offer first-year students the opportunity to collaborate in research projects and service activities. You will also find many opportunities to become involved in campus organizations. Getting involved in out-of-class opportunities will help you develop relationships with others on campus.

> Use *Facebook* to connect with other students and with campus activities and groups. Join in discussions that are happening in those groups.

CHECKLIST FOR SUCCESS

BECOME MORE ENGAGED

☐ **Practice the behaviors of engagement.** These behaviors include listening attentively, taking notes, and contributing to class discussion. But engagement also means participating in out-of-class activities without being "required" to do so.

☐ **Be aware of all the "senses" you have to aid your learning.** Which ones do you use the most? Try to increase your use of the other senses.

☐ **Prepare for class before class; it is one of the simplest and most important things you can do.** Read your notes from the previous class and do the assigned readings.

☐ **Go to class:** Ninety-five percent of success is simply showing up. You have no chance of becoming engaged in learning if you're not there.

☐ **Identify the different types of note taking covered in this chapter and decide which one(s) might work best for you.** Compare your notes with those of another good student to make sure you are covering the most important points.

☐ **As you review your notes before each class starts, make a list of any questions you have, and ask both fellow students and your professor for help.** Don't wait until just before the exam to try to find answers to your questions.

☐ **Seek professors who practice "active" teaching.** Ask other students, your seminar instructor, and your adviser to suggest the most engaging professors.

BUILD YOUR EXPERIENCE 1 3 2 4

1 STAY ON TRACK

Successful college students stay focused. They "stay on track." They know what they have to do to be successful, they set goals, and they monitor their progress toward their goals.

Reflect on what you have learned about college success in this chapter and how you are going to apply the chapter information or strategies in college and in your career. List your ideas.

1. _____

_____

_____

2. _____

_____

_____

3. _____

_____

_____

2 ONE-MINUTE PAPER

This chapter explores multiple strategies for being an effective listener and being engaged in class. What new strategies did you learn that you had never thought about or used before? What questions about effective note taking do you still have?

No matter how well prepared you are in your teaching, what a student hears and understands might not always be what you think you have said. The one-minute paper is a quick and easy assessment tool that will help alert you when students don't understand what was said or discussed in class. The one-minute paper will also give timid students an opportunity to ask questions and seek clarification. Ideally, you should ask for such a paper several minutes before the end of a class. The paper will also help you begin your next class by clarifying points your students seem to be unsure of.

3 APPLYING WHAT YOU HAVE LEARNED

Now that you have read and discussed this chapter, consider how you can apply what you have learned to your academic and personal life. The following prompts will help you to reflect on chapter material and its relevance to you both now and in the future.

1. Review the Using Your Senses in the Learning Process section of this chapter. Which modes of learning seem to work best for you? If you are not an aural learner, how can you use your preferred ways of learning to master the information that is presented in lecture-style courses? Brainstorm ways to convert lecture material into a format that is a better match for how you best use your five senses in the learning process.

2. Making an intentional effort to learn is not easy. As you try the suggestions in this chapter, consider ways in which you can encourage yourself to keep up the hard work. For example, if you have a big project, try breaking it up into several smaller pieces. As you complete each piece, reward yourself by hanging out with friends or taking time to do something you enjoy.

4 BUILDING YOUR PORTFOLIO

MAKING MEANING   Chapter 6 includes several examples of note-taking strategies, but did you catch the emphasis on what you should do with your notes after class? Sometimes it is helpful to associate a concept with an interest you have. And preparing to teach someone else how to do something or explaining a complex idea to others can help you to understand the information more fully. Test this idea for yourself.

1. Choose a set of current class notes (it doesn't matter which class they are from), and specifically look for connections between the subject matter and your personal interests and goals (future career, social issue, sports, hobbies, etc.).

2. Next, develop a 5-minute presentation using *PowerPoint* that both outlines your class notes and shows the connection to your interests. Develop the presentation as though you were going to teach a group of students about the concept. Use a combination of graphics, photos, music, and video clips to help your imaginary audience to connect with the material in a new and interesting way.

3. Save the *PowerPoint* in your portfolio. Use your *PowerPoint* presentation as one way to study for your next exam in that course.

You probably won't be creating *PowerPoint* presentations for all of your class notes, but making a habit of connecting class content to your life is an easy way to help yourself remember information. When it is time to prepare for a test, try pulling your notes into a presentation that you would feel comfortable giving to your classmates.

For more on this topic watch
French Fries Are Not Vegetables and Other College Lessons

WHERE TO GO FOR HELP...

ON CAMPUS

> **Learning Assistance Center** Almost every campus has one of these, and this chapter's topic is one of their specialties. More and more, the best students—and good students who want to be better students—use learning centers as much as students who are having academic difficulties. Services at learning centers are offered by both full-time professionals and highly skilled student tutors.

> **Fellow College Students** Often, the best help we can get comes from those who are closest to us: fellow students. Keep an eye out in your classes, residence hall, co-curricular groups, and other places for the most serious, purposeful, and directed students. Those are the ones to seek out. Find a tutor. Join a study group. Students who do these things are most likely to stay in college and be successful. It does not diminish you in any way to seek assistance from your peers.

ONLINE

> Toastmasters International offers public speaking tips at **http://www.toastmasters.org.**

> See guidelines for speaking in class at **http://www.school-for-champions.com/grades/speaking.htm.**

MY INSTITUTION'S RESOURCES

_____

_____

_____

_____

_____

_____

_____

_____

CHAPTER 7
Reading to Learn from College Textbooks

IN THIS CHAPTER YOU WILL EXPLORE

How to prepare to read

How to preview reading material

How to read your textbooks efficiently

How to mark your textbooks

How to review your reading

How to adjust your reading style to the material

How to develop a more extensive vocabulary

❝ **While my habits have worked well for me, students should get to know their own learning habits and find a reading method that works best for them.**

Kameron Fehrmann, 18
Communication Design major
Texas State University

Kameron Fehrmann was born in Texas and then spent most of her childhood in Lafayette, Louisiana, where she learned study habits that have helped throughout her education. Just before junior high, her family moved back to Texas. She decided to go to Texas State University in San Marcos because it was one of the only public colleges that offered a degree in Communication Design. In addition, she thought the campus was beautiful and she liked the community. Last, it put her only 30 minutes from Austin, one of her favorite places in Texas.

As someone who loves to learn, Kameron came to college with some strategies in place. "There is definitely a lot more reading involved in college than in high school. However, the good thing is that professors give out syllabi that detail when readings will be due so you can plan accordingly." Like many first-year students, she also had to learn to balance the amount of reading required. "I had to get used to measuring how long it took to read and then manage my time accordingly."

Kameron Fehrmann ▶

Many of the other strategies Kameron employs revolve around good time management and organization. "Learning how to juggle all other coursework, meals, a social life, and sleep can be difficult, but it is possible. I mostly organize my time in order of priorities, usually based on due dates and how much time it takes to do [the assignment]. [Once I start reading] I usually write down headings within the chapter as I go to keep me guided in the right direction and so that I know what the main point of upcoming sections will be. I then read through and write down any important dates, names, words, or anything that better explains the concept or explains it in a different way. This way I have multiple views on the subject that further enhance my understanding. It also doesn't hurt to reread sections and go over notes." She adds an important note: "While my habits have worked well for me, students should get to know their own learning habits and find a reading method that works best for them."

And Kameron has some pretty simple advice for other first-year students: "As much work as college is and as overwhelming as it can feel sometimes, *don't stress too much*. College is one of the best times of life. Enjoy it!"

As Kameron mentioned, reading college textbooks is more challenging than reading high school texts or reading for pleasure. College texts are loaded with concepts, terms, and complex information that you are expected to learn on your own in a short period of time. To accomplish all this, you will find it helpful to learn and use the active reading strategies in this chapter. They are intended to help you get the most out of your college reading.

A Plan for Active Reading

The following plan for active reading is designed to help you read college textbooks. When you read actively, you use strategies that help you stay focused. Active reading is different from reading novels or magazines for pleasure. Pleasure reading doesn't require you to annotate, highlight, or take notes. But as you read college textbooks, you'll use all these strategies and more. This plan will increase your focus and concentration, promote greater understanding of what you read, and prepare you to study for tests and exams. The four steps in active reading are

1. Previewing
2. Marking
3. Reading with Concentration
4. Reviewing

> **YOUR TURN**
>
> Which of these four steps do you always, sometimes, or never do? Do any of them seem unnecessary? If so, why? After you read this chapter, go back and see whether you have changed your mind.

IN CLASS: Ask students to practice previewing with one of their texts for another class by talking their way through it with a study partner.

IN CLASS: In response to the inevitable argument that a systematic reading method takes too much time, emphasize that students will understand more of the chapter using this method and will therefore spend less time rereading.

PREVIEWING

The purpose of previewing is to get the big picture, that is, to understand how what you are about to read connects with what you already know and to the material the instructor covers in class. Begin by reading the title of the chapter. Ask yourself: What do I already know about this subject? Next, quickly read through the introductory paragraphs. Then read the summary at

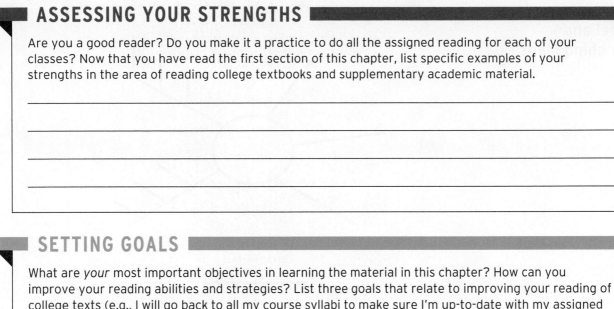

ASSESSING YOUR STRENGTHS

Are you a good reader? Do you make it a practice to do all the assigned reading for each of your classes? Now that you have read the first section of this chapter, list specific examples of your strengths in the area of reading college textbooks and supplementary academic material.

SETTING GOALS

What are *your* most important objectives in learning the material in this chapter? How can you improve your reading abilities and strategies? List three goals that relate to improving your reading of college texts (e.g., I will go back to all my course syllabi to make sure I'm up-to-date with my assigned reading. If not, I will catch up this week).

1.
2.
3.

the beginning or end of the chapter if there is one. Finally, take a few minutes to skim the chapter, looking at the headings and subheadings. Note any study exercises at the end of the chapter.

As part of your preview, note how many pages the chapter contains. It's a good idea to decide in advance how many pages you can reasonably expect to cover in your first study period. This can help build your concentration as you work toward your goal of reading a specific number of pages. Before long, you'll know how many pages are practical for you.

Keep in mind that different types of textbooks can require more or less time to read. For example, depending on your interests and previous knowledge, you might be able to read a psychology text more quickly than a logic text that presents a whole new symbol system.

Mapping. Mapping the chapter as you preview it provides a visual guide for how different chapter ideas fit together. Because many students identify themselves as visual learners, visual mapping is an excellent learning tool for test preparation, as well as reading (see Chapter 4, Discovering How You Learn). To map a chapter, use either a wheel structure or a branching

■ RETENTION STRATEGY: The inability to read and comprehend college textbooks is one of the most significant academic problems of new college students today and therefore is a factor in student dropout. Be on the lookout for students who do not read at a college level and help them seek assistance at your institution.

mapping A preview strategy of drawing a wheel or branching structure to show relationships between main ideas and secondary ideas and how different concepts and terms fit together and help you make connections to what you already know about the subject.

FIGURE 7.1

Wheel and Branching Maps

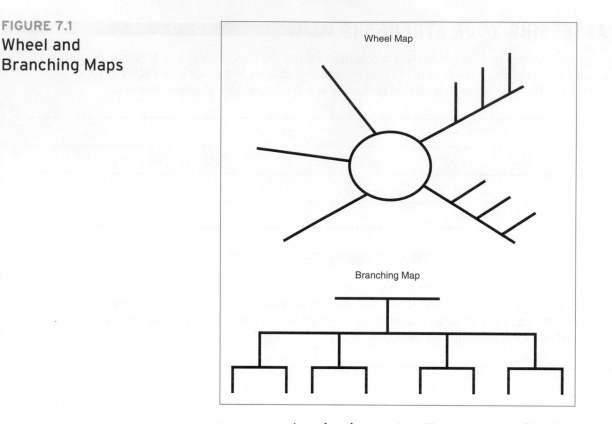

Wheel Map

Branching Map

OUTSIDE CLASS: After discussing how to map a chapter, have students map a chapter from a textbook they are using in another course.

IN CLASS: Have students bring the maps to class for sharing.

chunking A previewing method that involves making a list of terms and definitions from the reading and then dividing the terms into smaller clusters of five, seven, or nine to more effectively learn the material.

structure as you preview the chapter (see Figure 7.1). In the wheel structure, place the central idea of the chapter in the circle. The central idea should be in the introduction to the chapter and might be apparent in the chapter title. Place secondary ideas on the spokes emanating from the circle, and place off-shoots of those ideas on the lines attached to the spokes. In the branching map, the main idea goes at the top, followed by supporting ideas on the second tier and so forth. Fill in the title first. Then, as you skim the chapter, use the headings and subheadings to fill in the key ideas.

Alternatives to Mapping. Perhaps you prefer a more linear visual image. If so, consider making an outline of the headings and subheadings in the chapter. You can fill in the outline after you read. Alternatively, make a list. A list can be particularly effective when you are dealing with a text that introduces many new terms and their definitions. Set up the list with the terms in the left column, and fill in definitions, descriptions, and examples on the right after you read. Divide the terms on your list into groups of five, seven, or nine, and leave white space between the clusters so that you can visualize each group in your mind. This practice is known as **chunking**. Research indicates that we learn material best when it is in chunks of five, seven, or nine.

If you are an interactive learner, make lists or create a flash card for each heading and subheading. Then fill in the back of each card after reading each section in the text. Use the lists or flash cards to review with a partner, or recite the material to yourself.

Previewing, combined with mapping, outlining, or flash cards, might require more time up front, but it will save you time later because you will have created an excellent review tool for quizzes and tests. You will be using your visual learning skills as you create advanced organizers to help you associate details of the chapter with the larger ideas. Such associations will come in handy later. As you preview the text material, look for connections between the text and the related lecture material. Call to mind the related terms and concepts that you recorded in the lecture. Use these strategies to warm up. Ask yourself: Why am I reading this? What do I want to know?

MARKING YOUR TEXTBOOK

After completing your preview, you are ready to read the text actively. With your skeleton map or outline, you should be able to read more quickly and with greater comprehension. To avoid marking too much or marking the wrong information, first read without using your pencil or highlighter.

Think a moment about your goals for making marks in your own texts. Some students report that **marking** is an active reading strategy that helps them to focus and concentrate on the material as they read. In addition, most students expect to use their text notations when they study for tests. To meet these goals, some students like to underline, some prefer to highlight, and others use margin notes or annotations. Figure 7.2 provides an example of each method. No matter what method you prefer, remember these two important guidelines:

1. **Read before you mark.** Finish reading a section before you decide which are the most important ideas and concepts. Mark only those particular ideas, using your preferred methods (highlighting, underlining, circling key terms, annotating).

2. **Think before you mark.** When you read a text for the first time, everything can seem important. Only after you have completed a section and have reflected on it will you be ready to identify the key ideas. Ask yourself: What are the most important ideas? What will I see on the test? This can help you avoid marking too much material.

Two other considerations might affect your decisions about textbook marking. First, if you just make notes or underline directly on the pages of your textbook, you are committing yourself to at least one more viewing of all the pages that you have already read—all or most pages of your anatomy or art history textbook, for instance. A more productive use of your time might be taking notes, creating flash cards, making lists, or outlining textbook chapters. These methods are also more practical if you intend to review with a friend or study group.

Second, sometimes highlighting or underlining can provide you with a false sense of security. You might have determined what is most important, but you have not necessarily tested yourself on your understanding of the material. When you force yourself to put something in your own words while taking notes, you are not only predicting exam questions but also assessing whether you can answer them. Although these active reading strategies take more time initially, they can save you time in the long run because they not only promote concentration as you read but also make it easy to review. If you can use these strategies effectively, you probably won't have to pull an all-nighter before an exam.

IN CLASS: Students might complain that a marked book won't get a high buyback price when the course is over. As an exercise in values, ask them to consider which they value more: the cash or the better grade. Ask them to check buyback policies at local bookstores to find out how much of the book's value they will lose by marking in their books.

marking An active reading strategy of making marks in the text by underlining, highlighting, and writing margin notes or annotations.

IN CLASS: Explain that flash cards, lists, and outlines might also include students' reactions to the material or questions they need to ask about it.

CULTURE AND HUMAN BEHAVIOR 12.1

The Stress of Adapting to a New Culture

(marginal note: differences affecting cultural stress)

Refugees and immigrants are often unprepared for the dramatically different values, language, food, customs, and climate that await them in their new land. Coping with a new culture can be extremely stress-producing (Johnson & others, 1995). The process of changing one's values and customs as a result of contact with another culture is referred to as *acculturation*. Thus, the term **acculturative stress** describes the stress that results from the pressure of adapting to a new culture (Berry, 1994, 2003).

(marginal note: acceptance of new culture reduces stress also speaking new language, education, & social support)

Many factors can influence the degree of acculturative stress that a person experiences. For example, when the new society is one that accepts ethnic and cultural diversity, acculturative stress is reduced (Shuval, 1993). The ease of transition is also enhanced when the person has some familiarity with the new language and customs, advanced education, and social support from friends, family members, and cultural associations (Finch & Vega, 2003).

(marginal note: how attitudes affect stress)

Cross-cultural psychologist John Berry has found that a person's *attitudes* are important in determining how much acculturative stress is experienced. When people encounter a new cultural environment, they are faced with two fundamental questions: (1) Should I seek positive relations with the dominant society? (2) Is my original cultural identity of value to me, and should I try to maintain it?

(marginal note: 4 patterns of acculturation)

The answers to these questions result in one of four possible patterns of acculturation: integration, assimilation, separation, or marginalization (see the diagram). Each pattern represents a different way of cop-

Patterns of Adapting to a New Culture According to cross-cultural psychologist John Berry (1994, 2003), there are four basic patterns of adapting to a new culture. Which pattern is followed depends on how the person responds to the two key questions shown.

		Question 1: Should I seek positive relations with the dominant society?	
		Yes	**No**
Question 2: Is my original cultural identity of value to me, and should I try to maintain it?	**Yes**	Integration	Separation
	No	Assimilation	Marginalization

ing with the stress of adapting to a new culture (Berry, 1994, 2003).

1* *Integrated* individuals continue to value their original cultural customs but also seek to become part of the dominant society. Ideally, the integrated individual feels *comfortable* in both her culture of origin and the culture of the dominant society, moving easily from one to the other (LaFromboise, Coleman, & Gerton, 1993). The successfully integrated individual's level of acculturative stress will be low (Ward & Rana-Deuba, 1999).

2* *Assimilated* individuals give up their old cultural identity and try to become part of the new society. They may adopt the new clothing, religion, and social values of the new environment and *abandon* their old customs and language.

Assimilation usually involves a moderate level of stress, partly because it involves a psychological loss—one's previous cultural identity. People who follow this pattern also

(marginal note: possible rejection by both cultures)

face the possibility of being rejected either by members of the majority culture or by members of their original culture (LaFromboise & others, 1993). The process of learning new behaviors and suppressing old behaviors can also be moderately stressful.

3* Individuals who follow the pattern of *separation* maintain their cultural identity and avoid contact with the new culture. They may refuse to learn the new language, live in a neighborhood that is primarily populated by others of the same ethnic background, and socialize only with members of their own ethnic group.

*(marginal note: *separation may be self-imposed or discriminating)*

In some instances, such withdrawal from the larger society is self-imposed. However, separation can also be the result of discrimination by the dominant society, as when people of a particular ethnic group are discouraged from fully participating in the dominant society. Not surprisingly, the level of acculturative stress associated with separation is likely to be very high.

(marginal note: higher stress with separation)

4* Finally, the *marginalized* person lacks cultural and psychological contact with *both* his traditional cultural group and the culture of his new society. By taking the path of marginalization, he has lost the important features of his traditional culture but has not replaced them with a new cultural identity.

*(marginal note: *marginalized = higher level of stress)*

Marginalized individuals are likely to experience the greatest degree of acculturative stress, feeling as if they don't really belong anywhere. Essentially, they are stuck in an unresolved conflict between the traditional culture and the new social environment. They are also likely to experience feelings of alienation and a loss of identity (Berry & Kim, 1988).

Acculturative Stress As this Sikh family crossing a busy street in Chicago has discovered, adapting to a new culture can be a stressful process. What factors can make the transition less stressful? How can the acculturation process be eased?

FIGURE 7.2 Examples of Marking

Using a combination of highlighting, lines, and marginal notes, the reader has boiled down the content of this page for easy review. Without reading the text, note the highlighted words and phrases and the marginal notes, and see how much information you can gather from them. Then read the text itself. Does the markup serve as a study aid? Does it cover the essential points? Would you have marked this page any differently? Why or why not?

Source: "The Stress of Adapting to a New Culture," from *Discovering Psychology*, 4th ed., p. 481, by D. H. Hockenbury and S. E. Hockenbury. Copyright © 2007 by Worth Publishers. Used with permission of the publisher.

READING WITH CONCENTRATION

Students commonly have trouble concentrating or understanding the content when they read textbooks. Many factors can affect your ability to concentrate and understand texts: the time of day, your energy level, your interest in the material, and your study location.

Consider these suggestions, and decide which would help you improve your reading ability:

- Find a study location that is removed from traffic and distracting noises such as the campus library. Turn off your cell phone's ringer, and store the phone in your purse or book bag (someplace where you can't easily feel it vibrating). If you are reading an electronic document on your computer, download the information that you need and disconnect from the network to keep you from easily going online and chatting, e-mailing, or checking *Facebook* or *Twitter*.

- Read in blocks of time, with short breaks in between. Some students can read for 50 minutes; others find that a 50-minute reading period is too long. By reading for small blocks of time throughout the day instead of cramming in all your reading at the end of the day, you should be able to process material more easily.

- Set goals for your study period, such as "I will read twenty pages of my psychology text in the next 50 minutes." Reward yourself with a 10-minute break after each 50-minute study period.

- If you have trouble concentrating or staying awake, take a quick walk around the library or down the hall. Stretch or take some deep breaths, and think positively about your study goals. Then resume studying.

- Jot study questions in the margins, take notes, or recite key ideas. Reread confusing parts of the text, and make a note to ask your instructor for clarification.

- Focus on the important portions of the text. Pay attention to the first and last sentences of paragraphs and to words in italics or bold print.

- Use the glossary in the text or a dictionary to define unfamiliar terms.

> **YOUR TURN**
>
> Do you have trouble concentrating while you read your textbooks? What strategies do you use to make sure that your mind doesn't wander?

OUTSIDE CLASS: Divide the class into groups of four students. In each group, ask students to choose two or more of the tips for building concentration and understanding. Ask them to practice during the next few days and report on what worked, what did not work, and why.

REVIEWING

The final step in active textbook reading is reviewing. Many students expect to read through their text material once and be able to remember the ideas four, six, or even twelve weeks later at test time. More realistically, you will need to include regular reviews in your study process. Here is where your notes, study questions, annotations, flash cards, visual maps, or outlines will be most useful. Your study goal should be to review the material from each chapter every week.

Consider ways to use your many senses to review. Recite aloud. Tick off each item in a list on each of your fingertips. Post diagrams, maps, or outlines around your living space so that you will see them often and will likely be able to visualize them while taking the test.

OUTSIDE CLASS: Encourage students to use the learning center's reading resources to improve their reading rate and to master various methods of remembering material.

Strategies for Reading Textbooks

IN CLASS: Ask students how they usually read a textbook chapter. Do they just read? Do they highlight or take notes as they go? Use the discussion to introduce this section on reading from a textbook.

As you begin reading, be sure to learn more about the textbook and its author by reading the frontmatter in the book, such as the preface, foreword, introduction, and author's biographical sketch. The preface is usually written by the author (or authors) and will tell you why they wrote the book and what material it covers. Textbooks often have a preface written to the instructor and a separate preface for the students. The foreword is often an endorsement of the book written by someone other than the author, which can add to your understanding of the book and its purpose. Some books have an additional introduction that reviews the book's overall organization and its contents chapter by chapter. Frontmatter might also include biographical information about the authors that will give you important details about their background.

Some textbooks include questions at the end of each chapter that you can use as a study guide or as a quick check on your understanding of the chapter's main points. Take time to read and respond to these questions, whether or not your instructor requires you to do so.

Textbooks must try to cover a lot of material in a fairly limited space. Although many textbooks seem detailed, they won't necessarily provide all the things you want to know about a topic—the things that can make your reading more interesting. If you find yourself fascinated by a particular topic, go to the **primary sources**—the original research or document. You'll find those referenced in many textbooks, either at the end of the chapters or in the back of the book. You can read more information about primary and supplementary sources on page 137.

You might also go to other related sources that are credible—whatever makes the text more interesting and informative for you. Remember that most texts are not designed to treat topics in depth. Your textbook reading will be much more interesting if you dig a bit further in related sources. Because some textbooks are sold with test banks that are available to instructors, your instructors might draw their examinations directly from the text, or they might use the textbook only to supplement the lectures. Ask your instructors, if they have not made it clear, what the tests will cover and the types of questions that will be used. In addition, you might try to find a student who has taken a course with your instructor so that you can get a better idea of how that instructor designs tests. Some instructors expect that you will learn the kinds of detail that you can get only through the textbook. Other instructors are much more concerned that you be able to understand broad concepts that come from lectures in addition to texts and other readings.

Finally, not all textbooks are equal. Some are simply better designed and written than others. If your textbook is exceptionally hard to understand

---

> **YOUR TURN**
>
> Look at the front material in this book. What does it tell you about the authors and their purpose in writing this book? How do the authors' biographies influence the way you think about what's written in this book?

primary sources The original research or documentation on a topic, usually referenced either at the end of a chapter or at the back of the book.

> **YOUR TURN**
>
> What is your favorite text in one of your current courses? Why? Which is your least favorite text? Why?

or seems disorganized, let your instructor know your opinion. On the basis of what you say, your instructor might focus on explaining the text and how it is organized or might decide to use a different text for future classes.

MATH TEXTS

While the previous suggestions about textbook reading apply across the board, mathematics textbooks present some special challenges because they tend to have lots of symbols and very few words. Each statement and every line in the solution of a problem need to be considered and digested slowly. Typically, the author presents the material through definitions, theorems, and sample problems. As you read, pay special attention to definitions. Learning all the terms that relate to a new topic is the first step toward understanding.

Math texts usually include derivations of formulas and proofs of theorems. You must understand and be able to apply the formulas and theorems, but unless your course has a particularly theoretical emphasis, you are less likely to be responsible for all the proofs. So if you get lost in the proof of a theorem, go on to the next item in the section. When you come to a sample problem, it's time to get busy. Pick up pencil and paper, and work through the problem in the book. Then cover the solution and think through the problem on your own. Of course, the exercises that follow each text section form the heart of any math book. A large portion of the time you devote to the course will be spent completing assigned textbook exercises. It is absolutely vital that you do this homework in a timely manner, whether or not your instructor collects it. Success in mathematics requires regular practice, and students who keep up with math homework, either alone or in groups, perform better than students who don't.

After you complete the assignment, skim through the other exercises in the problem set. Reading the unassigned problems will deepen your understanding of the topic and its scope. Finally, talk the material through to yourself, and be sure your focus is on understanding the problem and its solution, not on memorization. Memorizing something might help you remember how to work through one problem, but it does not help you understand the steps involved so that you can employ them for other problems.

SCIENCE TEXTS

Your approach to your science textbook will depend somewhat on whether you are studying a math-based science, such as physics, or a text-based science, such as biology. In either case, you need to become acquainted with the overall format of the book. Review the table of contents and the glossary, and check the material in the appendices. There, you will find lists of physical constants, unit conversions, and various charts and tables. Many physics and chemistry books also include a minireview of the math you will need in science courses.

Notice the organization of each chapter, and pay special attention to graphs, charts, and boxes. The amount of technical detail might seem overwhelming, but—believe it or not—the authors have sincerely tried to present

IN CLASS: Ask a reading specialist from your campus developmental skills or learning center to come to class to provide tips on how to approach a science textbook.

All Textbooks Are Not Created Equal

Science texts are filled with graphs and figures that you will need to understand in order to grasp the content and the classroom presentations. If you have trouble reading and understanding your science textbooks, get help from your instructor or your learning center.

the material in an easy-to-follow format. Each chapter might begin with chapter objectives and conclude with a short summary, sections that can be useful to study both before and after reading the chapter. You will usually find answers to selected problems in the back of the book. Use the answer key or the student solutions manual to promote your mastery of each chapter.

As you begin an assigned section in a science text, skim the material quickly to gain a general idea of the topic. Begin to absorb the new vocabulary and technical symbols. Then skim the end-of-chapter problems so you'll know what to look for in your detailed reading of the chapter. State a specific goal: "I'm going to learn about recent developments in plate tectonics," or "I'm going to distinguish between mitosis and meiosis," or "Tonight I'm going to focus on the topics in this chapter that were stressed in class."

Should you underline and highlight, or should you outline the material in your science textbooks? You might decide to underline or highlight for a subject such as anatomy, which involves a lot of memorization. But use restraint with a highlighter; it should pull your eye only to important terms and facts. If highlighting is actually a form of procrastination for you (you are reading through the material but planning to learn it at a later date) or if you are highlighting nearly everything you read, your highlighting might be doing you more harm than good. You won't be able to identify important concepts quickly if they're lost in a sea of color. Ask yourself whether the frequency of your highlighting is helping you be more active in your learning process. If not, you might want to highlight less or try a different technique such as margin notes or annotations.

In most sciences, it is best to outline the text chapters. You can usually identify main topics, subtopics, and specific terms under each subtopic in your text by the size of the print. For instance, in each chapter of this textbook, the main topics (or level-1 headings) are in large orange letters with a line below. Following each major topic heading, you will find subtopics, or level-2 headings, printed in smaller, capital orange letters. The level-3 headings, which tell more about the subtopics, are in bold, orange letters, but are much smaller than the level-1 headings.

To save time when you are outlining, you won't write full sentences, but you will include clear explanations of new technical terms and symbols. Pay special attention to topics that the instructor covered in class. If you aren't sure whether your outlines contain too much or too little detail, compare them with the outlines members of your study group have made. You could also consult with your instructor during office hours. In preparing for a test, it's a good idea to make condensed versions of your chapter outlines so that you can see how everything fits together.

SOCIAL SCIENCE AND HUMANITIES TEXTS

Many of the suggestions that apply to science textbooks also apply to reading in the social sciences (sociology, psychology, anthropology, economics, political science, and history). Social science texts are filled with special terms or jargon that is unique to the particular field of study. These texts also describe research and theory building and contain references to many primary sources. Your social science texts might also describe differences in opinions or perspectives. Social scientists do not all agree on any one issue, and you might be introduced to a number of ongoing debates about particular issues. In fact, your reading can become more interesting if you seek out different opinions about a common issue. You might have to go beyond your particular textbook, but your library will be a good source of various viewpoints about ongoing controversies.

Textbooks in the **humanities** (philosophy, religion, literature, music, and art) provide facts, examples, opinions, and original material, such as stories or essays. You will often be asked to react to your reading by identifying central themes or characters.

Some instructors believe that the way in which colleges and universities structure courses and majors artificially divides human knowledge and experience. For instance, they argue that subjects such as history, political science, and philosophy are closely linked and that studying each subject separately results in only partial understanding. By stressing the links between courses, these instructors encourage students to think in an **interdisciplinary** manner. You might be asked to consider how the book or story you're reading or the music you're studying reflects the political atmosphere or the culture of the period. Your art history instructor might direct you to think about how a particular painting gives you a window on the painter's psychological makeup or religious beliefs.

IN CLASS: Explain that a large percentage of students have difficulty with introductory or "gateway" science and mathematics courses such as calculus, physics, or organic chemistry. Discuss why doing well in these courses is especially critical for some majors.

humanities Branches of knowledge that investigate human beings, their culture, and their self-expression. They include the study of philosophy, religion, literature, music, and art.

interdisciplinary Linking two or more academic fields of study, such as history and religion. Encouraging an interdisciplinary approach to teaching can offer a better understanding of modern society.

YOUR TURN

Are you ever tempted not to buy a textbook for one of your courses? Why? What can you do as an alternative? How important do you think textbooks are in your courses? In what other ways can you access the information you want and need to learn?

TECH TIP EMBRACE THE E-BOOK

1 ▶ THE PROBLEM

You're getting a hunchback from carrying twenty books around all day.

2 ▶ THE FIX

Discover how a digital reader differs from (and can even be better than) reading traditional ink-on-paper books.

3 ▶ HOW TO DO IT

THE PROS

- Digital reading devices are eminently portable—most weigh about a pound—and can carry thousands of books. (They're fantastic for those transatlantic flights when you don't want to pack the entire Sookie Stackhouse series.)
- They can hold a range of media, from books to newspapers to magazines.
- They save trees: no shipping costs, low carbon footprint.
- They let you buy books online from anywhere; you can start reading within minutes.
- They let you shop internationally. Even if you're in a remote Chinese village, you can easily find plenty of cyber books in English.
- You can type notes in an e-book, highlight passages, or copy and paste sections.
- You can print out pages simply by hooking the device up to your printer.
- Many of the books you can access are free: You can download books from the public library; you can even click to the British Library's Online Gallery to peruse some of the oldest and rarest books on record.
- Some e-books come with bonus audio, video, or animation features.
- Many digital reading devices even accept audio books and can read to you aloud.
- The backlit screen means you can read in bed with the light off, without keeping your roommate awake.
- You can adjust the size of the text, making it easier to read.
- E-books are searchable, and even sharable.

THE CONS

- Digital reading devices are expensive.
- Unlike books, they can break if you drop them.
- It's harder to flip through pages of an e-book.
- Textbooks are not yet widely available for digital reading devices.
- You miss out on the romantic sensation of opening, smelling, and carrying a real book.

GOOD TO KNOW

The most popular electronic e-readers include the iPad, Amazon's Kindle, Barnes & Noble's Nook, and Spring Design's Alex. The Kindle is the most popular basic model; others offer touch color screens, Web browsers, calculators, and even music.

PERSONAL BEST

Do you use an e-reader? How does using an e-book differ when reading a textbook versus reading a trade book?

_____

_____

_____

_____

_____

_____

_____

_____

SUPPLEMENTARY MATERIAL

Whether or not your instructor requires you to read material in addition to the textbook, your understanding will be enriched if you go to some of the primary and supplementary sources that are referenced in each chapter of your text. These sources can take the form of journal articles, research papers, dissertations (the major research papers that students write to earn a doctoral degree), or original essays, and they can be found in your library and on the Internet. Reading source material will give you a depth of detail that few textbooks accomplish.

Many sources were originally written for other instructors or researchers. Therefore they often use language and refer to concepts that are familiar to other scholars but not necessarily to first-year college students. If you are reading a journal article that describes a theory or research study, one technique for easier understanding is to read from the end to the beginning. Read the article's conclusion and discussion sections. Then go back to see how the author performed the experiment or formulated the ideas. If you aren't concerned about the specific method used to collect the data, you can skip over the "methodology" section. In almost all scholarly journals, articles are introduced by an abstract, a paragraph-length summary of the methods and major findings. Reading the **abstract** is a quick way to get the gist of a research article before you dive in. As you're reading research articles, always ask yourself: So what? Was the research important to what we know about the topic, or, in your opinion, was it unnecessary?

abstract A paragraph-length summary of the methods and major findings of an article in a scholarly journal.

Monitoring Your Reading

An important step in textbook reading is to monitor your comprehension. As you read, ask yourself: Do I understand this? If not, stop and reread the material. Look up words that are not clear. Try to clarify the main points and how they relate to one another.

Another way to check comprehension is to try to recite the material aloud, either to yourself or to your study partner. Using a study group to monitor your comprehension gives you immediate feedback and is highly motivating. After you have read and marked or taken notes on key ideas from the first section of the chapter, proceed to each subsequent section until you have finished the chapter.

After you have completed each section and before you move on to the next section, ask again: What are the key ideas? What will I see on the test? At the end of each section, try to guess what information the author will present in the next section.

> **YOUR TURN**
>
> How do you monitor your own reading comprehension? On the basis of the material in this chapter, what are some strategies you could use to ensure you understand what you are reading?

IN CLASS: Ask students to practice this method of monitoring with a study partner in class. Ask them to share what they learn with the rest of the class.

Improving Your Reading

With effort, you can improve your reading dramatically, but remember to be flexible. How you read should depend on the material. Assess the relative importance and difficulty of the assigned readings, and adjust your reading style and the time you allot accordingly. Connect one important idea to another by asking yourself: Why am I reading this? Where does this fit in?

When the textbook material is virtually identical to the lecture material, you can save time by concentrating mainly on one or the other. It takes a planned approach to read textbook materials and other assigned readings with good understanding and recall.

DEVELOPING YOUR VOCABULARY

Textbooks are full of new terminology. In fact, one could argue that learning chemistry is largely a matter of learning the language of chemists and that mastering philosophy, history, or sociology requires a mastery of the terminology of each particular **discipline**.

discipline An area of academic study, such as sociology, anthropology, or engineering.

If words are such a basic and essential component of our knowledge, what is the best way to learn them? Follow the basic vocabulary-building strategies outlined in the box at the bottom of the page.

IF ENGLISH IS NOT YOUR FIRST LANGUAGE

■ RETENTION STRATEGY: Non-native English speakers are at risk for poor academic performance and loss of self-confidence. Although many such students are highly intelligent and motivated to persist and may have been successful in school in another country, they will likely experience barriers to their academic progress. Make sure that these students and their families understand the policies and procedures of higher education and that ESL students are given the help they need to improve their English-language skills.

The English language is one of the most difficult languages to learn. Words are often spelled differently from the way they sound, and the language is full of idioms—phrases that are peculiar and cannot be understood from the individual meanings of the words. If you are learning English and are having trouble reading your texts, don't give up. Reading slowly and reading more than once can help you improve your comprehension. Make sure that you have two good dictionaries—one in English and one that links English with your primary language—and look up every word that you don't know. Be sure to practice thinking, writing, and speaking in English, and take advantage of your college's helping services. Your campus might have ESL (English as a Second Language) tutoring and workshops. Ask your adviser or your first-year seminar instructor to help you locate those services.

Listening, note taking, and reading are the essentials for success in each of your classes. You can perform these tasks without a plan, or you can practice some of the ideas presented in this chapter. If your notes are already working, great. If not, now you know what to do.

VOCABULARY-BUILDING STRATEGIES

> During your overview of the chapter, notice and jot down unfamiliar terms. Consider making a flash card for each term or making a list of terms.

> When you encounter challenging words, consider the context. See whether you can predict the meaning of an unfamiliar term by using the surrounding words.

> If context by itself is not enough, try analyzing the term to discover the root, or base part, or other meaningful parts of the word. For example, *emissary* has the root "to emit" or "to send forth," so we can guess that an emissary is someone who is sent forth with a message. Similarly, note prefixes and suffixes. For example, *anti* means "against," and *pro* means "for."

Use the glossary of the text, a dictionary, or the online **Merriam-Webster Dictionary (http://www.merriam-webster .com)** to locate the definition. Note any multiple definitions, and search for the meaning that fits this usage.

> Take every opportunity to use these new terms in your writing and speaking. If you use a new term a few times, you'll soon know it. In addition, studying new terms on flash cards or study sheets can be handy at exam time.

CHECKLIST FOR SUCCESS

READING IN COLLEGE

☐ **Be sure to practice the four steps of active reading: previewing, marking, concentrating while you read, and then reviewing.** If you practice these steps, you will understand and retain more of what you read.

☐ **Take your course textbooks seriously.** They contain essential information you'll be expected to learn and understand. Never try to "get by" without the text.

☐ **Remember that not all textbooks are the same.** They vary by subject area and style of writing. Some may be easier to comprehend than others, but don't give up if the reading level is challenging.

☐ **Learn and practice the different techniques suggested in this chapter for reading and understanding texts on different subjects.** Which texts come easiest for you? Which are the hardest? Why?

☐ **In addition to the textbook, be sure to read all supplemental assigned reading material.** Also, try to find additional materials to take your reading beyond just what is required. The more you read, the more you will understand, and the better your performance will be.

☐ **As you read, be sure to take notes on the material.** Indicate in your notes what specific ideas you need help in understanding.

☐ **Get help with difficult material before much time elapses.** College courses use sequential material that builds on previous material. You will need to master the material as you go along.

☐ **Discuss difficult readings in study groups.** Explain to each other what you do and don't understand.

☐ **Find out what kind of assistance your campus offers to increase reading comprehension and speed.** Check out your learning and counseling centers for free workshops. Even faculty and staff sometimes take advantage of these. Most everyone wants to improve reading speed and comprehension.

☐ **Use reading as a means to build your vocabulary.** Learning new words is a critical learning skill and outcome of college. The more words you know, the more you'll understand, and your grades will show it.

BUILD YOUR EXPERIENCE

1 STAY ON TRACK

Successful college students stay focused. They "stay on track." They know what they have to do to be successful, they set goals, and they monitor their progress toward their goals.

Reflect on what you have learned about college success in this chapter and how you are going to apply the chapter information or strategies in college and in your career. List your ideas.

1. _____

_____

_____

2. _____

_____

_____

3. _____

_____

_____

2 ONE-MINUTE PAPER

This chapter is full of suggestions for effectively reading your college textbooks. What suggestions did you find the most doable? What do you think is your biggest challenge in using these suggestions to improve your reading habits?

No matter how well prepared you are in your teaching, what a student hears and understands might not always be what you think you have said. The one-minute paper is a quick and easy assessment tool that will help alert you when students don't understand what was said or discussed in class. The one-minute paper will also give timid students an opportunity to ask questions and seek clarification. Ideally, you should ask for such a paper several minutes before the end of a class. The paper will also help you begin your next class by clarifying points your students seem to be unsure of.

3 APPLYING WHAT YOU HAVE LEARNED

Now that you have read and discussed this chapter, consider how you can apply what you have learned to your academic life and your personal life. The following prompts will help you reflect on the chapter material and its relevance to you both now and in the future.

1. Choose a reading assignment for one of your upcoming classes. After previewing the material, begin reading until you reach a major heading or until you have read at least a page or two. Now stop and write down what you remember from the material. Go back and review what you read. Were you able to remember all of the main ideas?

2. It is easy to say that there is not enough time in the day to get everything done, especially a long reading assignment. However, your future depends on how well you do in college. Challenge yourself not to use that excuse. How can you modify your daily activities to make time for reading?

4 BUILDING YOUR PORTFOLIO

The Big Picture   This chapter introduces a reading strategy called **mapping** as a visual tool for getting the "big picture" of what you are preparing to read. Mapping a textbook chapter can help you quickly recognize how different concepts and terms fit together and make connections to what you already know about the subject. A number of ways of mapping, including wheel maps and branching maps, are described in this chapter. You might also use other types of maps, such as *matrixes* to compare and contrast ideas or show cause and effect, a *spider web* to connect themes, or *sketches* to illustrate images, relationships, or descriptions.

1. Look through your course syllabi, and identify a reading assignment that you need to complete in the next week.

2. Begin by previewing the first chapter of the reading assignment.

3. Practice mapping the chapter by creating your own map using the drawing toolbar in *Microsoft Word*.

4. Save your map in your portfolio.

For an example of this exercise, go to the book's Web site at **bedfordstmartins.com/gardner**.

Reading a textbook efficiently and effectively requires that you develop reading strategies that will help you to make the most of your study time. Mapping can help you to organize and retain what you have read, making it a good reading and study tool. Writing, reciting, and organizing the main points, supporting ideas, and key details of the chapter will help you to recall the information on test day.

For more on this topic watch
French Fries Are Not Vegetables and Other College Lessons

WHERE TO GO FOR HELP...

ON CAMPUS

> **Learning Assistance Center** Most campuses have learning centers that specialize in reading assistance. Both the best students and struggling students use learning centers, where full-time professionals and skilled student tutors offer services.

> **Fellow Students** Your best help can come from a fellow student. Look for the best students—those who appear to be the most serious and conscientious. Hire a tutor if you can, or join a study group. You are much more likely to be successful.

ONLINE

> Middle Tennessee State University has a guide to "Reading Your Textbooks" at **http://frank.mtsu.edu/~studskl/Txtbook.html.**

> Niagara University's Office for Academic Support offers "21 Tips for Better Textbook Reading" at **www.niagara.edu/oas-21-tips.**

MY INSTITUTION'S RESOURCES

_____

_____

_____

_____

_____

_____

_____

_____

CHAPTER 8

Learning to Study, Comprehend, and Remember

IN THIS CHAPTER YOU WILL EXPLORE

How study groups can help you prepare

How commonsense study methods can produce greater learning

Common myths about memory

How to improve your ability to memorize

Why a good memory can be an asset but is not all that you need if you are to do well in college

66 **It sounds like a cliché, but don't procrastinate! If you get your study time in early, you won't have to worry about being up late studying.**

Noelle Green, 19
Accounting major
Missouri Southern State University

Noelle Green didn't struggle with study skills in high school. She grew up in Carthage, Missouri, where she finished tenth in her class and immediately enrolled in the honors program at Missouri Southern State University for its high-quality accounting program and a location that allowed her to commute from home and save money. "During high school, I was pretty good at studying, but it wasn't something I had to do very often at all. I could wait until the night before a test and make a few note cards with the information I needed to study."

In college, studying was a different story. Noelle found that she needed to study more—and more frequently—for tests that were less frequent and counted for a much larger portion of her grade. "I learned that I needed to set aside a long time to study so that I could go over all my notes several times." And even though she's an accounting major, Noelle's favorite course so far has been theater appreciation—a course that required disciplined study habits as well. "The tests were based on a thorough knowledge of our notes and the assigned reading. Flash cards are my favorite tool for studying, so I made sure to keep a stack on hand."

Noelle Green ▶

As a visual learner, Noelle also understands the importance of those flash cards—as well as reading, writing, and diagrams—when she is trying to retain a lot of information. (She also knows that she's *not* an auditory learner, meaning she can't just sit in class and listen and expect to retain all the necessary information.) She creates her own flash cards or rewrites lists and quizzes herself repeatedly until she is confident she has retained the information. Nolle works between 23 and 27 hours a week and volunteers with Koinonia, a Christian Campus Ministry Organization, so she knows that managing her time is important. She recommends combating the age-old problem of procrastination. "It sounds like a cliché, but don't procrastinate! If you get your study time in early, you won't have to worry about being up late studying and you can just do a quick skim of your information the next morning."

You might have learned to study effectively while you were in high school, or like Noelle, you might be finding that you need to learn more about how to study. In college you will need to spend time out of class reviewing course material, doing assigned reading, and keeping up with your homework. Occasionally, you will also want to go the extra mile by doing additional (unassigned) reading and investigating particular topics that interest you.

Studying, comprehending, and remembering are essential to getting the most out of your college experience. Although many students think that the only reason for studying is to do well on exams, a far more important reason is to learn and understand course information. If you study to increase your understanding, you are more likely to remember and apply what you learn not only to tests, but also to future courses and to life beyond college.

This chapter offers you a number of strategies for making the best use of your study time. It also addresses the important topic of memory. There's no getting around it: If you can't remember what you have read or heard, you won't do well on course exams.

Studying to Understand and Remember

■ RETENTION STRATEGY: One of the reasons that first-year seminars are correlated with retention is that these courses focus on study skills essential for college success. Even if your students tell you they have heard all of this before, do not neglect this important component of your seminar class. Also remind them that college-level study skills are, in fact, different skills. If you don't feel comfortable teaching study skills, find someone on your campus who can be a resource person for you.

Studying will help you accomplish two goals: understanding and remembering. While memory is a necessary tool for learning, what's most important is that you study to develop a deep understanding of course information. When you truly comprehend what you are learning, you will be able to place names, dates, and specific facts in context. You will also be able to exercise your critical-thinking abilities.

The human mind has discovered ingenious ways to understand and remember information. Here are some methods that might be useful to you as you're trying to nail down the causes of World War I, remember the steps in a chemistry problem, or absorb a mathematical formula:

1. **Pay attention to what you're hearing or reading.** This suggestion is perhaps the most basic and the most important. If you're sitting in class thinking about everything except what the professor is

YOUR TURN

When you're in class, how would you rate your level of concentration on what the instructor is saying? Is it good, fair, or poor? In which classes do you concentrate best? In which is your concentration worst? Why do you think it's easier to concentrate in some classes than in others?

▰ ASSESSING YOUR STRENGTHS ▰

What study skills have you learned and practiced, and how do you need to improve? Now that you have read the first section of this chapter, list specific examples of your strengths in studying and remembering course material.

_____

_____

_____

_____

▰ SETTING GOALS ▰

What are _your_ most important objectives in learning the material in this chapter? How do you need to improve your study skills and your memory? List three goals in this area (e.g., I will make sure that I am not distracted when I am studying; I will find a space where I can be alone, either the library or a study lounge; and I will turn off my cell phone during study time).

1. _____

_____

2. _____

_____

3. _____

_____

saying or if you're reading and you find that your mind is wandering, you're wasting your time. Force yourself to focus.

2. **"Overlearn" the material.** After you know and think you understand the material you're studying, go over it again to make sure that you'll retain it for a long time. Test yourself, or ask someone else to test you. Recite aloud, in your own words, what you're trying to remember.

3. **Check the Internet.** If you're having trouble remembering what you have learned, Google a key word, and try to find interesting details that will engage you in learning more, not less, about the subject. Many first-year courses cover such a large amount of material that you'll miss the more interesting details unless you seek them out for yourself. As your interest increases, so will your memory for the topic.

4. **Be sure you have the big picture.** Whenever you begin a course, make sure that you're clear on what

IN CLASS: Advise students that it is important to be conscious of times when their minds wander. They can bring themselves back if they are aware that their focus is not on the material.

YOUR TURN

Look around your room and at your computer desktop. Is your living environment neat and organized? How about your "electronic environment"? Does a lack of organization ever cause you to waste time? What strategies could you use to become better organized?

the course will cover. You can talk with someone who has already taken the course, or you can take a brief look at all the reading assignments. Having the big picture will help you understand and remember the details of what you're learning.

5. **Look for connections between your life and what's going on in your courses.** College courses might seem irrelevant to you, but if you look more carefully, you'll find many connections between course material and your daily life. Seeing those connections will make your courses more interesting and will help you remember what you're learning. For example, if you're taking a music theory course and studying chord patterns, listen for those patterns in contemporary music.

6. **Get organized.** If your desk or your computer is organized, you'll spend less time trying to remember a file name or where you put a particular document. And as you rewrite your notes, putting them in a logical order (either chronological or thematic) that makes sense to you will help you learn and remember them.

7. **Reduce stressors in your life.** Although there's no way to determine the extent to which worry or stress causes you to be unable to focus or to forget, most people will agree that stress can be a distraction. Healthy, stress-reducing behaviors, such as meditation, exercise, and sleep, are especially important for college students. Many campuses have counseling or health centers that can provide resources to help you deal with whatever might be causing stress in your daily life.

DID YOU KNOW?

92% of students study with others in their first year.

8. **Collaborate with others.** One of the most effective ways to study is in a group with other students. In your first year of college, gather a group of students who study together. Study groups can meet throughout the term or can review for midterm or final exams.

Work Together

One way to enhance your memory is through working collaboratively with others. Each of you can share your own memory strategies such as mnemonics or acrostics. You can also check specific facts and details through group consensus.

TECH TIP DON'T BE A VIRTUAL WALLFLOWER

1 ▶ THE PROBLEM

How do you create community in an online course?

2 ▶ THE FIX

Jump out of your cyber box and make some connections.

3 ▶ HOW TO DO IT

Studies show that you'll retain more of what you learn online if you like your school, your teacher, and your fellow classmates. Who says that taking a class remotely means you have to feel like a lonely hermit?

1. Don't pass up online discussion forums or Web casts that let you interact with your instructor and other students.

2. As in a traditional course, your instructor may ask students to say a few things about themselves. To foster conversation, give people something to work with. Don't just say, "I'm John from Fresno" and leave it at that. You need a lure. Try questions like "What's the worst boss you've ever worked for and why?" Then everyone can chime in with a shared experience.

3. Go ahead and e-mail three or four students privately: "Hi, I'm John in the online leadership course. I wondered if you're really getting our latest assignment. I noticed last night that you had a question, too." Students like to sympathize with each other.

4. Reach out to your instructor with thoughtful questions, too: "Are there any conferences that have to do with leadership that students can attend?"

5. Extra credit: To enrich your learning experience, find out if you can create a class wiki page or *Facebook* account so students can share articles, offer feedback, and have more of a presence.

PERSONAL BEST

How can you apply some of these skills to a traditional course? Get to class early and talk to some other students or your professor, for starters. If you have a group assignment, write down the e-mail addresses and phone numbers of the people on your team. (If you get sick, at least you'll be able to find out what you missed.) Single out the biggest brains in your class and form a study group. And remember: A college class is a safe zone for exploring opposing views. Be prepared to disagree with others and have others disagree with you.

How Memory Works

Kenneth Higbee describes two different processes involved in memory (see Table 8.1). The first is **short-term memory,** defined as how many items you are able to perceive at one time. Higbee found that information stored in short-term memory is forgotten in less than 30 seconds (and sometimes much

short-term memory How many items you are able to perceive at one time. Memory that disappears in less than 30 seconds (sometimes faster) unless the items are moved to long-term memory.

TABLE 8.1   Short-Term and Long-Term Memory

Short-Term Memory	Long-Term Memory
Stores information for about 30 seconds	Procedural: remembering how to do something
Can contain from five to nine chunks of information at one time	Semantic: remembering facts and meanings
Information either forgotten or moved to long-term memory	Episodic: remembering the time and place of events

IN CLASS: Ask students why they think the authors included material in this book about memory. Is memory related to learning and academic success? Why or why not? Can memory be improved? If so, how?

long-term memory The type of memory that is used to retain information and can be described in three ways: procedural, semantic, and episodic.

faster) unless you take action to either keep that information in short-term memory or move it to long-term memory.[1]

Although short-term memory is significantly limited, it has a number of uses. It serves as an immediate but temporary holding tank for information, some of which might not be needed for long. It helps you maintain a reasonable attention span so that you can keep track of topics mentioned in conversation, and it enables you to stay on task with the goals you are pursuing at any moment. But even these simple functions of short-term memory fail on occasion. If the telephone rings, if someone asks you a question, or if you're interrupted in any way, you might find that your attention suffers and that you essentially have to start over in reconstructing short-term memory.

The second memory process is **long-term memory**, and this is the type of memory that you will need to improve so that you will remember what you're learning in college. Long-term memory can be described in three ways. *Procedural memory* is knowing how to do something, such as solving a mathematical problem or playing a musical instrument. *Semantic memory* involves facts and meanings without regard to where and when you learned those things. *Episodic memory* deals with particular events, their time, and their place.[2]

You are using your procedural memory when you get on a bicycle you haven't ridden in years, when you can recall the first piece you learned to play on the piano, when you effortlessly type a letter or class report, and when you drive a car. Your semantic memory is used continuously to recall word meanings or important dates, such as your mother's birthday. Episodic memory allows you to remember events in your life—a vacation, your first day in school, the moment you opened your college acceptance letter. Some people can recall not only the event but also the very date and time the event happened. For others, although the event stands out, the dates and times are harder to remember immediately.

CONNECTING MEMORY TO DEEP LEARNING

It can be easy to blame a poor memory on the way we live; multitasking has become the norm for college students and instructors. Admittedly, it's hard

[1]K. Higbee, *Your Memory: How It Works and How to Improve It* (New York: Marlowet, 1996).

[2]W. F. Brewer and J. R. Pani, "The Structure of Human Memory," in G. H. Bower (Ed.), *The Psychology of Learning and Motivation: Advances in Research and Theory*, vol. 17 (New York: Academic Press, 1983), pp. 1–38.

to focus on anything for very long if your life is full of daily distractions and competing responsibilities or if you're not getting the sleep you need. Have you ever had the experience of walking into a room with a particular task in mind and immediately forgetting what that task was? You were probably interrupted either by your own thoughts or by someone or something else. Or have you ever felt the panic that comes from blanking on a test, even though you studied hard and thought you knew the material? You might have pulled an all-nighter, and studying and exhaustion raised your stress level, causing your mind to go blank. Such experiences happen to everyone at one time or another. But obviously, to do well in college—and in life—it's important that you improve your ability to remember what you read, hear, and experience. As one writer put it, "there is no learning without memory."[3] On the other hand, not all memory involves real learning.

Is a good memory all you need to do well in college? Most memory strategies tend to focus on helping you remember names, dates, numbers, vocabulary, graphic materials, formulas—the bits and pieces of knowledge. However, if you know the date the Civil War began and the fort where the first shots were fired but you don't really know why the Civil War was fought, you're missing the point of a college education. College is about **deep learning**, understanding the "why" and "how" behind the details. So don't forget that while recall of specific facts is certainly necessary, it isn't sufficient. To do well in college courses, you will need to understand major themes and ideas, and you will also need to hone your ability to think critically about what you're learning. Critical thinking is discussed in depth in Chapter 5 of this book.

deep learning Understanding the "why" and "how" behind the details.

IN CLASS: Remind students of the difference between memorization and learning. Explain that once they have mastered important concepts, using memory techniques will be an easy way to file facts for future use.

MYTHS ABOUT MEMORY

Although scientific knowledge about how our brains function is increasing all the time, Kenneth Higbee suggests that you might have heard some myths about memory (and maybe you even believe them). Here are five of these memory myths, and what experts say about them:

IN CLASS: Assign groups of students to read and discuss the myths about memory. Which of these myths do most students believe are true? Why?

1. **Myth:** Some people are stuck with bad memories.

   Reality: Although there are probably some differences among people in innate memory (the memory ability a person is born with), what really gives you the edge are memory skills that you can learn and use. Virtually anyone can improve the ability to remember and recall.

2. **Myth:** Some people have photographic memories.

   Reality: Although a few individuals have truly exceptional memories, most research has found that these abilities result more often from learned strategies, interest, and practice than from some innate ability. Even though you might not have what psychologists would classify as an exceptional memory, applying the memory strategies presented later in this chapter can help you improve it.

[3]Harry Lorayne, *Super Memory, Super Student: How to Raise Your Grades in 30 Days* (Boston: Little, Brown and Company, 1990).

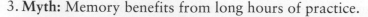

3. **Myth:** Memory benefits from long hours of practice.

   Reality: Practicing memorizing can help improve memory. If you have ever been a server in a restaurant, you might have been required to memorize the menu. You might even have surprised yourself at your ability to memorize not only the main entrees, but also sauces and side dishes. Experts acknowledge that practice often improves memory, but they argue that the way you practice, such as using special creative strategies, is more important than how long you practice.

4. **Myth:** Remembering too much can clutter your mind.

   Reality: For all practical purposes, the storage capacity of your memory is unlimited. In fact, the more you learn about a particular topic, the easier it is to learn even more. How you organize the information is more important than the quantity.

5. **Myth:** People only use 10 percent of their brain power.

   Reality: No scientific research is available to accurately measure how much of our brain we actually use. However, most psychologists and learning specialists believe that we all have far more mental ability than we actually tap.

Improving Your Memory

Throughout history, human memory has been a topic of great interest and fascination for scientists and the general public. Although severe problems with memory are extremely rare, you're in good company if you find that your memory occasionally lets you down, especially if you're nervous or stressed or when grades depend on immediate recall of what you have read, heard, or written.

So how can you improve your ability to store information in your brain for future use? Psychologists and learning specialists have conducted research on memory and have developed a number of strategies that you can use as part of a study-skills regimen. Some of these strategies might be new to you, but others will be simple commonsense ways to maximize your learning—ideas that you've heard before, though perhaps not in the context of improving your memory.

The benefits of having a good memory are obvious. In college, your memory will help you retain information and ace tests. After college, the ability to recall names, procedures, presentations, and appointments will save you energy and time and will prevent a lot of embarrassment.

There are many ways to go about remembering. Have you ever had to memorize a speech or lines from a play? How you approach committing the lines to memory might depend on your learning style. If you're an aural learner, you might choose to record your lines as well as lines of other characters and listen to them on tape. If you're a visual learner, you might remember best by visualizing where your lines appear on the page in the script. If you learn best by reading, you

> **YOUR TURN**
>
> How can you apply your learning style to remembering material for an exam? List some strategies that you already use or might want to try in the future.

"Is this the memory seminar?"

An Elephant (Almost) Never Forgets

While elephants apparently do have pretty good memories, they're like the rest of us in that they occasionally forget. Work to develop your memory by using the specific strategies in this chapter. One of the most important strategies you can use is understanding the big-picture context behind bits and pieces of information.

might simply read the script over and over. If you're a kinesthetic learner, you might need to walk or move across an imaginary stage as you read the script.

Although knowing specific words will help, remembering concepts and ideas can be much more important. To embed such ideas in your mind, ask yourself these questions as you review your notes and books:

1. What is the essence of the idea?
2. Why does the idea make sense? What is the logic behind it?
3. How does this idea connect to other ideas in the material?
4. What are some possible arguments against the idea?

MNEMONICS

Mnemonics (pronounced "ne MON iks") are various methods or tricks to aid the memory. Mnemonics tend to fall into four basic categories:

1. **Acronyms.** New words created from the first letters of several words can be helpful in remembering. The Great Lakes can be more easily recalled by remembering the word "HOMES" for Huron, Ontario, Michigan, Erie, and Superior.
2. **Acrostics.** An acrostic is a verse in which certain letters of each word or line form a message. Many piano students were taught the notes on the treble clef lines (E, G, B, D, F) by remembering the acrostic "Every Good Boy Deserves Fudge."

3. **Rhymes or songs.** Do you remember learning "Thirty days hath September, April, June, and November. All the rest have 31, excepting February alone. It has 28 days time, but in leap years it has 29"? If so, you were using a mnemonic rhyming technique to remember the days in each month.

4. **Visualization.** You use visualization to associate words, concepts, or stories with visual images. The more ridiculous the image, the more likely you are to remember it. So use your imagination to create mental images when you're studying important words or concepts. For example, as you're driving to campus, choose some landmarks along the way to help you remember material for your history test. The next day, as you pass those landmarks, relate them to something from your class notes or readings. A white picket fence might remind you of the British army's eighteenth-century approach to warfare, with its official uniforms and straight lines of infantry, while a stand of trees of various shapes and sizes might remind you of the Continental army's less organized approach.

Mnemonics work because they make information meaningful through the use of rhymes, patterns, and associations. They impose meaning where meaning might be hard to recognize. Mnemonics provide a way of organizing material, a sort of mental filing system. Mnemonics probably aren't needed if what you are studying is very logical and organized, but they can be quite useful for other types of material.

Although mnemonics are a time-tested way of remembering, the method has some limitations. The first is time. Thinking up rhymes, associations, or visual images can take longer than simply learning the words themselves through repetition. Also, it is often difficult to convert abstract concepts into concrete words or images, and you run the risk of being able to remember an image without recalling the underlying concept. Finally, memory specialists debate whether learning through mnemonics actually helps with long-term knowledge retention and whether this technique helps or interferes with deeper understanding.

USING REVIEW SHEETS, MIND MAPS, AND OTHER TOOLS

To prepare for an exam that will cover large amounts of material, you need to condense the volume of notes and text pages into manageable study units. Review your materials with these questions in mind: Is this one of the key ideas in the chapter or unit? Will I see this on the test? As suggested in Chapter 7, you might prefer to highlight, underline, or annotate the most important ideas or create outlines, lists, or visual maps.

Use your notes to develop review sheets. Make lists of key terms and ideas (from the recall column if you've used the Cornell method) that you need to remember. Also, don't underestimate the value of using your lecture notes to test yourself or others on information presented in class.

A **mind map** is essentially a review sheet with a visual element. Its word and visual patterns provide you with highly charged clues to jog your memory. Because they are visual, mind maps help many students recall information more easily.

IN CLASS: Have students select information taught in one of their courses or textbooks and use a mnemonic to aid their memory of this information. Ask students to demonstrate the mnemonic in class.

mind map A review sheet with words and visual elements that jog the memory to help you recall information more easily.

Figure 8.1 shows what a mind map might look like for a chapter on listening and learning in the classroom. Try to reconstruct the ideas in the chapter by following the connections in the map. Then make a visual mind map for this chapter, and see how much more you can remember after studying it a number of times.

In addition to review sheets and mind maps, you might want to create flash cards. One of the advantages of flash cards is that you can keep them in a pocket of your backpack or jacket and pull them out to study anywhere, even when you might not think that you have enough time to take out your notebook to study. Also, you always know where you left off. Flash cards can help you make good use of time that might otherwise be wasted, such as time spent on the bus or waiting for a friend.

OUTSIDE CLASS: Have students create a mind map of this chapter.

IN CLASS: Have students compare their maps and discuss any differences between them. Are the differences based on different interpretations of the information, or do they indicate errors?

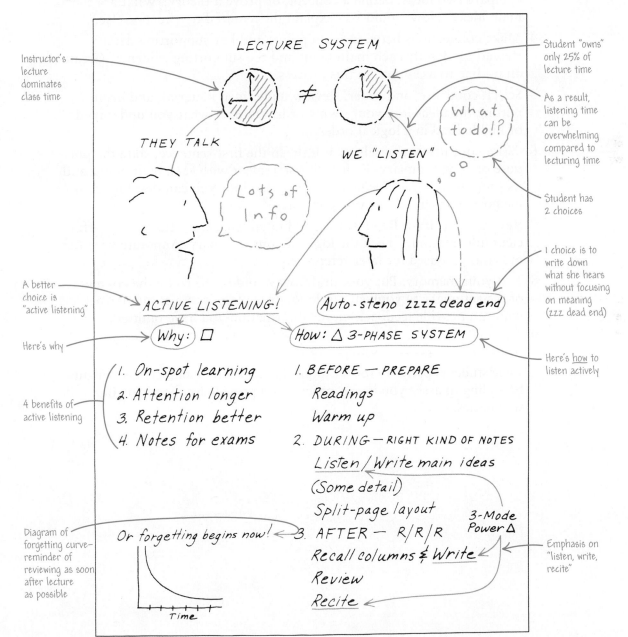

FIGURE 8.1

Sample Mind Map on Listening and Learning in the Classroom

SUMMARIES

Writing summaries of class topics can be helpful in preparing for essay and short-answer exams. By condensing the main ideas into a concise written summary, you store information in your long-term memory so you can retrieve it to answer an essay question. Here's how:

OUTSIDE CLASS: Have students write a summary of this chapter by following the outlined steps on this page. Ask students to discuss the differences between the mind map and the summary. Which was more helpful to them? Why?

1. Predict a test question from your lecture notes or other resources.

2. Read the chapter, supplemental articles, notes, or other resources. Underline or mark main ideas as you go, make notations, or make an outline on a separate sheet of paper.

3. Analyze and abstract. What is the purpose of the material? Does it compare two ideas, define a concept, or prove a theory? What are the main ideas? How would you explain the material to someone else?

4. Make connections between main points and key supporting details. Reread to identify each main point and the supporting evidence. Create an outline to assist you in this process.

5. Select, condense, and order. Review underlined material, and begin putting the ideas into your own words. Number what you underlined or highlighted in a logical order.

6. Write your ideas precisely in a draft. In the first sentence, state the purpose of your summary. Follow this statement with each main point and its supporting ideas. See how much of the draft you can develop from memory without relying on your notes.

7. Review your draft. Read it over, adding missing transitions or insufficient information. Check the logic of your summary. Annotate with the material you used for later reference.

8. Test your memory. Put your draft away, and try to recite the contents of the summary to yourself out loud, or explain it to a study partner who can provide feedback on the information you have omitted.

9. Schedule time to review summaries, and double-check your memory shortly before the test. You might want to do this with a partner, but some students prefer to review alone. Some faculty members also might be willing to assist you in this process and provide feedback on your summaries.

CHECKLIST FOR SUCCESS

GET THE MOST OUT OF YOUR STUDY TIME

☐ **Make studying a part of your daily routine.** Don't allow days to go by when you don't crack a book or keep up with course assignments.

☐ **Manage your study time wisely.** Create a schedule that will allow you to prepare for exams and complete course assignments on time. Be aware of "crunch times" when you might have several exams or papers due at once. Create some flexibility in your schedule to allow for unexpected distractions.

☐ **Collaborate with others.** One of the most effective ways to study is in a group with other students.

☐ **Be confident that you can improve your memory.** Remind yourself occasionally of things you have learned in the past that you didn't think you could or would remember.

☐ **Choose the memory improvement strategies that best fit your preferred learning styles: aural, visual, reading, kinesthetic.** Identify the courses where you can make the best use of each memory strategy.

☐ **Go beyond simply trying to memorize words and focus on trying to understand and then remember the big concepts and ideas.** Keep asking yourself: What is the main point here? Is there a big idea? Am I getting this?

☐ **Be alert for external distractions.** Choose a place to study where you can concentrate and allow yourself uninterrupted time to focus on the material you are studying.

☐ **Get a tutor.** Tutoring is not just for students who are failing. Often the best students seek assistance to ensure that they understand course material. Most tutors are students, and most campus tutoring services are free.

BUILD YOUR EXPERIENCE

1 STAY ON TRACK

Successful college students stay focused. They "stay on track." They know what they have to do to be successful, they set goals, and they monitor their progress toward their goals.

Reflect on what you have learned about college success in this chapter and how you are going to apply the chapter information or strategies in college and in your career. List your ideas.

1. _____

_____

_____

2. _____

_____

_____

3. _____

_____

_____

2 ONE-MINUTE PAPER

Doing well on exams is important, but being able to study, comprehend, and remember what you learn has bigger implications for your life. After reading this chapter, do you find yourself thinking about these concepts in a different way? If so, how? What kinds of questions would you ask your instructor about this chapter?

No matter how well prepared you are in your teaching, what a student hears and understands might not always be what you think you have said. The one-minute paper is a quick and easy assessment tool that will help alert you when students don't understand what was said or discussed in class. The one-minute paper will also give timid students an opportunity to ask questions and seek clarification. Ideally, you should ask for such a paper several minutes before the end of a class. The paper will also help you begin your next class by clarifying points your students seem to be unsure of.

 APPLYING WHAT
YOU HAVE LEARNED

Now that you have read and discussed this chapter, consider how you can apply what you have learned to your academic and personal life. The following prompts will help you reflect on the chapter material and its relevance to you both now and in the future.

1. Give mnemonics a try. Choose a set of class notes that you need to study for an upcoming quiz or exam. As you study, pick one concept, and create your own acronym, acrostic, rhyme, song, or visualization to help you remember.

2. The way in which students study in high school is often very different from the way they need to study in college. It can be difficult to adapt to new ways of doing things. Describe the way in which you studied in high school. Describe how you can improve on those habits to do well in college.

BUILDING YOUR PORTFOLIO

Takes Me Back Is there a song that reminds you, every time you hear it, of a certain time in your life or even the exact moment when something happened? Or maybe you have a photo that you take out every so often for a trip down memory lane? Our senses often trigger memories.

1. Recall a photo, song, or object that prompts you to remember a life event or time period. Create a new document in your word processing software, and describe just what it is about the photo, song, or object that reminds you of something else.

2. Describe your memory in as much detail as possible.

3. Describe how this memory makes you feel.

4. Describe how you might use photos or drawings, songs, or mnemonics to remember ideas or concepts in one of the classes you are currently taking.

5. Save these musings in your portfolio. If possible, save the photos or music files that you described along with your document.

For more on this topic watch
French Fries Are Not Vegetables and Other College Lessons

WHERE TO GO FOR HELP...

ON CAMPUS

Your campus probably has a study skills center or learning center that can help you develop effective memory strategies. Other students and faculty members can also give you tips on how they remember course material. And your college library will have many books on the topic of memory. Some were written by researchers for the research community, but others were written for people like you who are trying to improve their memory.

BOOKS

> Buzan, Tony. *Use Your Perfect Memory*, 3rd rev. ed. New York: Penguin Books, 1991.

> Higbee, Kenneth L., Ph.D. *Your Memory: How It Works and How to Improve It*, 2nd rev. ed. New York: Marlowe, 2001.

> Lorayne, Harry. *Super Memory, Super Student: How to Raise Your Grades in 30 Days*. Boston: Little, Brown, 1990.

ONLINE

> Memorization Techniques: **http://www.alamo .edu/sac/history/keller/ACCDitg/SSMT.htm.** This excellent Web site is maintained by the Alamo Community College District.

MY INSTITUTION'S RESOURCES

_____

_____

_____

_____

_____

_____

_____

_____

CHAPTER 9

Improving Your Performance on Exams and Tests

IN THIS CHAPTER YOU WILL EXPLORE

Ways to prepare yourself for exams physically, emotionally, and academically

How study groups can help you prepare for exams

How to devise a study plan for an exam

How to reduce test anxiety

What to do during the exam

How to take different types of tests

How cheating hurts you, your friends, and your college or university

> 66 **The first step to improving my test-taking abilities was changing my attitude about my 'academic self.'**

Kenzie Snyderman, 22
Business major
University of Alaska Anchorage

Kenzie Snyderman grew up all over the "lower 48," moving with her parents as part of a ministry. "My parents were young and adventurous and willing to move wherever the ministry sent them." At age seventeen, she landed in Fairbanks, Alaska, and attempted to finish high school. Soon after the move, Kenzie gave birth to a daughter and found herself working to support herself and her child. For a while, college was the furthest thing from her mind, but eventually she realized that she wanted more for her daughter—and for herself. "Ultimately being a single mother is what motivates me, not only to provide a better life for both of us but also to set an example that was not always set for me."

Part of going to college and raising a family involves finding that ever-elusive work-life balance in areas such as test taking. Kenzie always thought she just wasn't good at taking tests or learning, and so she usually finished at the middle of the pack on tests and exams. "The first step to improving my test-taking abilities," she tells us, "was changing my attitude about my 'academic self.'" Once Kenzie had worked to improve her attitude,

Kenzie Snyderman ▶

she began looking at the strategies that worked best for her. One thing she figured out was that note taking was integral to a good performance on tests. "I found that I remember things best by relating them to things that I already know." Now she knows to take careful notes during class, underline key terms, and make additional marginal notes so that when she gets home she can create associations to help with memory. She also knows that her brain works best when the rest of her body is well cared for and has plenty of rest, good food, exercise, and often meditation and relaxation. "It works better than cram studying, and I get a lot more out of my courses and do better on my exams."

As with many things in life, Kenzie realizes that with test taking you sometimes have to get it wrong before you get it right. Her advice to other first-year students? "Go back over the questions you got wrong on a test and try to figure out what you got wrong. Never stop learning new ways to study."

You can prepare for exams in many ways, and certain methods are more effective than others, depending on the subject matter, your preferred learning style, and the type of test you'll be taking. Kenzie identified the strategies that worked best for her, and you should do the same. Sometimes you'll need to be able to recall names, dates, and other specific bits of information, especially if you are taking a multiple-choice or short-answer exam. Many instructors, especially in humanities and social science courses such as literature, history, and political science, will expect you to go beyond names and dates and have a good conceptual understanding of the subject matter. They often prefer essay exams that require you to use higher-level critical-thinking skills, such as *analysis, synthesis*, and *evaluation*. They expect you to be able to provide the reasons, arguments, and assumptions on which a given position is based, and the evidence that you believe confirms or discounts it. They want you to be able to support your opinions so they can see how you think. They are not looking for answers that merely prove you can memorize the material presented in lecture and the text. Even in math and science courses, your instructors want you not only to remember the correct theory, formula, or equation but also to understand and apply what you have learned.

Knowing your preferred learning style will also help you decide the best ways for you to study, no matter what kind of text or exam you are facing. Remember your VARK score, and review the material in Chapter 4 that helps you link your learning style to strategies for exam preparation.

Getting Prepared for Tests and Exams

Believe it or not, you actually begin preparing for a test on the first day of the term. All of your lecture notes, assigned readings, and homework are part of that preparation. As the test day nears, you should know how much additional time you will need for review, what material the test will cover, and what format the test will take. It is very important to double-check the exam dates on your syllabi, as in Figure 9.1, and to incorporate these dates into your overall plans for time management—for example, in your daily and weekly to-do lists.

■ RETENTION STRATEGY: Many of us tell our students that "learning is more important than grades"; however, we should acknowledge that grades do matter. First-year students who have earned A's and B's in high school may be shocked to see their first C, D, or worse. The material in this chapter will help students do their best to earn good grades, but make sure that you also encourage students not to give up on college because they received a disappointing grade on a test or exam.

ASSESSING YOUR STRENGTHS

Tests and exams are an unavoidable component of college life. Good students will practice strategies to improve their exam scores. Now that you have read the first section of this chapter, list specific examples of your strengths in preparing for and taking different kinds of exams.

_____

_____

_____

_____

SETTING GOALS

What are _your_ most important objectives in learning the material in this chapter? Do you need to improve your abilities as a test taker, or do you need to deal with test anxiety that prevents you from doing your best? List three goals in this area (e.g., I will not wait until the last minute to study for my next exam; I will begin studying at least one week before the exam date).

1. _____

_____

2. _____

_____

3. _____

_____

Here are some specific suggestions to help you prepare well for any exam:

1. **Ask your instructor.** Find out the purpose, types of questions, conditions (how much time you will have to complete the exam), and content to be covered on the exam. Talk with your instructor to clarify any misunderstandings you might have about your reading or lecture notes. Some instructors might let you see copies of old exams so you can see the types of questions they use. Never miss the last class before an exam, because your instructor might summarize valuable information.

2. **Manage your preparation time wisely.** Create a schedule that will give you time to review effectively for the exam without waiting until the night before. Make sure your schedule has some flexibility to allow for unexpected distractions. If you are able to spread your study sessions over several days, your mind will continue to process the information between study sessions, which will help you during the test. Also, let your friends and family know when you have important exams coming up and how that will affect your time with them.

3. **Focus your study.** Figure out what you can effectively review that is likely to be on the exam. Collaborate with other students to share information, and try to attend all test or exam review sessions offered by your instructor.

IN CLASS: Ask students what they know about midterm and final exam periods. Why do colleges set these times aside for examinations?

IN CLASS: Have your students check their schedules and make sure that they have written down all their exam dates for each of their classes.

IN CLASS: Most college instructors would agree that essay exams measure learning far better than objective tests do. Explain why so many objective tests are given (e.g., large classes, easier to grade). Why do students need to alter their study methods according to the type of exam?

FIGURE 9.1

Exam Schedule from Sample Course Syllabus

History 111, US History to 1865
Fall 2012

Examinations
Note: In this course, most of your exams will be on Fridays, except for the Wednesday before Thanksgiving and the final. This is to give you a full week to study for the exam and permit me to grade them over the weekend and return the exams to you on Monday. I believe in using a variety of types of measurements. In addition to those scheduled below, I reserve the right to give you unannounced quizzes on daily reading assignments. Also, current events are fair game on any exam! Midterm and final exams will be cumulative (on all material since beginning of the course). Other exams cover all classroom material and all readings covered since the prior exam. The schedule is as follows:

Friday, 9/9: Objective type

Friday, 9/23: Essay type

Friday, 10/21: Midterm: essay and objective

Friday, 11/4: Objective

Wednesday, 11/23: Essay

Tuesday, 12/13: Final exam: essay and objective

PREPARE PHYSICALLY

Maintain your regular sleep routine. To do well on exams, you will need to be alert so that you can think clearly. And you are more likely to be alert when you are well rested. Last-minute, late-night cramming that robs you of sufficient sleep isn't an effective study strategy.

Follow your regular exercise program. Another way to prepare physically for exams is by walking, jogging, or engaging in other kinds of physical activity. Exercise is a positive way to relieve stress and to give yourself a needed break from long hours of studying.

Eat right. Eat a light breakfast before a morning exam, and avoid greasy or acidic foods that might upset your stomach. Limit the amount of caffeinated beverages you drink on exam day, because caffeine can make you jittery. Choose fruits, vegetables, and other foods that are high in energy-rich complex carbohydrates. Avoid eating sweets before an exam. The immediate energy boost they create can be quickly followed by a loss of energy and alertness. Ask the instructor whether you may bring a bottle of water with you to the exam.

IN CLASS: Have your students fill out an anonymous survey that asks (a) how many hours of sleep they get each night, (b) how much exercise they get every day, and (c) what kinds of foods they are most likely to eat each day. Compile and discuss the results. A staff member from the health and wellness center can be invited to class for this discussion.

PREPARE EMOTIONALLY

Know your material. If you have given yourself adequate time to review, you will enter the classroom confident that you are in control. Study by testing yourself or quizzing others in a study group or learning community so that you will be sure you really know the material.

Practice relaxing. Some students experience upset stomachs, sweaty palms, racing hearts, or other unpleasant physical symptoms of test anxiety. Consult your counseling center about relaxation techniques. Some campus learning centers also provide workshops on reducing test anxiety. If this is a problem you experience, read the section on test anxiety later in this chapter.

Use positive self-talk. Instead of telling yourself, "I never do well on math tests" or "I'll never be able to learn all the information for my history essay exam," make positive statements, such as "I have attended all the lectures, done my homework, and passed the quizzes. Now I'm ready to do well on the test!"

> **YOUR TURN**
>
> Are there times when you engage in negative predictions about your academic performance? What do you think causes you to be so hard on yourself? Do you think that changing your predictions could change your performance? Why or why not? How can you reverse your thinking and compliment yourself on your work?

PREPARE FOR TEST TAKING

Find out about the test. Ask your instructor what format the test will have, such as essay, multiple-choice, true/false, fill-in-the-blank, short-answer, or something else. Ask how long the test will last and how it will be graded. Ask whether all questions will have the same point value.

Design an exam plan. Use the information about the test as you design a plan for preparing. Build that preparation into a schedule of review dates. Develop a to-do list of the major steps you need to take to be ready. Be sure you have read and learned all the material by one week before the exam. That way, you will be able to use the final week to review and prepare for the exam. The week before the exam, set aside a schedule of one-hour blocks of time for review, and make notes on specifically what you plan to accomplish during each hour.

Join a study group. You have seen the suggestion to join or form a study group in other chapters because this is one of the most effective strategies for doing well in college, especially in preparing for exams. You can benefit from different views of your instructors' goals, objectives, and emphasis; have your study partners quiz you on facts and concepts; and gain the support and friendship of others to help sustain your motivation.

Some instructors will provide time in class for the formation of study groups. Otherwise, ask your teacher, adviser, or campus tutoring or learning center to help you identify interested students and decide on guidelines for the group. Study groups can meet throughout the term, or they can just review for midterms or final exams. Group members should complete their assignments before the group meets and prepare study questions or points of discussion ahead of time. If your study group decides to meet just before exams, allow enough time to share notes and ideas.

Get a tutor. Most campus tutoring services offer their services for free. Ask your academic adviser or counselor or campus learning center about arranging for tutoring. Many learning centers employ student tutors who have done well in the same courses you are taking. These students might have some good advice on how to prepare for tests given by particular instructors. Learning centers often have computer tutorials that can help you refresh basic skills.

PREPARE FOR MATH AND SCIENCE EXAMS

Math and science exams often require additional preparation techniques. Here are some suggestions for doing well on these exams:

1. Do your homework regularly, even if it is not graded, and do all the assigned problems. As you do your homework, write out your work as carefully and clearly as you will be expected to do on your tests. This practice will allow you to use your homework as a review for the test.

2. Attend each class, and always be on time. Many instructors use the time at the beginning of class to review homework.

3. Create a review guide throughout the term. As you begin your homework each day, write out a random problem from each homework section in a notebook that you have set up for reviewing material for that course. As you review later, you will be able to come back to these problems to make sure you have a representative problem from each section you've studied.

4. Throughout the term, keep a list of definitions or important formulas. (These are great to put on flash cards.) Review one or two of these as part of every study session. Another technique is to post the formulas and definitions in prominent areas in your living space (e.g., on the bathroom wall, around your computer work area, or on the door of the microwave). Seeing this information frequently will help embed it in your mind.

Taking Tests and Exams

Throughout your college career you will take tests in many different formats, in many subject areas, and with many different types of questions. The following box offers test-taking tips that apply to any test situation.

TIPS FOR SUCCESSFUL TEST TAKING

1. Write your name on the test (unless you are directed not to) and on the answer sheet.

2. Analyze, ask, and stay calm. Before you start the test, take a long, deep breath and slowly exhale. Carefully read all the directions before beginning the test so that you understand what to do. Ask the instructor or exam monitor for clarification if you don't understand something. Be confident. Don't panic. Answer one question at a time.

3. Make the best use of your time. Quickly survey the entire test and decide how much time you will spend on each section. Be aware of the point values of different sections of the test. If some questions are worth more points than others, they deserve more of your time.

4. Jot down idea-starters before the test. Before you even look at the test questions, turn the test paper over and take a moment to write down the formulas, definitions, and major ideas that you have been studying. (Check with your instructor ahead of time to be sure that this is okay.) This will help you go into the test with a feeling of confidence and knowledge, and it will provide quick access to the information while you are taking the test.

5. Answer the easy questions first. Expect that you'll be puzzled by some questions. Make a note to come back to them later. If different sections consist of different types of questions (such as multiple-choice, short-answer, and essay questions), complete the types of questions you are most comfortable with first. Be sure to leave enough time for any essays.

6. If you feel yourself starting to panic or go blank, stop whatever you are doing. Take a long, deep breath and slowly exhale. Remind yourself you will be okay and that you do know the material and can do well on this test. Then take another deep breath. If necessary, go to another section of the test and come back later to the item that triggered your anxiety.

7. If you finish early, don't leave. Stay and check your work for errors. Reread the directions one last time. If you are using a Scantron answer sheet, make sure that all bubbles are filled in accurately and completely.

ESSAY QUESTIONS

Many college instructors have a strong preference for essay exams for a simple reason: Essay exams promote higher-order critical thinking, whereas other types of exams tend to be exercises in memorization. Generally, advanced courses are more likely to include essay exams. To be successful on essay exams, follow these guidelines:

1. **Budget your exam time.** Quickly survey the entire exam, and note the questions that are the easiest for you, along with their point values. Take a moment to weigh their values, estimate the approximate time you should allot to each question, and write the time beside each item number. Be sure you know whether you must answer all the questions or choose among questions. Remember, writing profusely on easy questions that have low value can be a costly error because it takes up precious time you might need for more important questions. Wear a watch so you can monitor your time, and include time at the end for a quick review.

2. **Develop a very brief outline of your answer before you begin to write.** Start working on the questions that are easiest for you, and jot down a few

ideas before you begin to write. First, make sure that your outline responds to all parts of the question. Then use your first paragraph to introduce the main points and subsequent paragraphs to describe each point in more depth. If you begin to lose your concentration, you will be glad to have the outline to help you regain your focus. If you find that you are running out of time and cannot complete an essay, provide an outline of key ideas at the very least. Instructors usually assign points on the basis of your coverage of the main topics from the material. Thus you will usually earn more points by responding briefly to all parts of the question than by addressing just one aspect of the question in detail. An outline will often earn you partial credit even if you leave the essay unfinished.

3. **Write concise, organized answers.** Many well-prepared students write good answers to questions that were not asked because they did not read a question carefully or didn't respond to all parts of the question. Other students hastily write down everything they know on a topic. Instructors will give lower grades for answers that are vague and tend to ramble or for articulate answers that don't address the actual question.

4. **Know the key task words in essay questions.** Being familiar with the key task word in an essay question will help you answer it more specifically. The key task words in Table 9.1 appear frequently on essay tests. Take time to learn them so that you can answer essay questions as accurately and precisely as possible.

MULTIPLE-CHOICE QUESTIONS

Preparing for multiple-choice tests requires you to actively review all of the material that has been covered in the course. Reciting from flash cards, summary sheets, mind maps, or the recall column in your lecture notes is a good way to review large amounts of material.

Take advantage of the many cues that multiple-choice questions contain. Careful reading of each item might uncover the correct answer. Always question choices that use absolute words such as *always*, *never*, and *only*. These choices are often (but not always) incorrect. Also, read carefully for terms such as *not*, *except*, and *but*, which are introduced before the choices. Often, the answer that is the most inclusive is correct. Generally, options that do not agree grammatically with the first part of the item are incorrect. For instance, what answer could you rule out in the example in Figure 9.2?

Some students are easily confused by multiple-choice answers that sound alike. The best way to respond to a multiple-choice question is to read the first part of the item and then predict your own answer before reading the options. Choose the letter that corresponds to the option that best matches your prediction.

If you are totally confused by a question, place a check mark in the margin, leave it, and come back later, but always double-check that you are filling in the answer for the right question. Sometimes another question will provide a clue for a question you are unsure about. If you have absolutely no idea, look for an answer that at least contains some shred of information.

IN CLASS: If you test your students in this course, expose them to all types of test items: essay, multiple-choice, true/false, and matching. Consider telling them that you will deliberately attempt to mislead them on the multiple-choice and true/false questions so that they will learn how to take such tests successfully in other classes.

IN CLASS: Provide a tip on taking multiple-choice tests: The first answer that comes to your mind is usually the correct one. Generally, students should try not to second-guess themselves.

IN CLASS: Ask the class how often they have crammed in a last review of their notes just before a test is to begin. Tell the class that last-minute cramming usually will not improve a test score. It is better to prepare early and try to relax before the test starts.

YOUR TURN

Do you think that essay exams are more appropriate in upper-level courses and multiple-choice exams are more appropriate in first-year courses? Why or why not?

TABLE 9.1 Key Task Words

Analyze	Divide something into its parts in order to understand it better; show how the parts work together to produce the overall pattern.
Compare	Look at the characteristics or qualities of several things, and identify their similarities or differences. Don't just describe the traits; define how the things are alike and how they are different.
Contrast	Identify the differences between things.
Criticize/ Critique	Analyze and judge something. Criticism can be positive, negative, or both. A criticism should generally contain your own judgments (supported by evidence) and those of authorities who can support your point.
Define	Give the meaning of a word or expression. Giving an example sometimes helps to clarify a definition, but an example by itself is not a definition.
Describe	Give a general verbal sketch of something in narrative or other form.
Discuss	Examine or analyze something in a broad and detailed way. Discussion often includes identifying the important questions related to an issue and attempting to answer these questions. A good discussion explores all relevant evidence and information.
Evaluate	Discuss the strengths and weaknesses of something. Evaluation is similar to criticism, but the word *evaluate* stresses the idea of how well something meets a certain standard or fulfills some specific purpose.
Explain	Clarify something. Explanations generally focus on why or how something has come about.
Interpret	Explain the meaning of something. In science you might explain what an experiment shows and what conclusions can be drawn from it. In a literature course you might explain—or interpret—what a poem means beyond the literal meaning of the words.
Justify	Argue in support of some decision or conclusion by showing sufficient evidence or reasons in its favor. Try to support your argument with both logical and concrete examples.
Narrate	Relate a series of events in the order in which they occurred. Generally, you will also be asked to explain something about the events you are narrating.
Outline	Present a series of main points in an appropriate order. Some instructors want an outline with Roman numerals for main points followed by letters for supporting details. If you are in doubt, ask the instructor whether he or she wants a formal outline.
Prove	Give a convincing logical argument and evidence in support of some statement.
Review	Summarize and comment on the main parts of a problem or a series of statements. A review question usually also asks you to evaluate or criticize.
Summarize	Give information in brief form, omitting examples and details. A summary is short but covers all important points.
Trace	Narrate a course of events. Whenever possible, you should show connections from one event to the next.

IN CLASS: Divide the class into groups of four to five. Ask each group to prepare several potential essay questions from their notes, using the key task words you have assigned to them.

IN CLASS: Use overheads or a *PowerPoint* presentation to show some typical college essay questions. Incorporate key task words in your examples. Show how essay items generally require conceptual thinking rather than memorization of specifics, although both skills will be useful in writing the answers.

FIGURE 9.2

Example of a Multiple-Choice Question

Name ___Jack Brown_____ Date __9/9/11_____

Examination 1

1. Margaret Mead was an
   a. psychologist
   b. anthropologist
   c. environmental scientist
   d. astronomer

If there is no penalty for guessing, fill in an answer for every question, even if it is just a guess. If there is a penalty for guessing, don't just choose an answer at random; leaving the answer blank might be a wiser choice.

FILL-IN-THE-BLANK QUESTIONS

In many ways preparing for fill-in-the-blank questions is similar to getting ready for multiple-choice items, but fill-in-the-blank questions can be harder because you do not have a choice of possible answers right in front of you. Not all fill-in-the-blank questions are constructed the same way. Some teachers will provide a series of blanks to give you a clue about the number of words in the answer, but if just one long blank is provided, you can't assume that the answer is just one word. If possible, ask the teacher whether the answer is supposed to be a single word per blank or can be a longer phrase.

TRUE/FALSE QUESTIONS

Remember that for a statement to be true, every detail of the sentence must be true. Questions containing words such as *always*, *never*, and *only* tend to be false, whereas less definite terms such as *often* and *frequently* suggest the statement might be true. Read through the entire exam to see whether information in one question will help you answer another. Do not begin to second-guess what you know or doubt your answers just because a sequence of questions appears to be all true or all false.

MATCHING QUESTIONS

The matching question is the hardest type of question to answer by guessing. In one column you will find the terms, and in the other you will find their descriptions. Before answering any question, review all of the terms and descriptions. Then match the terms you are sure of. As you do so, cross out both the term and its description, and use the process of elimination to assist you in answering the remaining items. To prepare for matching questions, try using flash cards and lists that you create from the recall column in your notes.

Types of Tests

While you are in college, you will encounter many types of tests. Some tend to be used in particular disciplines; others can be used in any class you might take.

PROBLEM-SOLVING TESTS

In the physical and biological sciences, mathematics, engineering, statistics, and symbolic logic, some tests will require you to solve problems showing all steps. Even if you know a shortcut, it is important to document how you got from step A to step B. On other tests, all that will matter will be whether you have the correct solution to the problem, but doing all the steps will still help ensure that you get the right answer. For these tests, you must also be very careful that you have made no errors in your scientific notation. A misplaced sign, parenthesis, bracket, or exponent can make all the difference.

If you are allowed to use a calculator during the exam, it is important to check that your input is accurate. The calculator does what you tell it to, and if you miss a zero or a negative sign, the calculator will not give you the correct answer to the problem.

Be sure that you read all directions carefully. Are you required to reduce the answer to simplest terms? Are you supposed to graph the solution? Be careful when canceling terms, cross-multiplying, distributing terms, and combining fractions. Whenever possible, after you complete the problem, work it in reverse to check your solution, or plug your solution back into the equation and make sure it adds up. Also check to be sure that your solution makes sense. You can't have negative bushels of apples, for example, or a fraction of a person, or a correlation less than negative 1 or greater than 1. Write out each step clearly, with everything lined

Ace the Test

You have almost certainly taken machine-scored tests in high school. One of the simplest and most important steps you can take to do well on these tests is to make sure you align the questions with your answer sheet. But you must also read each question carefully so that you have the best chance of selecting the right answer.

up as the instructor has indicated in class (lining up the equal signs with each other, for example).

MACHINE-SCORED TESTS

It is important that you carefully follow the directions for machine-scored tests. In addition to your name, be sure to provide all the necessary information on the answer sheet, such as the instructor's name, the number for the class section, or your student ID number. Each time you fill in an answer, make sure that the number on the answer sheet corresponds to the number of the item on the test. If you have questions that you want to come back to (if you are allowed to do so), mark them on the test rather than on the answer sheet.

Although scoring machines have become more sophisticated over time, stray marks on your answer sheet can still be misread and throw off the scoring. When a machine-scored test is returned to you, check your answer sheet against the scoring key, if one is provided, to make sure that you receive credit for all the questions you answered correctly.

COMPUTERIZED TESTS

Your comfort with taking computerized tests might depend on how computer literate you are in general for objective tests as well as your keyboarding skills for essay exams. If your instructor provides the opportunity for practice tests, be sure to take advantage of this chance to get a better sense of how the tests will be structured. There can be significant variations depending on the kind of test, the academic subject, and whether the test was constructed by the teacher, a textbook company, or by another source.

For multiple-choice and other objective forms of computerized tests, you might be allowed to scroll down and back through the entire test, but this is not always the case. Sometimes you are allowed to see only one question at a time, and after you complete that question, you might not be allowed to go back to it. In this situation you cannot skip questions that are hard and come back to them later, so be sure that you try to answer every question.

For computerized tests in math and other subjects that require you to solve each problem, record an answer and then move to the next problem. Be sure to check each answer before you submit it. Also, know in advance what materials you are allowed to have on hand, including a calculator and scratch paper for working the problems.

LABORATORY TESTS

In many science courses and in some other academic disciplines, you will be required to take lab tests during which you rotate from one lab station to the next and solve problems, identify parts of models or specimens, explain chemical reactions, and complete other tasks similar to those that you have been performing in lab. At some colleges and universities, lab tests are now administered at computer terminals via simulations. To prepare for lab tests, always attend lab; take good notes, including diagrams and other visual representations as necessary; and be sure to study your lab notebook carefully before the test. If possible, create your own diagrams or models, and then see whether you can label them without looking at your book.

You might also have lab tests in foreign language courses. These tests can include both oral and written components. Work with a partner or study group to prepare for oral exams. Ask each other questions that require using key vocabulary words. Try recording your answers to work on your pronunciation. You might also have computerized lab tests that require you to identify syllables or words and indicate the order and direction of the strokes required to create them, particularly in a foreign language that uses a different symbol system, such as Chinese. The best way to prepare for these tests is to learn the meanings and parts of the symbols and regularly practice writing them.

OPEN-BOOK AND OPEN-NOTE TESTS

If you never had open-book or open-note tests in high school, you might be tempted to study less thoroughly, thinking that you will have access to all the information you need during the test. This is a common misjudgment on the part of first-year students. Open-book and open-note tests are usually harder than other exams, not easier.

IN CLASS: Ask students to think about the challenges of an open-book or open-note test. As an exercise, give the class an open-book test and ask them to work together in groups to complete the test. Then ask them what worked and what did not.

Most students don't really have time to spend looking things up during an open-book exam. The best way to prepare is to begin the same way you would study for a test in which you cannot refer to your notes or text. But as you do so, develop a list of topics and the page numbers where they are covered in your text. You might want to use the same strategy in organizing your lecture notes. Number the pages in your notebook. Later, type a three-column grid (or use an *Excel* spreadsheet) with your list of topics in alphabetical order in the first column and corresponding pages from your textbook and notebook in the second and third columns so that you can refer to them quickly if necessary. Or you might want to stick colored tabs onto your textbook or notebook pages for different topics. But whatever you do, study as completely as you would for any other test, and do not be fooled into thinking that you don't need to know the material thoroughly.

During the test, monitor your time carefully. Don't waste time unnecessarily looking up information in your text or notes to double-check yourself if you are reasonably confident of your answers. Instead, wait until you have finished the test, and then, if you have extra time, go back and look up answers and make any necessary changes. But if you have really studied, you probably will not find this necessary.

Sometimes the only reason a teacher allows open books or open notes is for students to properly reference their sources when responding to essay or short-answer tests. Make sure to clarify whether you are expected to document your answers and provide a reference or Works Cited list.

TAKE-HOME TESTS

Like open-book and open-note tests, take-home tests are usually more difficult than in-class tests. Many take-home tests are essay tests, though some teachers will give take-home objective tests. Be sure to allow plenty of time to complete a take-home test. Read the directions and questions as soon as you

TECH TIP FEAR NOT THE ONLINE TEST

1 ▶ THE PROBLEM

You don't know how to take an online test.

2 ▶ THE FIX

Learn to dodge rookie errors that can trip you up.

3 ▶ HOW TO DO IT

Here, our top ten strategies:

1. Don't wait until the last minute to study. Whether this online test is part of a self-paced online course or a face-to-face course, start a study group (either in person or online) as far in advance as possible.

2. Get organized. An open-book quiz can take longer than a normal test if you're not sure where to locate the information you need. Note: Having a solid grasp of the material going in is key; your notes and books should be for occasional reference only.

3. Resist the temptation to surf the Web for answers. The answer you pick might not be what your instructor is looking for. It's much better to check your notes to see what you were taught in class.

4. If your instructor doesn't forbid collaboration on tests, open up an instant message window with a fellow student. Take the test together and early.

5. Don't get distracted. When you're taking a cyber exam, it's easy to fall prey to real-life diversions like *Facebook*, *iTunes*, or a sudden urge to rearrange your closet. Whatever you do, take the test seriously. Go somewhere quiet where you can concentrate—not Starbucks. A quiet, remote spot in the library is ideal. You get bonus points if you wear noise-canceling headphones!

6. While taking the test, budget your time. Keep an eye on the clock so you'll be sure to finish the whole test.

7. Tackle easy questions first. Once you get those out of the way, you can revisit the harder ones.

8. Find out in advance if there's any penalty for wrong answers. If not, bluffing is allowed, so you want to be sure to fill in all the blanks.

9. Beware: There's always the risk of losing your Internet connection mid-test. To be on the safe side, type all of your answers and essays into a *Word* document. Then leave time at the end to cut and paste them into the test itself.

10. Finish early? Take a few minutes to obsessively check your answers and spelling. (That's good advice for traditional tests, too.)

PERSONAL BEST

What additional challenges might present themselves during an online test? List three challenges and some strategies for working through them:

1. _____

_____

_____

_____

2. _____

_____

_____

_____

3. _____

_____

_____

_____

receive the test to help you gauge how much time you will need. If the test is all essays, consider how much time you might allocate to writing several papers of the same length. Remember that your teacher will expect your essay answers to look more like assigned out-of-class papers than like the essays you would write during an in-class test.

Unfortunately, issues of academic honesty can arise for take-home tests. If you are accustomed to working with a study group or in a learning community for the course, check with the teacher in advance to determine the extent to which collaboration is allowed on the test. One thing that can be very confusing for students is to be encouraged to work together throughout the academic term and then to be told that there should be no communication outside of class about a take-home test.

Overcoming Test Anxiety

Test anxiety takes many different forms. Part of combating test anxiety is understanding its sources and identifying its symptoms. Whatever the source, be assured that test anxiety is common.

Test anxiety has many sources. It can be the result of the pressure that students put on themselves to succeed. Without any pressure, students would not be motivated to study; some stress connected with taking exams is natural and can enhance performance. However, when students put too much pressure on themselves or set unrealistic goals, the result is stress that is no longer motivating, only debilitating.

The expectations of parents, a spouse, friends, and other people who are close to you can also induce test anxiety. Sometimes, for example, students who are the first in their families to attend college bear the weight of generations before them who have not had this opportunity. The pressure can be overwhelming!

Finally, some test anxiety is caused by lack of preparation—by not keeping up with assigned reading, homework, and other academic commitments leading up to the test. Procrastination can begin a downward spiral because after you do poorly on the first test in a course, there is even more pressure to do well on subsequent tests to pull up your course grade. This situation becomes even more dire if the units of the course build on one another, as in math and foreign languages, or if the final exam is cumulative. While you are having to master the new material after the test, you are still trying to catch up on the old material as well.

Some test anxiety comes from a negative prior experience. Transcending the memory of negative past experiences can be a challenge. But remember that the past is not the present. Perhaps there are good reasons why you performed poorly in the past. You might not have prepared for the test, you might not have read the questions carefully, or you might not have studied with other students or sought prior assistance from your professor or a tutor. If you carefully follow the strategies in this chapter, you are very likely to do well on all your tests. Remember that a little anxiety is okay. But if you find that anxiety is getting

IN CLASS: Ask students to share their experiences with test anxiety. Discuss the underlying roots of test anxiety.

IN CLASS: Invite to class a student development counselor or other staff member who has experience helping students with test anxiety. Ask this person to share his or her expertise and provide practical ways to control or overcome test anxiety.

> **YOUR TURN**
>
> Do you experience any type of test anxiety? If so, what causes you to be anxious? If not, what strategies do you use to stay calm?

in the way of your performance on tests and exams, be sure to seek help from your campus counseling center.

TYPES OF TEST ANXIETY

Students who experience test anxiety under some circumstances don't necessarily feel it in all testing situations. For example, you might do fine on classroom tests but feel anxious during standardized examinations such as the SAT and ACT. One reason standardized tests are so anxiety provoking is the notion that they determine your future. Believing that the stakes are so high can create unbearable pressure. One way of dealing with this type of test anxiety is to ask yourself: What is the worst that can happen? Remember that no matter what the result, it is not the end of the world. How you do on standardized tests might limit some of your options, but going into these tests with a negative attitude will certainly not improve your chances. Attending preparation workshops and taking practice exams not only can better prepare you for standardized tests, but also can assist you in overcoming your anxiety. And remember that many standardized tests can be taken again at a later time, giving you the opportunity to prepare better and pull up your score.

Some students are anxious only about some types of classroom tests. Practice always helps in overcoming test anxiety; if you fear essay exams, try predicting exam questions and writing sample essays as a means of reducing your anxiety.

Some students have difficulty taking tests at a computer terminal. Some of this anxiety might be related to lack of computer experience. On the other hand, not all computerized tests are user-friendly. You might be allowed to see only one item at a time. Often, you do not have the option of going back and checking over all your answers before submitting them. In preparation for computerized tests, ask the instructor questions about how the test will be structured. Also, make sure you take any opportunities to take practice tests at a learning center or lab.

Test anxiety can often be subject-specific. For example, some students have math test anxiety. It is important to distinguish between anxiety that arises from the subject matter itself and more generalized test anxiety. Perhaps subject-specific test anxiety relates to old beliefs about yourself, such as "I'm no good at math" or "I can't write well." Now is the time to try some positive self-talk and realize that by preparing well, you can be successful even in your hardest courses. If the problem persists, talk to someone in your campus counseling center to develop strategies to overcome irrational fears that can prevent you from doing your best.

SYMPTOMS OF TEST ANXIETY

IN CLASS: Share your personal experiences with test anxiety. What memories do you have, particularly with high-stakes tests such as the SAT or GRE?

Test anxiety can manifest itself in many ways. Some students feel it on the very first day of class. Other students begin showing symptoms of test anxiety when it's time to start studying for a test. Others do not get nervous until the night before the test or the morning of an exam day. And some students experience symptoms only while they are actually taking a test.

Symptoms of test anxiety can include butterflies in the stomach, queasiness or nausea, severe headaches, a faster heartbeat, hyperventilating, shaking, sweating, or muscle cramps. During the exam itself, students who are overcome with test anxiety can experience the sensation of "going blank," that is, being unable to remember what they actually know. At this point, students can undermine both their emotional and academic preparation for the test and convince themselves that they cannot succeed.

Test anxiety can impede the success of any college student, no matter how intelligent, motivated, and prepared. That is why it is critical to seek help from your college's or university's counseling service or another professional if you think that you have significant test anxiety. If you are not sure where to go for help, ask your adviser, but seek help promptly! If your symptoms are so severe that you become physically ill (with migraine headaches, hyperventilating, or vomiting), you should also consult your physician or campus health service.

STRATEGIES FOR COMBATING TEST ANXIETY

In addition to studying, eating right, and getting plenty of sleep, there are a number of simple strategies you can use to overcome the physical and emotional impact of test anxiety. First, any time that you begin to feel nervous or upset, take a long, deep breath and slowly exhale to restore your breathing to a normal level. This is the quickest and easiest relaxation device, and no one even needs to know that you are doing it.

Before you go into the test room, especially before a multiple-hour final exam or before sitting through several exams on the same day, it can help to stretch your muscles just as you would when preparing to exercise. Stretch your calf and hamstring muscles, and roll your ankles. Stretch your arms, and roll your shoulders. Tilt your head to the right, front, and left to stretch your neck muscles.

When you sit down to take the test, pay attention to the way you are sitting. Sit with your shoulders back and relaxed, rather than shrugged forward, and put your feet flat on the floor. Smooth out your facial muscles rather than wrinkling your forehead or frowning. Resist the temptation to clutch your pencil or pen tightly in your fist; take a break and stretch your fingers now and then.

Anxiety-reducing techniques that might be available through your campus counseling center include systematic desensitization, progressive muscle relaxation, and visualization. One of the most popular techniques is creating your own peaceful scene and mentally taking yourself there when you need to relax. Try to use all five senses to re-create your peaceful scene in your mind: What would you see, hear, feel, taste, or smell?

These strategies can assist you in relaxing physically, but meanwhile, you must also pay attention to the mental messages that you are sending yourself. Focus on the positive! If you are telling yourself that you are not smart enough, that you did not study the right material, or that you are going to fail, you need to turn those messages around with a technique called **cognitive restructuring**. We all talk to ourselves, so make sure that your messages are encouraging rather than stress provoking. When you are studying, practice sending yourself positive messages: I really know this stuff. I am going to ace this test!

Similarly, do not allow others, including classmates, your spouse, parents, or friends, to undermine your confidence. If you belong to a study group,

OUTSIDE CLASS: Assign students to do an Internet search on test anxiety. Claude Steele, a professor at Stanford University, conducted interesting research on student performance on high-stakes exams. His research deals with the theory of stereotype threat, which is the idea that individuals sometimes underperform in a manner consistent with the way they are stereotyped. A team of students who are interested can research Steele's work.

IN CLASS: Have the group make a class presentation on what they learned from their Internet research on test anxiety.

IN CLASS: Ask students how breathing, meditation, and exercise can reduce test anxiety. If you feel comfortable doing so, lead the class in a short breathing and relaxation exercise, or invite a physical education or health instructor to come to class. Students can practice outside class. You might already have students in class who meditate regularly. If so, ask them whether they would be willing to show their classmates how it's done.

OUTSIDE CLASS: Encourage your students to attend a workshop offered by the campus counseling or health center on anxiety-reducing techniques.

IN CLASS: Have students report back and share tips they plan to use.

■ RETENTION STRATEGY: While extreme test anxiety is rare, it does happen and can cause some students to leave college. Encourage any student who suffers from a high level of anxiety when being tested in certain subjects to see you for a referral to a counselor. Anxiety management is a skill that can be both taught and learned in college.

cognitive restructuring
A technique of applying positive thinking and giving oneself encouraging messages rather than self-defeating negative ones.

discuss the need to stay positive. Sometimes, getting to the test room early will expose you to other students who are asking questions or making comments that are only going to make you nervous. Get to the building early, but wait until just a few minutes before the exam begins to approach the classroom itself. If at any point during a test you begin to feel like you cannot think clearly, or you have trouble remembering or you come to a question you cannot answer, stop for a brief moment, and take another long, deep breath and slowly exhale. Then remind yourself of the positive self-messages you have been practicing.

GETTING THE TEST BACK

Students react differently when they receive their test grades and papers. For some students the thought of seeing the actual graded test produces high levels of anxiety. But unless you look at the instructor's comments and your answers (the correct and incorrect ones), you will have no way to evaluate your own knowledge and test-taking strengths. You might also find that the instructor made an error in the grade that might have cost you a point or two. Be sure to let the instructor know if you find an error.

It is important that you review your graded test. You might find that your mistakes were caused by failing to follow directions, being careless with words or numbers, or overanalyzing a multiple-choice question. If you have any questions about your grade, be sure to talk to the instructor. You might be able to negotiate a few points in your favor, but in any case, you will let your instructor know that you are concerned and want to learn how to do better on graded tests and examinations.

> **YOUR TURN**
>
> What actions do you take when you look at graded tests? Take a look at an exam you got back in one of your classes. What can you learn from it? Would you challenge an instructor if you thought he or she had made a mistake in your grade? Why or why not?

Academic Honesty and Misconduct

Imagine what our world would be like if researchers reported fraudulent results that were then used to develop new machines or medical treatments or to build bridges, airplanes, or subway systems. Integrity is a cornerstone of higher education, and activities that compromise that integrity damage everyone: your country, your community, your college or university, your classmates, and yourself.

CHEATING

IN CLASS: Academic honesty is a serious issue. Review the types of misconduct, and discuss the impact of the Internet on academic honesty. Bring in your campus's academic honesty policy for the class to discuss.

Institutions vary widely in how they define broad terms such as *lying* or *cheating*. One university defines cheating as "intentionally using or attempting to use unauthorized materials, information, notes, study aids, or other devices . . . [including] unauthorized communication of information during an academic exercise." This would apply to looking over a classmate's shoulder for an answer, using a calculator when it is not authorized, obtaining or discussing an exam (or individual questions from an exam) without permission, copying someone else's lab notes, purchasing term papers over the Internet, watching the video instead of reading the book, and duplicating computer files.

PLAGIARISM

Plagiarism, or taking another person's ideas or work and presenting them as your own, is especially intolerable in academic culture. Just as taking someone else's property constitutes physical theft, taking credit for someone else's ideas constitutes intellectual theft.

On most tests, you don't have to credit specific sources. (But some instructors do require this. When in doubt, ask!) In written reports and papers, however, you must give credit any time you use (a) another person's actual words, (b) another person's ideas or theories—even if you don't quote them directly, or (c) any other information that is not considered common knowledge.

Many schools prohibit certain activities in addition to lying, cheating, unauthorized assistance, and plagiarism. Some examples of prohibited behaviors are intentionally inventing information or results, earning credit more than once for the same piece of academic work without permission, giving your work or exam answers to another student to copy during the actual exam or before that exam is given to another section, and bribing in exchange for any kind of academic advantage. Most schools also outlaw helping or attempting to help another student commit a dishonest act.

Stop! Thief!

When students are seated close to each other while taking a test, they may be tempted to let their eyes wander to someone else's answers. But don't let this happen to you. Cheating is equivalent to stealing. Also, don't make it easy for other students to copy your work. Reduce that temptation by covering your answer sheet.

plagiarism The act of taking another person's ideas or work and presenting it as your own. This gross academic misconduct can result in suspension or expulsion, and even the revocation of the violator's college degree.

CONSEQUENCES OF CHEATING AND PLAGIARISM

Although you might see some students who seem to be getting away with cheating or plagiarizing, the consequences of such behaviors can be severe and life-changing. Recent cases of cheating on examinations and plagiarizing major papers have caused some college students to be suspended or expelled and even to have their college degrees revoked. Writers and journalists whose plagiarism has been discovered, such as Jayson Blair, formerly of the *New York Times*, and Stephen Glass, formerly of the *New Republic*, have lost their jobs

DID YOU KNOW?

Despite serious consequences, 42% of students witness academic dishonesty or cheating in their first year.

and their journalistic careers. Even college presidents have occasionally been found guilty of "borrowing" the words of others and using them as their own in speeches and written documents. Such discoveries result not only in embarrassment and shame, but also in lawsuits and criminal actions.

Because plagiarism can be a problem on college campuses, faculty members are now using electronic systems such as **www.turnitin.com** to identify passages in student papers that have been plagiarized. Many instructors routinely check their students' papers to make sure that the writing is original. So even though the temptation to cheat or plagiarize might be strong, the chance of possibly getting a better grade isn't worth misrepresenting yourself or your knowledge and suffering the potential consequences.

OUTSIDE CLASS: Ask the class to submit a written summary of their thoughts on this section, Reducing the Likelihood of Academic Dishonesty. What experiences have students had with these issues?

REDUCING THE LIKELIHOOD OF ACADEMIC DISHONESTY

To avoid becoming intentionally or unintentionally involved in academic misconduct, consider the reasons why it could happen:

- **Ignorance.** In a survey at the University of South Carolina, 20 percent of students incorrectly thought that buying a term paper wasn't cheating. Forty percent thought using a test file (a collection of actual tests from previous terms) was fair behavior. Sixty percent thought it was

GUIDELINES FOR ACADEMIC HONESTY

1. Know the rules. Learn the academic code for your college by going to its Web site. Also learn about any department guidelines on cheating or plagiarism. Study course syllabi. If a teacher does not clarify standards and expectations, ask exactly what they are.

2. Set clear boundaries. Refuse when others ask you to help them cheat. This might be hard to do, but you must say no. In test settings, keep your answers covered and your eyes down, and put all extraneous materials away, including cell phones. Because that cell phones enable text messaging, instructors are rightfully suspicious when they see students looking at their cell phones during an exam.

3. Improve time management. Be well prepared for all quizzes, exams, projects, and papers. This might mean unlearning habits such as procrastination (see Chapter 2, Managing Your Time).

4. Seek help. Find out where you can obtain assistance with study skills, time management, and test taking. If your methods are in good shape but the content of the course is too difficult, consult your instructor, join a study group, or visit your campus learning center or tutorial service.

5. Withdraw from the course. Your institution has a policy about dropping courses and a deadline to drop without penalty. You might decide to drop only the course that's giving you

trouble. Some students choose to withdraw from all classes and take time off before returning to school if they find themselves in over their heads or if a long illness, a family crisis, or some other unexpected occurrence has caused them to fall behind. Before withdrawing, you should ask about campus policies as well as ramifications in terms of federal financial aid and other scholarship programs. See your adviser or counselor.

6. Reexamine goals. Stick to your own realistic goals instead of giving in to pressure from family members or friends to achieve impossibly high standards. You might also feel pressure to enter a particular career or profession that is of little or no interest to you. If that happens, sit down with counseling or career services professionals or your academic adviser and explore alternatives.

acceptable to get answers from someone who had taken the exam earlier in the same or in a prior term. What do you think?

- **Cultural and campus differences.** In other countries and on some U.S. campuses, students are encouraged to review past exams as practice exercises. Some student government associations maintain test files for use by students. Some campuses permit sharing answers and information for homework and other assignments with friends. Make sure you know the policy on your specific campus.

- **Different policies among instructors.** Because there is no universal code that dictates such behaviors, ask your instructors for clarification. When a student is caught violating the academic code of a particular school or instructor, pleading ignorance of the rules is a weak defense.

- **A belief that grades are all that matter.** This might reflect our society's competitive atmosphere. It also might be the result of pressure from parents, peers, or teachers. In truth, grades are nothing if one has cheated to earn them. Even if your grades help you get a job, it is what you have actually learned that will help you keep the job and be promoted. If you haven't learned what you need to know, you won't be ready to work in your chosen field.

- **Lack of preparation or inability to manage time and activities.** If you are tempted to cheat because you are unprepared, ask an instructor to extend a deadline so that a project can be done well.

The box on page 178 outlines some steps you can take to reduce the likelihood of problems.

CHECKLIST FOR SUCCESS

DOING YOUR BEST ON EXAMS AND TESTS

☐ **Learn as much as you can about the type of test you will be taking.** You will study differently for an essay exam than you will for a multiple-choice test.

☐ **Start preparing for test taking the very first day of the course.** Classes early in the term are the most important ones NOT to miss.

☐ **Prepare yourself physically through proper sleep, diet, and exercise.** These behaviors are as important as studying the actual material. You may not control what is on the exams, but you can control your physical readiness to do your best.

☐ **Prepare yourself emotionally by being relaxed and confident.** Confidence comes from the knowledge that you have prepared well and know the material.

☐ **If you experience severe test anxiety, seek help from your counseling center.** There are professionals who understand how to help you deal with this problem.

☐ **Develop a systematic plan of preparation for every test.** Be specific about when you are going to study, how long, and what material you will cover.

☐ **Join a study group and participate conscientiously and regularly.** Students who join study groups perform better on tests. It's a habit you should practice.

☐ **Never cheat or plagiarize.** Experience the satisfaction that comes from learning and doing your own work and from knowing you don't have to worry about getting caught or using material that may be incorrect.

☐ **Make sure you understand what constitutes cheating and plagiarism on your campus so you don't inadvertently do either.** If you are not clear, ask your instructors or the professionals in your campus learning center or writing center.

BUILD YOUR EXPERIENCE

1 STAY ON TRACK

Successful college students stay focused. They "stay on track." They know what they have to do to be successful, they set goals, and they monitor their progress toward their goals.

Reflect on what you have learned about college success in this chapter and how you are going to apply the chapter information or strategies in college and in your career. List your ideas.

1. _____

_____

_____

2. _____

_____

_____

3. _____

_____

_____

2 ONE-MINUTE PAPER

As you were reading the tips for improving your performance on exams and tests, were you surprised to see different tips for different subjects, such as math and science, and for different kinds of tests, such as multiple-choice and essay? What did you find to be the most useful information in this chapter? What material was unclear to you?

No matter how well prepared you are in your teaching, what a student hears and understands might not always be what you think you have said. The one-minute paper is a quick and easy assessment tool that will help alert you when students don't understand what was said or discussed in class. The one-minute paper will also give timid students an opportunity to ask questions and seek clarification. Ideally, you should ask for such a paper several minutes before the end of a class. The paper will also help you begin your next class by clarifying points your students seem to be unsure of.

3 APPLYING WHAT YOU HAVE LEARNED

Now that you have read and discussed this chapter, consider how you can apply what you have learned to your academic and personal life. The following prompts will help you reflect on the chapter material and its relevance to you both now and in the future.

1. Identify your next upcoming test or exam. What time of day is it scheduled, and what type of test will it be? What strategies have you read that will help you prepare for and take this test?

2. Is there one course that you find most difficult? If you are anxious about taking tests in that class, adopt a positive self-message to help yourself stay focused. It would be a favorite quote or even something as simple as "I know I can do this!"

4 BUILDING YOUR PORTFOLIO

A High Price to Pay Academic integrity is a supreme value on college and university campuses. Faculty members, staff, and students are held to a strict code of academic integrity, and the consequences of breaking that code can be severe and life-changing. Create a *Word* document to record your responses to the following activity.

1. Imagine that your college or university has hired you to conduct a month-long academic integrity awareness campaign so that students will learn about and take seriously your campus's guidelines for academic integrity. To prepare for your "new job":

   a. Visit your institution's Web site and use the search feature to find the academic integrity code or policy. Take the time to read through the code, violations, and sanctions.

   b. Visit the judicial affairs office on your campus to learn more about the way your institution deals with violations of academic integrity policies.

   c. Research online resources from other campuses, such as information from the Center for Academic Integrity, hosted by Clemson University (**http://www.academicintegrity.org/**).

   d. Check out several other college and university academic integrity policies and/or honor codes. How do they compare to your institution's code or policy?

2. Outline your month-long awareness campaign. Here are a few ideas to get you started:

   - Plan a new theme every week. Don't forget Internet-related violations.

   - Develop eye-catching posters to display around campus. (Check out the posters designed by students at Elizabethtown College in Pennsylvania, found at **http://www.rubberpaw .com/integrity**.)

   - Consider guest speakers, debates, skits, or other presentations.

   - Come up with catchy slogans or phrases.

   - Send students a postcard highlighting your institution's policies or honor code.

   - Consider the most effective ways to communicate your message to different groups on campus.

3. Save your work in your portfolio.

For more on this topic watch
French Fries Are Not Vegetables and Other College Lessons

WHERE TO GO FOR HELP. . .

ON CAMPUS

> **Learning Assistance Support Center** Almost every campus has one of these, and studying for tests is one of its specialties. The best students, good students who want to be the best students, and students with academic difficulties use learning centers and tutoring services. These services are offered by both full-time professionals and highly skilled student tutors and usually are free.

> **Counseling Services** College and university counseling centers offer a wide array of services, often including workshops and individual or group counseling for test anxiety. Sometimes these services are also offered by the campus health center.

> **Fellow College Students** Often the best help we can get is the closest to us. Keep an eye out in your classes, residence hall, and extracurricular activities for the best students, those who appear to be the most serious, purposeful, and directed. Find a tutor. Join a study group. Students who do these things are much more likely to be successful.

ONLINE

> Florida Atlantic University's Center for Learning and Student Success (CLASS) offers a list of tips to help you prepare for exams: **www.fau.edu/CLASS/ success/keys_to_success.php.**

> Learning Centre of the University of New South Wales in Sydney, Australia: **http://www.lc.unsw .edu.au/onlib/exam.html.** Includes the popular SQ3R method.

MY INSTITUTION'S RESOURCES

_____

_____

_____

_____

_____

_____

_____

CHAPTER 10

Writing and Speaking Effectively

IN THIS CHAPTER YOU WILL EXPLORE

How writing is a process that leads to a product

Ways to review and revise your writing

The importance of recognizing the difference between formal and informal writing

Six steps to success in preparing a speech

How best to use your voice and body language

How to sound organized when speaking on the spot

> " I've learned that academic writing is all about preparation. It is just like anything else that we do in life.

Jason Hardtke, 39
Business Management major
University of Phoenix

Jason Hardtke found himself at a crossroads when he graduated from high school. He received a full scholarship to play baseball at Arizona State University. At the same time, he was drafted in the third round by the Cleveland Indians. While he chose baseball and wound up playing for both the New York Mets and the Chicago Cubs, the lack of a college education always lingered at the back of his mind. Now, he coaches for the Arizona Diamondbacks as well as runs his own baseball academy, and he thought the timing was perfect to head back to college. An online degree fit his needs and lifestyle perfectly. "I travel half the year with the Diamondbacks, and it would be impossible for me to attend college in the traditional fashion."

Now that Jason is in college, he's found that applying the same level of commitment to his academic work as he does to his professional work helps him succeed. "I've learned that academic writing is all about preparation. It is just like anything else

Jason Hardtke ▶

that we do in life." Jason knows that his writing process begins with careful research and note taking. Next, he creates an outline to help him organize his thoughts, followed by a rough draft. The most important step, though, comes with rewriting and editing—and being sure he has the time to work these essential steps into his overall process. "It takes a while to check everything, from spelling and grammar to the flow and rhythm of the writing; all of them are pivotal in keeping the interest of the reader."

Like many adult students, Jason has skills that translate easily to an academic setting and that give him an advantage in his classes. His communication skills had already been honed by his years of work. "I was running my business prior to entering college and had to be very professional in communicating with customers on the phone and in person. I got a crash course on marketing, budgeting, and HR as well, and that taught me the importance of professionalism and making a good first impression." However, presenting in online classes offered him the opportunity to develop some new skills. "I have made a few different *PowerPoint* presentations in my classes. The first one I did I had to learn as I went. I had no idea how the *PowerPoint* process worked, but to my surprise it was easy, and I like the format."

Now, as Jason works toward finishing his degree, his advice to other students is "Be prepared, not only in doing the research and properly constructing a paper, but also in making sure that you have ample time to get the job done the right way without having to cut corners."

As Jason's story illustrates, the ability to write well and speak well makes a tremendous difference in how the rest of the world perceives you and how well you will be able to communicate throughout your life. But you will find that you often need to communicate differently depending on who is reading or listening to your words. Each time you speak or write, you are addressing an audience. The audience might be one person—a friend, family member, professor, or a potential employer—or your audience might be a group, such as your classmates in college. Some audiences might be unknown to you. For instance, if you're writing a book or an article for publication, a blog entry, or something on your *Facebook* page, you never know who might read your words. To communicate effectively, it's important to think about your audience, what they will understand and expect, and how they will react to what you are saying or writing. It's generally okay to use informal language with your friends, family, and other college students, for example, but your instructors and potential employers will expect more formal writing and speaking.

Experts suggest that there's no single, universally accepted standard for how to speak or write American English. Even so, school systems, professional communicators, and businesses all have standards, and, not surprisingly, the rules do not vary dramatically from place to place. If they did, we would have a hard time understanding one another. Our purpose in this chapter is not to teach you grammar and punctuation (we'll save that for your English classes), but to get you to think of writing and speaking as processes (how you get there) as well as products (the final paper or script) and to help you overcome those writer's and speaker's blocks we all encounter from time to time.

You might wonder: Why can't more people express themselves effectively? The answers vary, but all come back to the same theme: Most people do not

---

IN CLASS: Have students freewrite anonymously for 10 minutes in response to the following questions: What is keeping me from being a better writer? What are the major problems I have when I want to begin writing? Collect the papers, read some aloud, and ask students to identify common themes and problems.

OUTSIDE CLASS: Ask students to look in the *Wall Street Journal* or *New York Times* to find descriptions of professional jobs in which they might be interested after they graduate. Have them bring the descriptions to class.

IN CLASS: Ask why writing is such an important skill in all their job choices (ability to write letters, reports, proposals, etc.). Stress that the ability to write well is a major criterion for almost any job.

IN CLASS: Ask students to discuss how writing and speaking are both processes and products. Consider brainstorming on the board, first listing how writing and speaking are processes and then creating a second list of how they are products. Discuss the topic further with your students.

IN CLASS: Have students share their thoughts on writing and speaking blocks. Have any students had bad experiences with blocks? Were they able to turn their experiences into something positive? If so, how?

◤ ASSESSING YOUR STRENGTHS ◢

Writing and speaking are essential skills for college and for life. Success in your career will depend on your ability to communicate your ideas clearly to others. Now that you have read the first section of this chapter, list specific examples of your strengths as a writer or speaker.

_____

_____

_____

_____

◤ SETTING GOALS ◢

What are _your_ most important objectives in learning the material in this chapter? Do you need to improve your abilities as a writer or speaker? List three goals in this area (e.g., I will visit the writing center before submitting my next paper so that I can get some feedback on my writing).

1. _____

_____

2. _____

_____

3. _____

_____

think of writing and speaking as processes to be mastered step by step. Instead, they view writing and speaking as products; you knock them out and you're done. Nothing could be further from the truth.

Whatever career you choose, you will be expected to think, create, communicate, manage, and lead. A 2002 survey by the Plain English Network found that 96 percent of the nation's 1,000 largest employers say that employees must have good communication skills to get ahead. This means you will have to be able to write and speak well. You will have to write reports about your work and the performance of others, e-mails to describe problems and propose solutions, and position papers to explain and justify to your superiors why the organization must make certain changes.

As you lead and manage others, you also will need strong speaking skills in order to explain, report, motivate, direct, encourage, and inspire. You might have to give presentations in meetings to your superiors and their subordinates and then follow up with a written report or e-mail. So as you prepare yourself for a career, you need to start thinking of yourself as a person who is both a good thinker and an outstanding communicator.

■ RETENTION STRATEGY: Students who are focused on a career after college are more likely to be retained, and virtually all careers require good skills in writing. Help your students see the importance of writing to their future careers.

WRITING

William Zinsser, author of several books on writing, claims, "The act of writing gives the teacher a window into the mind of the student."[1] In other words, your writing provides tangible evidence of how well you think and how well you understand concepts related to the courses you are taking. Your writing might also reveal a good sense of humor, a compassion for the less fortunate, a respect for family, and many other things. Zinsser reminds us that writing is not merely something that writers do; it is a basic skill for getting through life. He claims that far too many Americans cannot perform useful work because they never learned to express themselves.

Using Freewriting to Discover What You Want to Say

Writing expert Peter Elbow asserts that it's impossible to write effectively if you simultaneously try to organize, check grammar and spelling, and offer intelligent thoughts to your readers.[2] He argues that it can't all be done at once, mainly because you use the right—or creative—side of your brain to create thoughts, whereas you use the left—or logical—side for grammar, spelling, organization, and so forth.

Elbow argues that we can free up our writing and bring more energy and voice into it by writing more like the way we speak and trying to avoid the heavy overlay of editing in our initial efforts to write. This preliminary step in the writing process is called "freewriting." By freewriting, Elbow simply means writing that is temporarily unencumbered by mechanical processes, such as punctuation, grammar, spelling, and context. Freewriting is also a way to break the habit of trying to write and edit at the same time.

The freewriting process can be difficult at first because it goes against the grain of how we are accustomed to writing. We normally edit as we write, pausing to collect our thoughts, to recollect the correct spelling of a word, to cross out a sentence that does not belong, to reject a paragraph that doesn't fit with the argument that we are making, or to mentally outline a structure of the argument that we are trying to make. Once you get the hang of it, though, it can become second nature.

> ### YOUR TURN
>
> Have you tried freewriting before? To see what freewriting feels like, write, "My writing speaks for me." Write for at least 10 minutes, nonstop, about that statement. Don't think about organization, grammar, punctuation, or spelling, and don't stop writing until the time is up. Discuss with your classmates your reactions to writing this way and what each of you wrote.

IN CLASS: Practice freewriting in class. Have fun with this; tell students they can freewrite on any humorous topic, picture, or sound. Ask students why focus is important (as in the Robert Pirsig example on the next page).

[1] William Zinsser, *On Writing Well* (New York: Harper, 2001).
[2] Peter Elbow, *Writing without Teachers* (New York: Oxford University Press, 1973).

NARROWING YOUR TOPIC

In *Zen and the Art of Motorcycle Maintenance*,[3] Robert Pirsig tells a story about a first-year English class he had taught. Each week he assigned students a 500-word essay to write. One week, a student failed to submit her paper about the town where the college was located, explaining that she had "thought and thought, but couldn't think of anything to write about." Pirsig gave her an additional weekend to complete the assignment. As he said this, an idea flashed through his mind. "I want you to write a 500-word paper just about Main Street, not the whole town," he said. She gasped and stared at him angrily. How was she to narrow her thinking to just one street when she couldn't think of a thing to write about the entire town? On Monday she arrived in tears. "I'll never learn to write," she said. Pirsig's answer: "Write a paper about one building on Main Street. The opera house. And start with the first brick on the lower left side. I want it next class."

The student's eyes opened wide. She walked into the next class with a 5,000-word paper on the opera house. In writing this paper, she had been freewriting but hadn't realized it. "I don't know what happened," she exclaimed. "I sat across the street and wrote about the first brick, then the second, and all of a sudden I couldn't stop." What had Pirsig done for this person? He had helped her find a focus and a place to begin. Getting started is what blocks most students from approaching writing properly. Faced with an ultimatum, the student probably began to see the beauty of the opera house for the first time and had gone on to describe it, to find out more about it in the library, to ask others about it, and to comment on its setting among the other buildings on the block.

Very few writers—even professionally published ones—say what they want to say on their first try. And the sad fact is that really good writers are in the minority. But through practice, an understanding of the writing process, and dedication, more people can improve their writing skills. And good writers can make good money.

EXPLORATORY WRITING

Another way to think about writing is to distinguish between exploratory writing and explanatory writing. Those terms practically define themselves, but here are some clearer definitions: **Exploratory writing**, like freewriting, helps you discover what you want to say; **explanatory writing** then allows you to transmit those ideas to others. Explanatory writing is "published," meaning you have chosen to allow others to read it (your teacher, your friends, other students, or the public at large), but it is important that most or all of your exploratory writing be private, to be read only by you as a series of steps toward your published work. Keeping your early drafts private frees you to say what you mean and mean what you say. Later, you will come back and make adjustments, and each revision will strengthen your message.

Some writers say they gather their best thoughts through exploratory writing: by researching their topic, writing down ideas from their research,

exploratory writing Writing that helps you first discover what you want to say. It is private and is used only as a series of steps toward a published work.

explanatory writing Writing that is "published," meaning that others can read it.

---

[3]Robert Pirsig, *Zen and the Art of Motorcycle Maintenance* (New York: Bantam Books, 1984).

TECH TIP BLOG FOR BRILLIANCE

1 ▶ THE PROBLEM

You need to improve your writing skills.

2 ▶ THE FIX

Express yourself. Keeping a diary, either on paper or onscreen in a blog, is a great way to get in some writing practice.

3 ▶ HOW TO DO IT

We know: Inside your head, you're the world's most articulate person. But trying to get your thoughts down on paper is another story, so it makes sense to flex those muscles. Any type of writing exercise is helpful simply because it gets you accustomed to organizing your thoughts, presenting a persuasive argument, and speaking in the language of the written word. It doesn't matter what you write about: politics, sports, your cat, ancient civilizations, whatever. Just get thinking and typing. Later on, when you sit down to write a masterpiece for an actual grade, you'll have valuable experience under your belt.

Remember, if you write about something related to your major or the kind of career that interests you—and you put some time into making your blog shine—you can always use it on your résumé or grad school application.

THE PROCESS:

To set up your own free blog:

1. Open your Web browser and go to **Blogger.com** or **Wordpress.com**. Click on the "Get Started" or "Sign Up Now" button.

2. Follow the prompts to create a blogger account and choose a display name. (Feel free to use your own name or an ingenious nom de plume.)

3. Name your blog, too: It needs a title and an address that people can use to visit it.

4. Follow the prompts to select a template. Once that's in place, you can start posting. Bonus: You can use plug-ins to make your blog more fun and functional.

5. Finished blogging for the day? Click the sign-out button at the top of the screen.

and adding their questions and reactions to what they have gathered. As they write, their minds begin to make connections between ideas. At this stage, they don't attempt to organize, to find exactly the right words, or to think about structure. But when they move from exploratory writing to explanatory writing, their preparation will help them form crystal clear sentences, spell correctly, and have their thoughts organized so that their material flows naturally from one point to the next.

The Writing Process

One of the more popular ways of thinking about the writing process includes the following steps:

1. **Prewriting or rehearsing (freewriting).** This step includes preparing to write by filling your mind with information from other sources. It is generally considered the first stage of exploratory writing.

2. **Writing or drafting.** This step is converting exploratory writing so that it becomes a rough explanatory draft.

3. **Rewriting or revision.** This step is polishing your work until it clearly explains what you want to communicate and is ready for your audience.

Many students turn in poorly written papers because they skip the first and last steps and make do with the middle one. Perhaps they don't have time because they have overloaded their schedule or they put off things until the night before the paper is due. Whatever the reason, the result is often a poorly written assignment, since the best writing is usually done over an extended period of time, not as a last-minute task. Most professional writers and speakers would never start preparing an assignment only a day or hours before it has to be delivered. For one thing, the mere anxiety such a situation creates would be more than enough to shut down any manner of intelligent thinking. Worrying about your grammar and spelling as you write what might be your only draft can lead to a low grade or a rejection from a career inquiry.

> **YOUR TURN**
>
> Describe your writing process. What steps do you go through when you write a major paper?

PREWRITING: THE IDEA STAGE

Many writing experts, such as Donald Murray,[4] believe that of all the steps, **prewriting** (or freewriting) should take the longest. During freewriting you might question things that seem illogical. You might recall what you've heard other people say. This should lead you to write more, to ask yourself whether your views are more reliable than those of others, whether the topic might be too broad or too narrow, and so forth.

prewriting The first stage of the writing process. It may include planning, research, and outlining.

What constitutes an appropriate topic or thesis? When is it neither too broad nor too narrow? Test your topic by writing, "The purpose of this paper is to convince my readers that . . ." (but don't use that stilted line in your eventual paper). Pay attention to the assignment. Know the limits of your knowledge, the limitations on your time, and your ability to do the necessary research.

WRITING: THE BEGINNING OF ORGANIZATION

Once you have completed your research and feel you have exhausted the information sources and ideas, it's time to move to the writing, or drafting, stage. It might be a good idea to begin with a **thesis statement** and an outline

thesis statement A short statement that clearly defines the purpose of the paper.

[4]Donald Murray, *Learning by Teaching: Selected Articles on Writing and Teaching* (Portsmouth, NH: Boynton/Cook, 1982).

Write. Revise. Repeat.

Good writers spend more time editing and revising their written work than they spend writing the original version, and computers have made this task much easier than it used to be. Never turn in your first draft; spend the necessary time to reread and improve your work.

so that you can put things where they logically belong. A thesis statement is a short statement that clearly defines the purpose of the paper (see Figure 10.1).

Once you have a workable outline and thesis, you can begin paying attention to the flow of ideas from one sentence to the next and from one paragraph to the next, including subheadings where needed. If you have chosen the thesis carefully, it will help you check to see that each sentence relates to your main idea. When you have completed this stage, you will have the first draft of your paper in hand.

REWRITING: THE POLISHING STAGE

Are you finished? Not by a long shot. Next comes the stage at which you take a good piece of writing and do your best to make it great. The essence of good writing is rewriting. You read. You correct. You add smoother transitions. You slash through wordy sentences and paragraphs, removing anything that is repetitious or adds nothing of value to your paper. You substitute stronger words for weaker ones. You double-check spelling and grammar. It also might help to share your paper with one or more of your classmates to get their feedback. This is typically called "peer review." Once you have talked with your reviewers about their suggested changes, you can either accept or reject them. At this point, you are ready to finalize your writing and "publish" (turn in) your paper.

ALLOCATING TIME

When Donald Murray was asked how long a writer should spend on each of the three stages, he suggested the following:

Prewriting: 85 percent (including research and rumination)

Writing: 1 percent (the first draft)

Rewriting: 14 percent (revising until it's suitable for "publication")

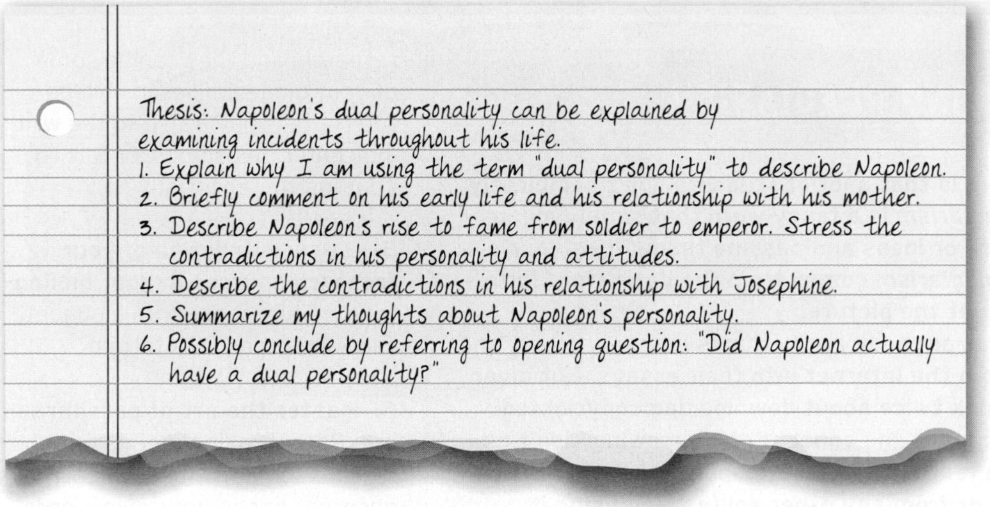

Thesis: Napoleon's dual personality can be explained by examining incidents throughout his life.
1. Explain why I am using the term "dual personality" to describe Napoleon.
2. Briefly comment on his early life and his relationship with his mother.
3. Describe Napoleon's rise to fame from soldier to emperor. Stress the contradictions in his personality and attitudes.
4. Describe the contradictions in his relationship with Josephine.
5. Summarize my thoughts about Napoleon's personality.
6. Possibly conclude by referring to opening question: "Did Napoleon actually have a dual personality?"

FIGURE 10.1

Example of a Thesis Statement

IN CLASS: Share your online resources for research and writing. Students might know of other sources that they can share with their classmates. One helpful and free tool is available at www.answers.com. Download "1-Click Answers" to be able to "alt-click" on any word in any program on your computer to get instant definitions and facts. The information will appear as a bubble on your screen. With this resource, there is no excuse for not looking up any word you don't understand.

When readers offer meaningful feedback, you might want to begin the process again, returning to prewriting, then writing, then rewriting (Figure 10.2).

If Murray's figures surprise you, here's a true story about a writer who was assigned to create a brochure. He had other jobs to do and kept avoiding that one. But the other work he was doing had a direct bearing on the brochure he was asked to write. So as he was putting this assignment off, he was also "researching" material for it.

After nearly three months, he finally decided it was time to move forward on the brochure. He sat at his computer and dashed the words off in just under 30 minutes. The more he wrote, the faster the ideas popped into his head. He actually was afraid to stop until he had finished. He read his words, made revisions, sent the result around the office for peer review, incorporated some suggestions, and the brochure was published.

He had spent a long time prewriting (working with related information without trying to write the brochure). He went through the writing stage

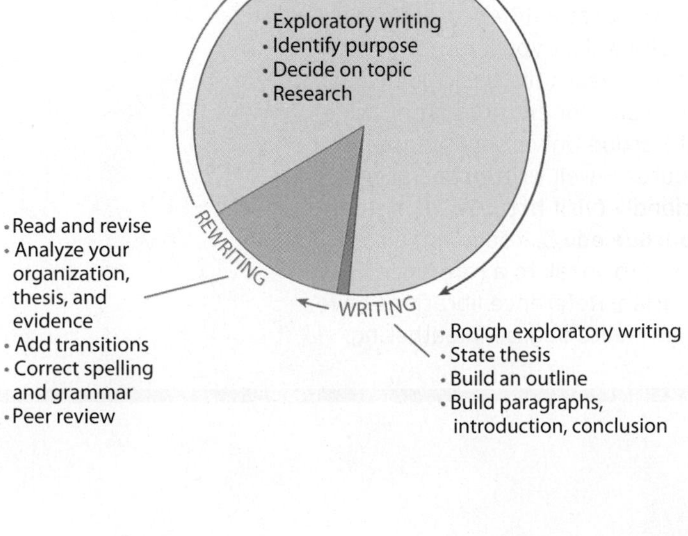

IN CLASS: Professional writer Donald Murray says that 1 percent of a writer's time should be spent on the writing stage. This seems so short. Ask students why Murray would make such a statement.

FIGURE 10.2

The Writing Process

- Read and revise
- Analyze your organization, thesis, and evidence
- Add transitions
- Correct spelling and grammar
- Peer review

PREWRITING
- Exploratory writing
- Identify purpose
- Decide on topic
- Research

REWRITING

WRITING
- Rough exploratory writing
- State thesis
- Build an outline
- Build paragraphs, introduction, conclusion

AVOIDING PLAGIARISM

The trouble with plagiarism is that a lot of students don't completely understand what it is. *Plagiarism* is a fancy word that simply means taking someone else's work or ideas and passing them off as your own. Fun fact: The word *plagiarism* comes from the Latin word for *kidnapping.* You probably get the picture.

It's hard to believe that anybody *really* thinks it's okay to cut and paste whole sentences from the Internet into their essays. But given that some people don't think twice about downloading copyrighted music tracks and videos, maybe the concept of "borrowing" isn't as clear as it used to be. The fact remains that copying or paraphrasing anything off the Internet, or from any other source, and using it without citing the source is cheating.

Plagiarizing with intent is one thing. But many college students get convicted of plagiarism simply because they forget to define which parts of an essay are their own and which parts belong to another author.

How *Not* to Cheat: 8 Essential Tips

1. Don't procrastinate. Here's the deal: If you want to write a thorough and honest essay, you need to start early. College papers aren't like movie reviews. You're required to do lots of outside research on your topic. Then you have to weed through it all to figure out what's valuable. Next, you have to incorporate the highlights into an outline, a first draft, and, ultimately, an original work that's all your own. All of that takes time. If you leave things too late, you'll be more tempted to cheat.

2. Don't muddle your notes. It's vital that you keep your own writing separate from the material you've gathered from other sources. Why? Because it's surprisingly easy to mistake someone else's words for your own, especially after you get 2 hours into writing and your brain turns numb. So document everything. Be obsessive about this.

3. Be a stickler for footnotes. It happens all the time: At the end of an essay, a student provides a full bibliography listing all the works he or she has cited. But in the paper itself, there are no references to be found. Without footnotes, you've made it impossible for your instructor to tell the difference between your writing and your references.

4. Familiarize yourself with the proper formatting for a research paper. The MLA style is pretty much standard. If your instructor requires a different style, he or she will let you know. If you need to learn the basic guidelines and rules for citations, *The Owl* at Purdue University is a great source—well written and user-friendly (visit **http://owl.english .purdue.edu/**). You might also want to speak to a reference librarian. Reference librarians have a graduate degree in gathering research, and they can be some of your biggest allies in college. Alternately, pay a visit to the writing center on campus, or talk to your instructor for advice.

5. Be sure to list all of your research sources in your bibliography. They should run alphabetically, in proper MLA format.

6. Master the art of paraphrasing. Paraphrasing means to restate someone else's ideas or observations in your own words. You don't have to put the text in quotation marks, but a citation acknowledging the original source is still essential.

7. If you need help, seek it early. This sounds painfully obvious, but it's important to go to the writing center or the librarian *well before your paper is actually due.* Proofreading takes time, and chances are, your paper will need more than a few tweaks.

8. If you hand something in and then realize that you used material without giving credit to the source, alert your instructor to your mistake immediately. Don't just hope it will slip through. Better to risk half a grade point on one essay than your whole college career.

quickly because his mind was primed for the task. As a result, he had time to polish his work before the first draft.

You can use a similar process. Begin writing the day you get the assignment, even if it's only for 10 or 15 minutes. That way, you won't be confronting a blank screen or piece of paper later. Write something on the assignment every day; the more you write, the better you'll write. Dig for ideas. *Reject nothing* at first, and then revise later. Read good writing; it will help you find your own writing style. Above all, know that becoming a better thinker and writer takes hard work, but practice can make it nearly perfect.

Choosing the Best Way to Communicate with Your Audience

OUTSIDE CLASS: Ask students to bring in examples of their e-mail messages.

IN CLASS: Discuss how e-mail has affected the ways in which we write and communicate.

Before you came to college, you probably spent much more time writing informally than writing formally. Think about all the time you've spent writing e-mails, *Facebook* and blog comments, text messages, and "tweets." Now think about all the time you've spent writing papers for school or work. Typically, writing for wired communications is informal. This can be a detriment to your writing skills. The grammar and structure of e-mail and other types of electronic communication resemble a conversation instead of a formal piece of writing. Additionally, communications via text messaging often use spelling and grammar conventions all their own. As a shortcut, people often condense text messages by using abbreviations such as "brb," "lol," "y?," and "ttyl." They are abbreviated for good reason—imagine how long it would take to type this sentence into a text message. The downside of these shortcuts is that they have gradually crept into our writing habits and caused many of us to become careless in our formal writing. It is important to be aware of when it's okay to be sloppy and when you have to be meticulous.

Electronic communication does not convey emotions as well as face-to-face or even telephone conversations do. Electronic communication lacks vocal inflection, visible gestures, and a shared environment. Your correspondent might have difficulty telling whether you are serious or kidding, happy or sad, frustrated or euphoric. Sarcasm is particularly dangerous to use in electronic messages. Therefore your electronic compositions will be different from both your paper compositions and your speech.

IN CLASS: Discuss with students the implications of different audiences when sending e-mail. Ask how they would send an e-mail to a friend versus sending one to a professor. Discuss the difference between formal and informal e-mailing.

Being aware of the differences between formal writing and informal writing will help you build appropriate writing skills for college work. How would you write an e-mail to friends telling them about the volunteer work you did this past weekend? How would you write that same e-mail to a potential employer who might hire you for your first job after college? Another way to improve your writing is to consider the reader's point of view. For the next week, before sending any *Facebook* messages, e-mails, or text messages, reread them and consider how the people who will receive them will perceive your tone. What

YOUR TURN

Have you ever sent or received an e-mail or text message that could be interpreted in more than one way? What did you learn from that experience?

kind of mood will they think you are in? Will they feel that you are happy to have them as a friend? In how many different ways might your message be interpreted?

Writing for class projects might be a challenge at first. Visit your institution's writing center when you are starting to work on your paper. Professional staff and trained peer consultants who work in writing centers are available to help students express their ideas clearly through writing. Ask your instructor for examples of papers that have received good grades. You might also ask your instructor to help you review your writing after you have worked with the writing center. Most important, you can practice by using a correct writing style when text messaging. You'll find that your friends won't fault you for it. (Have you ever seen a text asking you to "pls stop using proper grammar"?) Since you spend more time with online forms of communication, it's a great way to get real-world practice in the art of academic writing.

SPEAKING

The advice about writing also applies to speaking in public. The major difference, of course, is that you not only have to write the speech, you also have to present it to an audience. Because many people believe that fear of public speaking ranks up there with the fear of death, you might be thinking: What if I plan, organize, prepare, and rehearse, but calamity strikes anyway? What if my mind goes completely blank, I drop my note cards, or I say something totally embarrassing? Remember that people in your audience have been in your position and will understand your anxiety. Just accentuate the positive, rely on your wit, and keep speaking. Your recovery is what they are most likely to recognize; your success is what they are most likely to remember. The guidelines in this chapter can help you improve your speaking skills significantly, including losing your fear of speaking publicly.

Preparing a Speech

Successful speaking involves six fundamental steps:

Step 1. Clarify your objective.
Step 2. Analyze your audience.
Step 3. Collect and organize your information.
Step 4. Choose your visual aids.
Step 5. Prepare your notes.
Step 6. Practice your delivery.

STEP 1. CLARIFY YOUR OBJECTIVE

Begin by identifying what you want to accomplish. Do you want to persuade your listeners that your campus needs additional student parking? Inform

IN CLASS: Review college core requirements to determine whether a communications or speech course is mandated. If it is, show the students the course description, and discuss why speech and communication skills are important as students become successful professionals.

IN CLASS: If you asked your students to bring in professional job descriptions to discuss the importance of writing, ask them to review the job descriptions again and see how many of them also require strong speaking and communication skills. Ask students why these jobs require such skills. Remind students that they will need both types of skills when they apply for a job. Well-written résumés will help win them an interview, and good communication will help win them the job.

IN CLASS: Ask students whether they have ever attended a bad presentation. Ask them to describe the negative characteristics of those presentations. Write these characteristics on the board. Follow up by having students brainstorm solutions that could have improved the presentations. This should give you a lead-in to discussing the six steps to successful speaking.

■ RETENTION STRATEGY: For some students, formal public speaking is a terrifying activity, and they will do everything they can to avoid giving a class presentation. Give students the opportunity to practice in front of you or in front of the class, and help them understand the link between developing these skills and getting and keeping a job.

your listeners about the student government's accomplishments? What do you want your listeners to know, believe, or do when you are finished?

STEP 2. ANALYZE YOUR AUDIENCE

You need to understand the people you'll be talking to. Ask yourself:

- **What do they already know about my topic?** If you're going to give a presentation on the health risks of fast food, you'll want to find out how much your listeners already know about fast food so you don't risk boring them or wasting their time.
- **What do they want or need to know?** If your presentation will be about fast food and health, how much interest do your classmates have in nutrition? Would they be more interested in some other aspect of college life?
- **Who are my listeners?** What do the members of your audience have in common with you? How are they different from you?
- **What are their attitudes toward me, my ideas, and my topic?** How are they likely to feel about the ideas you are planning to present? For instance, what are your classmates' attitudes about fast food?

STEP 3. COLLECT AND ORGANIZE YOUR INFORMATION

Now comes the most critical part of the process: building your presentation by selecting and arranging blocks of information. One useful analogy is to think of yourself as guiding your listeners through the maze of ideas they already have to the new knowledge, attitudes, and beliefs you would like them to have. You can apply the suggestions from earlier in the chapter for creating an outline for writing to actually composing an outline for a speech.

STEP 4. CHOOSE YOUR VISUAL AIDS

Research has shown that when visual aids are added to presentations, listeners can absorb 35 percent more information and over time they can recall 55 percent more. You might choose to prepare a chart, show a video clip, write on the board, or distribute handouts. You might also use your computer to prepare overhead transparencies or dynamic *PowerPoint* presentations. As you select and use your visual aids, consider these rules of thumb:

- Make visuals easy to follow. Use readable lettering, and don't overload your audience by trying to cover too much on one slide.
- Explain each visual clearly.
- Allow your listeners enough time to process visuals.
- Proofread carefully. Misspelled words hurt your credibility as a speaker.
- Maintain eye contact with your listeners while you discuss the visuals. Don't turn around and address the screen.

A fancy *PowerPoint* slideshow can't make up for inadequate preparation or poor delivery skills, but using clear, attractive visual aids can help you organize your material and help your listeners understand what they're hearing. The quality of your visual aids and your skill in using them can contribute to making your presentation effective (see Figure 10.3).

FIGURE 10.3

Examples of Good and Bad Presentation Slides

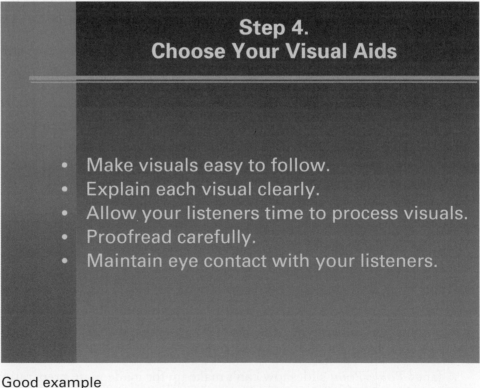

Bad example

Good example

STEP 5. PREPARE YOUR NOTES

If you are like most speakers, having an entire written copy of your speech in front of you might tempt you to read much of your presentation. Even if you can resist that temptation, your presentation could sound canned. On the other hand, your memory might fail you, so speaking without any material at all could be risky. A better strategy is to memorize only the introduction and conclusion of your speech so that you can maintain eye contact during the rest of your speech and thus build rapport with your listeners.

The best speaking aid is a minimal outline, carefully prepared, from which you can speak extemporaneously. Rehearse thoroughly in advance, and you'll be better prepared for how and when you want to present your points. Because you are speaking from brief notes, your words will be slightly different each time you give your presentation. That's okay; you'll sound prepared but natural. You might want to use some unobtrusive note cards. If so, it's not a bad idea to number them, just in case you accidentally drop the stack; this has happened to the best of speakers! When you become more comfortable with speaking, you might decide to let your visuals serve as notes. A paper copy of the *PowerPoint* slides can also serve as your basic outline. Eventually, you might find that you no longer need notes.

STEP 6. PRACTICE YOUR DELIVERY

As you rehearse, form a mental image of success rather than one of failure. Practice your presentation aloud several times beforehand to harness that energy-producing anxiety.

Begin a few days before your target date, and continue until you're about to present it. Rehearse aloud. Talking through your speech can help you much more than thinking through your speech. Practice before an audience—your roommate, a friend, your dog, even the mirror. Talking to something or someone helps simulate the distraction that listeners cause. Consider recording or videotaping yourself to help you pinpoint your own mistakes and to reinforce your strengths. If you ask your practice audience to critique you, you'll have some idea of what changes it might be helpful to make.

> ### YOUR TURN
>
> Think about public speakers you have heard either in person or on TV. Which ones were the most effective? Why? What are some of the specific ways in which the best public speakers communicate with an audience?

OUTSIDE CLASS: Assign students to groups, and have each group select a topic and prepare a short (5-minute) speech that one member of the group will deliver. Ask the students to follow the six steps to successful speaking and document the process.

IN CLASS: Have group members present their short speech, and have the students share results of the process.

Using Your Voice and Body Language

OUTSIDE CLASS: Ask students either to attend a speech on campus or to watch a speech on TV and to observe and comment on voice and body language.

Let your hands hang comfortably at your sides, reserving them for natural, spontaneous gestures. Unless you must stay close to a fixed microphone, plan to move comfortably and casually around the room. Some experts suggest that you change positions between major points to punctuate your presentation, signaling to your audience, "I've finished with that point; let's shift topics."

Body Language

Your posture and body language can add to or distract from the effectiveness of your oral presentations. Be sure to stand up straight. Unlike this student, don't lean on the podium, and keep your hands at your side or use them to emphasize the points you are making. Eye contact with the listeners is extremely important in U.S. culture and will let your audience know that you are confident and in control.

Following are some other tips for using your voice and body language:

- Make eye contact with as many listeners as you can. This helps you to read their reactions, demonstrate confidence, and establish command.

- A smile helps to warm up your listeners, although you should avoid smiling excessively or inappropriately. Smiling through a presentation on world hunger would send your listeners a mixed message.

- As you practice your speech, pay attention to the pitch of your voice, your rate of speaking, and your volume. Project confidence and enthusiasm by varying your pitch. Speak at a rate that mirrors normal conversation—not too fast and not too slow. Consider varying your volume for the same reasons you vary pitch and rate: to engage your listeners and to emphasize important points.

- Pronunciation and word choice are important. A poorly articulated word (such as *gonna* for *going to*), a mispronounced word (such as *nuculer* for *nuclear*), or a misused word (such as *anecdote* for *antidote*) can quickly erode your credibility. Check meanings and pronunciations in a dictionary if you're not sure, and use a thesaurus for word variety. Fillers such as *um*, *uh*, *like*, and *you know* are distracting, too.

- Consider your appearance. Convey a look of competence, preparedness, and success by dressing professionally.

The GUIDE Checklist

Imagine you've been selected as a campus tour guide for next year's prospective first-year students and their families who are visiting your campus. Picture yourself in front of the administration building with a group of people assembled around you. You want to get and keep their attention in order to achieve your objective: increasing their interest in your school. Using the GUIDE method shown in Figure 10.4, you would do the following:

THE GUIDE CHECKLIST

G Get your audience's attention

U "You" – don't forget yourself

I Ideas, ideas, ideas!

D Develop an organizational structure

E Exit gracefully and memorably

FIGURE 10.4
The GUIDE Checklist

G: GET YOUR AUDIENCE'S ATTENTION

You can relate the topic to your listeners: "Let me tell you what to expect during your college years here—at the best school in the state." Or you can state the significance of the topic: "Deciding which college to attend is one of the most important decisions you'll ever make." Or you can arouse their curiosity: "Do you know the three most important factors that students and their families consider when choosing a college?"

You can also tell a joke (but only if it relates to your topic and isn't offensive or in questionable taste), startle the audience, tell a story, or ask a rhetorical question (a question that is asked to produce an effect, especially to make an assertion, rather than to elicit a reply). Regardless of which method you select, remember that a well-designed introduction must not only gain the attention of your listeners, but also develop rapport with them, motivate them to continue listening, and preview what you are going to say during the rest of your speech.

U: "YOU"—DON'T FORGET YOURSELF

In preparing any speech, don't exclude the most important source of your presentation: you. Even in a formal presentation, you will be most successful if

IN CLASS: Show a tape of a speech in class. Have students critique the speech using the GUIDE checklist (Figure 10.4). Follow up with a discussion.

OUTSIDE CLASS: Have students select a familiar topic and follow the GUIDE checklist to develop a short presentation. Have students document their strategy for each step.

IN CLASS: As each student presents in class, have the other students evaluate the presentation by confirming whether the speaker completed each step. Provide verbal feedback by pointing out the strongest feature of the presentations. This activity is intended to increase confidence by following a process.

you develop a comfortable style that's easy to listen to. Don't play a role. Instead, be yourself at your best, letting your wit and personality shine through.

I: IDEAS, IDEAS, IDEAS!

Create a list of all the possible points you could make. Then write them out as conclusions you want your listeners to accept. For example, imagine that on your campus tour for prospective new students and their parents, you want to make the following points:

Tuition is reasonable.

The faculty is composed of good teachers.

The school is committed to student success.

College can prepare you to get a good job.

Student life is awesome.

The campus is attractive.

The library has great resources.

The campus is safe.

Faculty members conduct prestigious research.

This college is the best choice.

For a typical presentation, most listeners can process no more than five main points. After considering your list for some time, you decide that the following five points are crucial:

- Tuition is reasonable.
- The faculty is composed of good teachers.
- The school is committed to student success.
- The campus is attractive.
- The campus is safe.

Try to generate more ideas than you think you'll need so that you can select the best ones. As with writing, don't judge your ideas at first; rather, think up as many possibilities as you can. Then use critical thinking to decide which are most relevant to your objectives.

As you formulate your main ideas, keep these guidelines in mind:

- **Main points should be parallel if possible.** Each main point should be a full sentence with a construction similar to that of the others. A poor, *nonparallel* structure might look like this:

  1. Student life is awesome. (a full-sentence main point)
  2. Tuition (a one-word main point that doesn't parallel the first point)

  For a *parallel* second point, try instead:

  2. Tuition is low. (a full-sentence main point)

- **Each main point should include a single idea.** Don't crowd main points with multiple messages, as in the following:

  1. Tuition is reasonable, and the campus is safe.
  2. Faculty members are good teachers and researchers.

Ideas rarely stand on their own merit. To ensure that your main ideas work, use a variety of supporting materials. The three most widely used forms of supporting materials are examples, statistics, and testimony.

- **Examples** include stories and illustrations, hypothetical events, and specific cases. They can be compelling ways to dramatize and clarify main ideas, but make sure they're relevant, representative, and reasonable.

- **Statistics** are widely used as evidence in speeches. Of course, numbers can be manipulated, and unscrupulous speakers sometimes mislead with statistics. If you use statistics, make sure they are clear, concise, accurate, and easy to understand.

- **Testimony** includes quoting outside experts, paraphrasing reliable sources, and emphasizing the quality of individuals who agree with your main points. When you use testimony, make sure that it is accurate, expert, and credible.

Finally, because each person in your audience is unique, you can best add interest, clarity, and credibility to your presentation by varying and combining the types of support you provide.

D: DEVELOP AN ORGANIZATIONAL STRUCTURE

For example, you might decide to use a chronological narrative approach, discussing the history of the college from its early years to the present. Or you might decide on a problem-solution format in which you describe a problem (such as choosing a school), present the pros and cons of several solutions (the strengths and weaknesses of several schools), and finally identify the best solution (your school!).

Begin with your most important ideas. Writing an outline can be the most useful way to begin organizing. List each main point and subpoint separately on a note card. Spread the cards out on a large surface (such as the floor), and arrange, rearrange, add, and delete cards until you find the most effective arrangement. Then simply number the cards, pick them up, and use them to prepare your final outline.

As you organize your presentation, remember that your overall purpose is to guide your listeners. This means you must not neglect transitions between your main points. For example:

"Now that we've looked at the library, let's move on to the gymnasium."

"The first half of my presentation has identified our recreational facilities. Now let's look at the academic hubs on campus."

"So much for the academic buildings on campus. What about the campus social scene?"

In speaking, as in writing, transitions make the difference between keeping your audience with you and losing them at an important juncture.

E: EXIT GRACEFULLY AND MEMORABLY

Plan your ending carefully, realizing that most of the suggestions for introductions also apply to conclusions.

Whatever else you do, go out with style, impact, and dignity. Don't leave your listeners asking, "So that's it?" Subtly signal that the end is in sight (without the overused "So in conclusion . . ."), briefly summarize your major points, and then conclude confidently.

Speaking on the Spot

Most of the speaking you will do in college and afterward will be on the spot. When your instructor asks your opinion of last night's reading, when another member of your study group asks for your position on an issue, or when your best friend asks you to defend your views, you have to give an impromptu speech.

When you must speak on the spot, it helps to use a framework that allows you to sound organized and competent. Suppose your instructor asks, "Do you think the world's governments are working together effectively to ensure a healthy environment?" One of the most popular ways to arrange your thoughts is through the PREP formula.[5] Short for "preparation," this plan requires the following:

IN CLASS: Have students practice impromptu speeches. Write the PREP formula on the board, and provide a list of common topics. List them in a question format—for example, "Do you think that bars should be smoke-free?" Ask some students to volunteer to stand up and answer the question using the PREP formula. Do not allow the impromptu speeches to turn into a debate. The purpose of this activity is to follow a process in communicating on the spot.

YOUR TURN

Write about your experience of speaking in front of a group. Is public speaking something you enjoy or dread? Are you an anxious or a comfortable speaker? What strategies could you suggest to anyone who wants to become more comfortable when speaking in front of a group?

P: **Point of view**   Provide an overview—a clear, direct statement or generalization: "After listening to yesterday's lecture, yes, I do."

R: **Reasons**   Broadly state why you hold this point of view: "I was surprised by the efforts of the United Nations General Assembly to focus on the environment."

E: **Evidence or examples**   Present specific facts or data supporting your point of view: "For example, the industrialized nations have set stringent goals on air pollution and greenhouse gases for the year 2012."

P: **Point of view, restated**   To make sure you are understood clearly, end with a restatement of your position: "So, yes, the world's governments seem to be concerned and working to improve the situation."

[5]Kenneth Wydro, *Think on Your Feet* (Englewood Cliffs, NJ: Prentice-Hall, 1981). © 1981. Reprinted with permission of the author.

CHECKLIST FOR SUCCESS

COMMUNICATE CLEARLY

☐ **Take the time and effort to develop your writing and speaking skills.** Effective writing and speaking are skills for success in college and in life after college. They are skills that employers desire for all employees.

☐ **Understand the differences between formal and informal communication.** When you are in doubt about what's appropriate, use a more formal writing style.

☐ **Learn and practice the distinct stages of writing:** prewriting, drafting, revising, and polishing. Going through each step will improve the finished product.

☐ **Learn and practice the six fundamental steps of effective speaking:** clarify your objective, analyze your audience, organize your presentation, choose appropriate visual aids, prepare your notes, and practice delivery.

☐ **Ask for feedback from others on your writing and speaking.** You will improve if you accept both positive and negative feedback.

☐ **Before making a formal presentation, practice before a friend or the mirror.** Use eye contact, smile, vary your pitch and rate of speaking, pay attention to word choice and pronunciation, and when you are presenting formally, dress appropriately.

BUILD YOUR EXPERIENCE

1 STAY ON TRACK

Successful college students stay focused. They "stay on track." They know what they have to do to be successful, they set goals, and they monitor their progress toward their goals.

Reflect on what you have learned about college success in this chapter and how you are going to apply the chapter information or strategies in college and in your career. List your ideas.

1. _____

_____

_____

2. _____

_____

_____

3. _____

_____

_____

2 ONE-MINUTE PAPER

This chapter has information that you can use to improve your writing and speaking skills. Which strategies struck you as methods that you could or should put into practice? If your instructor could cover one area in more depth, what would you want it to be?

No matter how well prepared you are in your teaching, what a student hears and understands might not always be what you think you have said. The one-minute paper is a quick and easy assessment tool that will help alert you when students don't understand what was said or discussed in class. The one-minute paper will also give timid students an opportunity to ask questions and seek clarification. Ideally, you should ask for such a paper several minutes before the end of a class. The paper will also help you begin your next class by clarifying points your students seem to be unsure of.

3 APPLYING WHAT YOU HAVE LEARNED

Now that you have read and discussed this chapter, consider how you can apply what you've learned to your academic and personal life. The following prompts will help you reflect on chapter material and its relevance to you both now and in the future.

1. Develop a five-slide *PowerPoint* presentation to introduce yourself to your classmates in a new way. You might include slides that contain points about your high school years, your hobbies, your jobs, your family, and so forth. Use the effective speaking strategies in this chapter to help you outline your presentation. In addition to text, use visuals such as photos, video clips, and art to engage your audience.

2. Before reading this chapter, had you considered the differences between writing an exam response and writing a blog post or responding to someone on *Facebook*? Think about the online communications you've had in the last week. Can you say for certain that you knew exactly who your audience was? Did you send anything that could be misinterpreted or end up being read by someone outside your intended audience? What advice about online communications would you give to other students?

4 BUILDING YOUR PORTFOLIO

In the Public Eye   The media provide ample opportunities for celebrities and public figures to show off their public speaking skills. As you have probably noticed, some celebrities are much better speakers than others. However, being a good public speaker is not important just for those who are "in the public eye." Whether you want to be a movie star or a marine biologist, potential employers tend to put excellent communication skills at the top of their "must have" list.

1. Identify a public figure who, in your opinion, is a good public speaker.

2. In a *Word* document, explain why it is important for that person to speak well. List the specific qualities (e.g., humor, eye contact) that you think make that person a good public speaker. For an example, go to the book's Web site at **bedford.stmartins.com/gardner.**

3. Save your responses in your portfolio. The next time you make a presentation, revisit the chart and spend extra time preparing in the areas in which you rated yourself less than "good."

For more on this topic watch
French Fries Are Not Vegetables and Other College Lessons

WHERE TO GO FOR HELP. . .

ON CAMPUS

> Writing Center Most campuses have one. Frequently, it is found within the English department.

> Learning Assistance Center In addition to help on many other topics, these centers offer help on writing.

> Departments of Speech, Theater, and Communications These offer both resources and specific courses to help you develop your speaking skills.

> Student Activities One of the best ways to learn and practice speaking skills is to become active in student organizations, especially those like the Student Government Association and the Debate Club.

ONLINE

> Writing tips: http://www.uiowa.edu/~histwrit/ website/grammar%20help.htm. The University of Iowa's History Department offers help on common writing mistakes.

> Plain Language Have you ever been confused by government gobbledygook? Here's a guide to writing user-friendly documents for federal employees: **http://www.plainlanguage.gov/howto/ guidelines/FederalPLGuidelines/index.cfm.**

> Toastmasters International offers public speaking tips at **http://www.toastmasters.org/tips.asp.**

MY INSTITUTION'S RESOURCES

_____

_____

_____

_____

_____

_____

_____

_____

CHAPTER 11

Developing Library, Research, and Information Literacy Skills

> ❝ **In college, professors don't check your progress on papers every step of the way. However, I have found that when I do have a question, they are more than willing to meet with me.**

Paul Govoni, 18
Undecided major
Tufts University

When Paul Govoni was looking into going to college, Tufts University in Massachusetts had everything he wanted: It was a midsized university that offered great academics, and it was located close to both Boston and to Cape Cod, where he grew up. It also has a well-regarded research library that he started using almost immediately.

Paul enrolled in a small history seminar called Boston's American Revolution, in which each student signed up for a research project to be presented at the end of the semester. The library was the obvious place to start. Paul quickly found that conducting research for a college-level paper was quite different from his experiences in high school. "Tisch Library is huge and can be quite overwhelming if you don't know how to use it. The biggest difference between high school and college is the amount of resources." Luckily, Paul was able to take advantage of a library tutorial offered at the beginning of the course and his instructor's expertise. "In college, professors don't check your progress on papers every step of the way. However, I have found that when I do have a question, they are more than willing to meet with me."

Paul Govoni ▶

Once Paul was comfortable using the library, he was able to get started on the project. "I checked out several books and found several articles on a database called JSTOR." But he didn't stop there. Because his research was centered around Boston, he was able to head to the city to find even more. "Since I was writing a paper on Paul Revere and the Old State House, I thought the best type of research I could do was actually visit these sites." And his research was put to the test at the end of the semester when the students in the class gave one another a tour of the city. "Another cool thing about this class was that during our final class period we gave a tour of Boston to one another. Each student presented his or her findings when the class walked around Boston together."

Now that Paul has completed his first semester of college, what's his advice to other students facing their first research project? "Use your resources and talk to your professors. When you're writing college papers, *Wikipedia* and Google don't really get the job done."

As Paul's story illustrates, developing the skills to locate, analyze, and use information will significantly enhance your ability to keep up with what is going on in the world; to participate in activities that interest you; and to succeed in college, career, and community. The research skills you learn and use as a student will serve you well as a successful professional. That holds true for whatever career path you choose. Whether you're a student of biology, engineering, business, or public relations, your task in college is to manage information for projects and presentations, both oral and written. In a few years, as a lab technician, a project coordinator, a loss prevention specialist, or a campaign manager for a gubernatorial candidate, your task will be the same: to manage and present information for your employers and clients. All colleges and many companies provide libraries for this purpose. But finding and using information involve more than operating a computer or wandering the stacks. To make sense of the vast amount of information at your fingertips in a reasonable amount of time, you'll need to develop a few key research and information literacy skills.

Information Literacy

During the Agricultural Age, most people farmed. Now only a tiny fraction of us work the land, yet edible goods continue to fill our silos and dairy transfer stations and feedlots. During the Industrial Age, we made things.

> ### YOUR TURN
>
> Why do you think the chapter states that "information literacy is the premier survival skill for the modern world"? Do you agree? Why or why not?

We still do, of course, but automation has made it possible for more goods to be produced by fewer people. Now we live in the Information Age, a name that was created to signify the importance of information in today's economy and our lives.

Most of the global workforce is employed in one way or another in creating, managing, or transferring information. The gross national product (GNP) of the United States is substantially information based. Library science is one of the fastest-growing career opportunities around. Companies such as Google and Yahoo! have earned billions of dollars by simply

■ ASSESSING YOUR STRENGTHS ■

Information literacy is one of the most important skills you will learn in college. There is so much available information that you will also use your critical-thinking skills to determine what's really valid and important. Now that you have read the first section of this chapter, list your experiences in finding and using information successfully.

_____

_____

_____

_____

■ SETTING GOALS ■

What are your most important objectives in learning the material in this chapter? Do you need to improve your information literacy skills? List three goals in this area (e.g., I will visit the library and learn about the resources that relate to my classes).

1. _____

_____

2. _____

_____

3. _____

_____

offering, organizing, and selling information. Put another way, information has value: You can determine its benefits in dollars, and you can compute the cost of not having it.

The challenge is managing it all. There is more information than ever before, and it doubles at rapidly shortening intervals. Because abundance and electronic access combine to produce enormous amounts of retrievable information, people need highly developed **sorting** skills to cope. Information literacy is the premier survival skill for the modern world.

What is information literacy? Simply put, it's the ability to find, interpret, and use information to meet your needs. Information literacy has many facets, among them the following:

- **Computer literacy:** Facility with electronic tools, both for conducting inquiries and for presenting to others what you have found and analyzed.
- **Media literacy:** The ability to think critically about material distributed to a wide audience through television, film, advertising, radio, magazines, books, and the Internet.

sorting The process of sifting through available information and selecting what is most relevant.

■ **Cultural literacy:** Knowing what has gone on and is going on around you. You have to understand the difference between the Civil War and the Revolutionary War, U2 and YouTube, Eminem and M&Ms, or you will not understand everyday conversation.

Information matters. It helps empower people to make good choices. The choices people make often determine their success in business, their happiness as friends and family members, and their well-being as citizens on this planet.

LEARNING TO BE INFORMATION LITERATE

People marvel at the information explosion, paper inflation, and the Internet. Many confuse mounds of information with knowledge and conclude that they are informed or can easily become informed. But most of us are unprepared for the huge number of available sources and the unsorted, unevaluated mass of information that pours over us at the press of a button. What, then, is the antidote for information overload? To become an informed and successful user of information, keep three basic goals in mind:

1. **Know how to find the information you need.** If you are sick, you need to know whose help to seek. If you lose your scholarship, you need to know where to get financial assistance. If you want to win a lawsuit, you need to know how to find the outcomes of similar cases. Once you have determined where to look for information, you'll need to ask good questions and to make educated searches of information systems, such as the Internet, libraries, and databases. You'll also want to cultivate relationships with information professionals, such as librarians, who can help you frame questions, broaden and narrow searches, and retrieve the information you need.

2. **Learn how to interpret the information you find.** It is very important to retrieve information. It is even more important to make sense of that information. What does the information mean? Have you selected a source you can understand? Is the information accurate? Is the source reliable?

3. **Have a purpose.** Even the best information won't do much good if you don't know what to do with it. True, sometimes you'll hunt down a fact simply for your own satisfaction. More often, you'll communicate what you've learned to someone else. You should know not only what form that communication will take—a research paper for a class, a proposal for your boss, a presentation at a hearing—but also what you want to accomplish. Will you use the information to make a decision, develop a new solution to a problem, influence a course of action, prove a point, or something else?

We'll be spending most of this chapter exploring ways to pursue each of these goals.

WHAT'S RESEARCH—AND WHAT'S NOT?

To discover good information that you can use for a given purpose, you'll have to conduct research. You might be working on a college research paper right now—or anxious about one that's ahead of you. As you contemplate these projects, be sure you understand what research involves.

In the past, you might have completed assignments that asked you to demonstrate how to use a library's electronic book catalog, periodical index, e-mail delivery system, government documents collection, map depository, and interlibrary loan service. Or you might have been given a subject, such as ethics, and assigned to find a definition or a related book, journal article, or Web page. If so, what you accomplished was retrieval. And while retrieving information is an essential element of research, it's not an end in itself.

Nor is research a matter of copying passages or finding a handful of sources and patching together bits and pieces without commentary. In fact, such behavior could easily slip into the category of **plagiarism**, a serious misstep that could result in a failing grade or worse (see p. 224). At the very least, repeating information or ideas without interpreting them puts you at risk of careless use of sources that might be new or old, useful or dangerously in error, reliable or shaky, research based or anecdotal, or objective or biased beyond credibility.

Good research, by contrast, is information literacy in action. Let's take up the ethics topic again. If you were assigned to select and report on an ethics issue, you might pick ethics in politics, accumulate a dozen sources, evaluate them, interpret them, select a few and discard a few, organize the keepers into a coherent arrangement, extract portions that hang together, write a paper or presentation that cites your sources, compose an introduction that explains what you have done, draw some conclusions of your own, and submit the results. That's research. And if you learn to do it well, you'll experience the rush that comes with discovery and the pleasure that accompanies making a statement or taking a stand. The conclusion that you compose on the basis of your research is new information!

EMPLOYING INFORMATION LITERACY SKILLS

By the time you graduate, you should have attained a level of information literacy that will carry you through your professional life. The Association of College and Research Libraries has developed the following best practices for the information-literate student. Learn how to apply them, and you'll do well no matter where your educational and career paths take you.

- **Determine the nature and extent of the information needed.** In general, this involves first defining and articulating what information you need, then identifying a variety of potential sources.
- **Access information effectively and efficiently.** Select the most appropriate research methods, use well-designed search strategies, refine those strategies along the way, and keep organized notes on what you find and where you find it.
- **Evaluate information and its sources critically.** As an information-literate person, you'll be able to apply criteria for judging the usefulness

plagiarism The act of taking another person's ideas or work and presenting it as your own. This gross academic misconduct can result in suspension or expulsion, and even the revocation of the violator's college degree.

Many of your students will equate finding information with winning the battle. They might have had instructors who instructed them to "find a book about Abraham Lincoln" or to "locate a magazine article on the future of government in Cuba," and they even might have been told, "Try looking on your own before you ask the librarians for help." These instructors have confused retrieval for research and might have unintentionally deprived students of the opportunity to get help and counsel from information professionals. You know that while locating information is an essential step, how students evaluate, analyze, and use retrieved information will determine whether they have benefited from the experience.

and reliability of both information and its sources. You'll also become skilled at summarizing the main ideas presented by others and comparing new information with what you already know.

- **Incorporate information into your knowledge base and value system.** To do this, you'll determine what information is new, unique, or contradictory and consider whether it has an impact on what's important to you. You'll also validate, understand, or interpret the information through talking with other people. Finally, you'll combine elements of different ideas to construct new concepts of your own making.

- **Use information effectively to accomplish a specific purpose.** You'll apply information to planning and creating a particular product or performance, revising the development process as necessary, and communicating the results to others.

- **Access and use information ethically and legally.** There are economic, legal, and social issues surrounding the retrieval and use of information. You'll need to understand and follow laws, regulations, institutional policies, and etiquette related to copyright and intellectual property. Most important, you should acknowledge the use of information from sources in everything you write, record, or broadcast.[1]

IN CLASS: Information literacy is a skill that is acquired through practice, so the most helpful step a teacher can take at this point is to provide a practice opportunity. Most first-year students have at least one class in which they have to write a research paper. Why not help them get started? Ask a librarian to speak to your class. If students don't have a topic yet, ask the librarian to show them the Library of Congress Subject Headings, the *New York Times* Index, or Facts on File.

Choosing, Narrowing, and Researching a Topic

Assignments that require the use of library materials can take many forms and will come in many of your classes. There are numerous ways to search for information to complete an assignment, and we'll consider some of those later in the chapter. Before you start searching, however, you need to have an idea of what you're looking for.

Choosing a topic is often the most difficult part of a research project. Even if an instructor assigns a general topic, you'll need to narrow it down to a particular aspect that interests you enough to make worthwhile the time and energy you'll spend pursuing it. Imagine, for example, that you have been assigned to write a research paper on the topic of political ethics. What steps should you take?

Your first job is to get an overview of your topic. You can begin by looking at general and specific dictionaries and encyclopedias. To learn something about political ethics, for example, you might consult a political dictionary and the *Encyclopedia of American Political History*. Similar broad sources are available for just about any subject area, from marketing to sports psychology to colonial American literature. Check your library's reference area or consult with a librarian for leads.

Once you've acquired some basic information to guide you toward an understanding of the nature of your topic, you have a decision to make: What aspects of the subject will you pursue? Even if you launch the most

[1]Adapted from *Information Literacy Competency Standards for Higher Education* (2000), http://www.ala.org/ala/acrl/acrlstandards/standards.pdf.

general of inquiries, you will discover very quickly that your topic is vast and includes many related subtopics. If you look up "political ethics" in the Library of Congress Subject Headings or your library's online catalog, for instance, you will discover some choices:

Civil service, ethics	Judicial ethics
Conflict of interests	Justice
Corporations— corrupt practices	Legislative ethics
	Political corruption
Environmental ethics	Political ethics
Ethics, modern	Social ethics
Fairness	
Gifts to politicians	

Because the topic is broad, every one of these headings leads to books and articles on political ethics. What you want is a dozen or so focused, highly relevant hits on an aspect of the topic that you can fashion into a coherent, well-organized essay. Begin by assessing what you already know and asking what you would like to learn more about. Perhaps you know a little about the efforts of lobbyists and political action committees to influence legislation, and you're curious about recent efforts to limit what gifts politicians may accept; in that case you might decide on a three-pronged topic: gifts to politicians, political corruption, and lobbyists.

You can follow these steps to focus any topic. By simply consulting a few general sources, you'll find that you can narrow a broad topic to something that interests you and is a manageable size. From reference works and a quick search of a library catalog, periodicals database, or the Internet you will find definitions, introductory materials, some current and historical examples of your topic in action, and related information. You are now ready to launch a purposeful search.

Get Thee to a Library

How often do you go to your campus library? Beyond having a library tour, have you explored this important academic resource? Although information is available from many sources, the most reliable resource will be a professional librarian, who can guide you to relevant books, articles, and online information.

OUTSIDE CLASS: Create an assignment that shows students how important it is to narrow the topic. They can also practice key word searches as described later in the chapter.

Using the Library

Whenever you have research to do—whether for a class, your job, or your personal life—visit a library. We can't stress this enough. Although the Internet is loaded with billions of pages of information, don't be fooled into thinking it will serve all of your needs. For one thing, you'll have to sort through a lot of junk to find your way to good-quality sources online. More important, if you limit yourself to the Web, you'll miss out on some of the best materials. Although we often think that everything is electronic and can

OUTSIDE CLASS: Many librarians are responsible for user education and will be glad to host a visit from you and your class. Tell the librarian what you want your students to do so that the librarian will know how to conduct the lesson. Provide a copy of your assignment, and the librarian will talk your students through retrieval processes, explaining how to narrow searches, how to select the terms that will deliver hits, how to find general and specific sources, when electronic and print sources are best used, how to recognize and deal with opinion and bias, how to construct good research logic, how to distinguish between database and Internet sources, and how to ask questions.

> ## YOUR TURN
>
> Is the library a necessary resource for learning in college? Why or why not?

be found through a computer, a great deal of valuable information is still stored in traditional formats and is most easily accessed through a library.

Every library has books and journals as well as a great number of items in electronic databases that aren't available on public Web sites. Most libraries also have several other types of collections, such as government documents, microfilm, rare books, manuscripts, dissertations, fine art, photographs, historical documents, maps, and music and films, including archival and documentary productions. Remember that information has been recorded and stored in many forms over the centuries. Libraries maintain materials in whatever form they were first produced and provide access to these materials for free.

TAKING ADVANTAGE OF EVERYTHING YOUR LIBRARY HAS TO OFFER

Books and periodicals are essential, but a college or university library is far more than a document warehouse. For starters, most campus libraries have Web sites that offer lots of help for students. Some provide guidelines on writing research papers, conducting online searches, or navigating the stacks. And all of them provide invaluable services to students and faculty members, including virtual spaces for accessing library holdings and the Web, physical spaces where you can study in quiet or meet with other students, and perhaps even social and entertainment programs.

Of course, no one library can possibly own everything you might need, so groups of libraries share their holdings with each other. If your library does not have a journal or book that looks promising for your project, the interlibrary loan department will be happy to borrow the materials for you. In most cases you can expect to receive the materials in as little as a few days, but it's always a good idea to identify and request what you might need from other libraries as far in advance as possible, in case the material is in high demand.

Are you a commuter or distance education student who cannot easily visit your college library in person? Most libraries provide proxy access to their electronic materials to students off campus. Usually, the library's home page serves as an electronic gateway to its services, which may include the following:

- A searchable catalog of the library's physical holdings
- Electronic databases, some of which let you access the full text of newspaper, magazine, and journal articles from your computer
- Interlibrary loan requests
- Course reserve readings
- Downloadable e-books
- Indexes of Web sites that have been carefully screened for reliability and relevance to particular subject areas
- Online chats with librarians who can help you in real time

To learn more, poke around your library's Web site, or e-mail or phone the reference desk.

TECH TIP CHECK YOUR ENGINE

1 ▶ THE PROBLEM

You understand the basics of online research but don't know how to apply it to an academic setting.

2 ▶ THE FIX

Learn what research passes scholarly muster: peer-reviewed academic journals (e.g., the *Harvard Business Review*), government Web sites (which usually end in .gov), or newspaper Web sites (like the *New York Times* or the *Washington Post*).

3 ▶ HOW TO DO IT

Unlike the examples above, much of the information you find online isn't objective or factual; it's a digital free-for-all out there. When digging for academic research, you need to be fanatically picky and filter out all the garbage. That's called critical thinking, and it's what college is all about.

Your college library offers free access to a wealth of academic databases, LexisNexis, e-journals, etc. If you have questions about how to use them (and about what kinds of materials qualify as academic research in general), make an appointment with a reference librarian. In 30 minutes you'll probably be smarter than anyone else in your class.

Ask a Reference Librarian

SEARCH BY...	EXAMPLES	WHAT YOU GET
Key words separated by a space or a plus sign	sports + nutrition	Search results that contain both of the required words—*sports* and *nutrition*—in any order
Key words separated by the word *OR*	Patton OR warfare OR WWII	Search results that contain the word *Patton* or *warfare* or *WWII*
Key words plus words in brackets	Miami Florida [tourism OR hospitality]	Search results that contain both of the required words, *Miami* and *Florida*, and either the word *tourism* or *hospitality*
Key words and a minus sign	impressionism – Monet	Search results that feature the word *impressionism* but NOT *Monet*
Framing key words with asterisks	*Russian Revolution*	Search results that include the exact phrase *Russian Revolution*
Using an asterisk for a wildcard search	Gene*	Search results that include any word that starts with *gene*—genealogy, genetics, genesis, Gene Simmons, etc.

GOOD TO KNOW

Whatever online search engine you use (AltaVista, Bing, Google, Google Scholar, Yahoo, etc.), there are tricks to refining your search.

PERSONAL BEST

How to avoid Internet plagiarism: By now, you probably know that you can't cut and paste whole sentences from the Internet into your essays. (Professors have high-tech software to catch you, and the penalties range from an F on your paper to an F for your course to actual suspension or even expulsion.)

KEY TIPS

1. **Don't procrastinate.** If you leave a big paper till the last minute, you'll be more tempted to cut and paste, and less scrupulous about footnotes.

2. **Avoid *unintentional cheating*.** Whenever you copy online research into your notes, be sure to add a URL in brackets at the end. While you're at it, place quotation marks around all cited materials, or highlight them in a bright color. It's surprisingly easy to forget which words are your own and which words came from another author.

3. **When in doubt, footnote.** Paraphrasing anything off the Internet, or from any other source, and using it without attribution is cheating. Most colleges have a zero-tolerance policy on the subject.

Where Do You Work Out?

Look for ways to balance your life so that you give your body a workout in the gym and your brain a workout in the library.

Libraries also have a wide variety of physical spaces for students and faculty members to use. From individual study tables to private group rooms to comfortable chairs tucked in quiet corners, you should be able to find a study area that suits you and your needs. You might also discover places to eat, socialize, take in a movie or an art exhibit, check your e-mail and social networking page, search the Web, type your papers, make photocopies, edit videos, give presentations, hold meetings, or take a much-needed nap.

Be sure to use the handouts and guides that are available at the reference desk or online. You will also find tutorials and virtual tours that will help you to become familiar with the collections, services, and spaces available at your library.

IN CLASS: Share information with your students on what is available in your campus library.

ASKING A LIBRARIAN

Of all the resources available in a library, the most useful—and often the least used—are the people who staff it. Librarians thrive on helping you. If you're not sure how to start a search, if you're not successful in your first attempts at retrieving information, or if you just need some ideas about what you might try as you pursue a research project, ask a librarian. Librarians are information experts who are trained to assist and guide you to the resources you need. The librarians who work in the reference area or supervise the computer stations might look busy. But they are busy helping people with projects much like yours. You are not interrupting when you ask for assistance, and with rare exceptions, any librarian will be delighted to help you.

You can contact a reference librarian in several ways. E-mail a query, and you are likely to receive a quick reply. Or call the reference desk to ask a question, such as "Do you have a copy of the report *Problems with the*

Presidential Gifts System?" You can have a "live chat" online with a library staffer in real time. And of course, you can visit the reference desk in person or make an appointment for a tutorial or consultation. (Hint: You will be most successful if you bring a copy of your assignment and any written instructions you have to your meeting. Tell the librarian what you have tried—if anything.) Remember that there are no silly questions. A good librarian will treat your inquiries with respect.

The information professionals at your library are authorities on how to find information. Most important, they not only know where to find it, but also have the wonderful ability to help you use information to meet your needs, solve problems, provide explanations, open up new possibilities, and ultimately create new knowledge.

IN CLASS: Have your students select a method to contact a librarian and ask a question. Either assign each student a question or have students develop their own. Follow up with a short discussion about their experiences in contacting a librarian.

Electronic Resources

Online catalogs, periodical databases, and the World Wide Web allow you to quickly and easily locate materials in the vast universe of information. Learning how to use these resources efficiently will save you time and improve your odds of finding the information that best suits your needs.

LIBRARY CATALOGS

The card catalogs that were once common in libraries have been replaced by OPAC (online public access catalogs). These electronic catalogs tell you what books, magazines, newspapers, videos, and other materials are available in a particular library. They might also provide abstracts of the information presented in those materials, tables of contents for individual entries, and related search terms. Typically, they'll provide an identifying number that tells you where in the stacks to locate a particular document. A catalog might also inform you whether an item is already checked out and, if so, when it's due back. The catalog will also allow you to put the material on hold or give you the option of requesting it through interlibrary loan.

You can search the catalogs through terminals at the library or from your home computer or a laptop. The simplest way to search a catalog is by key word (see the guidelines for conducting an effective search on pp. 219–20). You might also search by subject, author, title, date, or a combination of these elements. Be sure to spend a few minutes on the catalog's help or FAQ page, which will guide you through the options and demonstrate ways to customize your search terms. Each system has its own preferences.

PERIODICAL DATABASES

A library catalog helps you search for books and the titles of magazines and journals owned by a particular library. By contrast, periodical databases let you hunt down articles published in hundreds (even thousands) of newspapers, magazines, and scholarly journals. Some databases might provide a full-text copy of the article as part of the record returned from your search; other times you'll have to use the information in the record to find a physical copy in your library or request it through interlibrary loan.

Subscription services such as EBSCOHost, LexisNexis, and Gale Research compile and maintain electronic periodical databases. These are not free to the general public and must be accessed through a library. (Ask at the circulation desk for a barcode number and PIN, which will allow you to access your library's databases from remote terminals.) Most libraries subscribe to multiple databases and subdivide them by broad general categories such as Humanities, Social Sciences, Science and Technology, Business, Health and Medicine, Government Information, or by major. Under "Social Sciences," for example, you might find International Political Science Abstracts (PAIS), America: History and Life, and over twenty other databases. There are also multidisciplinary databases, such as Academic Search Premier, InfoTrac, and Reader's Guide to Periodical Literature, that provide excellent material on most topics you will encounter during your first year of college.

Databases have their own specialties and different strengths, so you'll want to select the best ones for your particular subject or topic. Check your library's subscription list for an overview of what's available, and don't hesitate to ask a librarian to make recommendations about which databases are most relevant to your needs.

Information in a database is usually stored in a single location or on a server that is owned by the subscription service company. Human beings, not computers, do the indexing, so you can be fairly sure the information in a database meets certain criteria for inclusion, such as accuracy, timeliness, and authoritativeness. And because most of the material indexed in a database originally appeared in print, you can be fairly certain that it was reviewed for quality by other scholars or an editorial staff.

<aside>
IN CLASS: Students need to understand that knowing where to look for specific information is important. Use an analogy to illustrate that there are different tools (or databases) for different resources. For example, you wouldn't go to the grocery store to buy lumber. Not everything is available in the same location. This is why it's important that students ask their professor or a librarian where to look. Also point out that many libraries have database lists based on subject. It is helpful for students to look not only for their topics but also for subjects under which their topics might fall.
</aside>

THE WORLD WIDE WEB

Searching the Web is a totally different story. The material retrieved by Googling is an aggregation of information, opinion, and sales pitches from the vast universe of servers around the globe. Anybody can put up a Web site, which means you can't be sure of the Web site owner's credibility and reliability. The sources you find on the Web might be written by anyone—a fifth grader, a distinguished professor, a professional society, or a biased advocate.

A recent Google search on the subject "political corruption," for instance, generated over 10 million hits. The first page yielded some interesting results:

A collection of links on politics and political corruption

A Libertarian Party legislative program on political corruption

Two Amazon.com ads

A site that offers "research" on gambling and political corruption

A university site offering research on political corruption in Illinois

These varied results demonstrate that one must be alert when examining Internet sources. Mixed in with credible scholarship on this topic are sales promotions, some arguments against gambling, and useful links to other sources. It isn't always easy to evaluate the quality of Internet sources. Check pages 220–23 in this chapter for some helpful strategies you can use to determine whether a source is credible and authentic.

GUIDELINES FOR EFFECTIVE SEARCHES

Most searches of catalogs and databases are done by using key words. A key word is a single word that would appear in a discussion of the topic you are investigating. Other systems permit searching of phrases. A few databases and Web search engines allow a natural language search, in which you can ask a question or type in a sentence that describes what you are looking for. Some databases, such as the *New York Times* Index and ERIC (Education Resources Information Center), have their own approved lists of subject terms that you should consult before searching. Be careful to choose search terms that are relevant to your investigation; this will help you retrieve material you can use. And don't forget that a librarian can help you with this.

To become a successful and savvy user of electronic resources, follow these guidelines:

- **Consult the Help or FAQs link** the first time you use any catalog, database, or search engine to learn specific searching techniques. You will get the best results if you use the tips and strategies suggested by the database provider.

- **Write out your topic or problem as a statement or question.** "Is it right for politicians to take gifts from lobbyists?" Or "The influence of lobbyists or PACs has dramatically changed American political ethics." Doing so will help you identify potentially useful key words.

- **Understand Boolean operators.** Boolean operators are the words *and*, *or*, and *not*. The Bowling Green State University Library Web site describes these terms this way:

    A search for rock AND roll will locate all records containing both the word *rock* and the word *roll*. It will locate items about rock and roll music. It might also locate records that contain both words in a different context, such as "It recommends you roll the rock quickly."

    A search for rock OR roll will locate all records containing either the word *rock* or the word *roll*—not necessarily both. It will retrieve items about bakery rolls, tumbling, rocks, music, gemstones, etc.

    A search for rock NOT roll will locate records containing the word *rock* but NOT the word *roll*. It will retrieve items about rocks, gemstones, diamonds, etc.[2]

- **Write down several terms or synonyms for your topic** so that if one search does not yield any useful hits, you have some backup terms on hand. It's also a good idea to search more than one database or engine; different ones might pull up dramatically different sources.

- **Limit your search.** You can often limit a search by date, language, journal name, full text, or word(s) in title. If you still get too many hits, add more search terms.

> **YOUR TURN**
>
> Talk to a faculty member, a parent, or an older friend who went to college. Ask this person how he or she conducted research before the Internet. Write a short review of the strategies used by former generations to access and use information.

[2]http://www.bgsu.edu/colleges/library/infosrv/lue/boolean.html.

IN CLASS: Most of your students have probably conducted a search on the Web. You can ask the class to share what kinds of searches they do. Discuss their thoughts on how valuable the Web is for serious research.

OUTSIDE CLASS: Assign an exercise for students to follow these guidelines for electronic searching. Consider allowing students to use a topic for a paper that is due in another class.

- **Expand your search.** If you get too few hits, omit a search term. You can also truncate a word by using an asterisk to retrieve broader results. For instance, *lobby** will search for "lobby," "lobbying," "lobbyist," and "lobbyists."

- **Learn the quirks of the databases or search engines you use often.** Some yield better results from Boolean operators (e.g., "politicians AND lobbyists"); others are more attuned to natural language searches (e.g., "ethics in politics" or "gifts to politicians").

- **Check your library's electronic resources page** to see what else is available online. Most libraries have links to other commonly used electronic reference tools. These include online encyclopedias, dictionaries, almanacs, style guides, biographical and statistical resources, and news sources.

YOUR TURN

How do you find sources for an important paper? Do you go to the first several hits on Google, or do you use a more deliberate process? What strategies can you use to make sure your Internet or library research results in valid information?

Evaluating Sources

It's easy to assume that huge amounts of available information automatically provide knowledge. Some students might at first be excited about receiving 20,800,000 hits from a Google search on political ethics, but shock takes hold when they realize their discovery is utterly unsorted. They might respond by using only the first several hits, irrespective of quality. A more productive approach is to think critically about the usefulness of potential sources by measuring them against three important criteria: relevance, authority, and bias.

RELEVANCE

The first thing to consider in looking at a possible source is how well it fits your needs. That, in turn, will be affected by the nature of your research project and the kind of information you are seeking.

- **Is it introductory?** Introductory information is very basic and elementary. It neither assumes nor requires prior knowledge about the topic. Introductory sources can be useful when you're first learning about a subject. They are less useful when you're drawing conclusions about a particular aspect of the subject.

- **Is it definitional?** Definitional information provides some descriptive details about a subject. It might help you introduce a topic to others or clarify the focus of your investigation.

- **Is it analytical?** Analytical information supplies and interprets data about origins, behaviors, differences, and uses. In most cases it's the kind of information you want.

- **Is it comprehensive?** The more detail, the better. Avoid unsubstantiated opinions, and look instead for sources that consider the topic in depth and offer plenty of evidence to support their conclusions.

"It's a new syndrome we're seeing more of... "Google-itis"."

Google-itis

Search engines such as Google have made finding immediate answers to any question easier than ever before. But be careful: Although some Google hits may be authentic and valuable, others may take you to advertisements or biased reports that don't give you exactly THE answer you were looking for.

- **Is it current?** You should usually give preference to recent sources, although older ones can sometimes be useful (for instance, if your subject is historical or the source is still cited by others in a field).
- **Can you conclude anything from it?** Use the "so what?" test: How important is this information? Why does it matter to my project?

AUTHORITY

Once you have determined that a source is relevant to your project, check that it was created by somebody who has the qualifications to write or speak on the subject. This, too, will depend on your subject and the nature of your inquiry (a fifth grader's opinion might be exactly what you're looking for), but in most cases you'll want expert conclusions based on rigorous evidence.

Make sure you can identify the author and be ready to explain why that author is a reliable source. Good qualifications might include academic degrees, institutional affiliations, an established record of researching and publishing on a topic, or personal experience with a subject. Be wary, on the other hand, of anonymous or commercial sources or those written by someone whose credibility is questionable.

Understand, as well, whether your project calls for scholarly publications, popular magazines, or both. Do you know the difference?

You don't necessarily have to dismiss popular magazines. Many journalists and columnists are extremely well qualified, and their work might well be appropriate for your needs. But as a rule scholarly sources will be more credible.

Scholarly Journals	Popular Magazines
Long articles	Shorter articles
In-depth information on topic	Broad overview of topic
Written by academic experts	Written by journalists or reporters
Graphs, tables, and charts	Photos of people and events
Articles "refereed" or reviewed	Articles not rigidly evaluated
Formally documented	Sources credited informally

BIAS

When you are searching for sources, you should realize that there can be a heavy dose of bias or point of view in some of them. Although nothing is inherently wrong with someone's having a particular point of view, it is dangerous for a reader not to know that the bias is there. A great source for keeping you informed about potential bias is *Magazines for Libraries*,[3] which will tell you about a periodical's editorial and political leanings. *The Nation*, for instance, is generally considered liberal, while *National Review* is conservative.

Some signs of bias indicate that you should avoid using a source. If you detect overly positive or overly harsh language, hints of an agenda, or a stubborn refusal to consider other points of view, think carefully about how well you can trust the information in a document.

> ### YOUR TURN
>
> In your opinion, what newspapers, magazines, or TV networks are biased? Does a biased point of view make you more or less likely to read or watch? Why do you think many people expose themselves only to opinions or viewpoints like their own?

IN CLASS: Lead the class in a discussion of bias and point of view in articles. How can students determine whether the author is biased? What is the role of analytical thinking? You might bring in an opinion article to show students an example.

> ### YOUR TURN
>
> One of the most frequently visited sites on the Web is *Wikipedia*, a collaborative reference work written and maintained by hundreds of volunteers. Most of its articles can be (and have been) edited by anyone with Internet access. What are the pros and cons of using such a site as a source for a research project?

A NOTE ON INTERNET SOURCES

Be especially cautious of material you find online. It is often difficult to tell where something on the Internet came from or who wrote it. The lack of this information can make it very difficult to judge the credibility of the source. And while an editorial board reviews most print matter (books, articles, and so forth) for accuracy and overall quality, it's frequently difficult to confirm that the same is true for information on a Web site—with some exceptions. If you are searching through an online database such as the Human Genome Database or Eldis: The Gateway to Development Information (a poverty database), it is highly likely that documents in these collections have been reviewed. Online versions of print magazines and journals, likewise, have usually been checked out

[3]Cheryl LaGuardia, Bill Katz, and Linda S. Katz, *Magazines for Libraries*, 13th ed. (New Providence, NJ: RR Bowker LC, 2004).

by editors. And information from academic and government Web sites (those whose URLs end in .edu or .gov, respectively) is generally—but not always—trustworthy.

Making Use of What You Find

IN CLASS: Ask students to brainstorm ways to check the reliability of an Internet source. Suggest that they always include references from other media, such as books, periodicals (both popular and scholarly), and specialized databases, in their research.

You have probably heard the saying "Knowledge is power." While knowledge can certainly contribute to power, this is true only if that knowledge is put to use. When you retrieve, sort, interpret, analyze, and synthesize sources from an information center, whether it is the library, a computer database, or the Web, you can produce a product that has power.

But first, you have to decide what form that product will take and what kind of power you want it to hold. Who are you going to tell about your discoveries, and how? What do you hope to accomplish by sharing your conclusions? Remember that a major goal of information literacy is to use information effectively to accomplish a specific purpose (see p. 210). Make it a point to *do* something with the results of your research. Otherwise, why bother?

SYNTHESIZING INFORMATION AND IDEAS

Ultimately, the point of conducting research is that the process contributes to the development of new knowledge. As a researcher, you sought the answer to a question. Now is the time to formulate that answer and share it.

Many students satisfy themselves with a straightforward report that merely summarizes what they found. Sometimes, that's enough. More often, however, you'll want to apply the information to ideas of your own. To do that, first consider all of the information you found and how your sources relate to each other. What do they have in common, and where do they disagree? What conclusions can you draw from those similarities and differences? What new ideas did they spark? How can you use the information you have on hand to support your conclusions? (Refer to Chapter 5 for tips on drawing conclusions from different points of view and using evidence to construct an argument.)

Essentially, what you're doing at this stage of any research project is processing information, an activity known as **synthesis**. By accepting some ideas, rejecting others, combining related concepts, assessing the implications, and pulling it all together, you'll create new information and ideas that other people can use.

synthesis The process of combining separate information and ideas to formulate a more complete understanding.

CITING YOUR SOURCES

At some point you'll present your findings. Whether they take the form of an essay, a formal research paper, a script for a presentation or broadcast, a page for a Web site, or something else entirely, you must give credit to your sources.

Citing your sources serves many purposes. For one thing, acknowledging the information and ideas you've borrowed from other writers shows respect for their contributions; it also distinguishes between other writers' ideas and your own. Source citations demonstrate to your audience that you have based your conclusions on thoughtful consideration of good, reliable evidence. Source citations also provide a starting place for anyone who would like more information or is curious about how you reached your conclusions. Most important, citing your sources is the simplest way to avoid plagiarism.

The particular requirements of source citation can get complicated, but it all boils down to two basic rules. As you write, just remember:

- If you use somebody else's exact words, you must give that person credit.

- If you use somebody else's ideas, even if you use your own words to express those ideas, you must give that person credit.

Your instructors will indicate their preferred method for citation: footnotes, references in parentheses included in the text of your paper, or endnotes. If you're not provided with guidelines or if you simply want to be sure that you do it right, consult a handbook or writing style manual, such as those prepared by the Modern Language Association (*MLA Handbook for Writers of Research Papers*), the American Psychological Association (*Publication Manual of the American Psychological Association*), the University of Chicago Press (*The Chicago Manual of Style*), or the Council of Science Editors (*Scientific Style and Format: The CSE Manual for Authors, Editors, and Publishers*).

ABOUT PLAGIARISM

Several years ago, a serious candidate for the American presidency was forced to withdraw from the race when opponents discovered he had failed to give proper credit to a source he used in one of his speeches. A reporter at a top newspaper was fired for deliberately faking his sources, and a famous historian lost her peers' respect (and a portion of her royalties) when another writer noticed that the historian had included passages from her work in a book without citation.

All three writers were accused of plagiarism, but notice that only the reporter plagiarized on purpose. The political candidate and the historian were probably more guilty of poor note taking than of outright fraud, yet the consequences were just as dire. When information or ideas are put on paper, film, screen, or tape, they become intellectual property. Using those ideas without saying where you got them—even if you do this by mistake—is a form of theft and can cost you a grade, a course, a degree, maybe even a career.

It should go without saying (but we'll say it anyway) that deliberate cheating is a bad idea on many levels. Submitting a paper you purchased from an Internet source or from an individual will cause you to miss out on the discovery and skill development that research assignments are meant to teach. Intentional plagiarism is easily detected and will almost certainly earn you a failing grade, even expulsion.

Although most cases of plagiarism are the result of misunderstanding or carelessness, be aware that "I didn't know" is not a valid excuse. Although your instructors might acknowledge that plagiarism can be an "oops!" thing,

■ RETENTION STRATEGY: For some students, plagiarism is an innocent mistake; for others it is intentional cheating. The penalties for cheating may include academic failure or suspension. Either penalty reduces a student's likelihood of remaining on campus in good standing.

IN CLASS: Students often do not understand the complexities of plagiarism. Begin a discussion by brainstorming the meaning of plagiarism, especially as it relates to Internet sources.

IN CLASS: Some of your students will know about plagiarism; some will have only foggy impressions about what it is and why they should avoid it. Some students will have practiced it, thinking that they were doing nothing wrong. Others might come from a culture in which ideas, once expressed, become the free property of all who want to use them. Get your academic institution's statement about plagiarism, and discuss it with your students. Enforce the stated rules. You will be doing your students, and scholarship, a great favor.

they will still expect you to avoid errors, and they will call you on it if you don't. Luckily, plagiarism is relatively easy to avoid. Most important, always cite your sources. Keep careful notes as you conduct your research, so that later on you don't inadvertently mistake someone else's words or ideas for your own. Finally, be sure to check out your own campus's definition of what constitutes plagiarism, which you will find in the student handbook or in first-year English course materials. And if you have any questions or doubts about what is and isn't acceptable, ask.

CHECKLIST FOR SUCCESS

DEVELOPING RESEARCH SKILLS

☐ **Work to learn "information literacy" skills** because you will be working in the information economy, which uses and produces information. Most all professions that you could prepare for in college require that you be able to find, evaluate, and use information.

☐ **Become comfortable in your campus library.** Use it as a place to read, relax, study, or just be by yourself.

☐ **Accept that research projects and papers are part of college life.** Learn how to do them well. This will teach you how to "research" the information you need in life after college. After all, modern professional life is one big term paper after another!

☐ **Get to know your college librarians.** They are anxious to help you find the information you need. Ask them for help even if they look busy. If possible, get to know one as your personal "library consultant."

☐ **Take courses early in college that require you to do research and use your library skills.** Yes, they will demand more of you, especially in writing, but you will be thankful for them later. Go ahead—Bite the bullet.

☐ **Learn as many new electronic sources as possible.** You must be able to do research and seek the new information you need now and after college by doing more than using Google or *Wikipedia*.

☐ **When you use the ideas of others, it is important to give them credit and then create your own unique synthesis and conclusions.** Someday you will create what we call "intellectual property," and you will want others to give you credit for your ideas.

☐ **Consider becoming an information professional (librarian).** The world as we know it is going to need more and more of them. Explore this potential occupation in your campus's career center. If your campus is a university with a school of library and information science, drop by and see what you can learn.

BUILD YOUR EXPERIENCE

1 STAY ON TRACK

Successful college students stay focused. They "stay on track." They know what they have to do to be successful, they set goals, and they monitor their progress toward their goals.

Reflect on what you have learned about college success in this chapter and how you are going to apply the chapter information or strategies in college and in your career. List your ideas.

1. _____

_____

_____

2. _____

_____

_____

3. _____

_____

_____

2 ONE-MINUTE PAPER

Did the material in this chapter make you think about libraries and research in a new light? What did you find to be the most useful information in this chapter? What would you like to learn more about?

No matter how well prepared you are in your teaching, what a student hears and understands might not always be what you think you have said. The one-minute paper is a quick and easy assessment tool that will help alert you when students don't understand what was said or discussed in class. The one-minute paper will also give timid students an opportunity to ask questions and seek clarification. Ideally, you should ask for such a paper several minutes before the end of a class. The paper will also help you begin your next class by clarifying points your students seem to be unsure of.

3 APPLYING WHAT YOU HAVE LEARNED

Now that you have read and discussed this chapter, consider how you can apply what you have learned to your academic and personal life. The following prompts will help you reflect on chapter material and its relevance to you both now and in the future.

1. It is important to get comfortable with all of the resources in your campus library. Find out where your library keeps archived newspapers on microfiche. Search for a newspaper (such as the *New York Times*) that was published on the day you were born. What was the major headline that day? What movies were playing? What was happening in world news?

2. The importance of using information literacy skills in college is a no-brainer, but think beyond your college experience. How will improving your information literacy skills help you once you are out of college? Think of a career that you are interested in, and describe how you might use those skills in that career.

4 BUILDING YOUR PORTFOLIO

In the Know   Reviewing multiple sources of information can help you to get the whole story. This is especially important when using the Internet as a research tool. While the Internet is becoming a primary source of worldwide news, there is no overarching quality control system for information posted on the Internet. Regardless of where you are gathering your information, you need to read with a discerning eye to make sure the source is credible.

1. Choose a national current event. Carefully read about it in two places:
   a. On your favorite news Web site (e.g., **http://www.cnn.com**).
   b. In a traditional national newspaper (e.g., the *New York Times, Wall Street Journal, Christian Science Monitor*, or *USA Today*). Your campus library or local community library will have these national newspapers, or you can find them on the Web.

2. In a *Word* document, compare and contrast the differences in the way the event was portrayed by the two sources.
   - Are the authors' names or another source provided?
   - Are there clues that the authors are taking a biased stand in reporting? If so, describe these clues.
   - Whom do you think the authors were writing for (intended audience)? For example, were they writing for any reader or for people of a certain age or educational level?
   - Were the facts presented the same way by both the Internet source and the print source? Explain your answer.
   - Did one source cover more details than the other? If so, explain your answer.
   - Were the writers' information sources listed? If so, what were those sources?

3. Save your responses in your portfolio. Use this process as a tool to make sure you use valid resources the next time you are doing research for a project or paper.

For more on this topic watch
French Fries Are Not Vegetables and Other College Lessons

WHERE TO GO FOR HELP. . .

ON CAMPUS

> Your Instructor Be sure to ask your instructor for help with your information search, especially if you need to narrow your topic.

> Library Libraries offer a variety of forms of help, including library orientation sessions, workshops, and, on some campuses, credit-bearing courses to develop your library search and retrieval skills.

> Specialized Libraries/Collections At a large university, it is very common to find multiple libraries that are part of separate schools or colleges. For example, if you are a business administration major at such a university, there will probably be a separate business library that you will need to learn to use in addition to the central library. This is true for many majors.

> Technology Support Centers Many campuses have units staffed by personnel who are responsible for the institution's entire technology infrastructure. These units frequently offer noncredit workshops and help sessions. In addition, many of the depart-

ments in larger universities will have their own separate technology labs and centers where you can work and get assistance. It won't surprise you to find that much of the help provided to students comes from fellow students, who are often ahead of their faculty in these skills. Some campuses also provide such assistance in residence halls, where there might even be a "computing assistant" in addition to the resident assistant.

> Discipline-Based Courses Many academic majors will include specialized courses in discipline-based research methods. You will find these listed in your campus catalog or bulletin. Students don't usually take these courses in their first year, but check them out. If you are interested in credit courses dealing with technology, check out the courses in computer science.

ONLINE

> Research and documenting sources: http://owl .english.purdue.edu/owl/resource/584/02. Purdue University has an excellent resource on documenting sources, both print and electronic.

MY INSTITUTION'S RESOURCES

_____

_____

_____

_____

_____

_____

_____

_____

Preparing for
Success

PART 1

Preparing to
Study

PART 2

Preparing for
Life

PART 3

CHAPTER 12

Making the Right Choice for Majors and Careers

IN THIS CHAPTER YOU WILL EXPLORE

Tips for thriving in the current economy

How majors, interests, and careers are linked—but not always

How to plan a career itinerary for each year of college

The skills employers seek in college graduates

How to search for a job

> ❝ Choose a career and major you will love for the rest of your life. If you are not happy doing it now, you will most likely not be happy doing it twenty years from now.

Megan Henley, 23
English Literature major
Eastern Wyoming College

Megan Henley grew up all over the world, moving with her parents, who were in the military, to places like Germany, Georgia, California, and Kentucky before settling in Wyoming. She graduated from high school in 2006 and decided to take time off from academics before heading to college. She married, had a son, and, now that she is in the process of getting a divorce, has decided to enroll at Eastern Wyoming College and study English literature. She knew she would need a degree to provide for herself and her son, but why English literature? "My favorite classes so far have been English classes. I love the critical-thinking aspects and the ability to write analytically on the topics that are presented in class."

Megan has since taken that love of English and writing and transformed the passion into a career goal. She wants to teach English at either the high school or college level. She plans to finish her two-year degree at Eastern Wyoming College and then transfer to the University of Wyoming or Chadron State College. "In ten years," she says. "I plan to have my master's and a Ph.D. in English and writing and to be teaching."

Megan Henley ▶

When she's not in school or raising her son, Megan takes a little time out to enjoy martial arts and music. She also finds time to work eight hours a week as an information technology (IT) tech on campus, where she updates hardware and software and problem-solves computer glitches. She's lucky enough to have found a major that supports her ultimate career goals. "Choose a career and major you will love for the rest of your life," she says. "If you are not happy doing it now, you will most likely not be happy doing it twenty years from now."

Students come to college for many reasons, but for the majority of them, like Megan, a central purpose of college is gaining the knowledge and skills they will need for future employment. Your success in your work life will often depend on whether the profession or career you think you want to pursue is really right for you. But success in the workplace also depends on your ability to do simple things well, such as being on time, being honest, and doing your best.

IN CLASS: Misconceptions about career inventories and academic majors can cause major concerns. Ask students to make a list—in writing—of career-related concerns they have. Discuss the lists in class, and point students toward the proper resources.

Careers and the New Economy

In your lifetime, companies have restructured to remain competitive. As a result, major changes have taken place in how we work, where we work, and the ways in which we prepare for work while in college. In many ways, the following characteristics define today's economy:

OUTSIDE CLASS: Send students in small groups to research a multinational company such as Procter & Gamble or Coca-Cola. Ask them what they found out about the company's structure, the sorts of positions listed in the company profile, and whether or not the company markets the same brands worldwide.

- **Global.** Increasingly, industries have become multinational, not only moving into overseas markets but also seeking cheaper labor, capital, and resources abroad. Factories around the world built to similar standards can turn out essentially the same products. Your career is bound to be affected by the global economy, even if you never leave the United States. For example, when you call an 800 number for customer service, the person who talks to you might be answering your call in Iowa, Ireland, or India. In his best-selling book *The World Is Flat*, Thomas Friedman reminds his readers that talent has become more important than geography in determining a person's opportunity in life. College graduates in the United States are now competing for jobs with others around the world who are often willing to work longer hours for less money than American workers. And this is true not only in manufacturing jobs, which are routinely being outsourced to other countries, but also in professional occupations such as medicine and accounting.

- **Unstable.** In 2008 and 2009 the world economy suffered a series of events that led to downturns in stock markets, bankruptcies, foreclosures, failing businesses, and lost jobs. Scandals within the highest ranks of major companies and constant mergers and acquisitions of companies have destabilized the workforce. Depending on how long it takes to stabilize the economy in the United States and the rest of the world, your career goals might have to be refocused. Because the global economic situation is changing continuously, it's important to keep up-to-date on the economic situation as it relates to your prospective major and career.

ASSESSING YOUR STRENGTHS

One of the reasons most students go to a college or university is to acquire knowledge they will apply to a career. You may have thought about how your skills and interests will help you prepare for life after college. Now that you have read the first section of this chapter, list the steps you have already taken to find a major and a career that are right for you.

_____

_____

_____

_____

SETTING GOALS

What are your most important objectives in learning the material in this chapter? Do you need to make decisions about a major or a career? List three goals in this area (e.g., I will visit the career center and ask to have an evaluation of my skills and aptitudes so that I will know if I'm heading in the right career direction).

1. _____

_____

2. _____

_____

3. _____

_____

- **Innovative.** The economy depends on creativity in new products and services to generate consumer interest around the world. Especially in times of economic instability, the flexibility and responsiveness of companies to the changing economic climate will affect their ability to survive.

- **Boundaryless.** Teams of workers within an organization need to understand the missions of other teams because they most likely will have to work together. You might be an accountant and find yourself working with the public relations division of your company, or you might be a human resources manager who does training for a number of different divisions and in several different countries. You might even find yourself moved laterally to a unit that has a different function rather than being promoted to a higher position in your organization.

- **Customized.** More and more, consumers are demanding products and services tailored to their specific needs. You have probably noticed the seemingly endless varieties of a single brand of shampoo or cereal crowding store shelves. Such market segmentation requires constant adaptation of ideas to identify new products and services as new customer demands emerge.

RETENTION STRATEGY: Students are well aware of the "unstable" nature of the economy and are very anxious about the future. If they will take this chapter seriously and practice its advice, it may lessen their anxiety and improve their decision making about careers.

OUTSIDE CLASS: Have students work in teams to research where the growth in employment opportunities will be in the future. Assign categories (e.g., service, nonprofit, technology, manufacturing, health care), and ask students to report their findings to the class.

OUTSIDE CLASS: Ask students to find one or two examples of organizations that sponsor noncommercial causes. Ask students why they think companies sponsor such causes and how a company chooses a cause to sponsor.

IN CLASS: Talk about the amount of work you must bring home during the week and on weekends. Explain your attempts to strike a healthy balance between work and play. Ask students to discuss in small groups how their families handle this balance, how the students plan to handle this issue when they join the workforce, or how they do handle it if they are already in the workforce. Ask for comments.

- **Fast.** When computers became popular, people rejoiced because they believed the computer would reduce their workloads. Actually, the reverse happened. Whereas secretaries and other support workers once performed many tasks for executives, now executives design their own *PowerPoint* presentations and format their own documents. For better or worse, "We want it now" is the cry in the workplace, with product and service delivery time cut to a minimum (the "just-in-time" policy). Being fast requires constant thinking outside the lines to identify new approaches to designing and delivering products.

According to *Fast Company* magazine, the new economy has changed many of the rules about work. Leaders are now expected to teach and encourage others as well as to head up their divisions. Careers frequently zigzag into other areas. People who can anticipate the needs of the marketplace are in demand. Change has become the norm. Workers are being urged to continue their learning, and companies are volunteering to play a critical role in the welfare of all people through sponsorship of worthy causes. As the lines between work and the rest of life continue to blur, workers need to find healthy balance in their lives. Bringing work home might be inevitable at times, but it shouldn't be the rule.

As you work at your job, you'll be continually enhancing and expanding your skills and competencies. You can accomplish this on your own by taking evening courses or by attending conferences and workshops your employer sends you to. As you prepare for, continue, or change your career, remember the following:

- **You are, more or less, solely responsible for your career.** At one time, organizations often provided structured ladders that employees could climb in their moves to higher professional levels. In most cases such ladders have disappeared. Companies might assist you with assessments and information on available positions in the industry, but the ultimate task of creating a career path is yours.

- **To advance your career, you must accept the risks that accompany employment and plan for the future.** As organizations continue to restructure, merge, and either grow or downsize in response to economic conditions, you must do your best to prepare for the unexpected. Because you can quickly find yourself unemployed, it will be wise to keep all possible options in mind.

- **A college degree does not guarantee employment.** Of course, with a degree, you'll be able to hunt for more opportunities that are rewarding, financially and otherwise, than if you did not have a degree. But just because you want to work for a certain organization or in a certain field doesn't mean that there will always be a job for you there.

- **A commitment to lifelong learning will help keep you employable.** In college you have been learning a vital skill: how to learn. *Gradus*, the Latin root of "graduation," comes from the phrase *Gradus ad Parnassum*, or "steps to Parnassus," the home of the Muses. To move toward Parnassus means moving to a higher level of knowledge. Your learning has just begun when you receive your diploma.

Now the good news: Hundreds of thousands of graduates find jobs every year, even in recessionary times. Some of them might have to work longer to

What Do You Want to Be?

How do you envision your first job after graduation? Will you be working in a cubicle, behind an executive desk, or out in the fields or forests? As you plan for life after college, consider not only how you want to work, but also how you want to live.

get where they want to be, but persistence pays off. If you start now, you'll have time to build a portfolio of academic and **co-curricular experiences** that will begin to add substance to your career profile.

co-curricular experiences Learning that occurs outside of the classroom, through on-campus clubs and groups, co-op programs, internships, or other means.

Aligning Your Sense of Purpose and Your Career

Chapter 1 in this book suggested that you think very seriously about your purpose for being in college. Here are some additional questions to ask yourself as you continue thinking about why you're at this particular college or university:

- Am I here to find out who I am and to study a subject that I am truly passionate about, regardless of whether it leads to a career?
- Am I here to engage in an academic program that provides an array of possibilities when I graduate?
- Am I here to prepare myself for a graduate program or immediate employment?
- Am I here to obtain specific training in a field that I am committed to?
- Am I here to gain specific skills for a job I already have?

Remember these six simple, one-word questions. They can help you to prepare for a career and obtain that important first job:

Why? Why do you want to be a _____ ? Knowing your goals and values will help you pursue your career with passion and an

RETENTION STRATEGY: The questions on this page are very important for solidifying the connection between a student's sense of purpose for being in college and his or her career choice. Purposeful students are more likely to persist in college.

understanding of what motivates you. When you speak with an interviewer, avoid clichés such as "I'm a people person" or "I like to work with people." Sooner or later, most people have to work with people. And your interviewer has heard this much too often. Instead, be sure that you have crystallized your actual reasons for following your chosen career path. An interviewer will want to know why you are interested in the job, why it feels right for you at this time in your life, and whether you are committed to this career for the future.

Who? Who at your college or university or in your community can help you make career decisions? Network with people who can help you find out what work you want to do. Right now, those people might be instructors in your major, an academic adviser, and perhaps someone at your campus career center. Later, network with others who can help you attain your goal. Someone will almost always know someone else for you to talk to.

How? How will you develop the technical and communications skills required for working effectively? Don't be a technophobe. Learn how to do *PowerPoint* presentations, build Web pages, and create *Excel* spreadsheets. Take a speech course. Work on improving your writing. Even if you think your future job doesn't require these skills, you'll be more marketable with them.

What? What opportunities are available in your preferred career fields? Be aware of the range of job options an employer presents, as well as such threats as a company's decision to **outsource** certain jobs—that is, contracting with an external organization to perform particular functions at a lower cost. Clearly understand the employment requirements for the career field you have chosen. Know what training you will need if you want to remain and move up in your chosen profession.

Where? Where will your preferred career path take you? Will you be required to travel or live in a certain part of the country or the world? Or will job success require that you stay in one location? Although job requirements may change over the course of your lifetime, try to achieve a balance between your personal values and preferences and the predictable requirements of the career you are pursuing.

When? When will you need to start looking for your first job? Certain professions, such as teaching, tend to hire new employees at certain times of the year, generally spring or summer. Determine whether seasonal hiring is common for your preferred career.

CONNECTING YOUR MAJOR AND YOUR INTERESTS WITH YOUR CAREER

Some students are sure about their major when they enter college, but many others are at a loss. Either way, it's okay. At some point, you might ask yourself: Why am I in college? Although it sounds like an easy question to answer, it's not. Many students would immediately respond, "So I can get a

---

IN CLASS: Have students list tasks or goals for Why, Who, How, What, Where, and When, based on their current career plan or one that might interest them. Discuss their responses.

outsource To contract out jobs to an external organization in order to lower costs.

good job or education for a specific career." Yet most majors do not lead to a specific career path or job. You actually can enter most career paths from any number of academic majors. Marketing, a common undergraduate business major, is a field that recruits from a wide variety of majors, including advertising, communications, and psychology. Sociology majors find jobs in law enforcement, teaching, and public service.

DID YOU KNOW?

At the end of their first year, 35% of students decide to change majors and 22% remain undecided about their major.

Today, English majors are designing Web pages, philosophy majors are developing logic codes for operating systems, and history majors are sales representatives and business managers. You do not have to major in science to gain admittance to medical school. Of course, you do have to take the required science and math courses, but medical schools seek applicants with diverse backgrounds. Only a few technical or professional fields, such as accounting, nursing, and engineering, are tied to specific majors.

Exploring your interests is the best way to choose an academic major. If you're still not sure, take the advice of Patrick Combs, author of *Major in Success*, who recommends that you major in a subject about which you are really passionate. Most advisers would agree.

YOUR TURN

Would you describe your major as something you're really passionate about? Why or why not? If your answer is no, why are you pursuing this particular major?

Some students will find they're not ready to select an academic major in the first year. You can use your first year and even your second year to explore your interests and find out how they might connect to various academic programs. Over time, you might make different choices than you would have during your first year.

You can major in almost anything. As this chapter emphasizes, it is how you integrate your classes with your extracurricular activities and work experience that prepares you for a successful transition to your career. Try a major you think you'll like, and see what develops. But keep an open mind, and don't pin all your hopes on finding a career in that major alone. Your major and your career ultimately have to fit your overall life goals, purposes, values, and beliefs.

OUTSIDE CLASS: Have students use the college catalog to check the academic requirements for their major or intended major. As a larger project, consider having them develop a degree plan by tentatively selecting all their courses.

IN CLASS: Discuss the degree plan project in class, and have students share one or two things they learned.

IN CLASS: Require your students to read the academic regulations section in the college catalog. Ask students to write about the academic regulations that (a) they were surprised to discover, (b) they need to know immediately, and (c) they need to remember for future use.

EXPLORING YOUR INTERESTS

John Holland, a psychologist at Johns Hopkins University, developed a number of tools and concepts that can help you organize the various dimensions of yourself so that you can identify potential career choices (see Table 12.1).

Holland separates people into six general categories based on differences in their interests, skills, values, and personality characteristics—in short, their preferred approaches to life. Holland's system organizes career fields into the same six categories. Career fields are grouped according to what a particular career field requires of a person (the skills and personality characteristics most commonly associated with success in those fields) and what rewards those fields provide (interests and values most commonly associated with satisfaction).

TABLE 12.1   Holland Personality and Career Types

Category	Personality Characteristics	Career Fields
Realistic (R)	These people describe themselves as concrete, down-to-earth, and practical doers. They exhibit competitive/assertive behavior and show interest in activities that require motor coordination, skill, and physical strength. They prefer situations involving action solutions rather than tasks involving verbal or interpersonal skills, and they like taking a concrete approach to problem solving rather than relying on abstract theory. They tend to be interested in scientific or mechanical areas rather than the arts.	Environmental engineer, electrical contractor, industrial arts teacher, navy officer, fitness director, package engineer, electronics technician, Web designer
Investigative (I)	These people describe themselves as analytical, rational, and logical problem solvers. They value intellectual stimulation and intellectual achievement, and they prefer to think rather than to act and to organize and understand rather than to persuade. They usually have a strong interest in physical, biological, or social sciences. They are less apt to be people oriented.	Urban planner, chemical engineer, bacteriologist, flight engineer, genealogist, laboratory technician, marine scientist, nuclear medical technologist, obstetrician, quality-control technician, computer programmer, environmentalist, physician, college professor
Artistic (A)	These people describe themselves as creative, innovative, and independent. They value self-expression and relating with others through artistic expression and are also emotionally expressive. They dislike structure, preferring tasks involving personal or physical skills. They resemble investigative people but are more interested in the cultural or the aesthetic than the scientific.	Architect, film editor/director, actor, cartoonist, interior decorator, fashion model, graphic communications specialist, journalist, editor, orchestra leader, public relations specialist, sculptor, media specialist, librarian, reporter
Social (S)	These people describe themselves as kind, caring, helpful, and understanding of others. They value helping and making a contribution. They satisfy their needs in one-to-one or small-group interaction using strong speaking skills to teach, counsel, or advise. They are drawn to close interpersonal relationships and are less apt to engage in intellectual or extensive physical activity.	Nurse, teacher, social worker, genetic counselor, marriage counselor, rehabilitation counselor, school superintendent, geriatric specialist, insurance claims specialist, minister, travel agent, guidance counselor, convention planner
Enterprising (E)	These people describe themselves as assertive, risk taking, and persuasive. They value prestige, power, and status and are more inclined than other types to pursue it. They use verbal skills to supervise, lead, direct, and persuade rather than to support or guide. They are interested in people and in achieving organizational goals.	Banker, city manager, FBI agent, health administrator, judge, labor arbitrator, salary and wage administrator, insurance salesperson, sales engineer, lawyer, sales representative, marketing manager
Conventional (C)	These people describe themselves as neat, orderly, detail oriented, and persistent. They value order, structure, prestige, and status and possess a high degree of self-control. They are not opposed to rules and regulations. They are skilled in organizing, planning, and scheduling and are interested in data and people.	Accountant, statistician, census enumerator, data processor, hospital administrator, insurance administrator, office manager, underwriter, auditor, personnel specialist, database manager, abstractor/indexer

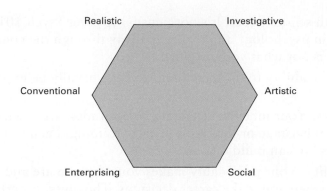

FIGURE 12.1

Holland's Hexagonal Model of Career Fields

Your career choices ultimately will involve a complex assessment of the factors that are most important to you. To display the relationship between career fields and the potential conflicts people face as they consider them, Holland's model is commonly presented in a hexagonal shape (Figure 12.1). The closer the types, the closer the relationships among the career fields; the farther apart the types, the more conflict between the career fields. For instance, individuals with "conventional" and "realistic" characteristics will find many similar characteristics in their career fields. However, careers preferred by "investigative" individuals will have little in common with careers chosen by individuals who are "enterprising."

Holland's model can help you address the problem of career choice in two ways. First, you can begin to identify many career fields that are consistent with what you know about yourself. Once you have identified potential fields, you can use the career library at your college to get more information about those fields, such as daily activities for specific jobs, interests and abilities required, preparation required for entry, working conditions, salary and benefits, and employment outlook. Second, you can begin to identify the harmony or conflicts in your career choices. This will help you to analyze the reasons for your career decisions and be more confident as you make choices.

Never feel you have to make a decision based on the results of only one assessment. Career choices are complex and involve many factors; furthermore, these decisions are reversible. Take time to talk your interests over with a career counselor. Another helpful approach is to shadow an individual in the occupation that interests you to obtain a better understanding of what the occupation entails in terms of skills, commitment, and opportunity.

FACTORS THAT AFFECT CAREER CHOICES

Some people have a definite self-image when they enter college, but most of us are still in the process of defining (or redefining) ourselves throughout life. We can look at ourselves in several useful ways with respect to possible careers:

- **Values.** Today, more than ever, knowing your core values (your most important beliefs) will be important in shaping your career path. In a faltering and unpredictable economy, having a strong rudder will help you steer through the turbulent times.

- **Interests.** Your interests will develop from experiences and beliefs and can continue to develop and change throughout your life. You might be interested in writing for the college newspaper because you wrote for

OUTSIDE CLASS: At the career center, students can seek information about the Holland areas in which they achieved high scores. You might assign an essay in which each student profiles a favorite field in the high-scoring category and evaluates it in terms of interests, skills, aptitudes, personality, life goals, and work values.

IN CLASS: Make the point that focusing on a major in the liberal arts might lead to any number of careers. Advise students to try a major they think they like and see what develops but not to pin all their hopes on finding a career in that major alone.

IN CLASS: Have students jot down five activities they find interesting. Collect their responses, and form small interest groups of students who listed similar activities. Have groups identify the kinds of careers in which their interests might be useful. For example, a passion for writing might lead to a career in communications but could also lead to a career in either business or information technology.

IN CLASS: Ask students what they believe are their natural abilities or what others have told them they are "a natural" at doing. Can they explain where such aptitudes came from?

your high school paper. It's not unusual to enter Psych 101 with a great interest in psychology and realize halfway through the course that psychology is not what you imagined.

- **Skills.** The ability to do something well can usually be improved with practice.
- **Aptitudes.** Your inherent strengths, or aptitudes, are often part of your biological heritage or the result of early training. Each of us has aptitudes we can build on.
- **Personality.** Your personality makes you who you are and can't be ignored when you make career decisions. The quiet, orderly, calm, detail-oriented person will probably make a different work choice than the aggressive, outgoing, argumentative person will.
- **Life goals and work values.** Each of us defines success and satisfaction in our own way. The process is complex and very personal. Two factors influence our conclusions about success and happiness: knowing that we are achieving the life goals we've set for ourselves and finding that we gain satisfaction from what we're receiving from our work. If your values conflict with the organizational values where you work, you might be in for trouble.

YOUR TURN

What kinds of jobs have you had, either for pay or as a volunteer? Which of your jobs was your favorite? Which did you dislike? What do your experiences tell you about your preferences for work in the future?

Planning for Your Career

The process of making a career choice begins with creating a career plan. A good career plan should eventually include:

- Researching possible occupations that match your skills, interests, and academic major
- Building on your strengths and developing your weaker skills
- Preparing a marketing strategy that sells you as a valued member of a professional team
- Writing a convincing résumé and cover letter

Table 12.2 on page 241 provides a guide to what you should be doing during each year of college. If you are in a two-year associate degree program, you will have to do more during your second year than this table suggests.

You might proceed through these steps at a different pace than your friends will, and that's okay. What you want is to develop your qualifications, make good choices, and take advantage of any opportunities on campus to learn more about the career search. Keep your goals in mind as you select courses and seek employment, but also keep an eye out for unique opportunities. The route you think you want to take might not be the best one for you.

TABLE 12.2   **Your Career Itinerary**

A. NO MATTER WHAT YEAR

- Get a job. Even a part-time job will develop your skills and might help you to make decisions about what you like—and what you don't—in a work environment. In any job, you can learn vital skills such as teamwork, communication, and interpersonal, computer, and time-management skills.

- Register with your college's online job listing system to find listings for part- and full-time, internship, co-op, and seasonal employment.

- Find on-campus interviewing opportunities for internships in your early years and for full-time employment after graduation.

- Network with family, friends, instructors, friends of family, and acquaintances to find contacts in your field(s) of interest so that you can learn more about those areas.

- Volunteer! This can help you explore careers and get some experience in an area that interests you as you help others.

- Conduct occupational and industry research for your field or area of geographic interest. Look for other options within and beyond those fields.

- Explore career options through informational interviews (interviewing to find out about a career) and job shadowing (observing someone at work—with his or her permission).

- Prepare a draft of your résumé and have it critiqued by a career counselor and perhaps by a professional in your chosen field.

- Get involved in clubs and organizations; work toward leadership positions.

- Explore study possibilities in other countries to gain a global perspective and learn a foreign language.

- Attend career fairs to connect with employers for internships and other career-related opportunities as well as to develop a professional network.

B. FIRST YEAR OF COLLEGE

- Take the Holland Self-Directed Search or a similar interest inventory at your career center.

- Take a variety of classes to get exposure to various skill and knowledge areas.

- Attend your campus's annual career fair to see what is being offered.

- Talk to a career counselor about your skills, aptitudes, and interests. Find out what the career center offers.

C. SECOND YEAR OF COLLEGE

- Attend career fairs to learn more about employers who hire graduates in your major.

- Spend some time talking with your college adviser or career counselor to discuss your career plans.

D. THIRD YEAR OF COLLEGE

- Take an advanced computerized career assessment to discover further career options and to refine your career plans. Visit your career center.

- Take on a leadership role in a club or organization.

(Continued)

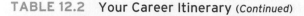

TABLE 12.2 Your Career Itinerary (Continued)

- Participate in mock interview activities to improve your interviewing skills.

- Attend workshops to learn more about résumé writing, looking for an internship, interviewing, and other job search skills.

- Explore the option of graduate school.

- Develop a top-10 list of employers of interest.

E. LAST YEAR OF COLLEGE

- Check on-campus interviewing opportunities on a daily basis, beginning in the fall term. Interview with organizations recruiting for your major.

- Conduct research on organizations of interest to you, interview with those coming to campus, and contact human resources professionals who represent organizations that won't be on campus. Find out if you can interview.

- Attend career fairs to network with employers and set up interviewing opportunities.

- If you're thinking about graduate school, request applications early in the fall, and send them out throughout the fall term.

- Target your geographic areas of interest by contacting local chambers of commerce and using local newspapers, phone books, and Internet resources.

Source: Developed by Michigan State University Career Services. Reprinted with permission of he Michigan State University Board of Trustees.

PLANNING FOR TWO-YEAR STUDENTS

Some students at two-year colleges pursue technical or professional degrees that prepare them for employment after two years. Others are planning to transfer to a four-year college or university. If you are a student attending a two-year college and plan to transfer to complete a four-year degree, you might find that once you get to the four-year institution, you have less time to make adjustments in your coursework and career opportunities. A major stumbling block is that transfers often arrive on their new campus with enough credits to declare a major; at this point, changing your major again can be costly, because it will mean adding time, and therefore expense, before graduation.

> **YOUR TURN**
>
> What kind of "marketing strategy" could you develop to sell yourself to a potential employer? Which of your characteristics or aptitudes would you emphasize?

Consider these early steps during your first three terms at your two-year college:

- Take a career interest inventory, and begin focusing on the career paths that most interest you.

- Visit with a career counselor to develop a short-term strategy to test your career interests.

- Enroll in a career decision-making class.

- Shadow a professional in the occupation(s) that you wish to enter.

- Attend a local career fair to learn about potential job opportunities.

Another consideration for students at community colleges is to determine whether transferring to another institution is necessary at all. More and more community colleges are offering bachelor's degrees. Check out your opportunities for advanced education right where you are.

During your last term at your two-year college, consider these options:

- Determine what academic majors best match your occupational interests.

- Investigate whether the college or university you will attend next has the majors you need and whether there are any prerequisite requirements you will have to meet before you can enroll in your chosen major. If you find you do not have a clear career focus by the time you transfer, meet again with the college's career adviser.

- Visit the campus to which you are transferring before you register. Meet with both a career adviser and an academic adviser there as soon as possible.

GETTING EXPERIENCE

Now that you have a handle on your interests, it's time to test the waters. Your campus has a variety of activities and programs in which you can participate to confirm those interests and your values and gain valuable skills. The list on page 244 provides a number of examples.

> **YOUR TURN**
>
> Have you explored your institution's career center? If so, what did you learn? If not, when in your college experience do you think going to the career center will be most important? Why?

IN CLASS: Tell interested students that they can visit the transfer center or see a transfer counselor to explore transfer options. Community college students sometimes select majors that are professionally oriented and later learn that their degrees might not be as transferable as they thought. This is an important area for community college students to investigate early in their first year.

DOS AND DON'TS OF CAREER PLANNING

As you start examining your aspirations and interests, keep in mind these simple dos and don'ts:

Do

1. Do explore a number of career possibilities and academic majors.

2. Do get involved through volunteer work, study abroad, and student organizations—especially those linked to your major.

3. Do follow your passion. Learn what you love to do, and go for it.

Don't

1. Don't just focus on a major and blindly hope to get a career out of it. That's backward.

2. Don't be motivated primarily by external stimuli, such as salary, prestige, and perks. All the money in the world won't make you happy if you hate what you're doing every day.

3. Don't select a major just because it seems trendy.

4. Don't choose courses simply because your roommate or friend said they were easy. That's wasting your valuable time, not to mention tuition.

First Impressions

A critical step on the way to any job is the personal interview. This is your chance to put your best foot forward. Remember to be on time, dress professionally, answer questions honestly, and smile!

IN CLASS: Have someone from your campus's service learning or community service office visit your class to acquaint students with all the possibilities for service learning in the local area.

OUTSIDE CLASS: Consider building a service-learning requirement into your course.

- **Volunteer/service learning.** Some instructors build service learning into their courses. Service learning allows you to apply academic theories and ideas to actual practice. Volunteering outside of class is also a valuable way to encounter different life situations and to gain work knowledge in areas such as teaching, health services, counseling, and tax preparation. A little time spent each week can provide immense personal and professional rewards.

- **Study abroad.** If possible, spend a term taking courses in another country so you can learn about a different culture, experience new traditions, and practice a different pace of life. Some study-abroad programs also include options for both work and service learning experiences. If this interests you, find out how financial aid applies to study abroad.

- **Internships and co-ops.** Many employers now expect these work experiences. They want to see that you have experience in the professional workplace and have gained an understanding of the skills and competencies necessary to succeed. Check with your academic department and your career center to find out what internships are available in your major. Many majors offer academic credit for internships. Remember that with an internship on your résumé, you'll be a step ahead of students who ignore this valuable experience.

- **On-campus employment.** On-campus jobs might not provide as much income as off-campus jobs, but on-campus jobs give you a chance to practice good work habits. On-campus employment also brings you into contact with faculty members and other academic professionals whom you can later consult as mentors or ask for those all-important reference letters.

- **Student projects/competitions.** In many fields, students engage in competitions based on what they have learned in the classroom. Civil engineers build concrete canoes, and marketing majors develop campaign strategies, for example. They might compete against teams from other colleges or universities. In the process, they learn teamwork, communication, and applied problem-solving skills.

- **Research.** An excellent way to extend your academic learning is to work with a faculty member on a research project. Research extends your critical-thinking skills and provides insight into a subject above and beyond your books and class notes.

Skills Employers Look For

One of the many important purposes and outcomes of your college experience is the acquisition of a combination of knowledge and skills. Two types of skills are essential to employment and to life: content skills and transferable skills.

CONTENT SKILLS

Content skills, often referred to as cognitive, intellectual, or "hard" skills, are acquired as you gain mastery in your academic field. They include writing proficiency, computer literacy, and foreign language skills. Computing knowledge and ability are now perceived as core skills that are equal in importance to reading, writing, and mathematics. In fact, employers' expectations regarding computer knowledge and application continue to rise.

Content skills include specific types of information, facts, principles, and rules. For instance, perhaps you have knowledge of civil engineering related to dam construction, or you have extensive experience working with telescopes. Maybe your work in the library and study of library science have trained you in several library databases. Or you might know the most common clinical diagnoses in psychology. We often forget some of the preparation we have gained that augments our mastery of specific academic material, especially statistics, research methods, foreign language aptitude, and computer literacy. You can apply all of this specific knowledge to jobs in a particular field or occupation.

Certain types of employers will expect extensive knowledge in your academic major before they will consider hiring you; for example, to get a job in accounting, you must demonstrate knowledge of that field. However, for most college students it's sufficient to have some fundamental knowledge. You will learn more on the job as you move from entry-level jobs to more advanced positions.

TRANSFERABLE SKILLS

Transferable skills are skills that are general and apply to or transfer to a variety of settings. By category, these transferable skills are as follows:

- Communication skills that demonstrate solid oral and listening abilities in addition to a good foundation in the basic content skill of writing

content skills Cognitive, intellectual, or "hard" skills, acquired as one gains mastery in an academic field. These include writing proficiency, computer literacy, and foreign language skills.

transferable skills General skills that apply to or transfer to a variety of settings. Examples include solid oral and listening abilities, leadership skills, critical thinking, and problem solving.

- Presentation skills, including the ability to justify and persuade as well as the ability to respond to questions and serious critiques of your presentation material
- Leadership skills, or the ability to take charge or relinquish control according to the needs of the organization
- Team skills, or the ability to work collaboratively with different people while maintaining autonomous control over some assignments
- Interpersonal abilities that allow you to relate to others, inspire others to participate, or ease conflict between coworkers
- Personal traits, including showing initiative and motivation, being adaptable to change, having a work ethic, being reliable and honest, possessing integrity, knowing how to plan and organize multiple tasks, and being able to respond positively to customer concerns
- Critical thinking and problem solving, or the ability to identify problems and their solutions by integrating information from a variety of sources and effectively weighing alternatives
- A willingness to learn quickly and continuously

IN CLASS: Refer students to Chapter 10 (Writing and Speaking Effectively), and ask them to discuss where one acquires these transferable skills. What are the roles of education and experience? Ask the class to make a list of places and opportunities to acquire these skills.

Transferable skills are valuable to many kinds of employers and professions. They give you flexibility in your career planning. You can gain transferable skills through a variety of activities. For example, volunteer work, study abroad, involvement in a student professional organization or club, and the pursuit of hobbies or interests can all build teamwork, leadership, interpersonal awareness, and effective communication abilities. Internships and career-related work are also valuable opportunities to practice these skills in the real world.

KEY COMPETENCIES

While employers expect skills and related work experience from today's college graduates, they also have begun to focus on additional key competencies that are critical for success in today's economy:

IN CLASS: Ask students why each of these competencies is important to employers.

IN CLASS: Ask students to do a self-assessment on which competencies they have and which they need to acquire. What kinds of positions would they hire themselves for? Why?

- **Integrity.** Your employment will depend on your being able to act in an ethical manner at work and in the community.
- **Innovation.** You should also be able to evaluate, synthesize, and create knowledge that will lead to new products and services. Employers seek individuals who are willing to take some risks and explore innovative and better ways to deliver products and services.
- **Initiative.** A great employee is able to recognize the need to take action, such as helping a team member, approaching a new client, or taking on assignments without being asked. Employers don't want employees who will wait passively for a supervisor to provide work assignments; they want people who will see what has to be done and do it.
- **Commitment.** Both employers and graduate schools look for a candidate's commitment to learning. They want you to express what you really love to study and are willing to learn on your own initiative. The best foundation for this competency is to be engaged in an academic program in which you wake up every morning eager to go to class.

Working in College

Do you hope to get a job while you are in college? Before you do, be really honest with yourself: Is this something you must do to pay for college? Is it something you want to do to maintain your lifestyle and acquire things you want? Or is it a combination of both? Most students work in paid jobs. Here are some things you should know about working in college.

Paid work can support the attainment of your college goals, provide you with the financial means to complete college, and help you structure your time so that you are a much better time manager. It can help you meet people who will later serve as important references for graduate school and/or employment. However, working too much can interfere with your college success, your ability to attend class, your homework, and your participation in many other valuable parts of college life, such as group study, foreign study and travel, and group activities. Take some time to determine how much you need to work, and stay within reasonable limits.

Stated very simply, students who work in paid jobs more than fifteen hours a week

Work Study

Often you will see students on campus who are studying while they work. While you might make more money working for a local business or industry, an on-campus job will generally provide more flexibility and more opportunities to connect with professors and administrators. Plus, your "boss" will understand that you occasionally need time off to study or take exams.

have a lower chance of success in college. Students who work on campus are more likely to graduate from college than are students who work off campus.

ON-CAMPUS JOBS

If you want or need to work, explore on-campus opportunities as soon as (or even before) you arrive at college. If you have a **work-study award**, a form of federal financial aid that covers a portion of college costs in return for on-campus employment, check with your student employment office for a listing of possible campus jobs for work-study students. Your career center can tell you how to access your college's online employment system. College employment systems generally channel all jobs listed by faculty, advisers, and career counselors into one database, so it is convenient for you to identify the sorts of jobs you are looking for.

Many campuses offer an on-campus job fair early in the fall term. Even if you might not be interested at the time, a visit to the job fair will give you a great idea of the range and type of jobs available on campus. You might be pleasantly surprised to learn that there are more opportunities than washing dishes in the cafeteria. Job fairs usually include off-campus community employers as well, in part because your institution must spend some of the work-study funds it receives in supporting off-campus work by students.

OUTSIDE CLASS: Assign the class to attend an on-campus job fair. There, students can see for themselves what kinds of jobs are available for college students. They can ask potential employers what skills they are looking for in an employee.

work-study award A form of federal financial aid that covers a portion of college costs in return for on-campus employment.

■ RETENTION STRATEGY: There is a very positive correlation between working on campus and persistence, as compared to working off campus. Use this finding to encourage students to work on campus if possible.

OFF-CAMPUS JOBS

The best places to start looking for off-campus jobs are your campus career center and your financial aid office. They might well have listings or Web sites with off-campus employment opportunities. Feel free to speak to a career counselor for suggestions. You can also use the following job-search strategies:

> ### DID YOU KNOW?
>
> 7% of first-year college students surveyed work full-time while attending college.

- Learn the names of the major employers in your college's geographic area: manufacturers, service industries, resorts, and so on. Once you know who the major employers are, check them out, visit their Web sites, and learn the details.

- Check out the Web site for the agency in your state that collects and disseminates information about available employment opportunities. Find out whether this agency has an office in the community where you are attending college.

- Visit employment agencies, particularly those that seek part-time, temporary workers. This is a convenient, low-risk (for both you and the employer) way to "shop" for a job and to obtain flexible, short-term, low-commitment employment.

- Visit online job boards, and look at the classified ads in the local newspaper, either in print or online. Don't forget the classifieds in the national press. Some national firms will have jobs that can be done part-time in your area or even from your own living space.

- Check your campus student newspaper. Employers who favor hiring college students often advertise there. Be cautious about work opportunities that seem unrealistic, such as those offering big salaries for working at home or those that ask you to pay an up-front fee for a job.

- Be aware that many jobs are never posted. Employers find it easier to hire people who are recommended to them by current employees, friends, or the person vacating the position. Faculty members often hire students for their research labs based on performance in the classroom.

- Realize that who you know is important. Your friends who already work on campus or who have had an internship can be the best people to help you when you are ready to search for your job. In fact, nearly 50 percent of all student jobs are found through family and friends.

College students often view the choice of a career as a monumental and irreversible decision. But in its broadest sense, a career is the sum of the decisions you make over a lifetime. There is no one right occupation just waiting to be discovered. Rather, there are many career choices you might find fulfilling and satisfying. The question to consider is: What is the best choice for me now?

OUTSIDE CLASS: Have students develop a résumé of their current skills and experience. They can build on this résumé as they gain more knowledge and experience.

BUILDING A RÉSUMÉ

Before you finish college, you'll need a résumé, whether it's for a part-time job, for an internship or co-op position, or to show to an instructor who agrees to

TECH TIP JOB SEARCH WISELY

Remember when career Web sites were just for job hunters? No? Neither do we. Today, virtual hiring sites are a requisite stop for anyone who wants to get a sense of the market: the coolest jobs, the most in-demand college majors, where the money is, and who's hiring.

1 ▶ THE PROBLEM

You have trouble navigating online job sites—all the options leave you dizzy.

2 ▶ THE FIX

Start with a few tried-and-true job search engines and a targeted hunt.

3 ▶ HOW TO DO IT

TIPS FOR GETTING STARTED

1. Use the "advanced search" option to narrow down your results. Some job sites even offer a handy "New Graduate" filter for entry-level positions.

2. Learn about the application process. You may need to submit your résumé through the hiring Web site or contact the employer directly.

3. Don't forget to check out the extras. Many job sites offer overviews of different fields along with helpful advice on how to write a compelling résumé and prepare for your interview.

4. Beware of scams. There are lots of them out there. Ideally, try to do some research on the company or organization before sending in your application. Also, when communicating with a potential employer, never e-mail any personal information (social security number, bank details, etc.) that could put you at risk of identity theft.

A FEW SITES WE LIKE

Job Site	Internet Address
BestJobsUSA	bestjobsusa.com
Career Builder	careerbuilder.com
Career Net	careernet.com
CareerXchange	careerxchange.com
CollegeGrad.com	collegegrad.com
College Recruiter	collegerecruiter.com
Experience.com	experience.com
Indeed.com	indeed.com
Job.com	job.com
Job Bank USA	jobbankusa.com
JobWeb	jobweb.com
Monster	monster.com
Simply Hired	simplyhired.com
USA Jobs	usajobs.gov
Volunteer Match	volunteermatch.org
Yahoo! Hot Jobs	hotjobs.yahoo.com

SOME THINGS YOU SHOULD EXPLORE:

1. How much does your chosen major figure into your career goals? Good question. Some jobs have fixed requirements. For instance, if your goal is to become a nurse, you probably shouldn't be a dance major. Likewise, if you've never taken essential biology courses, chances are you won't get into medical school. But most other majors offer plenty of flexibility. Which leads to our next question . . .

2. Do you have to major in business to make money? In a word, no. Students who major in the humanities learn valuable critical-thinking skills that can help them succeed as lawyers, editors, or gallery owners. If you're a women's studies or creative writing major, you might nab a job in account management, marketing, or public relations. Try to study what you like and figure out a way to make it work for your future. In the end, it's all about how you market yourself.

3. What kinds of jobs jump out at you? Even if you're still in school and just starting to think about career possibilities, it's wise to read up on job descriptions and look into internships in fields that appeal to you. Interning gives you something impressive to put on your résumé and is also one of the fastest ways to find out if you *don't* like a job.

PERSONAL BEST

Using two of the job search Web sites listed, find three positions you're interested in applying when you finish college. Make a table listing the required skills, the suggested majors, and the courses you should complete to qualify for those jobs upon graduation.

Job Description	Required Skills & Background	Courses You Need to Complete to Qualify
1. _____		
2. _____		
3. _____		

ONE STEP FURTHER

Create an Online Profile on LinkedIn.com. Remember: Your online profile should include your résumé and only the information you'd like potential employers to know.

249

write a letter of recommendation for you. Typically, there are two types of résumés; one is written in chronological format; the other is organized by skills. Generally, choose the chronological résumé if you have related job experience, and choose the skills résumé if you can group skills from a number of jobs or projects under several meaningful categories. Try for one page, but if you have a number of outstanding things to say that won't fit on a single page, add a second page.

WRITING A COVER LETTER

When sending a cover letter, heed the following suggestions:

- Find out whom to contact. It's not the same in all fields. If you were seeking a marketing position at an advertising agency, you would write to the director of account services. If you were approaching General Motors regarding a position in the engineering department, you might write either the director of human resources for the entire company or a special human resources director in charge of engineering. Your academic adviser or career counselor can help you address your letter to the right person. So can the Internet.

- Get the most recent name and address. Advisers or career counselors can guide you to references in your campus or career library. Never write, "To whom it may concern."

- Use the proper formats for date, address, and salutation.

INTERVIEWING

The first year of college might not seem like a time to be concerned about interviews. However, students often find themselves in interview situations soon after arriving on campus. They might be vying for positions on the student residence governing board, finding an on-campus job, competing for a second-year scholarship, applying for a residence hall assistant position, choosing a summer job opportunity, or being selected for an internship or as a research assistant. Preparing for an interview begins the moment you arrive on campus because the interview is about you and how college has changed you. Students who haven't clarified their sense of purpose or who have taken only a little time to reflect on who they are and how they have changed can feel lost in an interview.

The purpose of the interview is to exchange information. The interviewer's goal is to evaluate you on your abilities and competencies in terms of what the company is seeking. For you, the interview is an opportunity to learn more about the employer and whether the job would be a good fit with your aptitudes and preferences. Ideally, you will want to find a match between your interests and abilities and the position or experience you are seeking.

Here are some important tips as you prepare for an interview:

- Check with a career counselor to find out whether you can attend a mock interview. Usually designed only for seniors as they prep for their on-campus interviews, mock interviews help students strategize and feel comfortable in interview situations. Even if a mock interview session is not available, the career center can offer tips on handling an interview situation. Check your career center Web site for sample interview questions so that you can practice before an interview.

- Understand the nature of the **behavioral interview**. In a behavioral interview, the interviewer assumes that your past experiences are good predictors of your future abilities and performance. Interviewers want to hear stories about things you have done that can help them assess your skills and behaviors. Often, there is not a right or wrong answer. Answering a behavioral question can be hard. A method used at Michigan State University and other campuses to help students think through possible answers is the PARK method, which helps to focus on the most relevant aspects of your experience.

    P: The problem or situation (What happened?)

    A: The actions you took (What did you do?)

    R: The results or outcomes (What was the result of the actions you took?)

    K: The knowledge you gained and applied through the experience (What did you learn? How did you apply it?)

- Dress appropriately. Dress codes vary depending on the location of the interview and the type of interview (e.g., professional, student focused). First impressions matter, so as a rule of thumb, always dress neatly and conservatively. You can be somewhat casual for some types of employers, but it is better to dress too professionally than too informally.

behavioral interview
An interview in which the interviewer questions the candidate about past experiences and how they helped the candidate learn and grow. This type of interview helps assess your skills and behaviors.

IN CLASS: Have students role-play mock interviews. Identify some jobs for which your students could currently apply. Make a list of questions for each job to ask students. You could also involve more students by allowing some of them to be the mock interviewer and giving them specific questions to ask. Include a behavioral question for students to practice answering using the PARK method. Since this is an impromptu practice, you might need to help and encourage students who are struggling.

CHECKLIST FOR SUCCESS

MAKING THE RIGHT CHOICE FOR MAJORS AND CAREERS

☐ **Understand the nature of the new economy you will be entering.** It is global, unstable, innovative, boundaryless, customized, and fast.

☐ **Be responsible for planning your own career;** no one else is going to do it for you. But there are plenty of people on your campus willing to help you. Start by visiting your career center.

☐ **Align your life purpose(s) with your thinking about career options.** Do the two match? If not, you have to modify one or the other. If they aren't congruent, you are in for a life of discomfort, if not misery.

☐ **Learn how your personality characteristics have been shown to have affinity with particular career fields.** This won't tell you what to do, but it will help you narrow the field and get some good reality testing of your dreams.

☐ **Learn which of your characteristics could and should affect your career choices:** your interests, skills, aptitudes, personality, life goals, and work values. Talk these through with a career counselor. It's a normal thing for college students to do.

☐ **Start (not finish) developing a career plan this term.** After all, you will have plenty of time to refine this plan as you go through college.

☐ **Enhance your employability by getting different kinds of work and travel experience during college.** See your adviser and career center for examples and information. Learn what options for getting experience your college offers: volunteer or service learning, study abroad, internships and co-ops, employment on campus, student projects and juried competitions, and research.

☐ **Learn what particular skills employers are looking for.** A great resource is the Web site for Michigan State University's Collegiate Employment Research Institute: **http://www.ceri.msu.edu/.**

☐ **Get professional help from your career center** on writing your résumé and cover letters and on learning and practicing interview skills.

BUILD YOUR EXPERIENCE 1 3 2 4

1 STAY ON TRACK

Successful college students stay focused. They "stay on track." They know what they have to do to be successful, they set goals, and they monitor their progress toward their goals.

Reflect on what you have learned about college success in this chapter and how you are going to apply the chapter information or strategies in college and in your career. List your ideas.

1. _____

_____

_____

2. _____

_____

_____

3. _____

_____

_____

2 ONE-MINUTE PAPER

Making the right choices when it comes to picking a major and a career can be intimidating. What did you learn in this chapter that will help you prepare for declaring a major? Of the topics covered in this chapter, which would you like to learn more about?

No matter how well prepared you are in your teaching, what a student hears and understands might not always be what you think you have said. The one-minute paper is a quick and easy assessment tool that will help alert you when students don't understand what was said or discussed in class. The one-minute paper will also give timid students an opportunity to ask questions and seek clarification. Ideally, you should ask for such a paper several minutes before the end of a class. The paper will also help you begin your next class by clarifying points your students seem to be unsure of.

3 APPLYING WHAT YOU HAVE LEARNED

Now that you have read and discussed this chapter, consider how you can apply what you have learned to your academic and personal life. The following prompts will help you reflect on chapter material and its relevance to you both now and in the future.

1. Sometimes the best way to learn about a career is to talk to someone who is working or teaching in that field. Set up an appointment to talk with an instructor who teaches in the area in which you are interested. Find out as much as possible about the education required for a specific career in the field. Ask about the skills that are necessary to succeed and the outlook for the future. Ask the instructor to give you some advice for preparing for the major and the career.

2. Choosing a major is a big decision and should include consideration of your personal learning style, your personality, and your goals and values. Review what you learned about yourself in Chapter 3 (Understanding Emotional Intelligence) and Chapter 4 (Discovering How You Learn). How will those insights guide your exploration of majors and careers?

4 BUILDING YOUR PORTFOLIO

Investigating Occupations How can you select a major if you are not sure what you want to do when you graduate? College classes, out-of-class activities, and part-time jobs will help you narrow your choices and make decisions about a major and a potential career.

1. Create a *Word* document and list at least two majors that you are considering right now or that you would like to know more about. Why do you find these majors interesting?

2. Name two or more careers you think you might be interested in after you graduate. Explain your choice.

3. The U.S. Bureau of Labor Statistics publishes the online *Occupational Outlook Handbook*, which provides details about hundreds of jobs. You can search for a specific job, such as nursing, and learn about the training and education needed, median earnings, job prospects, roles and responsibilities on the job, and working conditions.

   a. Visit the *Occupational Outlook Handbook* online at **http://www.bls.gov/oco/**, and in the search field, enter one or two of the careers you listed above.

   b. Create a chart. Note the training or degree required, describe the job outlook, and list the median earnings for each career. Look through the other descriptions to learn more about the careers.

4. Save your findings in your portfolio. Even in your first college year it is important that you begin to think about what you are going to do after graduation. The more you investigate different types of careers, the easier it will be for you to identify a major or decide what kind of internship, part-time job, or service learning opportunity you want to experience while you are still in college. Exploring your strengths, interests, and goals will help you to find a career that you enjoy and that meets your lifestyle expectations.

For more on this topic watch
French Fries Are Not Vegetables and Other College Lessons

WHERE TO GO FOR HELP. . .

ON CAMPUS

> Your College Web Site Search your campus career resources. Larger campuses might have specialized career service centers for specific professional schools and clusters of majors. Often student professional organizations, academic advisers, and departments will provide relevant career information on their Web sites.

> Career Center Almost every college campus has a career center where you can obtain free counseling and information on careers. A career professional will work with you to help you define your interests, interpret the results of any assessment you complete, coach you on interview techniques, and critique your résumé. It's important to schedule an appointment. By the end of your first year you should be familiar with the career center, where it is located, and the counselor who is responsible for your academic major or interests. You might also find opportunities for internships and interview practice there.

> Academic Advising More and more advisers have been trained in what is known as "developmental advising," or helping you see beyond individual classes and working to help you initiate a career search. Talking to your adviser is often the best place to start. If you have not declared a major—which is true of many first-year students—your adviser might be able to help you with that decision as well.

> Faculty On many campuses, faculty members take an active role in helping students connect academic interests to careers. A faculty member can recommend specific courses that relate to a particular career. Faculty members in professional curricula, such as business and other applied fields, often have direct contact with companies and serve as contacts for internships. If you have an interest in attending graduate school, faculty sponsorship is critical to admission. Developing a relationship with a faculty mentor can open a number of important doors.

> Library Some campuses have a separate library in the career center staffed by librarians whose job is to help you locate career-related information

resources. Of course, all campuses have a main library that contains a wealth of information on careers. The reference librarian at the main desk will be glad to help you. If you are a student on a large university campus, you might find additional libraries that are specific to certain professional schools and colleges within the university, such as business, education, law, medicine, music, and engineering; these are also excellent sources for career information.

> Upperclass Students Ask whether more experienced students can help you navigate courses and find important resources. Upperclass students might also have practical experience gained from internships and volunteering. Since they have tested the waters, they can alert you to potential pitfalls or inform you of opportunities.

> Student Organizations Professional student organizations that focus on specific career interests meet regularly throughout the year. Join them now. Not only will they put you in contact with upperclass students, but also their programs often include employer representatives, helpful discussions on searching for internships or jobs, and exposure to current conditions in the workplace.

ONLINE

> Career Center Go to your campus career center's home page and check its resources, such as links to useful pages.

> Occupational Information Network: http://www.onetcenter.org. This federal government site has information on occupations, skill sets, and links to professional sites for selected occupations. This is a great place to get started thinking about your interests.

> Mapping Your Future: http://www.mappingyourfuture.org. This comprehensive site provides support for those who are just starting to explore careers.

> The Riley Guide: http://www.rileyguide.com. One of the best sites for interviewing, job search strategies, and other critical career tips.

MY INSTITUTION'S RESOURCES

_____

_____

_____

CHAPTER 13

Managing Your Money

IN THIS CHAPTER YOU WILL EXPLORE

How to create a budget that works for you

How to obtain and keep financial aid

What kinds of student loans are best

How to use and manage credit cards

Why you should plan for your financial future

> ❝ I think about my financial future constantly. Considering the uncertain economy, there is no guarantee that I will have a job right after graduation.

Cindy Kuriakose, 27
Nursing major
Labouré College

Cindy is currently in the middle of her second first year of college. She received a bachelor of science degree in psychology from the University of Florida in 2006. After graduation she spent some time working in banking and real estate, as well as traveling, but she recognized that her true passion is nursing and enrolled in a nursing program at Labouré College in Dorchester, Massachusetts.

There are many differences between Cindy's two college experiences, and money is certainly one of them. "During my first college experience, money was not too much of a concern because I had a full scholarship to the university. I did not have to worry about paying rent or finding money for books because my scholarship covered all of those expenses. Now, I have to work for every penny to cover my expenses. Very few scholarships are offered for the type of program that I am in, so keeping up with finances is much more difficult for me now."

To pay her tuition, rent, and other expenses, Cindy works four days a week as a nanny for two young children. "I chose Labouré College in part because the program allows me to schedule classes that coincide with a

Cindy Kuriakose ▶

full-time work schedule. At this time, it would not be the best option for me to stop working or work less."

Despite significant financial responsibilities, Cindy does not turn to credit cards regularly. "I never had any credit cards in my first college experience. I was rather uninformed about the dangers of irresponsible credit card usage. I worked at a bank after college, so I am now well educated on credit and I make it a point to manage it properly. I have two credit cards with credit limits of $8,000 and $4,000. I am able to manage my credit for the most part, although depending on the time of year I may carry a balance due to extra expenses. I think it is very difficult as a college student to manage credit and finances in general."

Cindy is already thinking about her financial future. "I think about my financial future constantly. Considering the uncertain economy, there is no guarantee that I will have a job right after graduation. Fortunately, I have a great job right now and have been putting away some money every month for emergencies. I also monitor my credit and pay down any debts I have on a monthly basis."

After graduation Cindy plans to either continue her education for an advanced nursing degree or start working full-time in a hospital, preferably in pediatrics. Her advice to first-year college students: "Educate yourselves about the dangers of credit card usage and the importance of credit in the long term. Many first-year students get roped into credit card companies' mass marketing and product offers without being educated on the big picture of personal credit. Credit cards should only be used for emergencies."

Although your primary goal in college should be a strong academic record, money or the lack of it can make it easier or more difficult to complete your degree. Cindy chose her college and program specifically because they allow her to work full-time to pay tuition. Educators recognize that not understanding personal finances can hinder a student's progress, and mandatory personal finance classes are now being added in high schools and are available as options at some colleges. The purpose of this chapter is to provide basic information and suggestions so that money will not be a barrier to your success in college. Think of this chapter as a summary of needed financial skills; if you want more information, consider taking a personal finance class at your college or in your community.

IN CLASS: Ask students to write about their financial situations anonymously (or with attribution). Without using names, summarize their responses during the next class, and ask students what they might do to solve any financial problems. Provide students information on where they can go for help on the campus or in the community.

YOUR TURN

So far, how well or poorly are you managing your money in college? Why is it difficult or easy?

Living on a Budget

Face it: College is expensive, and most students have limited financial resources. Not only is tuition a major cost, but day-to-day expenses can add up quickly. No matter what your financial situation, a budget for college is a must. While a budget might not completely eliminate debt after graduation, it can help you become realistic about your finances so that you can have a basis for future life planning.

A budget is a spending plan that tracks all sources of income (student loan disbursements, money from parents, etc.) and expenses (rent, tuition, etc.)

■ ASSESSING YOUR STRENGTHS ■

Whether they work, receive financial aid, or receive money from their family, successful college students will learn to live on a budget. Now that you have read the first section of this chapter, make a list of areas where you feel you have had some success in the past in managing your money.

_____

_____

_____

_____

■ SETTING GOALS ■

What are _your_ most important objectives in learning the material in this chapter? Think about challenges you have had in the past with money management or areas that confuse you or make you nervous. Write down three money-management goals (e.g., I will track my spending and expenses for one month and use the information to create a monthly budget).

1. _____

_____

2. _____

_____

3. _____

_____

during a set period of time (weekly, monthly, etc.). Creating and following a budget will allow you to pay your bills on time, cut costs, put some money away for emergencies, and finish college with as little debt as possible.

CREATING A BUDGET

A budget will condition you to live within your means, put money into savings, and possibly invest down the road. Here are a few tips to help you get started.

Step 1. Gather Basic Information. To create an effective budget, you need to learn more about your income and your spending behaviors.

First, determine how much money is coming in and when. Sources of income might include a job, your savings, gifts from relatives, student loans, scholarship dollars, or grants. Write them all down, making note of how often you receive each type of income (weekly paychecks, quarterly loan disbursements, one-time gifts, and so forth) and how much money you can expect each time.

■ RETENTION STRATEGY: Money and related financial problems are major causes of attrition during college. If your course is designed to promote retention, don't ignore this chapter.

IN CLASS: Share the methods you use to keep your finances in order (e.g., balancing the checkbook, saving credit card and debit slips, reviewing your credit report). Ask the class whether these methods seem appropriate and doable. Why or why not?

To determine where your money is going and when, track your spending for a week or two (or, even better, a full month) by recording every bill you pay and every purchase you make. It might surprise you to learn how much money you spend on coffee, bagels, and other incidentals. This information will help you to better understand your spending behaviors and where you might be able to cut costs in the future.

Step 2. Build a Plan.
Use the information you gathered in step 1 to set up three columns: one for income, one for expected cost, and one for actual cost. Table 13.1 is an example of such a plan. Knowing when your money is coming in will help you decide how to structure your budget. For example, if most of your income comes in on a monthly basis, you'll want to create a monthly budget. If you are paid every other week, a biweekly budget might work better.

Be sure to recognize which expenses are fixed and which are variable. A *fixed expense* is one that will cost you the same amount every time you pay it. For example, your rent is a fixed expense because you owe your landlord the same amount each month. A variable expense is one that may change. Your textbooks are a variable expense because the number and cost of them will be different each term.

Although you will know, more or less, how much your fixed expenses will be during each budget period, you might need to estimate your variable expenses in your anticipated expenses column. Use past bills, checking account statements, and spending behaviors from your tracking in step 1 to create an educated guess for your anticipated expenses in the variable categories. When you are in doubt, it is always better to overestimate your expenses to avoid shortfalls at the end of your budget period.

Step 3. Do a Test Run.
Use your budget plan from step 2 for a few weeks and see how things go, recording your actual expenses as you pay them. Don't be surprised to see differences between your expected and

TABLE 13.1 Sample Budget

Cost Category	Expected Cost	Actual Cost
Rent	$ 500	$ 500
Electric	50	47
Gas (heat)	75	75
Cell phone	45	50
Water	15	12
Gasoline	40	45
Groceries	150	135
Dining out	50	40
Books	200	170
Miscellaneous	100	120
Total	$1,225	$1,194

actual expense columns; budgeting is not an exact science, and you will likely never see a perfect match between these two columns. It might be wise to add a "miscellaneous" category for those unexpected and added expenses throughout the budget period.

Step 4. Make Adjustments. Although your budget might never be perfect, you can strive to improve it. Are there areas in which you spent much more or much less than expected? Do you need to reallocate funds to better meet the needs of your current situation? Be realistic and thoughtful in how you spend your money, and use your budget to help meet your goals, such as planning for a trip or getting a new pair of jeans.

Whatever you do, don't give up if your bottom line doesn't end up the way you expected it would. Budgeting is a lot like dieting; you might slip up and eat a pizza (or spend too much buying one), but all is not lost. If you stay focused and flexible, your budget can lead you to financial stability and independence.

CUTTING COSTS

Once you have put together a working budget, have tried it out, and have adjusted it, you're likely to discover that your expenses still exceed your income. Don't panic. Simply begin to look for ways to reduce those expenses. Here are some tips for saving money in college:

- **Recognize the difference between your *needs* and your *wants*.** A *need* is something you must have. For example, tuition and textbooks are considered *needs*. On the other hand, your *wants* are goods, services, or experiences that you wish to purchase but could reasonably live without. For example, concert tickets and mochas are *wants*. Your budget should always provide for your *needs* first.

- **Share expenses.** Having a roommate (or several) can be one of the easiest ways to cut costs on a regular basis. In exchange for giving up a little bit of privacy, you'll save hundreds of dollars on rent, utilities, and food. Make sure, however, that you work out a plan for sharing expenses equally and that everyone accepts his or her responsibilities. For instance, remember that if only your name is on the cable account, you (and only you) are legally responsible for that bill. You'll need to collect money from your roommates so that you can pay the bill in full and on time.

- **Consider the pros and cons of living on campus.** Depending on your school's location, off-campus housing might be less expensive than paying for a room and a meal plan on campus. However, be aware that while you might save some cash, you will give up a great deal of convenience by moving out of your campus residence. You almost certainly won't be able to roll out of bed ten minutes before class, and you will have to prepare your own meals. At the same time, living on campus makes it easier to make friends and develop a sense of connection to your college or university. Before you make the decision about where to live, weigh the advantages and disadvantages of each option, and then choose.

- **Use low-cost transportation.** If you live close to campus, consider whether or not you need to keep a car on campus. Take advantage of lower-cost options such as public transportation or biking to class to save money on gasoline and parking. If you live farther away, check to see whether your institution hosts a ride-sharing program for commuter students, or carpool with someone in your area.

- **Seek out discount entertainment options.** Take advantage of discounted or free programming through your college. Most institutions use a portion of their student fees to provide affordable entertainment options such as discounted or free tickets to concerts, movie theaters, sporting events, or other special events.

- **Embrace secondhand goods.** Use online resources such as Craigslist and thrift stores such as Goodwill to expand your wardrobe, purchase extras such as games and sports equipment, or furnish and decorate your room or apartment. You'll save money, and you won't mind as much when someone spills a drink on your "new" couch.

- **Avoid unnecessary fees.** Making late payments on credit cards and other bills can lead to expensive fees and can lower your credit score (which in turn will raise your interest rates). You might want to set up online, automatic payments to avoid making this costly mistake.

IN CLASS: Consider sharing a time when you didn't handle your finances very well, perhaps when you were in college. Explain what went wrong and how long it took you to resolve your financial problem. Students can certainly learn from another person's mistakes.

IN CLASS: Ask students to share their thoughts about financial aid and any experiences they have had in applying for financial aid. What advice would they give to other students about financial aid?

■ RETENTION STRATEGY: Even though the term has already begun, many of your students may have registered without fully understanding or taking advantage of all the options available to them for financial aid. Financial aid could make the difference between leaving and persisting in college.

Getting Financial Aid

Very few students can pay the costs of college tuition, fees, books, room and board, bills, and random expenses without some kind of help. Luckily, several sources of financial aid, including some you might not know about, are available to help cover your costs. With a combination of research, diligence, and luck, some students even manage to enroll and succeed in college with little or no financial support from their families because of the financial aid they receive.

TYPES OF AID

Financial aid seems complex because it can come from so many different sources. Each source may have different rules about how to receive the money and how not to lose it. The financial aid staff at your college can help you find the way to get the largest amount of money that doesn't need to be repaid, the lowest interest rate on loans, and work possibilities that fit your academic program. Whether or not your family can help you pay for college, you should not overlook this valuable campus resource. The financial aid office and its Web site are the best places to begin looking for all types of assistance. Other organizations that can help students to find the right college and money to help them attend are located across the United States. Many of these organizations are members of the National College Access Network or participate in a national effort called Know How to Go. Check their Web sites at **http://www.collegeaccess.org/accessprogramdirectory** and **http://www.knowhow2go.org**. Very few students complete college without some type of financial assistance, and it is rare for students to cover all college expenses with only scholarships. The majority of students pay for college through a combination of various types of financial assistance: scholarships, grants, loans, and paid employment. Financial aid professionals refer to this combination as a "package."

While scholarships and grants are unquestionably the best forms of aid because they do not have to be repaid, the federal government, states, and colleges offer many other forms of assistance, such as loans, work-study opportunities, and cooperative education. You might also be able to obtain funds from your employer, a local organization, or a private group.

- **Need-based scholarships** are based on both a talent and financial need. "Talent" can be past accomplishments in the arts or athletics, your potential for future accomplishments, or even where you are from. Some colleges and universities want to admit students from other states or countries. "Need" in this context means the cost of college minus a federal determination of what you and your family can afford to contribute toward those costs. Your institution might provide scholarships from its own resources or from individual donors. Donors themselves sometimes stipulate characteristics of scholarship recipients, such as age or academic major.

> **DID YOU KNOW?**
>
> 74% of first-year college students are concerned about being able to fund their education.

- **Merit scholarships** are based on talent as defined above but do not require you to demonstrate financial need. It can be challenging to match your talent with merit scholarships. Most of them come through colleges and are part of the admissions and financial aid processes, usually described on the college's Web site. Web-based scholarship search services are another good source to explore. Be certain the Web site you use is free, will keep your information confidential unless you release your name, and will send you a notice (usually through e-mail) when a new scholarship that matches your qualifications is posted. Also be sure to ask your employer, your family's employers, and social, community, or religious organizations about any available scholarships.

- **Grants** are based on financial need but, like scholarships, do not have to be repaid. Grants are awarded by the federal government and state government and by institutions themselves. Students meet academic qualifications for grants by being admitted to the college and maintaining grades that are acceptable to the grant provider.

- **Work-study** jobs are reserved for students with financial need. Students receive work-study notices as part of the overall financial aid notice and then can sign up to be interviewed for work-study jobs. Although some work-study jobs can be relatively menial, the best options provide experience related to your academic studies while allowing you to earn money for college. The salary is based on the skill required for a particular position and the hours involved. Keep in mind that you will be expected to accomplish specific tasks while on duty, although some employers might permit you to study during any down-time.

IN CLASS: Invite a financial aid officer to visit class and have the class meet in the financial aid office. Your students might not be aware of scholarship opportunities offered by your college or university. A financial-aid adviser can give them up-to-date information and encourage them to apply for available scholarships.

- **Cooperative (co-op) education** allows you to alternate a term of study (a semester or quarter) with a term of paid work. Engineering co-op opportunities are among the most common, and the number of co-op programs in health care fields is growing. Colleges make information about co-ops available through admissions and academic departments.

QUALIFYING FOR AID

Most financial assistance requires some form of application. The application used most often is the Free Application for Federal Student Aid (FAFSA). Every student should complete the FAFSA by the earliest deadline of the colleges you are considering. Additional forms, such as the College Board's Profile form and scholarship applications, might also be required and will be listed in colleges' financial aid or admissions materials or by organizations that offer scholarships.

The box on the next page outlines the steps you must take to qualify for most scholarships and grants, especially those sponsored by federal or state governments.

The amount of financial aid you receive will depend on the cost of your academic program and what you or your family can pay as determined by FAFSA. Cost includes average expenses for tuition and fees, books and supplies, room and board, transportation, and personal expenses. The financial aid office will subtract from the cost the amount you and your family are expected to pay. In some cases that amount can be as little as zero. Financial aid is designed to make up as much of the balance or "need" as possible.

Show Me the Money

Don't let the paperwork scare you away. If you're not already receiving financial aid, be sure to investigate all the available options. And remember that your institution may also offer scholarships or grants that you don't have to repay.

STEPS TO QUALIFY FOR FINANCIAL AID

1. Enroll half-time or more in a certificate or degree program at one of the more than 4,500 institutions that are certified to distribute federal financial aid. A few aid programs are available for less than half-time study; check with your department or college to see what your options are.

2. Complete the FAFSA. The first FAFSA you file is intimidating, especially if you rush to complete it right before the deadline. Completing the FAFSA in subsequent years is easier because you need to update only items that have changed. To make the process easier, get your personal identification number (PIN) a few weeks before the deadline. This PIN will be the same one you'll use throughout your college career. Try to do the form in sections rather than tackling all of it at once. Most of the information is basic: name, address, driver's license number, and things you will know or have in your billfold. For most undergraduates the financial section will require your own and your parents' information from tax materials. If you are at least twenty-four years of age, married, have dependents of your own, or areaveteran your tax information and that for your spouse will be needed.

3. If your school or award-granting organization requires it, complete the College Board Profile form. Review your college's admission information, or ask a financial aid adviser to determine if this applies to you.

4. Identify any additional applications that are required. These are usually scholarship applications with personal statements or short essays. The organizations, including colleges, that are giving the money will provide instructions about what is required. Most have Web sites with complete information.

5. Follow all instructions carefully, and submit each application on time. Financial aid is awarded from a fixed pool of funds. When money has been awarded, there is usually none left for those who file late.

6. Complete the classes for which you were given financial aid with at least a minimum grade point average as defined by your academic department or college or the organization that provided you the scholarship.

HOW TO AVOID LOSING YOUR FUNDING

If you earn average or better grades, complete your courses each term, and finish your program or degree on time, you should have no trouble maintaining your financial aid. It's a good idea to check with the financial aid office before you drop classes to make sure you will not lose any aid.

Some types of aid, especially scholarships, require that you maintain full-time enrollment and make satisfactory academic progress. Dropping or failing a class might jeopardize all or part of your financial aid unless you are enrolled in more credits than the minimum required for financial aid. Full-time financial aid is often defined as twelve credit hours per term. If you initially enrolled in fifteen credit hours and dropped one three-hour course, your aid should not change. Even so, talk with a financial aid counselor before making the decision to drop a course, just to be sure.

Remember that although the financial aid office is there to serve you, you must be your own advocate. The following tips should help:

■ File for financial aid every year. Even if you don't think you will receive aid for a certain year, you must file annually in case you become eligible in the future.

- Meet all filing deadlines. Students who do not meet filing deadlines risk losing aid from one year to the next.
- Talk with a financial aid officer immediately if you or your family experiences a significant loss (such as loss of a job or death of a parent or spouse). Don't wait for the next filing period; you might be eligible for funds for the current year.
- Inquire every year about criteria-based aid. Many colleges and universities have grants and scholarships for students who meet specific criteria. These might include grants for minority students, grants for students in specific academic majors, and grants for students of single parents. Sometimes a donor will give money to the school's scholarship fund for students who meet certain other criteria, even county or state of residence. Determine whether any of these fit your circumstances.
- Inquire about campus jobs throughout the year, as jobs after become available after the beginning of the term. If you do not have a job and want or need to work, keep asking.
- Consider asking for a reassessment of your eligibility for aid. If you have reviewed your financial aid package and think that your circumstances deserve additional consideration, you can ask the financial aid office to reassess your eligibility. The office is not always required to do so, but the request might be worth your effort.

Achieving a Balance between Working and Borrowing

- RETENTION STRATEGY: Even though it may sound counterintuitive to you and your students, explain to them that there is a positive correlation between degree attainment and borrowing money for tuition to enable full-time enrollment (versus not borrowing money, working more hours, and attending part-time).

After determining your budget, deciding what you can pay from savings (if any), and taking your scholarships and grants into consideration, you might still need additional income. Each term or year, you should decide how much you can work while maintaining good grades and how much you should borrow from student loans.

ADVANTAGES AND DISADVANTAGES OF WORKING

Paid employment while you are in college can be important for reasons other than money. Having a job in a field related to your major can help you develop a credential for graduate school and make you more employable later because it shows you have the capability to manage several priorities at the same time. Work can help you determine whether a career is what you will really want after you complete your education. And students who work a moderate amount (fifteen hours per week) typically get better grades than students who do not work at all.

On the other hand, it's almost impossible to get great grades if you work full-time while trying to be a full-time student. Some students prefer not to take a job during their first year in college while they're making adjustments to a new academic environment. You might find that you're able to work some terms while you are a student but not others. And family obligations or challenging classes can sometimes make the added burden of work impractical or impossible.

The majority of students today find that a combination of working and borrowing is the best way to gain experience, finance college, and complete their educational goals on time.

STUDENT LOANS

Although you should be careful not to borrow yourself into a lifetime of debt, avoiding loans altogether could delay your graduation and your progress up the career ladder. For most students, some level of borrowing is both necessary and prudent.

The following list provides information about the most common types of student loans. The list reflects the order in which you should apply for and accept loans to get the lowest interest rates and best repayment terms.

- **Subsidized federal student loans** are backed by the government, with interest paid on your behalf while you are enrolled in undergraduate, graduate, or professional school. These loans require at least half-time enrollment and a submitted FAFSA application (see page 262).

- **Unsubsidized federal student loans** may require that you make interest payments while you are enrolled. If not, the interest is added to the amount you owe, called "capitalization."

- **Parent Loan for Undergraduate Students (PLUS) loans** are applied for and owed by parents but disbursed directly to students. Interest is usually higher than that on federal student loans but lower than that on private loans. Parents who apply must provide information on the FAFSA.

- **Private student loans** are offered through banks and credit unions. Private loans often have stricter credit requirements and higher interest rates than federal loans do, and interest payments on private loans begin immediately. Student loans are a very important source of money for college, but like paid employment, loans should be considered carefully. Loans for costs such as books and tuition are good investments. Loans for a more lavish lifestyle are likely to weigh you down in the future. As one wise person put it, if by borrowing you live like a wealthy graduate while you're a student, you'll live like a student after you graduate. Student loans can be a good way to begin using credit wisely, a skill you are likely to need throughout your life.

Managing Credit Wisely

When you graduate, you will leave your institution with two significant numbers. The first is your grade point average (GPA), which represents the level of academic success you attained while in college. The second, your credit score, is a numerical representation of your fiscal responsibility. Although this second number might be less familiar to you, it could be the deciding factor that determines whether you get your dream job, regardless of your GPA. And twenty years from now, you're likely to have forgotten your GPA, while your credit score will be more important than ever.

■ RETENTION STRATEGY: There is evidence that some students do not persist because they abuse credit cards and accumulate unsustainable debt, especially for purposes unrelated to education. Hence, one of the financial literacy skills students must acquire is credit card management.

Your credit score is derived from a credit report that contains information about accounts in your name. These accounts include credit cards, student loans, utility bills, cell phones, and car loans, to name a few. This credit score can determine whether or not you will qualify for a loan (car, home, student, etc.), what interest rates you will pay, how much your car insurance will cost, and your chances of being hired by some organizations. Even if none of these things is in your immediate future, now is the time to start thinking about your credit score.

While using credit cards responsibly is a good way to build credit, acquiring a credit card has become much more difficult for college students. In May 2009, President Obama signed legislation that prohibits college students under the age of twenty-one from obtaining a credit card unless they can prove they are able to make the payments or the credit card application is co-signed by a parent or guardian.

UNDERSTANDING CREDIT

Even if you can prove you have the means to repay credit card debt, it is important for you to thoroughly understand how credit cards work and how they can both help and hurt you. Simply put, a credit card allows you to buy something now and pay for it later. Each month you will receive a statement listing all purchases you made using your credit card during the previous thirty days. The statement will request a payment toward your balance and will set a payment due date. Your payment options will vary: You can pay your entire balance, pay a specified amount of the balance, or pay only a minimum payment, which may be as low as $10.

But beware: If you make only a minimum payment, the remaining balance on your card will be charged a finance fee, or interest charge, causing your balance to increase before your next bill arrives even if you don't make any more purchases. Paying the minimum payment is almost never a good strategy and can add years to your repayment time. In fact, if you continue to pay only $10 per month toward a $500 credit card balance, it will take you more than seven years to pay it off! And assuming an 18 percent interest rate, you'll pay an extra $431 in interest—almost doubling the total amount you'll pay.

Avoid making late payments. Paying your bill even one day late can result in a finance charge of up to $30; it can also raise the interest rate not only on that card but also on any other credit accounts you have. If you decide to use a credit card to build credit, you might want to set up online, automatic payments to avoid incurring expensive late fees. Remember that the payment due date is the date the payment should be received by the credit card lender, not the date you send it.

If you decide to apply for a credit card while you're in college, remember that credit cards should be used to build credit and for emergencies. They should not be used to fund a lifestyle you cannot otherwise afford or to buy wants (see

YOUR TURN

Do you have your own credit card or one that you own jointly with your parents? If not, what are your reasons for not getting one? If you do have a card, do you feel you're in control of the way you use it? Why or why not? If you don't have a card, do you think you are ready for one? Why or why not?

IN CLASS: Ask students to share their opinions about the new credit card legislation and its effect on college students. Do they think the government was justified in changing the way credit cards are made available? Consider organizing an in-class debate on the pros and cons of the new legislation.

the section on budgeting earlier in this chapter). On the other hand, if you use your credit card just once a month and pay the balance as soon as the bill arrives, you will be on your way to a strong credit score in just a few years.

FREQUENTLY ASKED QUESTIONS ABOUT CREDIT CARDS

Here are some answers to common questions about credit cards:

- **I have a credit card with my name on it, but it is actually my parents' account number. Is this card building credit for me?** No. You are considered an authorized user on the account, but your parents are the primary account holders. To build credit, you must be the primary account holder or at least a joint account holder.

- **I choose the "credit" option every time I use my debit card. Is this building credit for me?** No. Using the credit function of your debit card is more like an electronic check because it is still taking money directly out of your checking account. Even if your debit card has a major credit card (Visa, MasterCard, etc.) logo on it, it is not building credit for you.

- **I have a few store credit cards (Target, Kohl's, Best Buy, etc.). Are these accounts included on my credit report?** Yes. Although they will affect your credit score, they do not carry as much weight as major credit cards (Visa, MasterCard, etc.). It is okay to have a few store credit cards, but a major credit card will do more to help you build credit.

- **Where can I apply for a major credit card?** A good place to begin is your bank or credit union. Remember that you will have to prove your ability to make payments in order to obtain a card.

- **If one credit card will help me build credit, will several build my credit even more?** Research shows that there is no benefit to having more than two major credit cards. And even if you're able to pay the required monthly amounts, having too many accounts open can make you appear risky to the credit bureaus determining your credit score.

- **What if I forget and make a late payment? Is my credit score ruined?** Your credit report reflects at least the past seven years of activity but puts the most emphasis on the most recent two years. In other words, the farther you get from your mistakes, the less impact they will have on your credit score. There is no quick fix for improving a credit score, so beware of advertisements that say otherwise.

CREDIT CARD DOS AND DON'TS

> **Don't** use your credit card to bridge the gap between the lifestyle you would like to have and the one you can actually afford.

> **Do** keep an eye on your credit report by visiting the free Web site **www.annualcreditreport.com** at least once a year.

> **Do** use your credit card to build credit by making small charges and paying them off each month.

> **Do** have a credit card for emergencies if possible, even if your parents co-sign for it. And remember: spring break is *not* an emergency!

TECH TIP CREATE WEALTH AND SECURITY

It doesn't matter whether your parents still control the purse strings or you're a working adult with a mortgage: If you want to become wealthy and successful, you need to learn how to be your own chief financial officer. Managing your credit is a key factor in making money; so is having goals and knowing where to invest.

1 ▸ THE PROBLEM

You don't know how to make money work for you or which financial Web sites you can trust.

2 ▸ THE FIX

Learn a few key tips and tricks for getting ahead, and then make an action plan. (No accounting degree required!)

3 ▸ HOW TO DO IT

THE BASICS

These three money-making tools can change your life.

1. Savings account: Offers a secure place to grow your money when you're starting out. There are different types of savings accounts, but they all accumulate interest (at varying rates) and are backed by federal insurance (the FDIC).

2. IRA (individual retirement account): Gives you a tax-deferred way to save for retirement. A traditional IRA accepts tax-deductible contributions of up to $5,000 a year. There may be a penalty if you withdraw money before the age of fifty-nine and a half, but there are exceptions if you're buying a house or paying for higher education.

3. 401(k): Gives you another smart way to save. A 401(k) is an employer-sponsored savings plan that lets you place a certain percentage of your earnings into a tax-deferred account. Some companies will even match your contribution as part of your benefits package.

GUIDELINES

- **Make an appointment** with a representative at your bank to get a clear understanding of bank fees and compound interest.
- **As a student,** you might want to join a campus investment group to learn about the stock market and how to navigate e-trade sites. Who knows? You could even invest in some penny stocks and end up rich by graduation.
- **Once you begin to see the possibilities,** you may want to gain even more financial know-how. That's when you'll want to visit the following Web sites.

GENERAL ADVICE

Bankrate.com	bankrate.com
Hands On Banking	handsonbanking.org
Loan.com	loan.com
Market Watch	marketwatch.com
The Motley Fool	fool.com
MSN Money	money.msn.com
My Money	mymoney.gov
National Endowment for Financial Education	nefe.org

STOCK MARKET

E*Trade	us.etrade.com
Merrill Lynch	ml.com
Morningstar	morningstar.com
Reuters	reuters.com/investing
Vanguard	vanguard.com

TAXES

H&R Block	hrblock.com
Internal Revenue Service	irs.gov
J.K. Lasser	jklasser.com

PERSONAL BEST

Visit your bank's Web page and register to manage your account online.

ONE STEP FURTHER

Learn how to avoid identity theft. Identity theft is an increasingly common crime in which someone assumes your identity, secretly opens up accounts in your name, and has the bills sent to another address. To protect yourself, check all of your monthly bank and credit card statements for discrepancies, and keep close tabs on your credit rating. You're entitled to one free credit rating a year from each of the three major credit bureaus. Make sure to order yours from the U.S. government Web site, **www.annualcreditreport.com.** For more information on avoiding identity theft, visit **www.ftc.gov/bcp/edu/microsites/idtheft.**

DEBIT CARDS

Although you might wish to use a credit card for emergencies and to establish a good credit rating, you might also look into the possibility of applying for a debit card (also called a checkcard). The big advantage of a debit card is that you don't always have to carry cash and thus don't run the risk of losing it. And since the amount of your purchases will be limited to the funds in your bank account, a debit card is a good form of constraint on your spending. The only real disadvantage is that a debit card provides direct access to your checking account, so it's very important that you keep your card in a safe place and away from your personal identification number (PIN). The safest way to protect your account is to commit your PIN to memory. If you lose your debit card or credit card, notify your bank immediately.

Planning for the Future

It's never too early to begin thinking about financing your life after graduation. Here are some tips that could open future opportunities and help you avoid future problems.

- Plan now for your next step, whether that's additional education or work. Get to know faculty members by using their office hours to learn about their specific areas of study and ask their advice about your career. Faculty members mention frequently that they wish more students came to talk with them, instead of just meeting them when a problem occurs.

- Keep your address current with the registrar even when you have finished your degree or program and especially if you stop classes for a term. This is doubly important if you have student loans; you do not want to get a negative report on your credit rating because you missed information about your loan.

- Make a point of establishing a savings account and adding to it regularly, even if you can manage only a few dollars a month. The sooner you start, the greater your returns will be.

Your education is the most productive investment you can make for your future and that of your family. Research shows that completion of programs or degrees after high school increases earnings, opens up career options, leads to greater satisfaction in work, results in more engaged citizenship such as voting and community service, and greatly increases the probability that your children will go on to college. College is a big investment of both time and money, but it's an investment of proven worth.

BUILD YOUR EXPERIENCE

1 STAY ON TRACK

Successful college students stay focused. They "stay on track." They know what they have to do to be successful, they set goals, and they monitor their progress toward their goals.

Reflect on what you have learned about college success in this chapter and how you are going to apply the chapter information or strategies in college and in your career. List your ideas.

1. _____

_____

_____

2. _____

_____

_____

3. _____

_____

_____

2 ONE-MINUTE PAPER

This chapter covers a lot of information about financing your college experience and managing your money. Planning ahead is an important part of managing your finances. What did you find to be the most useful information in this chapter? Did anything that was covered leave you with more questions than answers? If so, what?

No matter how well prepared you are in your teaching, what a student hears and understands might not always be what you think you have said. The one-minute paper is a quick and easy assessment tool that will help alert you when students don't understand what was said or discussed in class. The one-minute paper will also give timid students an opportunity to ask questions and seek clarification. Ideally, you should ask for such a paper several minutes before the end of a class. The paper will also help you begin your next class by clarifying points your students seem to be unsure of.

3 APPLYING WHAT YOU HAVE LEARNED

Now that you have read and discussed this chapter, consider how you can apply what you have learned to your academic and personal life. The following prompts will help you reflect on chapter material and its relevance to you both now and in the future.

1. Sometimes it's hard to plan for the future. Describe two ways you can save money each week, such as using public transportation to reduce the expense of owning a car.

2. Money is a difficult subject to talk about, and sometimes it seems easier not to worry about it. Ask yourself hard questions. Do you spend money without much thought? Do you have a lot of debt? Describe your ideal financial picture.

4 BUILDING YOUR PORTFOLIO

Credit Cards: A Slippery Slope Remember the saying "There is no free lunch"? That is a good maxim to keep in mind as you consider adding credit cards to your financial picture. College students are often targeted by credit card companies through an offer of a free T-shirt or other novelty if they sign up for a new card. While it might seem harmless at the time, signing up for multiple credit cards can have you in financial trouble—and fast!

A big factor in effectively managing your credit card debt is being aware of the terms and conditions that apply to each account you have.

1. If you already have credit cards (including gas cards and store credit cards), find your most recent billing statements. If you do not have a credit card, use an Internet search engine to search for "credit cards for college students." You will find several Internet offers specifically for college students. Find the terms and conditions for one of the offers.

2. Next, to understand the fees associated with your credit accounts, create a spreadsheet with the following headers (see **www.bedfordstmartins.com/gardner**):

   - Card Issuer and Card Type
   - Credit Limit
   - APR (Annual Percentage Rate)
   - Default APR (A default APR may be used when you fail to make the minimum payment on your credit card account or exceed your credit limit by a certain amount. The default APR is always higher than the stated APR for the credit account.)
   - Due On
   - Late Fee
   - Over Credit Limit Fee

3. List each credit card you have and enter the associated fees.

4. Save the file to your portfolio.

5. Update the file any time you open or close a credit account.

Understanding the terms and conditions of every credit card account you have can help you avoid paying extremely high interest rates and damaging your credit history.

For more on this topic watch
French Fries Are Not Vegetables and Other College Lessons

WHERE TO GO FOR HELP...

ON CAMPUS

> **Your Institution's Financial Aid Office** Professionals in this office will help you understand financial aid opportunities and how to apply for scholarships.

> **Local United Way Office** Many communities have credit counseling agencies within the local United Way.

> **Campus Programs** Be on the lookout for special campus programs on money management. These programs are often offered in residence halls or through the division of student affairs.

> **Business School or College** Faculty or staff members within a school or college of business or a division of continuing education sometimes offer a course in personal finance. Check your college catalog or Web site, or call the school, college, or division office.

> **Counseling Center** If money problems are related to compulsive shopping or gambling, your institution's counseling center can provide help.

ONLINE

> Budget Wizard: **http://www.cashcourse.org.** The National Endowment for Financial Education (NEFE) offers this free, secure, budgeting tool.

> Free Application for Federal Student Aid: **http://www.fafsa.ed.gov.** The online form allows you to set up an account, complete the application electronically, save your work, and monitor the progress of your application.

> FastWeb: **http://www.FastWeb.com.** Register for this free scholarship search service and discover sources of educational funding you never knew existed.

> Bankrate: **http://www.bankrate.com**. This free site provides unbiased information about the interest rates, fees, and penalties associated with major credit cards and private loans. It also provides calculators that let you determine the long-term costs of different kinds of borrowing.

OTHER

> Knox, Susan. *Financial Basics: A Money-Management Guide for Students.* Columbus: Ohio State University Press, 2004.

MY INSTITUTION'S RESOURCES

_____

_____

_____

_____

_____

_____

_____

CHAPTER 14

Establishing and Maintaining Relationships in College

IN THIS CHAPTER YOU WILL EXPLORE

How relationships are important to your success in college

How to have positive relationships with your college instructors

How to determine whether a serious relationship is right for you

What kinds of relationships you should avoid

What guidelines to use in establishing online relationships

How relationships with parents or family members change during college

> ❝ My wife's persistence and ongoing encouragement have given me more reasons to be proud of my upcoming graduation.

Benjamin Smock, 32
Music major
Bunker Hill Community College

Even before he enlisted in the U.S. Navy and served for nine years as an electronic technician, Benjamin Smock had a passion for music. He played guitar in high school and on his ship and recently discovered an interest in professional recording. However, if it hadn't been for his wife's encouragement, he may never have decided to enroll in Bunker Hill Community College in Boston and begin pursuing music as a career. "My wife initially encouraged me to enroll in college when I began simply throwing the idea around a couple of years ago. Her continued persistence and ongoing encouragement have given me more reasons to be proud of my upcoming graduation." He has also found plenty of support from friends and family. "My father and sisters back in Illinois continue to support me as I tell them what classes I take and how much closer I get to graduating. My friends have been supportive to

Benjamin Smock ▶

the point of expressing interest in the research papers I've written and attending events with me in support of my research."

Another important relationship that Benjamin developed in college was with one of his music instructors, Mari Black, who taught an arranging and composing course. Professor Black encouraged Benjamin to work with other students in order to learn different styles of music and composition. Her guidance allowed Benjamin to become a more disciplined and focused composer. Professor Black also agreed to mentor Benjamin when he decided to participate in the honors program. "It's been a wonderful experience to work so closely with a professor," he says. "She's encouraged me to become the first music major in BHCC history to graduate with honors."

Benjamin plans to continue his studies in the music education program at the University of Massachusetts, Boston, and because he is graduating with honors from BHCC he will be automatically enrolled in the honors program at UMass. Even as he looks toward his future career, Benjamin is excited to work with other musicians and develop relationships that will help them succeed. "My ultimate goal for the future is to work with students and help them achieve a sound that will set them apart from the rest of the crowd."

What does success in college have to do with relationships? As Benjamin's story shows, the quality of relationships students develop in college can have positive effects on their success. As college educators, we have also learned from our own experiences and the experiences of others that relationships can negatively affect success as well.

Relationships take many forms. An important set of relationships will be with your instructors. You might choose to get to know your instructors or to ignore them outside of class, but the quality and frequency of the interaction you have with them can affect how well you do academically.

Whether you live on or off campus, you will continue a relationship with your parents, spouse, children, or other family members. Sometimes the assumptions and expectations that define family interactions will change, and negotiating that change is not always easy. Parents sometimes have trouble letting go of a son or daughter, and if you are fresh out of high school, you might feel that your parents still want to control your life. If you are an adult with a spouse or partner, going to college will give you a new identity that might seem strange or threatening to your partner. If you have children, they might not understand what's going on as you try to balance your need for study time with their need for your undivided attention.

If your friends also go to college, you will have a great deal to share and compare. But if your friends are not college students, they, too, might feel threatened as you take on a new identity. And romantic relationships can support you or can create major conflict and heartbreak, depending on whether your partner shares your feelings and whether the relationship is healthy or dysfunctional.

This chapter will help you to think about all these different kinds of relationships, including those that are established and maintained online.

IN CLASS: Have students write, anonymously, about one thing that concerns them about relationships in college and one thing about relationships they are looking forward to. Compile a list of these concerns, and share them with the class. Students will be surprised to realize that many of them share the same kinds of concerns.

YOUR TURN

At this point in your life, what are your three most important relationships? Write about each of those three people and what makes them special to you.

◼ ASSESSING YOUR STRENGTHS ◼

One of the best aspects of college life is developing relationships with people your age, your instructors, and upperclass students. Now that you have read the first section of this chapter, create a list of the relationships you have developed since coming to college that mean the most to you.

_____

_____

_____

_____

◼ SETTING GOALS ◼

What are *your* most important objectives in learning the material in this chapter? Think about the relationship challenges you have had in the past, and write down three goals for the future (e.g., I will make an appointment to see my calculus instructor to get help for the next test and to learn more about his interests and career).

1. _____

_____

2. _____

_____

3. _____

_____

Building Relationships with College Instructors

One of the most important types of relationships you can develop in college is with your course instructors. The basis of such relationships is mutual respect. Instructors who respect students treat them fairly and are willing to help them both in and out of class. Students who respect instructors come to class regularly and take their work seriously.

WHAT YOUR INSTRUCTORS EXPECT FROM YOU

While instructors' expectations might vary depending on a particular course, most instructors will expect their students to exhibit attitudes and behaviors that are basic to student success. They will expect you to come to class, do the

◼ RETENTION STRATEGY: Good research dating back to 1980 suggests that there is a positive correlation between out-of-class interaction between students and faculty and retention to the second year. Encourage your students to get to know their professors by taking advantage of office hours and interacting with them after class.

DID YOU KNOW?

83% of first-year college students feel they understand what their professors expect of them academically.

YOUR TURN

Before you came to college, what had you heard about college professors? Write about what others told you and whether you have found those opinions to be accurate or inaccurate.

assigned work to the best of your ability, listen and participate, think critically about course material, and persist—that is, not give up when a concept is difficult to master. Instructors also expect honesty and candor. Many instructors will invite you to express your feelings about the course anonymously in writing through one-minute papers or other forms of class assessment.

Generally college instructors expect that you're going to be self-motivated to do your best. Your grade school and high school teachers might have spent a great deal of time thinking about how to motivate you, but college faculty will usually consider this to be your personal responsibility.

WHAT YOU CAN EXPECT FROM YOUR INSTRUCTORS

The expectations you have for college instructors may be based on what you have heard, both positive and negative, from friends, fellow students, and family members. But you will find that instructors vary in basic personality and in experience. You might have instructors who are in their first year of teaching, either as graduate students or as new professors. Other instructors might be seasoned professors who have taught generations of new students. Some will be introverted and difficult to approach; others will be open, friendly, and willing to talk to you and your classmates.

But no matter what their level of experience, basic personality, or skill as a lecturer, you should expect your instructors to grade you fairly and provide meaningful feedback on your papers and exams. They should be organized, prepared, and enthusiastic about their academic field. And they should be accessible. You should always be able to approach your instructors if you need assistance or if you have a personal problem that affects your academic work.

MAKING THE MOST OF THE LEARNING RELATIONSHIP

Contrary to what you might have heard, most college instructors appreciate your willingness to ask for appointments. Though it might seem a little scary, the best way to establish an appropriate relationship with an instructor is to schedule an appointment early in the term. At this meeting, introduce yourself, tell why you are taking the course (besides the fact that it's required), and say what you hope to learn from it. Ask about the instructor's academic background and why he or she chose college teaching as a career. You can learn a great deal about your instructor from simply looking around the office. There will often be pictures of family members or animals or travel locations.

The relationships you develop with instructors will be valuable to you both now and in the future. People who become college faculty members do so because they have a real passion for learning about a particular subject. If you and your professor share an interest in a particular field of study, you will have the opportunity to develop a true friendship based on mutual

The Instructor Is In

Of all the relationships you experience in college, those you have with course instructors may be among the most enjoyable and influential. But you must take the initiative to visit your instructors during their office hours. They are available to help you with your coursework, and you may also find one or more to be lifelong mentors and friends.

interests. Instructors who know you well can also write that all-important letter of reference when you are applying to graduate or professional school or seeking your first job after college.

UNDERSTANDING ACADEMIC FREEDOM

Colleges and universities have promoted the advancement of knowledge by granting professors **academic freedom**—the virtually unlimited freedom of speech and inquiry as long as human lives, rights, and privacy are not violated. Such freedom is not usually possible in other professions.

Most college instructors believe in the freedom to speak out, whether in a classroom discussion about economic policy or at a political rally. Think of where education would be if instructors were required to keep their own ideas to themselves. You won't always agree with your instructors, but you will benefit by listening to what they have to say and respecting their ideas and opinions.

Academic freedom also extends to students. Within the limits of civility and respect for others you will be free to express your opinions in a way that might be different from your experience in high school or work settings.

academic freedom The virtually unlimited freedom of speech and inquiry granted to professors to further the advancement of knowledge, as long as human lives, rights, and privacy are not violated.

WHEN THINGS GO WRONG BETWEEN YOU AND AN INSTRUCTOR

Although there is a potential in any environment for things to go wrong, problems between students and instructors that cannot be resolved are rare. First, ask for a meeting to discuss your problem. See whether the two of you can work things out. If the instructor refuses, go up the administrative ladder, starting at the bottom: department head to dean, and so on. If the problem is a grade, keep in mind that academic freedom includes the right of an instructor to grade you as he or she sees fit and that no one can force the instructor to change that grade. Most important, don't let a bad experience sour you on college. Even the most trying instructor will be out of your life by the end of the term. When all else fails, resolve to stick with class until the final exam is behind you. Then shop carefully for instructors for next term by asking fellow students, your academic adviser, and others whose advice you can trust.

Friendships in and beyond College

One of the best things about going to college is meeting new people. In fact, scholars who study college students have found that you'll learn as much—or more—from other students you meet as you'll learn from instructors. Although not everyone you hang out with will become a close friend, you will likely find a few relationships that are really special and might even last a lifetime.

ROOMMATES

Adjusting to a roommate is a significant transition experience. You might make a lifetime friend or end up with an exasperating acquaintance you wish you'd never known. A roommate doesn't have to be a best friend—just someone with whom you can share your living space comfortably. Furthermore, your best friend might not make the best roommate. In fact, many students have lost friends by rooming together.

With any roommate, it's important to establish your mutual rights and responsibilities in writing. Many colleges provide contract forms that you and your roommate might find useful if things go wrong later.

If you have problems with your roommate, talk them out promptly. Talk directly—politely but plainly. If problems persist or if you don't know how to talk them out, ask your residence hall counselor for help; he or she is trained to help resolve roommate conflicts.

Normally, you can tolerate (and learn from) a less than ideal situation; but if things get really bad and do not improve, insist on a change. If you are on campus, talk to your resident assistant (RA) or to a professional counselor in your campus's counseling center.

SOCIAL NETWORKING

Social networking Web sites such as *Facebook* and *Twitter* are very popular with college students. While there are both positives and negatives associated with using social networking sites, one thing is certain: Entering college students rarely examine what they post online, the effects their online

> **DID YOU KNOW?**
>
> 10% of first-year college students have difficulties getting along with roommates.

OUTSIDE CLASS: Problem roommates are one of the biggest threats to success, especially for new students. Use a regular form of written feedback (a weekly journal entry, an end-of-class note, etc.) for the students to reflect on "how I'm doing." If roommate problems surface, ask whether the student needs help solving the problem. Contact the residence hall adviser or the counseling center for assistance if the student grants you permission to do so.

■ RETENTION STRATEGY: The influence of roommates connects to a major finding on the most important of environmental influences during the college years: Very simply, the greatest influence is that of other students. Hence, roommates can have a profound impact on one another, for better or worse.

IN CLASS: Be alert for students who might be engaging in online relationships instead of (rather than in addition to) real-world involvements. While there is evidence that online connections might help some students in their adjustment to college (those who use the Internet for communication), there is also evidence that some students—those who use the Internet for purposes beyond necessary communications—can suffer negative emotional consequences from too much Internet use. Discuss sensible precautions that students should take with strangers online, but emphasize the positives of Internet socializing too.

TECH TIP MAINTAIN SOME MYSTERY

1 ▸ THE PROBLEM

You're open and honest with just about everyone online.

2 ▸ THE FIX

Protect yourself from predators and from losing potential jobs.

3 ▸ HOW TO DO IT

1. Honesty is the best policy. But oversharing is not, especially in the digital age. This goes double for students. Graduate school admissions directors are apt to look you up online. Likewise, companies are constantly rummaging the Web for information on potential employees.

2. The best way to manage your image online is to be proactive and aware. Make sure your privacy settings on *Facebook* are up to par. For instance, if you list your birthday, don't put the year. Don't express any controversial opinions that could work against you. Restrict your photos to friends only. If you find yourself tagged in a compromising picture that makes you look like an idiot or a drunkard, address it right away. You want to show the world that you're a responsible, go-getting genius. *Party animal* is not the moniker you're seeking.

3. Good to know: Free services like kgbPeople can dig up every mention of you online, drawing from regular search engines, social networks, and other video and photo sites. For more information on protecting your virtual reputation, visit **http://blog.kgbpeople.com/**.

OKAY TO LEAVE FLOATING OUT IN CYBERSPACE

Photos of you looking like an academic superstar.

NOT GOOD

Stuff like this.

PERSONAL BEST

Put yourself in the mind of a potential employer and search for yourself online. What can you find out without logging onto *Facebook* or *Twitter*? What kind of information about you is available on the Web?

---

statements have on others, and the benefits and pitfalls of using social networking sites.

Social networking Web sites are wonderful tools to help you keep connected to your friends from high school and to your new friends in college. What you might not know is that you can also use social networking sites for more than just staying in touch with friends. *Facebook* can help you become more engaged in life on your campus. If you are a returning adult student, you might feel that learning how to use something like *Facebook* will be a daunting task. However, returning adult students, like traditional-age students, can learn a great deal about academic life and the campus community from being involved on *Facebook*.

You might also use *Facebook* to help you learn more about your instructors. When students read an instructor's profile, they might be surprised to learn that instructors are people too and engage in everyday activities such as exercising and watching movies. Learning a bit more about your instructors can help you feel more comfortable participating in class discussion and asking for help.

YOUR TURN

Have you met someone online whom you consider interesting? If so, describe that person. If not, describe the kind of person you would like to meet online and why.

Now for the downside: It is easy to get lost in reading profiles, status updates, notes, and checking out your friends' photos. Students often describe social networking Web sites as "addicting," which could interfere with your academic success and your well-being. You might find that you spend much more time on *Facebook* than you expected and don't have enough time to finish your work. Some students use technology to the exclusion of other activities in their lives. If you find yourself struggling to keep up with your real-world commitments and relationships because you are spending so much time on *Facebook*, it might be a good idea to talk to someone at your campus counseling center.

Getting Serious with Relationships

Not only does college present an opportunity to make lots of new friends, it is also a place where romantic relationships flourish. Although some beginning college students are married or are already in long-term committed relationships, others might have their first serious romance with someone they meet on campus. If you are gay, lesbian, bisexual, or transgendered, you might find it much easier to meet romantic partners in college than you ever have before. Whatever your sexual orientation, you'll have many opportunities; some students will sample lots of different choices, and others will settle in with just one person. Either way, you'll grow and learn a great deal about yourself and those with whom you become involved. If you are seriously thinking about marriage or a long-term commitment, consider this: Studies show that the younger you are, the lower are your odds of a successful marriage. Also, a "trial marriage" or living together does not necessarily decrease your risk of later divorce. It is important not to marry before both you and your partner are certain about who you are and what you want in life. Many eighteen- to twenty-year-olds change their outlook and life goals drastically as they get older, which can negatively affect a romantic relationship.

IN CLASS: Ask students how much time they have for relationships, how often relationships and other outside activities help or interfere with their studies, and whether they have a plan to balance the two. Remind students that they will need to strike this balance throughout life by setting priorities according to their values.

BREAKING UP

IN CLASS: Engage students in a discussion about breaking up. Why do relationships end? How does being in college affect the way in which relationships start and end?

Breaking up is hard, but if it's time to end a relationship, do it cleanly and calmly. Explain your feelings and talk them out. If you don't get a mature reaction, take the high road; don't join someone else in the mud. If you decide to reunite after a trial separation, be sure enough time has passed for you to evaluate the situation effectively. If things fail a second time, you might need to move on.

If your partner breaks up with you, you might find yourself sad, angry, or even depressed. If your partner breaks up with you online or you learn about an imminent breakup through instant messaging, social networking Web sites, or blog postings, ask to discuss the matter over the phone or in person. Almost everyone has been rejected or "dumped" at one time or another. Let some time pass, be open to emotional support from your friends and your family, and, if necessary, pay a visit to your college counselor or a chaplain. These skilled professionals have assisted many students through similar experiences, and they can be there for you as well. Bookstores and your library will also have good information on the topic of surviving a breakup.

> **YOUR TURN**
>
> On the basis of your experience or the experience of someone close to you, what advice would you give other students who are dealing with breakups?

RELATIONSHIPS YOU SHOULD AVOID

It is never wise to become romantically involved with your professor or someone who works above or for you. Many of these relationships end in a breakup. Imagine how you would feel if your ex, who might be hurt or bitter or even want you back, still had control over your grades or your job! If you date a subordinate and the relationship ends, you might find yourself being accused of sexual harassment, fired, or sued. Even dating coworkers is risky; it will be much harder to heal from a breakup if you must continue to work together.

IN CLASS: Ask students why they think the authors take this stand. Ask them whether they have known people who "fished in forbidden waters" and, if so, what the outcomes were.

IN CLASS: Talk with students about the dangers of having a relationship with an instructor. What do they think a student can do if he or she feels pressured by an instructor or boss?

Family Connections

Almost all first-year students, no matter what their age, are connected to other family members. Your family might be a spouse and children, a partner, or your parents and siblings. The relationships you have with family members can be a source of support throughout your college years, and it's important that you do your part to maintain those relationships.

MARRIAGE AND PARENTING DURING COLLEGE

Can marriage and parenting coexist with being a college student? The answer, of course, is yes, although linking all of these identities—student, spouse, parent—will not be easy. If you are married or in a long-term relationship, with or without children, you will need to become an expert at time management. The responsibilities of your roles might come into conflict, and you'll need to know what comes first and when. Most college instructors will be flexible with requirements if you have genuine problems with meeting a deadline because of family obligations. But it's important that you explain your situation; don't expect your instructors to be able to guess what you need. As the demands on your time increase, it is important that you and your partner share the burdens equally.

Occasionally, deciding to go to college can create conflict within a family. Partners and children can be threatened and intimidated if you take on a new identity and set of responsibilities. Financial pressures are likely to put an extra strain on your relationship, so both you and your partner will have to work hard at paying attention to each other's needs. Be sure to involve your family members in your decision to go to college. Bring them to campus at every

IN CLASS: Ask your students whether they think marriage and parenting can coexist with being a college student. Married adult learners who return to college face a number of role conflicts. How many of these conflicts can the class identify?

It Takes an Armada

Benjamin Smock, a veteran of the U.S. Navy, credits his wife, Katherine Bates, with helping to create the right learning environment for him to graduate with high honors from Bunker Hill Community College in Boston. Ben is now enrolled at the University of Massachusetts, Boston, where he plans to get a B.A. in music education.

IN CLASS: Have the class members share thoughts about how their relationships with their parents have changed.

opportunity and let them read your papers and other assignments. Finally, it's very important to carve out time for your partner and your family just as carefully as you schedule your work and your classes.

RELATIONSHIPS WITH YOUR PARENTS

Whether you live on campus or at home, your relationship with your parents will never be quite the same as it was before. You might find that your parents hover over you and try to make decisions on your behalf, such as your major, where and how much you work, and what you do on weekends. In fact, some instructors and administrators have coined the term "helicopter parents" to describe parents who exhibit these hovering behaviors. You also might find that it's hard for you to make any decisions without talking to your parents first. While communication with your parents is important, don't let them make all your decisions. Your college or university will help you draw the line between what decisions should be yours alone and what decisions your parents should help you make.

Many college students are living in blended families, so more than one set of parents is involved in their college experience. If your father or mother has remarried, you might have to negotiate with both family units.

So how can you have a good relationship with your parents during this period of transition? A first step in establishing a good relationship with them is to be aware of their concerns. Parents are often worried that you'll harm yourself in some way. They might still see you as young and innocent, and they don't want you to make the same mistakes they might have made or experience situations that have been publicized in the media. They might be concerned that your family or cultural values will change or that you'll never really come home again. For some students, this is exactly what happens.

But remember that parents generally mean well. Most of them love their children even if their love isn't always expressed in the best way. They have genuine concerns that you will understand even better if and when you become a parent yourself. To help your parents feel more comfortable with your life in college, try setting aside regular times to update them on how things are going for you. Ask for and consider their advice. You don't have to take it, but it can be useful to think about what your parents suggest, along with the other factors that will help you make decisions.

Not every family is ideal. If your family is not supportive, find other people who can help you create the family you need. With your emotional needs satisfied, your reactions to your real family will be much less painful.

What should you do if your family falls apart? Divorce happens, and sometimes it happens when a son or daughter goes to college. It can be hard to proceed with life as usual when the family foundation seems to be cracking under you. But remember that your parents are adults. If your father and mother decide to go their separate ways, it's not your fault, and you should not feel responsible for their happiness.

Even if you're successful in determining appropriate boundaries between your life and your parents' lives, it's hard not to worry about what's happening at home. So seek help from your campus's counseling center or from a chaplain if you find yourself in the midst of a difficult family situation.

> **YOUR TURN**
>
> How is your family reacting to your college experience? Are they supportive, fearful, meddling, remote? If there are problems, how are you handling them?

Getting Involved

■ RETENTION STRATEGY: Long-standing research has determined that students who "get involved" are more likely to persist; urge your students to get involved on campus.

Colleges and universities can seem to be huge and unfriendly places, especially if you went to a small high school or grew up in a small town. To feel comfortable in this new environment, it is important for you to find your comfort zone or niche. It's not hard to find the place where you belong, but it will take some initiative on your part. Consider your interests and the high school activities you enjoyed most, and choose some activities to explore. You might be interested in joining an intramural team, performing community service, running for a student government office, or getting involved in your residence hall. Or you might prefer joining a more structured campus-wide club or organization.

Almost every college has numerous organizations you can join; usually, you can check them out through activity fairs, printed guides, open houses, Web pages, and so on. Even better, consider attending one of the organization's meetings before you make the decision to join. Find out what the organization is like, what the expectations of time and money are, and whether you feel comfortable with the members. New students who become involved with at least one organization are more likely to survive their first year and remain in college.

Be careful not to overextend yourself when it comes to campus activities. While it is important to get involved, joining too many clubs or organizations will make it difficult to focus on any given activity and will interfere with your studies. Future employers will see a balance in academics and campus involvement as a desirable quality in prospective employees. Don't fall into the trap of thinking that more is better. In campus involvement, as in many things, quality is much more important than quantity.

> **YOUR TURN**
>
> Have you already become involved in campus organizations? If so, what kinds of involvement have you experienced? If you haven't become involved, what club or organization most interests you? Explain why.

TO GREEK OR NOT TO GREEK?

Greek social organizations are not all alike, nor are their members. Fraternities and sororities can be a rich source of friends and support. Some students love them. Other students find them philosophically distasteful, too demanding of time and finances, or too constricting. Members of Greek organizations sometimes associate exclusively with other members, and this exclusivity can cause them to miss opportunities to have a more varied group of friends. Greek rush (member recruitment) on your campus might happen before you have had an opportunity to decide whether you want to go Greek or to determine which fraternity or sorority is right for you. There is nothing wrong with delaying a decision about Greek membership. In fact, we would argue that it's better to learn your way around campus and meet lots of different friends before committing to a particular organization. Fraternities and sororities are powerful social influences, so you'll definitely want to take a good look at the upperclass students who are in them. If what you see is what you want to be, consider joining. If not, steer clear.

If Greek life is not for you, consider the many other ways in which you can make close friends. Many campuses have residence halls or special floors for students with common interests or situations, such as first-year students; honors students; students in particular majors; students with strong ethnic or religious affiliations; students who do not use tobacco, alcohol, and drugs; students who are interested in protecting the environment; and so on. Check these out. Often, they provide very satisfying experiences.

WORKING

One of the best ways to develop relationships with instructors and administrators on your campus is to get an on-campus job. Generally, your on-campus supervisors will be much more flexible than off-campus employers in helping you balance your study demands and your work schedule. You might not make as much money working on campus as you would in an off-campus job, but the relationships you'll develop with influential people who really care about your success in college and who will write those all-important reference letters make on-campus employment well worth it. Consider finding a work experience that is related to your intended major. For instance, if you are a premed major, you might be able to find on-campus work in a biology or chemistry lab. That work could help you to gain knowledge and experience and to make connections with faculty experts in these fields.

If an on-campus job is not available or you don't find one that appeals to you, an off-campus job is also a good way to meet new people in the community. However, it's important that you restrict work to a reasonable number of hours per week. Although you might feel that you have to work in order to pay your tuition or living expenses, many college students work too many hours just to support a certain lifestyle. Be careful to maintain a reasonable balance between work and study. Don't fall into the trap of thinking, "I can do it all." Too many college students have found that doing it all means not doing anything well.

Many schools have **co-op programs** in which students spend some terms in regular classes and other terms in temporary paid employment in their field. Although such programs will usually prolong your education somewhat, they have many advantages. They offer an excellent preview of what work in your

---

IN CLASS: Many new students tend to flock to Greek rush on campuses where it is available. Make it clear that although the Greek system might be right for some students, the majority find ways to stay in touch on campus through other organizations. Tell students that if they feel pressured to join a Greek organization, it might not be the right choice for them. Ask whether any of the students have already been approached or involved with a Greek organization. Ask them to share their experiences.

IN CLASS: Students can be conflicted about whether to rush or not. What can they do to make the correct decision? Help students generate a list of questions that they can use to make an educated decision.

OUTSIDE CLASS: Give students an explicit assignment to investigate co-op programs if they are available on your campus.

co-op programs
Programs offered at many institutions that allow students to work in their field of study while enrolled in college. They offer valuable experiences and an excellent preview of what work in the chosen field is actually like. Also called cooperative education.

chosen field is actually like, thus helping you determine whether you have made the right choice. They give you valuable experience and contacts that will help you get a job when you finish school; in fact, many firms offer successful co-op students permanent jobs when they graduate.

Alternating work and school terms might be more suitable for you than eight or ten straight terms of classes, and it might help you keep your ultimate goal in mind. Co-op programs can help you pay for school too; some co-op students, especially in technical fields, make almost as much, or even more, during their co-op terms as their instructors do!

IN CLASS: Have someone from your career or placement office come to class and discuss the advantages of co-op programs. Share some success stories from former students. Most beginning students know little or nothing about co-op programs and do not realize how educational, helpful, and remunerative they can be.

COMMUNITY SERVICE

As a first-year student, you will spend much of your time on campus, either going to class, studying, or hanging out with other students. But there are also ways you can get involved in the surrounding community. Consider volunteering for a community service project such as helping at an animal shelter, serving the homeless at a soup kitchen, or helping to build or renovate homes for needy families. Your college might offer service opportunities as part of first-year courses (service learning), or your campus's division of student affairs might have a volunteer or community service office. You can also check Volunteer Match (**http://www.volunteermatch.org/**) for opportunities in your area. Simply enter your ZIP code and, if you wish, key words to help you find volunteer work in your field of interest.

CHECKLIST FOR SUCCESS

ESTABLISHING AND MAINTAINING RELATIONSHIPS IN COLLEGE

☐ **Seek out relationships with instructors outside of class.** Especially, visit them during their posted office hours.

☐ **Use social networking to help you develop supportive, stimulating, and motivating new relationships while in college.** These connections will help you be successful during and after college.

☐ **Be open to new relationships.** College may be a great time for you to test out serious relationships, including romantic ones.

☐ **Don't hesitate to get help from relationship experts in your campus counseling center.** When counselors are asked, "What is the most common type of problem you help students address?" the answer is relationships.

☐ **Work to have good relationships with your family during the college years.** They have your best interests at heart, and college is a time to set boundaries while also becoming closer to them.

☐ **Get involved.** Join other students in groups sponsored by the institution. Involved students are more likely to graduate from college. It's fun, easy, free, and rewarding. And employers are interested in your extracurricular activities.

☐ **Know that social organizations, such as fraternities and sororities, can be very supportive of college success.** But they can also be very disruptive. The choice will be yours.

☐ **Working during college is a good thing, depending on where you work, how much you work, and what you do.** Get help on this important decision from your adviser and career center.

☐ **Consider performing some kind(s) of service during college.** You will develop meaningful relationships that will help you clarify your career choice.

BUILD YOUR EXPERIENCE 13 24

1 STAY ON TRACK

Successful college students stay focused. They "stay on track." They know what they have to do to be successful, they set goals, and they monitor their progress toward their goals.

Reflect on what you have learned about college success in this chapter and how you are going to apply the chapter information or strategies in college and in your career. List your ideas.

1. _____

_____

_____

2. _____

_____

_____

3. _____

_____

_____

2 ONE-MINUTE PAPER

Chapter 14 provides a lot of information about establishing and maintaining relationships in college. What did you find to be the most useful information? Was there anything in this chapter that you didn't understand or that you disagreed with?

No matter how well prepared you are in your teaching, what a student hears and understands might not always be what you think you have said. The one-minute paper is a quick and easy assessment tool that will help alert you when students don't understand what was said or discussed in class. The one-minute paper will also give timid students an opportunity to ask questions and seek clarification. Ideally, you should ask for such a paper several minutes before the end of a class. The paper will also help you begin your next class by clarifying points your students seem to be unsure of.

3 APPLYING WHAT YOU HAVE LEARNED

Now that you have read and discussed this chapter, consider how you can apply what you have learned to your academic and personal life. The following prompts will help you reflect on chapter material and its relevance to you both now and in the future.

1. If you are not already involved in on-campus activities and clubs, visit your campus's Web site or activities office to learn more about the kinds of clubs, organizations, service learning opportunities, sports teams, or volunteer work that are offered. Find at least one activity that seems interesting to you, and learn more about it. When does the group meet and how often? How many students are involved?

2. Check out some of your fellow students' profiles on a social networking site such as *Facebook* or *Twitter*. What kinds of personal information do they share? What kinds of issues are they writing about? Do they use the privacy settings that are available? Do you think it is important for college students to be careful about the kind of information they post on social networking sites? Why or why not?

4 BUILDING YOUR PORTFOLIO

A Day in the Life Managing family relationships while in college can sometimes be a real challenge! Whether you are attending college in your hometown or across the country, relationships with those who are close to you will change. Sometimes parents or other family members have a hard time letting go, and it is sometimes difficult for new college students to start making independent decisions.

1. In a *Word* document, describe some of the ways in which your life has changed since you came to college (e.g., more independence, more personal responsibility, less free time). How have you handled these changes? What has been the most difficult aspect of your new college life so far? Why?

2. Have you considered how your family's day-to-day lives might also have changed since you began college? Conduct an in-person or phone interview with one (or more) of your family members about how life has changed for them. *Tip:*

   ■ Set up a mutually convenient time to talk.

   ■ Choose a quiet place, free of distractions.

   Here are a few questions to get you started:

   a. What do you feel has changed in your life since I began college?

   b. Is the family routine any different now? If so, in what way?

   c. Do you worry about me? If so, what is your biggest concern about my college experience?

   d. Do you feel that we communicate enough (by phone, e-mail, etc.)?

3. Save your responses in your portfolio. Reflect on what you learned from the interviews. How can you be sensitive to your family's needs and concerns while recognizing your own changing needs?

For more on this topic watch
French Fries Are Not Vegetables and Other College Lessons

WHERE TO GO FOR HELP. . .

ON CAMPUS

> Counseling Center Professional college counselors help students think and talk about their relationships and then make the most appropriate decisions. It is normal to seek such assistance. It's a rare student who doesn't have some relationship challenges in college, whether with roommates, friends, family members, romantic partners, teachers, supervisors, or other individuals. This kind of counseling is strictly confidential (unless you are a threat to yourself or others) and usually is provided at no charge, which is a great fringe benefit of being in college. But unless this is an emergency, be prepared to wait for your first appointment; these centers have very heavy caseloads because so many students are experiencing stress.

> Chaplains An often underrecognized resource in terms of getting help on relationships is a session (or more) with a campus chaplain. Many colleges, both public and private, have religiously affiliated chaplains, who usually have specialized training in pastoral counseling. They also organize and host group activities in campus religious centers that you might want to take advantage of. Your academic adviser might be able to refer you to an appropriate chaplain, or you can seek out the one who represents your faith. Most chaplains are happy to see students for counseling whether or not you attend their church, synagogue, or mosque.

> Student Organizations The variety of student groups designed to bring together students to help them with their relationships is virtually unlimited. Everything exists—from Greek letter social fraternities and sororities to organizations for single parents with children to gay/lesbian/bisexual/transgendered student groups.

ONLINE

> The University of Chicago's "Student Counseling Virtual Pamphlet Collection" (**http://www.dr-bob .org/vpc/**) takes you to dozens of Web sites devoted to problems in relationships. Browse among the many links to see whether any information applies to you.

> Healthy Romantic Relationships during College: (**http://cmhc.utexas.edu/healthyrelationships .html**) The University of Texas Counseling Center offers an online brochure that explores the ups and downs of romantic relationships.

MY INSTITUTION'S RESOURCES

_____

_____

_____

_____

_____

_____

_____

_____

CHAPTER 15

Appreciating Diversity

IN THIS CHAPTER YOU WILL EXPLORE

The value of living in a diverse nation

The concepts of culture, ethnicity, race, age, sexual orientation, physical ability, and gender as they relate to diversity

The value of gaining knowledge about various groups

The role colleges play in promoting diversity

How to identify and cope with discrimination and prejudice on campus

> ❝ Diversity is like a salad of people . . . mixed well.

Derrick Behm (20), elementary education; Lakeishia Brown (19), undecided; Ikumi Kawamata (22), social work; Kristy Ramos (19), studio art; Krishneer Sen (24), information technology; and Zulma Sewell (45), deaf studies
Gallaudet University

Diversity can mean many things to many people. For the purposes of introducing this chapter, we spoke to a number of students about their personal experiences with the topic. We started at Gallaudet University in Washington, D.C.—a university founded for the deaf community—and asked six students to tell us about themselves, where they were from, why they decided to attend college, and how diversity has played a part in their lives, both in college and elsewhere.

The students range in ages from nineteen to forty-five and grew up in Fiji, the state of Georgia (among other places), Japan, New York City, Poughkeepsie, N.Y., and Puerto Rico. Some of the students chose Gallaudet because of the opportunities it offers deaf students, whereas others chose the school for its high-quality academics. Kristy is the first person in her family to go to college. She was born and raised in a deaf

Gallaudet University students ▶

family and says, "The reason I decided to go to college was to show my family that if I can go to college, they can too!" Some of the students were born deaf, while others became deaf later in life. Some grew up signing; others did not. Lakeishia identifies as hard of hearing. She chose Gallaudet because she knew that "communication between students and teachers through sign language would be easier." Some were mainstreamed in grade school, others were homeschooled, and others went to schools for deaf children. The list of differences could go on and on, but each of them brings his or her own unique experience to Gallaudet, and each of them strives to learn about the differences and similarities among them.

We asked the students to talk a bit about diversity and how it has played a part in their education. Derrick believes it is important to seek out other people and other opinions: "Your view in life is one of billions. Get to know what your peers' thoughts are!" Lakeishia, Kristy, and Zulma emphasize getting involved on campus so that you can learn to work with many people toward a common goal. As Kristy puts it, "Diversity brings language skills, new ways of thinking, and creative solutions to different problems." Lakeishia mentions joining a summer program called Jumpstart that had people from all different backgrounds. "We worked together to reach our common goal, and when we were successful, it was as a group." Zulma adds, "I learned so much from working with [one group] that I started to appreciate my own heritage." Ikumi reminds us that diversity is international: "The Internet and improved transportation mean that contact between countries is increasing. Diversity is various people, various skins, various backgrounds, various beliefs, various philosophies, and various cultures. Learning about diversity equals learning people skills." Krishneer sums it all up: "Diversity is like a salad of people . . . mixed well."

We couldn't possibly capture all of the wonderful responses in a few short paragraphs. To read the full transcripts of the students' answers, please visit the Diversity section of the book's Web site.

As demonstrated by the diverse group profiled here, a college or university serves as a microcosm of the real world—a world that requires us all to work, live, and socialize with people from various ethnic and cultural groups. In few settings do members of ethnic and cultural groups interact in such close proximity to one another as they do on a college campus. Whether you are attending a four-year university or a community college, you will be exposed to new experiences and opportunities, all of which can enhance learning and a deeper sense of understanding.

Through self-assessment, discovery, and open-mindedness, you can begin to understand your perspectives on diversity. This work, although difficult at times, will intensify your educational experiences, personal growth, and development. Thinking critically about your personal values and belief systems will allow you to have a greater sense of belonging and to make a positive contribution to our multicultural society.

IN CLASS: Ask students what the term *diversity* means to them. Ask them to reflect on experiences they have had with people who are racially or ethnically different from themselves. Were the experiences positive or negative?

YOUR TURN

If you broadly define the term *diversity* as differences in race, gender, ethnicity, religion, political preference, and the like, is your college or university more or less diverse than your high school?

■ ASSESSING YOUR STRENGTHS ■

Your college or university campus has many opportunities for you to experience diversity. Through classes, clubs, and informal interactions, you will likely have experiences that enable you to explore diverse ideas or people who are from different countries, cultures, or religions. Now that you have read the first section of this chapter, list specific examples of the ways you have already experienced new ideas and people who are different from you.

_____

_____

_____

_____

■ SETTING GOALS ■

What are *your* most important objectives in learning the material in this chapter? Think about the challenges you have had in the past in the area of diversity, and write down three goals for the future (e.g., Next semester I will take a course that is part of the "diversity curriculum"; I will ask my academic adviser for help in choosing the course).

1. _____

_____

2. _____

_____

3. _____

_____

Understanding Diversity and the Source of Our Beliefs

Diversity is the variation in social and cultural identities among people living together. **Multiculturalism** is the active process of acknowledging and respecting social groups, cultures, religions, races, ethnicities, attitudes, and opinions. As your journey through higher education unfolds, you will find yourself immersed in this mixture of identities. Regardless of the size of the institution, going to college brings together people who have differing backgrounds and experiences but similar goals and aspirations. Each person brings to campus a unique combination of life story, upbringing, value system, view of the world, and set of judgments. Familiarizing yourself with such differences can greatly enhance your experiences in the classes you will take, the organizations you will join, and the relationships you will cultivate.

diversity Variations in social and cultural identities among people living together.

multiculturalism The active process of acknowledging and respecting the diverse social groups, cultures, religions, races, ethnicities, attitudes, and opinions within a community.

IN CLASS: Discuss with students why understanding perspectives on diversity is an important element of a college education. Why is this important for personal growth and development? Why will learning about others help us to better understand ourselves?

stereotype An oversimplified set of assumptions about another person or group.

IN CLASS: Ask students to define and discuss the terms *bias, stereotyping,* and *prejudice*. What are the sources of these attitudes and beliefs? You might want to introduce students to the lyrics of "You've Got to Be Carefully Taught," a song about prejudice from the Rodgers and Hammerstein musical *South Pacific*.

For many students college is the first time they have been exposed to so much diversity. Learning experiences and challenges await you both in and out of the classroom. College provides opportunities to learn not only about others but also about yourself.

Many of our beliefs grow out of personal experience and reinforcement. If you have had a negative experience or endured a series of incidents involving members of a particular group, you're more likely to develop **stereotypes**, or negative judgments, about people in that group. Or maybe you have heard repeatedly that everyone associated with a particular group behaves in a certain way, and you might have bought into that stereotype without even thinking about it. Children who grow up in an environment in which dislike and distrust of certain types of people are openly expressed might subscribe to those very judgments even if they have had no direct interaction with those being judged.

In college you might encounter beliefs about diversity that run counter to your basic values. When your friendships with others are affected by differing values, tolerance is generally a good goal. Talking about diversity with someone else whose beliefs seem to be in conflict with your own can be very rewarding. Your goal in this kind of discussion is not to reach agreement, but to enhance your understanding of why people see diversity differently—why some seem to flee from it and others allow experiences with diversity to enrich their college experience.

Before coming to college, you might never have coexisted with most of the groups you now see on campus. Your home community might not have

Expand Your Worldview

How has going to college changed your experience with diversity? Are you getting to know people of different races or ethnic groups? Do your classes have both traditional-aged and older students? Colleges and universities can be a microcosm of our world. Make it a point to seek out people who are different from you and share your personal stories and worldviews.

been very diverse, although possibly it seemed so before you reached campus. In college you have the opportunity to learn from many kinds of people. From your roommate in the residence hall to your lab partner in your biology class to the members of your sociology study group, your college experience will be enriched if you allow yourself to be open to the possibility of learning from members of all cultural groups.

> **YOUR TURN**
>
> Write about any specific lessons you learned in your family about the expectations you should have of diverse groups.

Forms of Diversity

When you think about diversity, you might first think of differences in race or ethnicity. While it is true that those are two forms of diversity, there are many other types of diversity that you will most likely experience in college and in the workplace, including age, religion, physical ability, gender, and sexual orientation.

ETHNICITY, CULTURE, RACE, AND RELIGION

Often the terms *ethnicity* and *culture* are used interchangeably, although their definitions are quite distinct. Throughout this chapter we will use these two words together and in isolation. Before we start using the terms, it's a good idea to learn their definitions so that you're clear on what they actually mean.

> **DID YOU KNOW?**
>
> 83% of first-year college students believe their college experiences have exposed them to diverse opinions, cultures, and values.

Ethnicity refers to the identity that is assigned to a specific group of people who are historically connected by a common national origin or language. For example, let's look at one of the largest ethnic groups: Latinos. Latin America encompasses over thirty countries within North, Central, and South America, all of which share the Spanish language. A notable exception is Brazil. However, although the national language is Portuguese, Brazilians are considered Latinos (both Spanish and Portuguese are languages that evolved from Latin). The countries also share many traditions and beliefs, with some variations. However, we shouldn't generalize. Not every Latino who speaks Spanish is of Mexican descent, and not every Latino speaks Spanish. Acknowledging that differences exist within ethnic groups is a big step in becoming ethnically aware.

Culture is defined as those aspects of a group of people that are passed on or learned. Traditions, food, language, clothing styles, artistic expression, and beliefs are all part of culture. Certainly, ethnic groups are also cultural groups: They share a language, foods, traditions, art, and clothing, which are passed from one generation to the next. But numerous other, nonethnic cultural groups can fit this concept of culture, too. Think of the hip-hop community, in which a common style of dress, specific terminology, and distinct forms of musical and artistic expression also constitute a culture but not an ethnicity.

ethnicity An affiliation assigned to a specific group of people historically connected by a common national heritage or language.

culture The aspects of a group of people that are passed on or learned. Traditions, food, language, clothing styles, artistic expression, and beliefs are all part of culture.

OUTSIDE CLASS: Ask students to write a short paper on their cultural backgrounds, using food, language, ceremonies, clothing, and arts as unifying themes.

race A term that refers to biological characteristics shared by groups of people, including skin tone, hair texture and color, and facial features.

IN CLASS: Ask students to share their cultural backgrounds and make a list of interesting examples of traditions in their cultures.

IN CLASS: Define *race*, and allow students to add their perspectives. Ask students to recall whether they have met anyone who defied racial categorization, that is, whose heritage was not obvious. What does this say about the whole concept of *race*? Is it perhaps an artificial way to describe groups or individuals? Why or why not?

OUTSIDE CLASS: Ask students to gather news from the Internet about religious discrimination.

IN CLASS: Have students discuss the findings from their Internet research on religious discrimination.

■ RETENTION STRATEGY: A campus characterized by respect for all is the kind of environment in which students will want to persist. Make sure that your class also exemplifies that respect.

Although we don't use the term **race** much in this chapter, it's important to understand this word as it is commonly used in everyday language. Race refers to biological characteristics that are shared by groups of people, including skin tone, hair texture and color, and facial features. Making generalizations about someone's racial group affiliation is risky. Even people who share some biological features—such as similar eye shape or dark skin—might be ethnically very distinct. For instance, people of Asian descent are not necessarily ethnically and culturally alike, since Asia is a vast region encompassing such disparate places as Mongolia, India, and Japan. Likewise, people of African descent come from very different backgrounds; the African continent is home to fifty-three countries and hundreds of different languages, and Africans are genetically very diverse. More and more individuals today, including President Obama, describe themselves as multiracial. You might meet fellow students whose families include parents, grandparents, and great-grandparents of several different racial groups.

All of us come into the world with our own unique characteristics—aspects of our physical appearance and personalities that make us who we are. But people around the world have one attribute in common: We want to be respected even if we are different from others in some ways. Whatever the color of your skin or hair, whatever your life experiences or cultural background, you will want others to treat you fairly and acknowledge and value your contribution to your communities and the world. And, of course, others will want the same from you.

Diversity of religion has been central to the American experience since our colonial origins. In fact, many settlers of the original thirteen colonies came to North America to escape religious persecution. Religious diversity might or might not have been obvious in your hometown or neighborhood, but unless you are attending an institution that enrolls only students of one religious sect, you will find religious diversity to be part of your college experience. Religious denominations might sponsor campus centers or organizations, and students' religious affiliations might determine their dress, attitudes, or avoidance of certain behaviors. While you are in college, your openness to religious diversity will add to your understanding of the many ways in which people are different from one another.

YOUR TURN

Other than your grandparents, do you know people who are significantly older than you? If so, what has been the nature of your interaction and your relationship? If not, how might you meet some older people on campus or in your community?

AGE

Although many students enter college around age eighteen, others choose to enter or return in their thirties and beyond. In the fall of 2006, over 37 percent of American college students were twenty-five years of age or older. Age diversity in the classroom gives everyone the opportunity to learn from others who have different life experiences. All kinds of factors determine when students enter higher education for the first time or stop and then reenter. Therefore, there is no such thing as "the norm" in considering the age of college students. If you are attending a college that has a large number of students who are older (or younger) than you, strive to see this as an advantage for learning. A campus where younger and older students learn together can be much more interesting than a campus where everyone is the same age.

LEARNING AND PHYSICAL ABILITIES

Although the majority of students have reasonably average learning and physical abilities, the numbers of students with physical and learning disabilities are rising on most college campuses, as are the services that are available to them. Physical disabilities can include deafness, blindness, paralysis, or a mental disorder. Also, many students have some form of learning disability (see Chapter 4) that makes college work a challenge.

People who have physical and learning disabilities want to be treated just as you would treat anyone else—with respect. If a student with a disability is in your class, treat him or her as you would any student; your overzealousness to help might be seen as an expression of pity.

If you have, or think you might have, a learning disability, consult your campus learning center for a diagnosis and advice on compensating for learning problems. Most campuses have a special office to serve students with both physical and learning disabilities.

> **IN CLASS:** Ask students whether they have been around people with learning or physical disabilities. If so, how did they act and feel in their company? Did the disability make them feel uncomfortable? If so, why? Would they do things differently now? Why or why not?

GENDER

A basic example of diversity is gender. But other than the obvious physical differences, are men and women really that different? Or do we believe they are because of our own biases?

While you're in college, make friends with people of both genders, avoid stereotyping what is "appropriate" for one group or another, and don't limit your own interests. In today's world, there is almost no activity or profession that isn't open to everyone, regardless of gender. If your college or university has a Gender Studies department, consider taking a course in this area. Gender studies courses are generally interdisciplinary and look at the subject matter from the perspective of gender. Such a course could open up new ways of thinking about many aspects of your world.

> ### YOUR TURN
>
> Can you remember any time in your life when you gave up a dream because you thought it was "inappropriate" for someone of your gender? Can you remember a time when you assumed you wouldn't be good at an activity, a sport, or a course because of your gender? What advice could you give to other students about not letting their gender narrow their range of life options?

SEXUAL ORIENTATION

In college you will likely meet students, staff members, and professors who are homosexual or bisexual. Because most colleges and universities openly accept gay, lesbian, bisexual, or transgendered people, many individuals who were in the closet in high school will come out in the collegiate environment. The subject of sexual orientation is highly personal and often emotionally charged, but whatever your own personal sexual orientation, it is important that you respect all individuals with whom you come in contact. Most colleges and universities have campus codes or standards of behavior that do not permit acts of harassment or discrimination based on race, ethnicity, gender, or sexual orientation.

Seeking Diversity on Campus

inclusive curriculum
A curriculum that offers courses that introduce students to diverse people, worldviews, and approaches. Gender studies, religious studies, and ethnic and cultural studies are some areas included in an inclusive curriculum.

Acknowledging the importance of diversity to education, colleges and universities have begun to take the concepts of diversity and apply them to student learning opportunities. We see this in efforts by colleges to embrace an **inclusive curriculum**. Today, you can find courses with a diversity focus in many departments of your college or university, such as Black Studies, Asian Studies, Latino or Hispanic Studies, Women's Studies, Gay and Lesbian Studies, and Religious Studies. Many of the courses in these departments meet graduation requirements. The college setting is ideal for promoting education about diversity because it allows students and faculty of varying backgrounds to come together for the common purpose of learning and critical thinking.

According to Gloria Ameny-Dixon, education about diversity can do the following:

> ## DID YOU KNOW?
>
> 10% of first-year college students believe there is a lot of racial tension on their campuses.

IN CLASS: An excellent video series on the civil rights movement is *Eyes on the Prize*. After watching parts of the series, the class can share their reactions. How could racism like this exist in the United States? What was the role of youth in the civil rights movement?

- Increase problem-solving skills through different perspectives applied to reaching solutions
- Increase positive relationships through the achievement of common goals, respect, appreciation, and commitment to equality
- Decrease stereotyping and prejudice through contact and interaction with diverse individuals
- Promote the development of a more in-depth view of the world[1]

Be it religious affiliation, sexual orientation, gender, ethnicity, age, culture, or ability, your campus provides the opportunity to interact with and learn alongside a kaleidoscope of individuals.

THE CURRICULUM

College students have led the movement for a curriculum that reflects disenfranchised groups such as women, people of color, the elderly, the disabled, gays, lesbians, bisexuals, and the transgendered. By protesting, walking out of classes, and staging sit-ins at the offices of campus officials, students have demanded the hiring of more faculty members from different ethnic groups, the creation of Ethnic Studies departments, and a variety of initiatives designed to support diverse students academically and socially. These initiatives have increased academic access for students from ethnic and cultural groups and have helped them stay in school. They exist today in the form of multicultural centers, women's resource centers, enabling services, and numerous academic support programs. The movement for multiculturalism in education has continued to gain momentum since it began during the civil rights era of the 1960s. By expressing their discontent over the lack of access and representation

---

[1]Gloria M. Ameny-Dixon, "Why Multicultural Education Is More Important in Higher Education Now Than Ever: A Global Perspective," McNeese State University (http://www.nationalforum.com).

Commit to Coexist

In a college or university environment, students often learn that there are more commonalities than differences between themselves and others who have been on the opposite side of the fence for centuries. By learning to coexist respectfully and peacefully, students can take the first step toward building a better world.

in many of society's niches, including higher education, ethnic and cultural groups have achieved acknowledgment of their presence on campus.

In almost all colleges and universities, you will be required to take some general education courses. The purpose of these courses is to expose you to a wide range of topics and issues so that you can develop and learn to express your own views. We hope you will include a course or two with a multicultural basis in your schedule. Such courses can provide you with new perspectives and an understanding of issues that affect your fellow students and community members—and affect you too, possibly in ways you had not considered. And just as your college or university campus is diverse, so, too, is the workforce you will be entering. A multicultural education can improve the quality of your entire life.

STUDENT-RUN ORGANIZATIONS

Student-run organizations can provide multiple avenues to express ideas, pursue interests, and cultivate relationships. According to our definition of culture, all student-run organizations are culturally based and provide an outlet for the promotion and celebration of a culture. Let's take, for instance, two very different student groups, a Muslim Student Union and an Animation Club, and apply the components of culture to them. Both groups promote a belief system that is common among their members: The first is based on religious beliefs, and the second is based on ideas about what constitutes animation as an art form. Both have aspects that can be taught and passed on: the teachings of the Muslim faith and the rules and techniques used in drawing. Both groups utilize language that is specific to the belief system of the group. Most campus organizations bring like-minded students together and are open to anyone who wants to become involved.

IN CLASS: How is multiculturalism reflected in the curriculum on your campus? Are there multicultural organizations? Ask students to discuss their feelings about multiculturalism. Are there any negative points of view? If so, what are they, and why do you think they exist?

OUTSIDE CLASS: Students will have fun seeking campus events that have multicultural themes. Assign students to attend such an event on their own or with classmates.

IN CLASS: Have students report back what they experienced at one or more multicultural events.

OUTSIDE CLASS: Have students attend an orientation event sponsored by a campus organization.

■ RETENTION STRATEGY: There is evidence that minority or underrepresented students who join co-curricular organizations devoted specifically to supporting those students realize higher retention and graduation rates. Recommend such participation to your students.

To promote learning and discovery not only inside the classroom but outside as well, colleges and universities provide programming that highlights ethnic and cultural celebrations, such as Chinese New Year and Kwanzaa; gender-related topics, such as Take Back the Night; and a broad range of entertainment, including concerts and art exhibits. These events expose you to new and exciting ideas and viewpoints, enhancing your education and challenging your current views.

Most college students, especially first-year students, are seeking their own niche and their own identity. Many have found that becoming involved in campus organizations eases the transition and helps them make connections with their fellow students.

FRATERNITIES AND SORORITIES

Fraternities and sororities provide a quick connection to a large number of individuals—a link to the social pipeline, camaraderie, and support. Fraternities and sororities differ in their philosophies and commitment to philanthropy. Some are committed to community service; others are more socially oriented. Fraternities and sororities created by and for specific ethnic groups have existed for years and were developed by students of color who felt the need for campus groups that allowed them to connect to their communities and cultures. Nu Alpha Kappa Fraternity, Alpha Rho Lambda Sorority, Omega Psi Phi Fraternity, Alpha Kappa Alpha Sorority, Lambda Phi Epsilon Fraternity, and Sigma Omicron Pi Sorority are just some of the many ethnically based fraternities and sororities that exist across the country. Such organizations have provided many students with a means to become familiar with their campus and to gain friendships and support while promoting their culture and ethnicity.

CAREER/MAJOR GROUPS

You can explore diversity through your major and career interests as well. Groups that focus on a specific field of study can be great assets as you explore your interests. Are you interested in helping minority and majority groups interact more effectively? Consider majoring in sociology or social work. Do you want to learn more about human behavior? Study psychology. If you join a club that is affiliated with the major that interests you, not only will you find out more about the major, but you can also make contacts in the field that could lead to career options. Many of these clubs participate in challenges and contests with similar groups from other colleges and contribute to campus activities through exhibitions and events. The Psychology Club; the Math, Engineering, and Science Association; and the Association of Student Filmmakers are examples of such groups.

POLITICAL/ACTIVIST ORGANIZATIONS

Adding to the diversity mix on campuses are organizations devoted to specific political affiliations and causes. Campus Republicans, Young Democrats, Amnesty International, Native Students in Social Action, and other groups provide students with a platform to express their political views and share their causes with others. Contributing to the diversity of ideas, organizations provide debating events and forums to address current issues and events.

SPECIAL-INTEREST GROUPS

Perhaps the largest subgroup of student organizations is the special-interest category, which encompasses everything from recreational interests to hobbies. On your campus you might find special-interest clubs such as the Brazilian Jujitsu Club, the Kite Flyers' Club, the Flamenco Club, and the Video Gamers' Society. Students can cultivate an interest in bird watching or indulge their curiosity about ballroom dance without ever leaving campus. Many of these clubs will sponsor campus events highlighting their specific interests and talents so that you can check them out. If a club for your special interest is not available, create one yourself.

Discrimination, Prejudice, and Insensitivity on College Campuses

You might feel uncomfortable when asked about your views of diversity. We all have **biases** against certain groups or value systems. Yet it is what we do with our individual beliefs that separates the average person from the racist, the bigot, and the extremist.

Unfortunately, some individuals opt not to seek education for the common good but instead respond negatively to groups that differ from their own. Documented acts of **discrimination** and **prejudice** on campuses span the country. You might be shocked to hear that these acts of violence, intimidation, and stupidity occur on campuses, when the assumption is that college students are "supposed to be above that."

RAISING AWARENESS

At a midwestern university, students arrived on campus to find racial slurs and demeaning images aimed at various ethnic groups spray-painted on the walls of the multicultural center. In the wake of the terrorist attacks on the World Trade Center and the Pentagon in September 2001, many students of Middle Eastern descent were subjected to both violence and intimidation because of their ancestry.

While actions like these are deliberate and hateful, others occur out of a lack of common sense. Consider a campus party to celebrate Cinco de Mayo. Party organizers asked everyone to wear sombreros. On arrival, guests encountered a mock-up of a border patrol station on the front lawn and were required to crawl under or climb over a section of chain-link fencing. Student groups voiced their disapproval over such insensitivity, which resulted in campus probationary measures for the organization that had thrown the party. At a Halloween party at a large university, members of a campus organization decided to dress in Ku Klux Klan outfits while other members dressed as slaves and wore black shoe polish on their faces. The group then simulated slave hangings during the party. When photos of the events surfaced, the university suspended the group from campus, and the community demanded that the group be banned indefinitely.

For a number of years stereotypes that are used to identify school sports teams and their supporters have disturbed ethnic and cultural groups such as

IN CLASS: Confusion can arise when students use *prejudice* and *racism* interchangeably. Racism is prejudice directed at a racial group that often stems from one group's fear of losing power and privilege to another. Ask students whether they understand the difference between prejudice and racism and how and why power often can be misdirected. The bottom line is this: Neither racism nor prejudice is tolerable; the latter is merely a prelude to the former.

bias The tendency to hold a certain perspective when there are valid alternatives.

discrimination The act of treating people differently because of their race, ethnicity, gender, socioeconomic class, or other identifying characteristics, rather than on their merits.

prejudice A preconceived judgment or opinion of someone based not on facts or knowledge, such as prejudging someone based entirely on his or her skin color.

OUTSIDE CLASS: Most college campuses have policies against discrimination and intolerance. Ask students to research your campus policy and write a short paper on the subject. Have there been any recent incidents involving discrimination, racism, or insensitivity? If so, how did students react? What would students do if they observed this kind of activity?

Native Americans. Mascots that incorporate a bow and arrow, a tomahawk, feathers, and war paint have raised awareness about the promotion and acceptance of stereotypes associated with the concept of the "savage Indian." Some schools have responded by altering the images while retaining the mascot. Other schools have changed their mascots altogether.

> ### YOUR TURN
>
> Have you ever witnessed or been a victim of harassment because of your gender, race, regional identity, religion, or ethnic group? What can colleges and universities do to reduce the incidence of harassment?

Colleges and universities are working to ensure that a welcoming and inclusive campus environment awaits all students, both current and prospective. Campus resources and centers focus on providing acknowledgment of and support to the diverse student population. Campus administrations have established policies against any and all forms of discriminatory actions, racism, and insensitivity, and many campuses have adopted zero-tolerance policies that prohibit verbal and nonverbal harassment, intimidation, and violence. Find out what resources are available on your campus to protect you and other students from discriminatory and racist behavior and what steps your college or university takes to promote the understanding of diversity and multiculturalism. If you have been a victim of a racist, insensitive, or discriminatory act, report it to the proper authorities.

WHAT YOU CAN DO TO FIGHT HATE ON CAMPUS

IN CLASS: Does your campus have a program that promotes diversity and understanding within the student body? If so, invite a speaker from this program to your class to describe the program's goals and activities.

Hate crimes, regardless of where they occur, should be taken very seriously. A hate crime is any prejudicial activity and can include physical assault, vandalism, and intimidation. One of the most common forms of hate crime on campus is graffiti that expresses racial, ethnic, and cultural slurs.

Whatever form these crimes might take on your campus, it is important to examine your thoughts and feelings about their occurrence. The most important question to ask yourself is: Will you do something about it, or do you think it is someone else's problem? If you or a group to which you belong is the target of the hate crime, you might feel compelled to take a stand and speak out against the incident. But what if the target is not a group you associate with? Will you feel strongly enough to express your discontent with the actions that are taken? Or will you feel that it is the problem only of the targeted group?

Many students, whether or not they were directly targeted in a hate crime, find strength in unity, forming action committees and making it clear that hate crimes will not be ignored or tolerated. In most cases, instead of dividing students, hate crimes bring students together to work toward denouncing hate. It is important not to respond to prejudice and hate crimes with violence. It is more effective to unite with fellow students, faculty, staff, campus police, and administrators to address the issue and educate the greater campus community.

IN CLASS: Talk with the class about the world of work in the future, when diversity will be a norm as demographics change. Preparing for the future will require a multicultural perspective.

How can you get involved? Work with existing campus services such as the campus police and the multicultural center as well as the faculty and administration to plan and host educational opportunities, such as training sessions, workshops, and symposiums centered on diversity, sensitivity, and multiculturalism. Organize an antidiscrimination event on campus in which campus and community leaders address the issues and provide solutions. Join prevention programs to come up with ideas to battle hate crimes on campus or in the

Take a Stand

By taking a strong position against discrimination, as these school mascots are doing, colleges and universities can have a major, positive influence on their local communities. Whether the issue is protection of lesbian, gay, bisexual, or transgendered individuals, immigrants, or low-wage campus employees, student groups have significant political power if they will only use it.

community. Finally, look into the antidiscrimination measures your college is employing and decide whether you think they need updating or revising.

Just because you or your particular group has not been targeted in a hate crime doesn't mean that you should do nothing. Commit to becoming involved in making your campus a safe place for students with diverse views, lifestyles, languages, politics, religions, and interests to come together and learn. If nothing happens to make it clear that hate crimes on campus will not be tolerated, it's anyone's guess as to who will be the next target.

Challenge Yourself to Experience Diversity

During his inaugural address, President Obama reiterated the value of diversity:

> For we know that our patchwork heritage is a strength, not a weakness. We are a nation of Christians and Muslims, Jews and Hindus, and non-believers. We are shaped by every language and culture, drawn from every end of this earth; and because we have tasted the bitter swill of civil war and segregation, and emerged from that dark chapter stronger and more united, we cannot help but believe that the old hatreds shall someday pass; that the lines of tribe shall soon dissolve; that as the world grows smaller, our common humanity shall reveal itself; and that America must play its role in ushering in a new era of peace.

TECH TIP THE CASE FOR VOLUNTEERING

1 ▸ THE PROBLEM

You need to build your résumé, explore career options, and broaden your horizons (and maybe save the world).

2 ▸ THE FIX

Roll up your sleeves and volunteer in an area that interests you.

3 ▸ HOW TO DO IT

WHAT'S IN IT FOR YOU?

Volunteering is about doing something you care about and gaining experience, but it's also about opening your mind. A few of the pluses:

1. You'll get to go to interesting places and do important work.

2. You'll learn to appreciate diversity. If you're like many college students, you may have led a pretty sheltered life. Volunteer work tests you in new ways and in new situations. It puts you in touch with lots of different people from different backgrounds. It also helps you connect with your community and the rest of the world on a deeper level.

3. Some volunteer positions let you travel internationally. Volunteer abroad and you'll probably get to polish your foreign language skills.

4. You'll gain valuable experience that could help you in your career. Volunteering adds depth to your résumé. Even if you volunteer close to home, you'll learn new skills and might discover talents you didn't know you had. You might even make some useful networking contacts.

5. More important, volunteering will help you become a happier, more fascinating, and less self-absorbed person. Studies show that helping others actually lowers your stress levels.

6. Need more motivation? Employers say that applicants who do volunteer work stand out from the pack. Being socially responsible tells the world that you're ambitious and a good team player.

GOOD TO KNOW

You can find rewarding volunteer opportunities in almost every field you can imagine: animal welfare, agriculture, the arts, education, the environment, fair trade, health care, human rights, politics, technology—you name it. Here is a list of national and international volunteer organizations to get you on your way:

Amigos de las Americas	amigoslink.org
Directory on International Voluntary Service	avso.org
Child Family Health International	cfhi.org
Cross-Cultural Solutions	crossculturalsolutions.org
Earthwatch Worldwide	earthwatch.org
Foundation for Sustainable Development	fsdinternational.org
Idealist.org: Action Without Borders	idealist.org
International Partnership for Service Learning	ipsl.org
International Volunteer Programs Association (IVPA)	volunteerinternational.org
Peace Corps	peacecorps.gov
Projects Abroad	projects-abroad.org
South American Explorers Volunteer Opportunities	saexplorers.org
Teach for America	teachforamerica.org
Volunteer Match	volunteermatch.com
Volunteers for Peace	vfp.org

PERSONAL BEST

What types of volunteer activities interest you most? List five here:

_____

_____

_____

_____

_____

Diversity enriches us all. Allowing yourself to become more culturally aware and more open to differing viewpoints will help you become a truly educated person. Understanding the value of working with others and the importance of an open mind will enhance your educational and career goals and provide gratifying experiences, both on and off campus. Making the decision to become active in your multicultural education will require you to be active and sometimes to step out of your comfort zone. There are many ways to become more culturally aware, including a variety of opportunities on your campus. Look into what cultural programming is being offered throughout the school year. From concerts to films, from guest speakers to information tables, you might not have to go far to gain additional insight into the value of diversity.

Challenge yourself to learn about various groups in and around your community, at both school and home. These two settings might differ ethnically and culturally, giving you an opportunity to develop the skills you need to function in and adjust to a variety of settings. Attend events and celebrations outside of your regular groups. Whether they are in the general community or on campus, this is a good way to see and hear traditions that are specific to the groups being represented. Exposing yourself to new experiences through events and celebrations can be gratifying. You can also become active in your own learning by making time for travel. Seeing the world and its people can be an uplifting experience. Finally, when in doubt, ask. If you do this in a tactful, genuine way, most people will be happy to share information about their viewpoints, traditions, and history. It is only through allowing ourselves to grow that we really learn.

CHECKLIST FOR SUCCESS

APPRECIATING DIVERSITY

☐ **Understand that successful college students have strong skills in understanding, appreciating, and embracing diversity.** Most employers now hold this as an expectation, too. This is just good business.

☐ **Use college as the ideal environment to learn about people who are different from you.** Practice acknowledging and respecting other people, even if you don't agree with them.

☐ **Use college to help you improve your understanding of the dynamics of diversity.** Yes, you can and should study it, in both the curriculum and the co-curriculum, that is, both diversity of people and diversity of ideas.

☐ **Be alert for examples of racism and discrimination.** College is a microcosm of our society. Therefore, you may see examples of discrimination, prejudice, and insensitivity on your campus. Become aware of what you can do to combat hate on campus.

☐ **Don't fear diversity.** The best students allow themselves to break out of their comfort zones and be challenged by new people and new experiences.

BUILD YOUR EXPERIENCE

1 STAY ON TRACK

Successful college students stay focused. They "stay on track." They know what they have to do to be successful, they set goals, and they monitor their progress toward their goals.

Reflect on what you have learned about college success in this chapter and how you are going to apply the chapter information or strategies in college and in your career. List your ideas.

1. _____

_____

_____

2. _____

_____

_____

3. _____

_____

_____

2 ONE-MINUTE PAPER

One aspect of a liberal arts education is learning about differences in cultures, races, and other groups. Were there any ideas in this chapter that influenced your personal opinions, viewpoints, or values? Was there anything that you disagreed with or found unsettling?

No matter how well prepared you are in your teaching, what a student hears and understands might not always be what you think you have said. The one-minute paper is a quick and easy assessment tool that will help alert you when students don't understand what was said or discussed in class. The one-minute paper will also give timid students an opportunity to ask questions and seek clarification. Ideally, you should ask for such a paper several minutes before the end of a class. The paper will also help you begin your next class by clarifying points your students seem to be unsure of.

3 APPLYING WHAT YOU HAVE LEARNED

Now that you have read and discussed this chapter, consider how you can apply what you have learned to your academic and personal life. The following prompts will help you reflect on the chapter material and its relevance to you both now and in the future.

1. Use your print or online campus course catalog to identify courses that focus on topics of multiculturalism and diversity. Why do you think academic departments have included these issues in the curriculum? How would studying diversity and multiculturalism help you prepare for different academic fields?

2. Reflecting on our personal identities and values is a step to increase self-awareness. Read and answer the following questions to the best of your ability:

   How do you identify and express yourself ethnically and culturally?

   Are there practices or beliefs in your culture to which you have difficulty subscribing? If so, what are they? Why do you have difficulty accepting these beliefs?

   What aspects of your identity do you truly enjoy?

4 BUILDING YOUR PORTFOLIO

It's a Small World after All!   The concepts of diversity, ethnicity, culture, and multiculturalism have been explored in this chapter. Reading about these controversial topics is one thing, but really stepping into someone else's shoes is another. Study-abroad and student-exchange programs are excellent ways of adding new perspectives to your college experience.

Consider the possibilities:

1. Visit your institution's International Programs/Study Abroad office, or, if you are at a college that does not have a study-abroad program, search for study-abroad opportunities on the Web. *Tip:* Look for the Center for Global Education (**http://www.lmu.edu/globaled/index.html**), the Council on International Education Exchange (**http://www.ciee.org/study.aspx**), or the International Partnership for Service Learning (**http://www.ipsl.org**).

Using a major or career that interests you, think about how you might spend time abroad to gain experience in your major field.

2. On the basis of your research, create a *PowerPoint* presentation to share with your class outlining the opportunities to study abroad or participate in an exchange program.

   ■ Describe the steps students need to take at your campus to include a study-abroad trip in their college plan (e.g., whom to contact, financial aid, the best time to study abroad, how to earn course credit).

   ■ Describe the benefits of study abroad, and include photos of the country or countries you would like to visit.

   ■ Include information about your current or intended major and career and how a study-abroad or exchange trip would fit into your plans.

   ■ Reference Web links you found useful in preparing your presentation.

3. Save your presentation in your portfolio.

For more on this topic watch
French Fries Are Not Vegetables and Other College Lessons

WHERE TO GO FOR HELP...

ON CAMPUS

Most colleges and university campuses take an active role in promoting diversity. In the effort to ensure a welcoming and supportive environment for all students, institutions have established offices, centers, and resources to provide students with educational opportunities, academic guidance, and support networks. Look into the availability of the following resources on your campus, and visit one or more: Office of Student Affairs; Office of Diversity; Multicultural Centers; Women's and Men's Centers; Lesbian, Gay, Bisexual, and Transgendered Student Alliances; Centers for Students with Disabilities; and academic support programs for under-represented groups.

ONLINE

> **Diversity Resources** Diversity Web: **http://www.diversityweb.org**. Resources related to diversity on campus.

Tolerance.org: **http://www.tolerance.org**. This Web site, a project of the Southern Poverty Law Center, provides numerous resources for dealing with discrimination and prejudice both on and off campus.

MY INSTITUTION'S RESOURCES

_____

_____

_____

_____

_____

_____

_____

_____

CHAPTER 16
Maintaining Wellness

IN THIS CHAPTER YOU WILL EXPLORE

The importance of managing stress

Warning signs of depression

The positive effects of exercise on your mind and body

Strategies for better nutrition and weight management

The many options you have for contraception and safer sex

The realities of alcohol use on campus

The consequences of abusing alcohol, tobacco, and drugs

❝ Once I moved out on my own, I felt like a kid in a candy store. All the foods that I wasn't allowed to eat at my parents' house were now all that I was eating.

Dalton Eidem, 19
Music Industry major
California State University, Chico

Dalton Eidem was born and raised in Paradise, California, a small town outside Chico. Music has always been a huge part of his life. "My childhood was largely impacted by music," he says. "At age four, I began playing piano, and at age thirteen I taught myself to play guitar." It was only natural that Dalton chose a school with a reputable music department. It didn't hurt that California State University, Chico, was close to friends and family and enabled Dalton to continue playing with his progressive metal band.

Even though Dalton attends school close to home, he moved out of his parents' house to be closer to campus. And while that works well with his exercise regime of walking to and from school every day, it was initially hard to establish good eating habits outside the structure of home. "Once I moved out on my own, I felt like a kid in a candy store. All the foods that I wasn't allowed to eat at my parents' house were now all that I

Dalton Eidem ▶

was eating: Hot Pockets, countless bags of chips, and various other processed foods that can't possibly be good for you. Also, my fast-food intake increased dramatically. With money being tight and fast food being, well, fast and cheap, I found myself eating pizza and cheeseburgers multiple times a week. And with no one there to regulate me, my eating habits were out of control. After my first year, I was able to move out of the dorms and into an apartment, where home-cooked meals became a regular thing, and going to a restaurant became a special occasion." These days Dalton walks to school every day. "It takes more time as opposed to riding the bus or a bike. But I find that the walk to and from school leaves me feeling good and awake for the rest of the day."

An unfortunate outcome of Dalton's first year of school was that he started to smoke cigarettes. "The biggest cause for me to start smoking when I began college was influences from friends and other residents of the dorms. It began as a social thing, but I quickly became addicted and not just due to the effect it had on my body, but the social aspect of it as well. I met many people that I never would have talked to, just by bumming the occasional cigarette whenever I ran out. I still have not quit smoking after more than a year. However, I am trying to quit, and I'm taking the quitting process in stride."

Dalton's "take-it-in-stride" attitude carries over to his outlook on stress. "College as a whole is very stressful in numerous ways, whether it's because you're stressed about grades or because you have a roommate that you just can't deal with. I find that the best way to deal with stress is to try not to worry about it too much. There is no point focusing on the past. All you can do is look to the future and make sure you know what you have to do in order to succeed. Stress will come and go, and the best thing you can do is not let it take you over."

After college Dalton hopes to make it big with his band, but should that dream not pan out he'll happily settle for a job somewhere in the music business. His advice to first-year students: "It's easy to let yourself fall into bad habits, such as smoking, drinking, and doing drugs. Everyone feels a pull in one direction or another at some point. However, it's important to remember exactly what it is you're doing and what the consequences are. I've witnessed countless college careers flushed down the drain just because somebody got a bit too drunk one night, or a bit too high. Be smart about what you do and don't fall prey to the party life in college."

College is a great time to explore. It's an opportunity to exercise your mind and expand your horizons. Unfortunately, for too many students, including Dalton, it becomes an opportunity to stop exercising their bodies and begin expanding their waistlines! Because the college environment might be new to you, you could forget to take care of yourself.

Many students can handle the transition to college easily, using various coping mechanisms. Others drink too much or smoke too much. Some overeat or develop an eating disorder such as bulimia or anorexia. Some become so stressed that their anxiety overwhelms them. Some ignore their sexual health and then have to deal with a sexually transmitted infection or an unplanned pregnancy.

This chapter explores the topic of wellness, which is a catchall term for taking care of your mind, body, and spirit. **Wellness** means making healthy choices and achieving balance. It includes reducing stress in positive ways, keeping fit, maintaining good sexual health, and taking a sensible approach to alcohol and other drugs.

IN CLASS: Begin this chapter by discussing how the mind, the spirit, and the body are all integral parts of a healthy person. Ask students what this means. Make a list under each category, and share thoughts on how the mind, the spirit, and the body each complement the other.

IN CLASS: Ask students how many of them feel they are constantly juggling one deadline to meet another or skipping one class to finish an assignment for another one. Assure them that although they will need to work on both time and stress management, most other students are facing the same challenges and most learn to handle them successfully.

wellness A catchall term for taking care of your mind, body, and spirit. This includes keeping fit, making healthy choices, achieving balance, and reducing stress in positive ways.

ASSESSING YOUR STRENGTHS

Maintaining your health in college will enable you to feel good about yourself and do well academically. By making smart choices, developing an exercise regime, and eating a healthy diet, you will be ready to make the most of your college experience. Now that you have read the first section of this chapter, list the healthy behaviors you already practice.

_____

_____

_____

_____

SETTING GOALS

What are _your_ most important objectives in learning the material in this chapter? Think about the challenges you have had in the past in the area of health and wellness, and write down three goals for the future (e.g., Next week I will schedule time to go to the gym every day).

1. _____

_____

2. _____

_____

3. _____

_____

Managing Stress

In the spring of 2010, according to a survey conducted by the American College Health Association, about one quarter of college students reported that stress had negatively affected either an exam grade or a course grade.[1] When you are stressed, your body undergoes rapid physiological, behavioral, and emotional changes. Your rate of breathing can become more rapid and shallow. Your heart rate begins to speed up, and the muscles in your shoulders and forehead, at the back of your neck, and perhaps across your chest begin to tighten. Your hands might become cold or sweaty. You might experience gastrointestinal symptoms such as an upset stomach. Your mouth and lips might feel dry and hot, and you might notice that your hands and knees begin to shake or tremble. Your voice might quiver or even go up an octave.

[1]American College Health Association, _National College Health Assessment II: Reference Group Data Report Spring 2010_ (Linthicum, MD: American College Health Association, 2010).

A number of psychological changes also occur when you are under stress. You might experience changes in your ability to think, such as confusion, trouble concentrating, inability to remember things, and poor problem solving. Emotions such as fear, anxiety, depression, irritability, anger, or frustration are common, and you might have trouble getting to sleep at night or wake up too early and not be able to go back to sleep.

Stress has many sources, but two seem to be prominent: life events and daily hassles. Life events are those that represent major adversity, such as the death of a parent, spouse, partner, or friend. Researchers believe that an accumulation of stress from life events, especially if many events occur over a short period of time, can cause physical and mental health problems. Daily hassles are the minor irritants that we experience every day, such as losing your keys, having three tests on the same day, quarreling with your roommate, or worrying about money.

The College Readjustment Rating Scale is a life events scale, adapted from Holmes and Rahe's Life Events Scale and modified for traditional-age college students. Complete the scale in the box on page 311. If you find that your score is 150 or higher, you have experienced a great deal of stress over the past year. You might consider what help you need or skills you must learn to be able to cope effectively.

On this scale, each event, such as one's first term in college, is assigned a value that represents the amount of readjustment a person has to make in life as a result of change. In some studies, people with serious illnesses have been found to have high scores on similar scales. People with scores of 300 and higher have a high health risk. People who score between 150 and 300 points have about a 50-50 chance of a serious health change within two years. People who score 150 and below have a one in three chance of a serious health change.

If your score is high enough to indicate potential health problems, it would benefit you to pay special attention to the stress-reduction and -management techniques discussed in this chapter and to select and implement some strategies to reduce your stress.[2]

The best starting point for handling stress is to be in good physical and mental shape. When your body and mind are healthy, it's like inoculating yourself against stress. This means you need to pay attention to your diet, exercise, sleep, and mental health.

YOUR TURN

How do you feel, both physically and mentally, when you are stressed? What specific changes do you notice in your behavior and feelings? How does stress affect your ability to concentrate, your breathing patterns, your patience, and so on?

DID YOU KNOW?

31% of first-year college students exercise 6 or more hours per week.

DIET AND EXERCISE

There is a clear connection between what you eat and drink, your overall health and well-being, and stress. Eating a lot of junk food will add pounds to your body and reduce your energy level. And when you can't keep up with your

[2]T. H. Holmes and R. H. Rahe, "The Social Readjustment Scale." First printed in the *Journal of Psychosomatic Research*, vol. 11, copyright © 1967. Reprinted with permission from Elsevier Limited, via Copyright Clearance Center.

WHAT IS YOUR STRESS SCORE?

To determine your stress score, circle the number of points corresponding to each event you have experienced in the past six months or are likely to experience in the next six months. Then add up the circled numbers.

Event	Points
Death of spouse	100
Pregnancy for unwed female	92
Death of parent	80
Male partner in unwed pregnancy	77
Divorce	73
Death of a close family member	70
Death of a close friend	65
Divorce between parents	63
Jail term	61
Major personal injury or illness	60
Flunked out of college	58
Marriage	55
Fired from job	50
Loss of financial support for college (scholarship)	48
Failing grade in important or required course	47
Sexual difficulties	45
Serious argument with significant other	40
Academic probation	39
Change in major	37
New love interest	36
Increased workload in college	31
Outstanding personal achievement	29
First term in college	28
Serious conflict with instructor	27
Lower grades than expected	25
Change in colleges (transfer)	24
Change in social activities	22
Change in sleeping habits	21
Change in eating habits	19
Minor violation of the law (for example, a traffic ticket)	15

My stress score is _____

work because you're sluggish or tired, you might experience more stress. One dietary substance that can be directly linked to higher stress levels is caffeine.

In moderate amounts (50 to 200 milligrams per day), caffeine increases alertness and reduces feelings of fatigue, but even at this low dosage it can make you perkier during part of the day and more tired later. Consumed in larger quantities, caffeine can cause nervousness, headaches, irritability, stomach irritation, and insomnia—all symptoms of stress. Many people who have heart conditions have been told to avoid caffeine, since it tends to speed up heart rates. How much caffeine do you consume? Total your caffeine intake on the basis of the figures in Table 16.1.

If the amount of caffeine is excessive (this will vary with individuals, so monitor such things as inability to sleep and when you are most alert and most tired), consider drinking water in place of caffeinated drinks, or choose decaf coffee or a caffeine-free soft drink.

Exercise is an excellent stress-management technique, the best way to stay fit, and a critical element of any worthwhile weight loss program. While any kind of recreation benefits your body and spirit, aerobic exercise is the best for stress management as well as weight management. In aerobic exercise, you work until your pulse is in a "target zone" and keep it in this zone for at least 30 minutes. You can reach your target heart rate through a variety of exercises: walking, jogging, running, swimming, biking, or using a stair climber.

IN CLASS: Have students write down the kinds of exercise they do regularly, including the type of activity, how long each day, and how many days a week they exercise (even walking counts). Ask some of the students to read what they wrote about their exercise regimen. It is generally accepted that it takes 30 to 40 minutes of aerobic exercise at least three times a week to gain the health benefits that exercise affords (lower cholesterol, weight loss, stress relief, increased strength, etc.). Ask how many of the students are meeting that requirement. Discuss the factors that are preventing any of them from getting the proper amount of exercise.

IN CLASS: Poll students to find out how many cups of coffee and how many caffeinated soft drinks they drink a day. Have them calculate the total number of milligrams of caffeine they ingest each day.

TABLE 16.1   Product Caffeine Content (milligrams per serving)

Coffee (5-oz. cup)

    Regular: 65–115

    Decaffeinated: 3

Tea (6-oz. cup)

    Hot steeped: 36

    Iced: 31

Soft drinks and energy drinks (12-oz. serving)

    Coca-Cola: 46

    Dr. Pepper: 61

    Full Throttle (16 oz.): 144

    Jolt Cola: 72

    Monster Energy (16 oz.): 160

    Mountain Dew: 54

    Red Bull: 80

    Rockstar Energy Drink (16 oz.): 160

Chocolate bar: 6–20

Caffeine gum (2 pieces): 115

Over-the-counter drugs

    NoDoz (2 tablets): 200

    Excedrin (2 tablets): 130

    Midol (2 tablets): 65

CALCULATING YOUR TARGET HEART RATE ZONE

1. Estimate your maximum heart rate:

220−age = _____ (maximum heart rate)

2. Determine your lower-limit exercise heart rate by multiplying your maximum heart rate by 0.6.

Max Heart Rate × 0.6 = _____

3. Determine your upper-limit exercise heart rate by multiplying your maximum heart rate by 0.9.

Max Heart Rate × 0.9 = _____

4. Your Target Heart Rate Zone is the range between your lower and upper limits.

Source: *ACSM Fitness Book: A Proven Step-by-Step Program from the Experts,* 3rd ed. (Indianapolis: American College of Sports Medicine, 2003).

What makes the exercise aerobic is the intensity of your activity. Choose activities that you enjoy so you will look forward to your exercise time. That way, it's more likely to become a regular part of your routine.

Besides doing wonders for your body, aerobic exercise keeps your mind healthy. When you do aerobic exercise, your body produces hormones called beta-endorphins. These natural narcotics cause feelings of contentment and happiness and help manage anxiety and depression. Your mood and general sense of competence improve with regular aerobic exercise. In fact, people who undertake aerobic exercise report more energy, less stress, better sleep, weight loss, and an improved self-image.

Think about ways to combine activities and use your time efficiently. Maybe you could leave the car at home and jog to class. Try going to the gym with a friend and asking each other study questions as you work out on treadmills. Park at the far end of the lot, and walk to classes. Take the stairs whenever possible. Remember that exercise does not have to be a chore. Find something you enjoy doing, and make it part of your daily schedule. Many campuses have recreation departments that offer activities such as intramural sports, rock climbing, aerobics classes, and much more. The most important thing about exercise is that you stay active and make it part of your day-to-day life.

SLEEP

Getting adequate sleep is another way to protect yourself from stress. According to the National Sleep Foundation, 63 percent of American adults do not get the recommended 8 hours of sleep per night. Lack of sleep can lead to anxiety, depression, and academic struggles. Researchers at Trent University in Ontario found that students who studied all week but then stayed up late partying on the weekends forgot as much as 30 percent of the

OUTSIDE CLASS: Ask students to do an Internet search on the effects of sleep deprivation. They might be surprised at what they find.

IN CLASS: Follow up the investigation of effects of sleep deprivation with a discussion. What happens to the body if we do not get sufficient sleep? Do class members think they are getting enough sleep? Why or why not?

Get Moving!

Whether it's running, walking, or playing a sport, every student needs to get moving. What are your exercise habits? Remember that daily exercise can be a great, no-cast way to reduce stress while keeping you in good physical and mental shape.

material they had learned during the prior week. Try the following suggestions to establish better sleep habits:

- Avoid long daytime naps.
- Try reading or listening to a relaxation tape before going to bed.
- Get exercise during the day.
- Get your clothes and school materials together before you go to bed.
- Sleep in the same room and bed every night.
- Set a regular schedule for going to bed and getting up.

TAKING CONTROL

Modifying your lifestyle is yet another approach to stress management. You have the power to change your life so that it is less stressful. Teachers, supervisors, parents, friends, and even your children influence you, but ultimately, you control how you run your life. Lifestyle modification involves identifying the parts of your life that do not serve you well, making plans for change, and then carrying out the plans. For instance, if you are stressed because you are always late for classes, get up 10 minutes earlier. If you get nervous before a test when you talk to a certain pessimistic classmate, avoid that person before a test. Learn test-taking skills so you can manage test anxiety better.

Relaxation techniques such as visualization and deep breathing can help you reduce stress. Learning these skills is just like learning any new skill. It takes knowledge and practice. Check your course catalog, college counseling center, health clinic, student newspaper, or fitness center for classes that teach relaxation. You'll find books as well as audiotapes and CDs that guide you through relaxation techniques.

IN CLASS: Have students identify their own stressors that they might be able to reduce through lifestyle modification. What would those modifications be?

OTHER WAYS TO RELIEVE STRESS

Your stress level plays a key role in your overall mental health. Here are several additional things you can do to improve your level of stress and your mental health:

- Reward yourself on a regular basis when you achieve small goals.
- Remember that a college degree is worth some temporary stress. Keep the payoff in mind.
- Laugh. A good laugh will almost always make you feel better.
- Get—or give—a hug.
- Pray or meditate.
- Do yoga.
- Practice a hobby.
- Get a massage.
- Practice deep breathing.

> **YOUR TURN**
>
> Review this list of ways to improve your stress level. Which of these ideas do you think makes the most sense for you? On the basis of your experience, which ideas would you suggest to other college students? Explain your choices.

Mental Health

According to the American Psychological Association, depression is one of the most common psychiatric disorders in the United States, affecting more than 15 million adults. College students are at especially high risk for depression as well as suicide.

DEPRESSION

The National Institutes of Health reports that depression is diagnosed more often in women than in men. Depression is not a weakness; it is an illness that requires medical attention. You will find that many college students suffer from some form of depression. The feelings are often temporary and may be situational. A romantic breakup, a disappointing grade, or an ongoing conflict with a friend or roommate can create feelings of despair. Although most depression goes away on its own, if you or a friend have any of the following symptoms for more than two weeks, it is important to talk to a health care provider:

- Feelings of helplessness and hopelessness
- Feeling useless, inadequate, bad, or guilty
- Self-hatred, constant questioning of one's thoughts and actions
- Loss of energy and motivation
- Weight loss or gain
- Difficulty going to sleep or excessive need for sleep
- Loss of interest in sex
- Difficulty concentrating for a significant length of time

OUTSIDE CLASS: Ask students to research the topic of depression in young adults and to be prepared to discuss their findings in class.

IN CLASS: Follow up with a discussion. What factors contribute to this problem? What experiences have they had with depression, either their own or that of someone else?

■ RETENTION STRATEGY: Depression is relatively commonplace in students, *very* disruptive to academic success, and potentially life-threatening. Therefore, it is important to have your students rate themselves as they read this chapter. Above all, make sure they know where to get help on campus in dealing with any of these warning signals.

SUICIDE

The Centers for Disease Control and Prevention (CDC) reports that students ages fifteen to twenty-four are more likely than any other age group to attempt suicide. Most people who commit suicide give a warning of their intentions. The following are common indicators of someone's intent to commit suicide:

- Recent loss and a seeming inability to let go of grief
- Change in personality—sadness, withdrawal, apathy
- Expressions of self-hatred
- Change in sleep patterns
- Change in eating habits
- A direct statement about committing suicide ("I might as well end it all.")
- A preoccupation with death

YOUR TURN

Why do you think that college students are at especially high risk for depression and suicide? Is there anything that colleges and universities can do to decrease this risk, or is this all up to the students themselves?

If you or someone you know threatens suicide or displays any of these signs, it's time to consult a mental health professional. Most campuses have counseling centers that offer one-on-one sessions as well as support groups for their students. Finally, remember that there is no shame attached to high levels of stress, depression, anxiety, or suicidal tendencies. Unavoidable life events or physiological imbalances can cause such feelings and behaviors. Proper counseling, medical attention, and, in some cases, prescription medication can help students cope with mental health issues.

Nutrition and Weight Management

"You are what you eat" is more than a catchphrase; it's an important reminder of the vital role diet plays in our lives. You've probably read news stories about how there are more and more obese young people than ever before in our history. The CDC reports that the rates of obesity have more than doubled in the United States since 1990: In 1990 an estimated 11.6 percent of U.S. citizens were obese; in 2009 an estimated 26.7 percent were classified as obese. One expert, Dr. James Hill, Director of Human Nutrition at the University of Colorado, predicts, "If obesity is left unchecked, almost all Americans will be obese by 2050." Many people attribute this situation to the explosion of fast-food restaurants, which place flavor and low prices before health. A Tufts University researcher found that 60 percent of college students eat too much saturated fat, which increases the risk for heart disease. Also, most of us do not consume enough fiber and whole grains. As a result, we are more likely to have long-term health problems, such as diabetes, heart disease, and cancer.

HEALTHY EATING

So what can you do about your eating habits? It's not easy at first, but if you commit to a new eating regimen, you will not only feel better, you'll be

"They major in nutrition."

You Are What You Eat

Think about what, when, and how much you eat day to day. When you're busy, it's easy to resort to a fast-food diet, but that regimen will add pounds while reducing your overall health and sense of well-being. By paying attention to nutrition guidelines, you can maintain your optimal weight both now and in the future.

healthier and probably happier. Your campus might have a registered dietitian available to help you make healthy changes in your diet. Check with your student health center. Meanwhile, here are some suggestions:

- Restrict your intake of red meat, butter, white rice, white bread, and sweets. "White foods" are made with refined flour, which has few nutrients. Instead, go for fish, poultry, soy products, and whole wheat or multigrain breads. Remember that brown bread is not necessarily whole wheat. Check the label.

- Eat plenty of vegetables and fruits daily. These are important building blocks for a balanced diet, and they contain lots of fiber (to help fight off cancer and heart disease). Instead of fruit juices, which contain concentrated amounts of sugar, opt for the actual fruit. When you sit down to eat any meal (including breakfast), make sure you have at least one fruit or vegetable on your plate.

- Avoid fried foods—french fries, fried chicken, and so forth. Choose grilled or broiled meats instead. Avoid foods with large amounts of fat and sugar, such as doughnuts.

- Keep your room stocked with healthy snacks, such as fruit, vegetables, yogurt, pretzels, and graham crackers.

- Eat a sensible amount of nuts and all the legumes (beans) you want to round out your fiber intake.

- Watch your portion size. Avoid "supersized" fast-food items and all-you-can-eat buffets.

- Eat breakfast! Your brain will function more efficiently if you eat a power-packed meal first thing in the morning. Eating breakfast can also jump-start your metabolism. If you are not normally a breakfast eater, try eating just a piece of fruit or half a bagel. You will notice a big difference in your energy level during your early morning classes. Avoid sugar-coated cereals. Go for healthier options that are loaded with fiber.

- Always read the government-required nutrition label on all packaged foods. Check the sodium content (sodium will make you retain fluids and increase your weight and possibly your blood pressure) and the number of grams of fat. Strive for a diet with only 20 percent fat.

YOUR TURN

Look at the preceding list of suggestions about healthy eating. Which one of these is the most difficult for you? Which ones do you think are difficult for most college students? Do you think that college students are less likely to eat a healthy diet than the general population? Why or why not?

Figure 16.1 shows the new "MyPlate" icon created by the U.S. Department of Agriculture in conjunction with First Lady Michelle Obama's anti-obesity team and federal health officials. Designed as a simpler replacement for the Food Guide Pyramid and introduced in June 2011, the plate is split into four sections: fruits, vegetables, grains, and protein. A smaller circle sits beside it for dairy products. Mrs. Obama said of the icon, "This is a quick, simple reminder for all of us to be more mindful of the foods that we're eating." The government Web site **ChooseMyPlate.gov** provides tips and recommendations for healthy eating and understanding the plate's design.

FIGURE 16.1
MyPlate Eating Guidelines

OBESITY

People have been joking about the "freshman 15" forever, but it's no joke that new college students tend to gain weight during their first term. Nutrition experts at Tufts University reported that the average weight gain is 6 pounds for men and about 4.5 pounds for women during the first year of college. Increased stress, lifestyle changes, new food choices, changes in physical activity, and alcohol consumption can all cause weight gain. Try eating smaller meals more often, getting regular exercise, keeping a food journal (to keep track of what you are actually consuming), and being realistic about dieting.

IN CLASS: Discuss the "freshman 15." Have your students experienced this weight problem yet? If so, what can they do about it? If not, how do they think they avoided it?

EATING DISORDERS

An increasing number of college students are obsessed with their bodies and food intake. This can lead to conditions such as anorexia, bulimia, or binge eating disorder, all of which affect women disproportionately more than men. Anorexia is characterized by self-induced starvation, extreme preoccupation with food, and a body weight less than 85 percent of a healthy weight. Bulimia is characterized by cycles of bingeing (eating large amounts of food) and purging by vomiting, abusing laxatives and/or diuretics, exercising excessively, and fasting. People with a binge eating disorder do not purge the calories after the binge. Individuals with binge eating disorder tend to eat secretively and are often clinically obese.

Some of the signs and symptoms of an eating disorder are as follows:

- Intense fear of gaining weight
- Restricting types of food, such as those containing any kind of fat
- Weighing less than 85 percent of recommended body weight based on height, or failure to make appropriate weight gain during a period of growth
- Stopping or never getting a monthly menstrual period
- Seeing one's body as fat, even though it is underweight
- Overexercising
- Secrecy about food and denial of a problem with eating

Anyone who is struggling with an eating disorder should seek medical attention. Eating disorders can be life-threatening if they are not treated by a health care professional. Many colleges and universities have eating disorder case management teams to help individuals on campus. Contact your student health center for more information, or contact the National Eating Disorder Association (**http://www.nationaleatingdisorders.org** or 1-800-931-2237) to find a professional in your area who specializes in the treatment of eating disorders.

Sexual Health

Numerous studies report that about 75 percent of traditional-age college students have engaged in sexual intercourse at least once. Whether or not

IN CLASS: Approach the subjects of sexuality and drinking with tact, confidence, and respect for a variety of viewpoints. Above all, don't preach or judge. Remember that you are presenting this material not as an expert but as an adult mentor. Students might claim, "It's all been covered in high school." However, it is unlikely that their prior education included a frank discussion of sexual issues with both genders present.

TECH TIP SURF FOR HEALTH

1 ▶ THE PROBLEM

You don't know how to evaluate the fitness and nutrition information that you find online.

2 ▶ THE FIX

Arm yourself with our list of trustworthy Web sites. Then log on and tone up.

3 ▶ HOW TO DO IT

To feel strong and live long, there are a few steps you have to take. Believing every health-related newsflash you encounter isn't one of them. When it comes to fitness and nutrition, there's a lot of conflicting advice and bad information out there—and more than a few scams. To protect yourself, it's essential to learn how to filter out the fiction.

- **Zero in on a few reputable, well-vetted Web sites.** On the ones listed below, you can find everything from healthy menu plans to yoga training to fitness tips.

FITNESS WEB SITES

FitDay	fitday.com
Fitness.com	fitness.com
Fitness Partner	primusweb.com/fitnesspartner
LIVESTRONG	livestrong.com
Men's Fitness	mensfitness.com
Nutrition Data	nutritiondata.self.com
Peer Trainer	peertrainer.com
Weight Watchers Points Calculator	weightwatchers.com
Whole Fitness	wholefitness.com

- **Clear some floor space.** You already know the first rule of healthy living: Don't spend too much time in front of your computer. But actually, the Internet can be a valuable ally if you're struggling to find time to work out. Free Web sites like *YouTube* and online services like *NetFlix* (which charges a low monthly fee) let you stream a huge variety of workout videos–no need to hit the gym.
- **Exergame.** Video gaming systems like *Nintendo Wii* and *Xbox* let you enjoy real-life workouts in the virtual world. Try Dance Dance Revolution or cyber baseball, bowling, boxing, golf, or tennis. While you're at it, get your lazy roommate or family member to join in.

GOOD TO KNOW

A quick workout can be the world's best study break. Exercise isn't just good for your waistline; it also reduces stress, improves the quality of your sleep, and even makes you smarter. Recent studies show that aerobically fit students score higher on cognitive tests.

EXTRA CREDIT

When searching for medical or health advice online, go for impartial, reputable Web sites (see the list below). And unless you want to turn into a crazed hypochondriac, try not to self-diagnose. Once you type in your symptoms, all sorts of unlikely yet horrifying possibilities will appear: You start with a headache and suddenly you're sure you have cholera.

HEALTH WEB SITES

The Centers for Disease Control & Prevention (CDC)	cdc.gov
Cleveland Clinic	my.clevelandclinic.org
HealthFinder	healthfinder.gov
Mayo Clinic	mayoclinic.com
WebMD	webmd.com

PERSONAL BEST

Click to a medical history site—like *Google Health*, *PersonalMD*, or *Web MD*—and create an online health profile.

you are part of this percentage, it can be helpful to explore your sexual values and to consider whether sex is right for you at this time. If it is the right time, you should choose a good birth control method and adopt some strategies for avoiding sexually transmitted infections (STIs) and unplanned pregnancies. What matters most is that you take care of yourself and your partner.

SEXUALLY TRANSMITTED INFECTIONS

The problem of STIs on college campuses has received growing attention in recent years as epidemic numbers of students have become infected. In general, STIs continue to increase faster than other illnesses on campuses today, and approximately 5 to 10 percent of visits by U.S. college students to college health services are for the diagnosis and treatment of STIs. The belief that it won't happen to you and you can't catch these sorts of infections is inaccurate and potentially more dangerous than ever before. If you choose to be sexually active, particularly with more than one partner but even if there is only one, exposure to an STI is a real possibility.

STIs are usually spread through genital contact. Sometimes, however, STIs can be transmitted through mouth-to-mouth or mouth-to-genital contact. There are more than twenty known types of STIs; Table 16.2 lists those that are most common on college campuses.

As you can see from the table, many of the STIs have similar symptoms or no symptoms at all. Many women show no symptoms and are therefore considered asymptomatic. Most health care professionals recommend that women who are sexually active be screened for all of the possible STIs during their yearly pap smear. These screenings are not part of the regular annual exam and must be specifically requested.

Not all STIs are curable. This means that medications will help alleviate the symptoms, but the virus will stay in an individual's system. Sexually transmitted infections that are left untreated can progress to pelvic inflammatory disease, which is now thought to be the leading cause of infertility in women.

One particularly common STI is the human papillomavirus (HPV). In fact, the CDC estimates that currently 20 million people in the United States are infected with HPV. HPV is a sexually transmitted infection that is closely linked to cervical cancer. Gardasil, a vaccine that became available in 2006, provides protection for both men and women against the types of HPV that cause genital warts, and cancer, anal cervical cancer. For more information about this vaccine or to receive the three injection series, contact your college or university health services or local health care provider.

NEGOTIATING FOR SAFER SEX

If you are sexually active, it's important that you talk with your partner about ways to protect against sexually transmitted infections and unwanted pregnancy.

Communicating with your partner about safer sex can be difficult and even embarrassing initially, but this communication can make your relationship

IN CLASS: Ask students to name characteristics of a person who is sexually healthy. This might require some probing questions to get actions rather than outcomes. For example, a sexually healthy person probably doesn't have sexually transmitted diseases (outcome), but more important, good sexual health results from practicing safe sex (action).

IN CLASS: This information is provided to make students aware of the variety and significance of STIs and to help them recognize symptoms so that they can seek proper treatment. As is true for much of the information in this chapter, you might want to ask a health educator to discuss this issue with your class.

■ RETENTION STRATEGY: STIs need to be a topical concern for instructors in this course because they are sources of great stress for affected students and hence interfere with concentration and academic success. And, of course, they also can have long-term negative health consequences. Make sure you tell students where they can go on campus to obtain confidential diagnosis and treatment.

TABLE 16.2   Sexually Transmitted Infections

SEXUALLY TRANSMITTED INFECTION	FEMALE SYMPTOMS	MALE SYMPTOMS	NUMBER OF NEW CASES IN THE UNITED STATES ANNUALLY	CURABLE OR TREATABLE
AIDS (acquired immunodeficiency syndrome)	Symptoms appear several months to several years after contact with HIV; unexplained weight loss; white spots in mouth; yeast infections that do not go away	Symptoms appear several months to several years after contact with HIV; unexplained weight loss; white spots in mouth	40,000	Treatable
Chlamydia	Yellowish discharge; bleeding between periods; burning or pain during urination	Painful and frequent urination; watery, puslike discharge from penis	3 million	Curable
Genital HPV (human papillomavirus)	Small, bumpy warts on the sex organs and/or anus; burning or itching around sex organs	Small, bumpy warts on the sex organs and/or anus; burning or itching around sex organs	5.5 million	Treatable
Gonorrhea	Thick yellow or gray discharge; abnormal periods or bleeding between periods; cramps or pain in lower abdomen	White, milky discharge from penis; painful, burning urination; swollen or tender testicles	600,000	Curable
Hepatitis B	Symptoms appear 1-9 months after contraction; flulike feelings that go away; tiredness; dark urine	Symptoms appear 1-9 months after contraction; flulike feelings that go away; tiredness; dark urine	46,000	Treatable
Herpes	Burning sensation and redness at the site of infection; painful blister that will crust over, dry up, and disappear	Burning sensation and redness at the site of infection; painful blister that will crust over, dry up, and disappear	1 million	Treatable
Syphilis	Painless chancre; rash or white patches on skin; lymph nodes enlarge	Painless chancre; rash or white patches on skin; lymph nodes enlarge	36,000	Curable in early stages
Trichomoniasis	Yellowish, unpleasant-smelling discharge accompanied by a burning sensation during urination	Watery, white drip from the penis; burning or pain during urination; need to urinate more often	8 million	Curable

Sources: Rebecca J. Donatelle and Larraine G. Davis, *Access to Health,* 8th ed. (San Francisco: Benjamin Cummings, 2004); Linda L. Alexander et al., *New Dimensions in Women's Health,* 3rd ed. (Sudbury, MA: Jones and Bartlett, 2004). Adapted from http://www.plannedparenthood.org, www.ashastd.org, and http://www.herpescounter.com.

stronger and more meaningful. The national organization Advocates for Youth offers these suggestions to help make this conversation easier and more effective:

- Use "I" statements when talking. For example, you might say, "I feel that abstinence is right for me at this time," or "I would feel more comfortable if we used a condom." Be assertive! Do not avoid talking about sex because you fear your partner's reaction.

- Be a good listener. Let your partner know that you hear, understand, and care about what he or she is saying and feeling.

- Be patient with your partner and remain firm in your decision that talking is important.

- Understand that success in talking does not mean getting your partner to agree to do something. It means that you both have said what you honestly think and feel and that you have both listened respectfully to one another.

- Avoid making assumptions. Ask open-ended questions to discuss relationship expectations, past and present sexual relationships, contraceptive use, and testing for STIs.

- Do not wait until you become sexually intimate to discuss safer sex with your partner. In the heat of the moment, you and your partner might be unable to talk effectively.

You can avoid STIs and unwanted pregnancies by avoiding sex entirely. Apparently, 25 percent of college students choose this option, according to national research. For many people, masturbation is a reasonable alternative to sex with a partner.

If you're in the remaining 75 percent, you'll be safer (in terms of STIs) if you have only one partner. Yet you might feel that you're at a point in your life when you would prefer to have multiple relationships simultaneously. Whether you're monogamous or not, you should always protect yourself by using a condom.

In addition to being a contraceptive, the condom can help prevent the spread of STIs, including HIV. The condom's effectiveness against disease holds true for anal, vaginal, and oral intercourse. The most current research indicates that the rate of protection provided by condoms against STIs is similar to its rate of protection against pregnancy (90 to 99 percent) when used correctly and consistently for each and every act of intercourse or oral sex. Note that only latex rubber condoms and polyurethane condoms—not lambskin or other types of "natural membrane" condoms—provide this protection. The polyurethane condom is a great alternative for individuals who have allergies to latex. Use only a water-based lubricant (such as K-Y Jelly) to keep the condom from breaking.

BIRTH CONTROL

Sexually active heterosexual students have to take steps to prevent unwanted pregnancy. Planning is the key. What is the best method of contraception? It is any method that you use correctly and consistently each time you have intercourse. Table 16.3 compares the major features of some of the most

IN CLASS: Topics such as masturbation, celibacy, monogamy, and condom negotiation are often uncomfortable to discuss and have stigmas and myths attached. Students should know that it is perfectly natural and normal for individuals to have sexual desires, feelings, and urges. The key point of this section is to let students know that there are alternatives to intercourse, including a range of behaviors on a continuum of varying risks.

IN CLASS: Although today's college students are more sophisticated and experienced than earlier generations, they are also exposed to a great deal of misinformation. They might have heard about abstinence and perhaps the importance of condoms, but have they learned how to negotiate for safer sex, how to communicate with potential partners, or how to be assertive about their own bodies and sexuality? If they had, would we be experiencing the high levels of unwanted pregnancies and sexually transmitted diseases that are still prevalent on college campuses?

TABLE 16.3 **Methods of Contraception**

METHOD	HOW EFFECTIVE IS THIS METHOD?	DOES IT PROTECT AGAINST HIV AND STIs?	AVERAGE COST	DO I NEED A PRESCRIPTION?
Abstinence	100%	Yes	Free	No
Cervical Cap	84%	No	$60-75	Yes
Contraceptive Injection	99%	No	$20-40 (visit to clinician); $35-75 (injection)	Yes
Diaphragm	94%	No	$15-75	Yes
Female Condom	95%	Yes	$4.00 per condom	No
Intrauterine Device (IUD)	99%	No	$175-500 (exam, insertion, and follow-up visit)	Yes
Male Condom	97%	Yes	$1.00; sometimes available for free	No
NuvaRing	99%	No	$15-50 monthly	Yes
Oral Contraceptive (The Pill)	99%	No	$15-50 monthly	Yes
Ortho Evra (The Patch)	99%	No	$15-50 monthly	Yes
Spermicide	94%	No	$8 per package	No
Tubal Ligation (Female Sterilization)	99%	No	$1,500-6,000	Yes
Vasectomy (Male Sterilization)	99%	No	$350-1,000	Yes

Source: Rebecca J. Donatelle and Larraine G. Davis, *Access to Health*, 8th ed. (San Francisco: Benjamin Cummings, 2004). Adapted from http://www.plannedparenthood.org.

common methods of birth control. You should be aware that the actual cost of some of these methods will vary depending on where you live and the kind of medical insurance you have. The costs listed in Table 16.3 will give you a general idea of how the costs of the various methods compare.

Always discuss birth control with your partner so that you both feel comfortable with the option you have selected. For more information about a particular method, consult a pharmacist, your student health center, a local family planning clinic, the local health department, or your private physician. The important thing is to resolve to protect yourself and your partner each and every time you have sexual intercourse.

What if the condom breaks or you forget to take your birth control pill? Emergency contraception pills can reduce the risk of pregnancy. According to Planned Parenthood Federation of America, if the pills are taken within 72 hours of unprotected intercourse, they can reduce the risk of pregnancy by 75 to 89 percent. Most campus health centers and local health clinics are now dispensing emergency contraception to individuals in need. Emergency contraception does come with side effects, such as nausea, vomiting, and cramping. In rare cases, serious health complications can result from emergency contraception. Be sure you ask your provider what symptoms to watch for.

Substance Abuse

In this section our purpose is not to make judgments, but to warn you about irresponsible use of some substances that can have a major negative impact on your college experience and your life: alcohol, tobacco, prescription drugs, and illegal drugs. While you're in college, you will likely be exposed to the reckless use of one or more of these substances. We hope that this information will help you think twice and avoid the trouble that can come from substance abuse.

MAKING DECISIONS ABOUT ALCOHOL

Even if you don't drink, you should read this information because 50 percent of college students reported helping a drunken friend, classmate, or study partner in the past year.

A number of surveys have confirmed that your peers aren't drinking as much as you think they are, so there's no need for you to try to "catch up." Most students' estimates of how much the average college student drinks are twice as high as the actual statistics. In the final analysis, it's your decision to drink or not to drink alcoholic beverages, to drink moderately or to drink heavily, to know when to stop or to be labeled as a drunk who isn't fun to be around. Between 10 and 20 percent of people in the United States become addicted to alcohol at some point in their lives. Alcohol can turn even people who don't drink into victims, such as people who are killed by drunk drivers or family members who suffer from the behavior of an alcoholic. Over the course of one year, about 20 to 30 percent of students report serious problems related to excessive alcohol use. You might have heard news reports about college students who died or were seriously or permanently injured as a result of excessive drinking. Just one occasion of heavy or high-risk drinking can lead to problems.

How alcohol affects behavior depends on the dose of alcohol, which is best measured by blood alcohol content, or BAC (see Table 16.4). Most of the pleasurable effects of alcoholic beverages are experienced at lower BAC levels, when alcohol acts as a behavioral stimulant. For most people, the stimulant level is around one drink per hour. Usually, problems begin to emerge at doses higher than .05, when alcohol acts as a sedative and begins to slow down areas of the brain. Most people who have more than four or five drinks on one occasion feel "buzzed," show signs of impairment, and are likely to be higher risks for alcohol-related problems. However, significant impairment at lower doses can occur.

How fast you drink makes a difference, too. Your body gets rid of alcohol at a rate of about one drink an hour. Drinking more than one drink an hour might cause a rise in BAC because the body is absorbing alcohol faster than it can eliminate it.

IN CLASS: Research shows that alcohol is often involved in unplanned, unintended sexual activity—whether consensual or not. Ask the class to brainstorm ideas for preventing and/or managing such a situation.

IN CLASS: Ask students to write for several minutes on what the statement "You do not have to be an alcoholic to experience problems with alcohol" means to them. Ask students to volunteer their answers, and discuss these as a class.

IN CLASS: Students might claim that they have heard this all before. Have them defend their right to party; that is, ask them to explain why campus authorities should have no business interfering with a student's social life.

■ RETENTION STRATEGY: There is a clear-cut relationship, as illustrated in this section, between whether students use or abuse alcohol, their level of academic functioning, and their retention.

IN CLASS: Ask students to identify as many effects of alcohol on the body as they can. What are some of the early effects? What are the later effects? Some research might be of interest here.

IN CLASS: Ask students to write anonymously whether they believe they drink more or less than their peers. Now ask them to estimate the number of drinks they consume in a week. Tell them to be as accurate as possible. Collect the unsigned papers, and determine the average number of drinks per week per student. What can the class derive from these data?

TABLE 16.4 **Effects of Blood Alcohol Content on Thinking, Feeling, and Behavior**

BAC RANGE	EFFECTS ON BEHAVIOR AND MAJOR DANGERS
0.02–0.03	Few obvious effects; slight intensification of mood. In some states, a BAC of .02 is the legal level of intoxication for individuals under 21 years of age.
0.05–0.06	Feeling of warmth, relaxation, mild sedation; exaggeration of emotion and behavior; slight decrease in reaction time and in fine muscle coordination; impaired judgment about continued drinking.
0.07–0.09	More noticeable speech impairment and disturbance of balance; impaired motor coordination, hearing, and vision; feeling of elation or depression; increased confidence; might not recognize impairment.
0.08	Legal definition of intoxication in all states for people twenty-one years of age and older.
0.11–0.12	Coordination and balance become difficult; distinct impairment of mental faculties and judgment.
0.14–0.15	Major impairment of mental and physical control; slurred speech, blurred vision, and lack of motor skills; needs medical evaluation.
0.20	Loss of motor control; must have assistance moving about; mental confusion; needs medical assistance.
0.30	Severe intoxication; minimum conscious control of mind and body; needs hospitalization.
0.30–0.60	This level of alcohol has been measured in people who have died of alcohol intoxication.
0.40	Unconsciousness; coma; needs hospitalization.

Source: Adapted from Brown University Health Education Web site: http://www.brown.edu/Student_Services/Health_Services/Health_Education/atod/alc_aayb.htm.

IN CLASS: Ask students to make a list of times or situations when it would be unwise to drink alcohol. Ask some of the students to volunteer what they wrote, and discuss their lists with the class.

IN CLASS: Ask the class to share their experiences with intoxicated friends. What was the situation? What was their role?

IN CLASS: Be aware that one or more students in the class might know someone who has died or has come close to dying from acute alcohol poisoning or might have suffered acute intoxication themselves. Be prepared for emotional reactions to this topic.

Professionals can estimate BAC from your behavior. When someone is stopped for suspicion of drunk driving, police might videotape the person completing a series of tasks such as walking on a line and tipping his or her head back or touching the nose with the eyes closed. The degree of impairment shown in these tests can be presented as evidence in court.

At BAC levels of .025 to .05 a drinker tends to feel animated and energized. At a BAC level of around .05 a drinker can feel rowdy or boisterous. This is where most people report feeling a buzz from alcohol. At a BAC level between .05 and .08, alcohol starts to act as a depressant. So as soon as you feel that buzz, remember that you are on the brink of losing coordination, clear thinking, and judgment. Driving is measurably impaired at BAC levels lower than the legal limit of .08. In fact, an accurate safe level for most people might be half the legal limit (.04). As BAC levels climb past .08, you will become progressively less coordinated and less able to make good decisions. Most people become severely uncoordinated with BAC levels higher than .08 and might begin falling asleep, falling down, or slurring their speech.

Most people pass out or fall asleep when the BAC is above .25. Unfortunately, even after you pass out and stop drinking, your BAC can continue to rise as alcohol in your stomach is released to the intestine and absorbed into the bloodstream. Your body might try to get rid of alcohol by vomiting, but you can choke if you are unconscious, semiconscious, or severely uncoordinated.

Worse yet, at BAC levels higher than .30, most people will show signs of severe alcohol poisoning, such as an inability to wake up, slowed breathing, a fast but weak pulse, cool or damp skin, and pale or bluish skin. People exhibiting these symptoms need medical assistance immediately. If you ever find someone in such a state, remember to keep the person on his or her side with the head lower than the rest of the body. Check to see that the airway is clear, especially if the person is vomiting or if the tongue is blocking the back of the throat.

There are many home remedies (such as coffee, water, or cold showers) for helping to sober someone up, but none has been proven to work. Time is the only remedy because your liver can metabolize only one ounce of alcohol per hour. Harvard University has developed the following guidelines for helping an intoxicated friend:

- Never leave a drunk person alone.
- Keep the person from driving, biking, or going anywhere alone.
- If your friend wants to lie down, turn the person onto his or her side to prevent the inhalation of vomit.
- Don't give the person any drugs or medications to try to sober him or her up.
- You can't prevent the alcohol from being absorbed once it has been consumed, so giving a drunken person food will not prevent or reduce intoxication but can increase the risk of vomiting.
- Do not assume that a drunk person is just "sleeping it off" if he or she cannot be awakened. This person needs urgent care.

We know that many students have been subjected to what they might regard as exaggerated scare tactics by well-intentioned educators. However, there are many compelling warning indicators related to heavy drinking. Think about the following statistics and their possible application to you and your friends. The effects of heavy drinking are nothing less than a tragedy for many college students:

- 1,700 college students between the ages of eighteen and twenty-four die each year from alcohol-related unintentional injuries, including motor vehicle crashes.
- 599,000 students between the ages of eighteen and twenty-four are unintentionally injured each year while under the influence of alcohol.

> **DID YOU KNOW?**
>
> When asked about the previous two weeks, 36% of first-year college students admitted to consuming five or more drinks on one occasion.

IN CLASS: Ask students to discuss how they define heavy drinking. Under what conditions might four or five drinks be problematic? Under what conditions would the same amount be less likely to be problematic? Why do so many people abuse alcohol?

■ More than 696,000 students between the ages of eighteen and twenty-four are assaulted each year by another student who has been drinking.[3]

Heavy, or binge, drinking is commonly defined as five or more drinks for males and four or more drinks for females on a single occasion. Presumably, for a very large person who drinks slowly over a long period of time (several hours), four or five drinks might not lead to a BAC associated with impairment. However, research suggests that in many cases the BAC of heavy drinkers exceeds the legal limit for impairment (.08).

The academic, medical, and social consequences of heavy drinking can seriously endanger a person's quality of life. Research based on surveys conducted by the Core Institute at Southern Illinois University (**http://www.siuc.edu/~coreinst**) provides substantial evidence that heavy drinkers have a significantly greater risk of adverse outcomes. Among other problems, the Core data identify heavy drinking with increased risk of poor test performance, missed classes, unlawful behavior, violence, memory loss, drunk driving, regretful behavior, and vandalism, compared with all drinkers and all students. At the same time, college health centers nationwide are reporting increasing occurrences of serious medical conditions—even death—resulting from excessive alcohol use:

■ Alcohol poisoning causing coma and shock

■ Respiratory depression, choking, and respiratory arrest

■ Head trauma and brain injury

■ Lacerations

■ Fractures

■ Unwanted or unsafe sexual activity causing STIs and pregnancies

■ Bleeding intestines

■ Anxiety attacks and other psychological crises

■ Worsening of underlying psychiatric conditions such as depression or anxiety

IN CLASS: Ask students to make a list of all the times they have been affected by someone else's drinking. Then have the class brainstorm ways to reduce such annoyances.

If you engage in heavy drinking for so long that your body can tolerate large amounts of alcohol, you might become an alcoholic. According to the medical definition, someone is alcohol-dependent or alcoholic if he or she exhibits three of the following symptoms:

1. A significant tolerance for alcohol

2. Withdrawal symptoms such as "the shakes"

3. Overuse of alcohol

4. Unsuccessful attempts to control or cut down on use

5. Preoccupation with drinking or becoming anxious when you do not have a drink

IN CLASS: Ask students whether drinking alcohol, especially during the week, affects one's schoolwork. Ask for examples. How can these issues be better managed?

6. Making new friends who drink and staying away from friends who do not drink or who do not drink to get drunk

7. Continued heavy drinking despite experiencing alcohol-related social, academic, legal, financial, or health problems

[3]R. Hingson et al., "Magnitude of Alcohol-Related Mortality and Morbidity among U.S. College Students Ages 18–24: Changes from 1998–2001," *Annual Review of Public Health*, 26 (2005): 259–79.

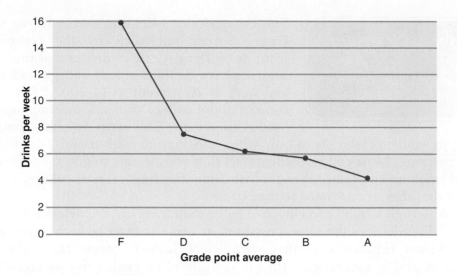

IN CLASS: Although this "grades versus drinking" graph seems simplistic, underscore that the data from which it was taken are very real and the reasons grades go down as drinking goes up are very obvious.

FIGURE 16.2 **Negative Correlation between Drinks per Week and Grade Point Average**

Source: Data from L. A. Rowald and J. L. Gillman, "Average Number of Drinks per Week by Grade Point Average," *AOD Risk Factors across Grade Point Averages: 2006-2008*, Core Institute Data, Southern Illinois University, unpublished manuscript (2011). Illustration adapted from C. A. Presley, P. W. Merriman, J. R. Cashin, and R. Lyeria, *Alcohol and Drugs on American College Campuses: Use, Consequences, and Perceptions of the Campus Environment*, vol. IV: 1992-1994. Published by The Core Institute, Southern Illinois University. Used by permission of The Core Institute.

Through its College Alcohol Study (CAS), the Harvard School of Public Health has found that consuming alcohol at binge levels has a negative effect on academic performance, social relationships, decision making, and health. Binge drinking is also associated with risky sexual behavior such as having unplanned or unprotected sex as well as antisocial behavior such as vandalism and getting in trouble with the police.

The College Alcohol Study also finds that a student's alcohol use affects others in the immediate environment. Roommates and neighbors complain of the following:

- Disruption of sleep or study
- Property damage
- Verbal, physical, or sexual violence
- Visits from the police[4]

Since the early 1990s, surveys conducted by the Southern Illinois University Core Institute have found a consistent negative correlation between grades and the number of drinks per week—and not just for heavy drinkers. Findings are similar for two-year and four-year institutions (see Figure 16.2).

TOBACCO—THE OTHER LEGAL DRUG

Tobacco use is clearly the cause of many serious medical conditions, including heart disease, some forms of cancer, and lung ailments. Over the years, tobacco has led to the deaths of hundreds of thousands of individuals.

[4]H. Wechsler and T. F. Nelson, "What We Have Learned from the Harvard School of Public Health College Alcohol Study: Focusing Attention on College Student Alcohol Consumption and the Environmental Conditions That Promote It," *Journal of Studies on Alcohol and Drugs* (July 2008): 481–90.

IN CLASS: Discuss why people choose to smoke tobacco. Why do young people start smoking? What is the role of peer pressure? Why do some athletes use smokeless tobacco? Is smoking cool?

DID YOU KNOW?

17% of first-year college students smoke tobacco.

The University of Michigan's Monitoring the Future Survey published by the National Institute on Drug Abuse estimates that rates of smoking have declined among college students and were at 20 percent as of 2007.[5] But one concern about college students and smoking is "social smoking." This term describes smoking by students who do so only when hanging out with friends, drinking, or partying. Most college students feel they will be able to give up their social smoking habit once they graduate, but after four years of college, some find that they are addicted to cigarettes.

Although a small percentage of college students use smokeless tobacco, one "dip" delivers the same amount of nicotine as three to four cigarettes. Smokeless tobacco contains twenty-eight known cancer-causing substances and is associated with the same level of health risk as cigarette smoking.

Although smoking is more prevalent among men than among women, according to the American Lung Association,[6] the differences are narrowing, and the rates of smoking-related cancers in women are rapidly approaching or surpassing rates in men. One explanation as to why women smoke is the enormous amount of pressure on young women to stay thin. While there is some evidence that smoking increases metabolism and suppresses the appetite, the problem of being two or three pounds heavier cannot begin to compare to the dangers of smoking. It has been noted that on the average, female smokers have their first heart attack nineteen years before nonsmoking females do.

YOUR TURN

In your opinion, given the cost and the dangers of smoking, what are the reasons that some college students continue to smoke?

Chemicals in tobacco are highly addictive, making it hard to quit. Although young people might not worry about long-term side effects, increased numbers of respiratory infections, worsening of asthma, bad breath, stained teeth, and the huge expense should be motivations not to start smoking at all. Smoking and the use of hormonal birth control can be a deadly combination. A study conducted at Boston University School of Medicine showed that women who smoke and use hormonal birth control are nearly ten times more likely to have a heart attack than are women who don't smoke and don't use hormonal methods of birth control. A final reason for smokers to quit is the cost (see Table 16.5).

Many institutions and local hospitals offer smoking cessation programs to help individuals who are addicted to nicotine to quit smoking. Contact your campus health center for more information about taking this step toward quitting.

[5]L. D. Johnston, P. M. O'Malley, J. G. Bachman, and J. E. Schulenberg, *Monitoring the Future: National Survey Results on Drug Use, 1975–2007*. Volume II: *College Students and Adults Ages 19–45* (NIH Publication No. 08-6418B). Bethesda, MD: National Institute on Drug Abuse, 2008.

[6]American Lung Association, *Quit Smoking: Smoking and Women Fact Sheet*, http://www.lungusa.org/site/c.dvLUK9O0E/b.33572.

TABLE 16.5   The Approximate Cost of Smoking across the United States

Half-Pack-a-Day Smoker

$6.25/pack × 3.5 packs/week = $21.88/week
$21.88/week × 52 weeks/year = $1,137.76/year
$1,137.76/year × 4 years of college = $4,551.04
In 25 years you will have spent $28,444.00.

Pack-a-Day Smoker

$6.25/pack × 7 packs/week = $43.75
$43.75/week × 52 weeks/year = $2,275.00
$2,275.00/year × 4 years of college = $9,100.00
In 25 years you will have spent $56,875.00.

PRESCRIPTION DRUG ABUSE AND ADDICTION

Researchers at the University of Michigan reported in 2008 that 11.2 percent of college students have used prescription stimulants for nonmedical purposes at some point and 6.9 percent have used them in the past year. Three classes of prescription drugs are the most commonly abused: opioids, central nervous system depressants, and stimulants. Some individuals might engage in "doctor shopping" to get multiple prescriptions for the drugs they abuse.

Opioids include morphine, codeine, and such branded drugs as OxyContin, Darvon, Vicodin, Demerol, and Dilaudid. Opioids work by blocking the transmission of pain messages to the brain. Chronic use can result in addiction. Taking a large single dose of an opioid can cause a severe reduction in your breathing rate that can lead to death.

IN CLASS: Invite a campus health professional or local physician to discuss the risks and benefits of taking prescription drugs and why only a physician can dispense them.

Taken under a doctor's care, central nervous system depressants, such as Valium, Librium, Xanax, and Halcion, can be useful in the treatment of anxiety and sleep disorders. The flip side is that exceeding the recommended dosage can create a drug tolerance, and the user will need larger doses to achieve the same result. If the user stops taking the drug, the brain's activity can rebound and race out of control, possibly leading to seizures and other harmful consequences.

Stimulants, such as ephedrine, Ritalin, and Dexadrine, enhance brain activity, causing an increase in alertness, attention, and energy accompanied by elevated blood pressure and increased heart rate. Legal use of stimulants to treat obesity, asthma, and other problems has dropped off as their potential for abuse and addiction has become apparent.[7]

Ritalin is prescribed for a condition called ADHD (attention deficit/ hyperactivity disorder) but is gaining recognition on college campuses as a "cramming drug." This prescription drug costs only about 50¢ per tablet but sells on the street for as much as $15. College students are using Ritalin to stay awake for long periods of time to study for exams. Many students think

[7]Adapted from *Prescription Drugs: Abuse and Addiction*. Bethesda, MD: National Institute on Drug Abuse, part of the National Institutes of Health, a division of the U.S. Department of Health and Human Services, 2009.

that since it is a prescribed drug, it must be harmless. The U.S. Department of Education's Higher Education Center for Alcohol and Other Drug Abuse and Violence Prevention lists the following as possible adverse effects from abusing Ritalin: nervousness, vomiting, changes in heart rate and blood pressure, dependency, fevers, convulsions, headaches, paranoia, hallucinations, and delusions.

Another class of drugs that is of concern in the college setting is anabolic steroids. When most people think of steroids, they think about collegiate and professional athletes. But it is important for all college students to know and understand the dangers of these synthetic substances. According to the National Institute on Drug Abuse, steroids are taken orally or injected into the body in cycles that last weeks or months. Steroid abuse has many major side effects, including liver tumors, cancer, jaundice, fluid retention, high blood pressure, kidney tumors, and severe acne. Most anabolic steroid users are male and therefore have gender-specific side effects, including shrinking of the testicles, reduced sperm count, infertility, baldness, development of breasts, and increased risk for prostate cancer. Abusers also put themselves at risk for contracting HIV or other blood-borne viruses from using or sharing infected needles.

The abuse rate for steroids is fairly low among the general population. The 2007 Monitoring the Future Survey found that 1.9 percent of young adults ages nineteen to twenty-eight reported using steroids at least once during their lifetimes. Just over half a percent (0.6 percent) reported using steroids at least once in the past year, and 0.3 percent reported using steroids in the past month.[8]

Drugs that can be purchased without a prescription are generally safe when taken according to directions on the bottle or package. But never take more than the recommended dose without consulting your physician.

Drugstores and health food stores also carry many supplements in pill or liquid form that are labeled "natural." This label does not mean that the product has been tested, is safe, or is worth your money. The Food and Drug Administration (FDA) does not regulate supplements as they do food or other medication, so it is very important to do thorough research and to consult your physician before starting any over-the-counter regimen.

ILLEGAL DRUGS

Illegal recreational drugs, such as marijuana, cocaine, methamphetamine, MDMA (ecstasy), and heroin, are used by a much smaller number of college students and far less frequently than alcohol. Yet these drugs are significant public health issues for college students. The penalties associated with the possession or use of illegal drugs tend to be much more severe than those associated with underage alcohol use.

Athletic departments, potential employers, and government agencies do routine screenings for many of these illegal drugs. Future employability, athletic scholarships, and insurability could be compromised if you have a

[8]L. D. Johnston, P. M. O'Malley, J. G. Bachman, and J. E. Schulenberg, *Monitoring the Future: National Survey Results on Drug Use, 1975–2007.* Volume II: *College Students and Adults Ages 19–45* (NIH Publication No. 08-6418B). Bethesda, MD: National Institute on Drug Abuse, 2008.

positive drug test for any of these substances. A brief summary of five of the most prevalent drugs follows.

Marijuana.

The effects of marijuana can linger for three to seven days, depending on the smoker and the potency of the drug. Chronic use of marijuana can lead to a lethargic state in which users might tend to forget about current responsibilities (such as going to class). Long-term use carries the same risks of lung infections and cancer that are associated with smoking tobacco.

Ecstasy.

MDMA, commonly known as ecstasy, is a synthetic (human-made) drug, in contrast to drugs that are derived from plants, such as marijuana and heroin. Many young people believe that MDMA is safe and offers nothing but a pleasant high for the $25 cost of a single tablet ("How bad can it be if it's that cheap?" is one rationalization); however, the reality is far different. Taken orally, the effects of MDMA last approximately four to six hours. Many people will take a second dose when the initial dose begins to fade. Some tablets contain drugs in addition to MDMA, including amphetamine, caffeine, dextromethorphan, ephedrine, and cocaine. MDMA significantly depletes serotonin, a substance in the brain that helps regulate mood, sleep, pain, emotion, and appetite as well as other behaviors. It takes the brain time to rebuild the serotonin needed to perform important physiological and psychological functions. Of great concern is MDMA's adverse effects on the pumping efficiency of the heart. Heavy users can experience obsessive traits, anxiety, paranoia, and sleep disturbance. One study indicates that MDMA can have long-lasting effects on memory.[9]

Heroin.

Numerous reports have suggested a rise in heroin use among college students. A highly addictive drug with the potential to be more damaging and fatal than other opioids, heroin is the most abused and most rapidly acting of this group. One of the most significant—and surest—effects of heroin use is addiction. The human body begins to develop tolerance to the drug on first use. Once tolerance is built up, the abuser must use more of the drug to achieve the same intensity. Within a short time, users must take the drug more and more often to alleviate the symptoms of addiction. Eventually, they don't get much of a high from the heroin but take the drug simply to avoid the discomfort of withdrawal. Heroin can be injected, smoked, or snorted. Injection is the most efficient way to administer low-purity heroin. However, the availability of high-purity heroin and the fear of infection by sharing needles have made snorting and smoking the drug more common. Some users believe that snorting or smoking heroin will not lead to addiction. They are 100 percent wrong.

Chronic users of intravenous drugs can develop collapsed veins, infection of the heart lining and valves, abscesses, and liver disease. Users are also at risk for pulmonary complications, including various types of pneumonia. In addition to the effects of the drug itself, users who inject heroin or share needles put themselves at risk of contracting HIV, hepatitis B and C, and

IN CLASS: Have a frank discussion of marijuana use. Is marijuana use widespread among the students at your college? What do the class members really think about marijuana use?

OUTSIDE CLASS: Ask students to do further research on the effects of ecstasy and similar drugs.

IN CLASS: Follow up in class with a discussion of what students found in their research on drugs.

IN CLASS: Invite someone from the drug and alcohol office on campus to answer questions in class. Ask ahead of time whether this person knows a drug "victim" who has been rehabilitated and is willing to speak openly.

IN CLASS: Heroin, cocaine, and methamphetamine are dangerous drugs. A student who uses any of these might be making a decision that could seriously affect the rest of his or her life. Ask students to think about why intelligent college students who have bright futures would jeopardize themselves by getting involved with these drugs.

[9]Excerpted from *Ecstasy: What We Know and Don't Know About MDMA: A Scientific Review.* Bethesda, MD: National Institute on Drug Abuse, part of the National Institutes of Health (NIH), a division of the U.S. Department of Health and Human Services, 2001.

other blood-borne viruses. A heroin overdose is known to cause slow and shallow breathing, convulsions, coma, and possibly death.

Cocaine.   Cocaine produces an intense experience that heightens senses. A cocaine high lasts only a short time; then the good feelings are gone. During the crash, the user might feel tired and unmotivated and find it impossible to sleep. Cocaine is highly addictive. In some instances, users have died of cardiac arrest while taking the drug. Some users are shocked into quitting when their nasal septum (the wall of cartilage separating the two nostrils) begins to develop holes caused by cocaine use.

Methamphetamine.   Methamphetamine, often abbreviated "meth," is particularly dangerous because it costs so little and is so easy to make. Much of it is produced in makeshift labs in homes or college residences, which means not only that the quality varies from batch to batch but also that it's virtually impossible to know what else is in the mixture.

The drug can initially produce euphoria, enhanced wakefulness, increased physical activity, and decreased appetite. Prolonged use can lead to binges, during which users take more meth every few hours for several days until they run out of the drug or become too disorganized to continue. Chronic abuse can lead to psychotic behavior, characterized by intense paranoia, visual and auditory hallucinations, and out-of-control rages that can be coupled with extremely violent behavior. Researchers have found that many former meth users have experienced long-term brain damage, and it is unknown whether the damage can ever be reversed.

OUTSIDE CLASS: Have students look into what kinds of health and wellness programs are available on your campus. What are the goals of these programs? Where are they housed?

IN CLASS: Have students share what they learned in their research into wellness programs.

CHECKLIST FOR SUCCESS

MAINTAINING WELLNESS

☐ **Remember: Managing stress is a key college success strategy.** This is because college, by its very demanding nature, both increases stress and can teach you how to reduce it.

☐ **Get in touch with your own stress levels and sources.** Heightened awareness is the first step in learning how to manage and reduce stress.

☐ **Consider the powerful connections between things you control through your decisions,** such as diet, exercise, and sleep, and your stress levels.

☐ **Recognize that college students are at especially high risk of mental health problems such as anxiety and depression.** Get help from your counseling center if you are not feeling like you would like to feel.

☐ **Practice good sexual health decision making.** This means making wise choices to protect yourself against sexually transmitted infections, developing and maintaining respectful relationships, and avoiding unplanned pregnancies.

☐ **Practice moderation.** Successful college students can still have a good time in college and not let alcohol use interfere with their academic success or personal health. Contrary to prevalent stereotypes, it is not the norm for students to abuse alcohol.

☐ **Don't get hooked!** The college years are the time when many young adults acquire what become lifetime behaviors. It would be a shame if one of the consequences of your college experience were addiction to tobacco, with its long-term negative expense and health effects.

☐ **Avoid experimenting with dangerous behaviors.** Keep thinking about your purpose(s) for being in college and for life and try to make decisions about your own choices accordingly.

BUILD YOUR EXPERIENCE

1 STAY ON TRACK

Successful college students stay focused. They "stay on track." They know what they have to do to be successful, they set goals, and they monitor their progress toward their goals.

Reflect on what you have learned about college success in this chapter and how you are going to apply the chapter information or strategies in college and in your career. List your ideas.

1. _____

_____

_____

2. _____

_____

_____

3. _____

_____

_____

2 ONE-MINUTE PAPER

This chapter provides a lot of tips and strategies for staying mentally and physically healthy. What was the most surprising or unexpected point made in this chapter? What interesting questions remain unanswered about these topics?

No matter how well prepared you are in your teaching, what a student hears and understands might not always be what you think you have said. The one-minute paper is a quick and easy assessment tool that will help alert you when students don't understand what was said or discussed in class. The one-minute paper will also give timid students an opportunity to ask questions and seek clarification. Ideally, you should ask for such a paper several minutes before the end of a class. The paper will also help you begin your next class by clarifying points your students seem to be unsure of.

3 APPLYING WHAT YOU HAVE LEARNED

Now that you have read and discussed this chapter, consider how you can apply what you have learned to your academic and personal life. The following prompts will help you reflect on the chapter material and its relevance to you both now and in the future.

1. Identify one area in your life in which you need to make changes to become healthier. How do you think becoming healthier will improve your performance in college? What are the challenges you face in becoming healthier?

2. If you could make only three recommendations to an incoming first-year college student about managing stress in college, what would they be? Use your personal experience and what you have learned in this chapter to make your recommendations.

4 BUILDING YOUR PORTFOLIO

Are You "Technostressed"? Ever-changing, ever-improving technology is a wonderful part of our modern world, but it can also be an additional stressor in our everyday lives. It seems the list of hot, new gadgets grows longer every day. How does being constantly accessible, being a multitasking marvel, having constant reminders of what you haven't done yet, and sorting an overload of information affect your stress level? Do you occasionally find yourself overwhelmed or even a bit lonely when you are face to face with your computer instead of your friends, families, or coworkers? The hurried, plugged-in life can be exhausting and nerve-racking, especially if you get an incomprehensible error message on your computer screen the night before a big paper is due!

How are you "plugged in"? Create a *Word* document in your portfolio.

1. Describe all the ways in which your life is affected by technology. How are your health and well-being affected, both positively and negatively, by the things you list? *Tip: Think of how you use technology for entertainment and for class or work.*

   Sometimes it seems as if all of the technology that is supposed to make our lives easier actually adds to the balancing act. Here are a few tips for reducing your stress level and avoiding a "technology takeover":

   - Schedule some downtime offline for yourself.
   - Don't become a text message junkie.
   - Don't try to multitask 24/7! Take advantage of time to exercise, eat, or just take a break without the demands of e-mail and cell phones.
   - Recognize the warning signs of Internet addiction, for example:
     - Using the Internet to escape from problems or responsibilities
     - Missing class, work, or appointments to spend time online
     - Always allowing the Internet to substitute for face-to-face interaction with others

2. Save your reflections in your portfolio. The next time you're feeling stressed out, revisit this activity and evaluate the role technology is playing in your life.

For more on this topic watch
French Fries Are Not Vegetables and Other College Lessons

WHERE TO GO FOR HELP...

ON CAMPUS

> **Counseling Center** Professionals here will offer individual and group assistance and lots of information. Remember that their support is confidential, and you will not be judged.

> **Health Center/Infirmary** On most campuses the professionals who staff the health center are especially interested in educational outreach and practicing prevention. You should be able to receive treatment as well.

> **Health Education and Wellness Programs** College campuses assume and recognize that for many students, problems and challenges with alcohol, other drugs, and sexual decision making and the consequences are part of the college universe. Student peer health educators who are trained and supervised by professionals can provide support. Taking part in such peer leadership is also a great way to develop and practice your own communication skills.

> **Campus Support Groups** Many campuses provide student support groups led by professionals for students dealing with problems related to excessive alcohol and drug use, abusive sexual relationships, and other issues.

ONLINE

> Advice about College Student Health Issues: **http://www.goaskalice.com.** This Web site, sponsored by Columbia University, has answers to many health questions.

> Dealing with stress: **http://www.stress.org.** Want to combat stress? Find out how at the American Institute of Stress Web site.

> Advice from the American Dietetic Association: **http://www.eatright.org.** This Web site provides information on healthy eating and nutrition.

> How tobacco affects your health: **http://www .cancer.org.** To learn more about the health effects of tobacco, visit the American Cancer Society.

> The Center for Young Women's Health: **http:// www.youngwomenshealth.org/collegehealth10 .html.** This Web site has helpful advice on sexual health as well as other issues.

> National Clearinghouse for Alcohol and Drug Information: **http://www.ncadi.samhsa.gov/.** This organization provides up-to-date information about the effects of alcohol and drug use.

> Drug-Rehab: **http://www.drug-rehab.org.** This is a private, nonprofit referral service for drug and alcohol rehab treatment.

> Methamphetamine addiction: **http://www .methamphetamineaddiction.com.** Learn more about the dangers of methamphetamine at this Web site.

> The Centers for Disease Control and Prevention: **http://www.cdc.gov.** This Web site is an excellent resource for all of the topics in this chapter.

> If you have questions about suicide prevention, contact the National Suicide Prevention Lifeline at 1-800-273-TALK or on the organization's Web site **http://www.suicidepreventionlifeline.org.**

> National Eating Disorders Association: **http://www.nationaleatingdisorders.org**

> U.S. Government's Nutrition Information: **http://www.nutrition.gov**

> Shape Up America: **http://www.shapeup.org**

> National Health Information Center: **http://www .healthfinder.org**

> Planned Parenthood Federation of America: **http://www.plannedparenthood.org**

> U.S. Food and Drug Administration: **http//www .fda.gov**

MY INSTITUTION'S RESOURCES

_____

_____

EPILOGUE

Maintaining Your Momentum as a Successful Student

The great baseball player Yogi Berra is often quoted as having said, "It ain't over 'til it's over!" This course is over—or is it? One thing is for sure: College isn't over for you, and what you learned in this course isn't over. But finishing this course has to feel good. It is something you have accomplished early in college.

Because there has been so much research done on students like you, we can confidently tell you that successful completion of this course is a good predictor for overall success in college. In this last chapter we are going to provide you with some concrete action steps that you can put in place for next term and next year.

When you finish any of your courses in college, take some time to step back, reflect, and ask yourself some thoughtful questions:

- What did I learn in this course?
- Can I apply what I learned to other courses?
- How will I use what I learned both in and out of class?
- What did I learn that I am most likely to remember?
- Do I want to stay in touch with this instructor?
- Did I improve my basic skills?
- How do I feel about what I accomplished?
- Did I do better than I thought I would?
- What did I do that helped me progress, and how can I repeat those kinds of successful efforts in other courses?
- What challenges do I still face?

Whether you are finishing this course at the end of your first term in college or at the end of your first year in college, you have learned many success strategies that will continue to help you as you move through the rest of your college experience.

Unfortunately, many students, and many college educators too, think that when you finish the first year of college and, hopefully, have achieved sophomore status, you are over the hump. The rest is downhill because the most difficult part is behind you. Well, there is some truth to those beliefs. For many students the first year is by far the most challenging, especially in terms of adjustment to college life. But there are still many decisions you will have to make and many opportunities that await you. We know that you will need a set of strategies to succeed beyond the first year.

TAKING THE NEXT STEPS TO SUCCESS

You are still at the beginning of your college journey. Here are some suggestions for next steps you can take as you make your way toward graduation.

Keep in Touch with Your Instructors. We suggest that you consider keeping in touch with the instructor of this course. Educators who volunteer to teach a college success course or first-year seminar really do care about students and enjoy staying in touch with them over time and noting their progress. You will also want to stay in touch with your other instructors. Later in college you may need to ask them to write letters of reference for you as you seek employment or admission to graduate school. When an instructor becomes part of your larger support group, this is a form of networking.

In particular, discuss with the instructor of this course what your options might be for staying in touch. If you have enjoyed this class and would like to take another course from your instructor, find out what other courses he or she teaches. Choosing courses by selecting excellent instructors is a very important success strategy for the entire college experience.

Stay in Touch with Your Fellow Students. If you developed some good friendships in this class and discovered one or more students with whom you really connected, stay in touch with them. As we have explained in this book, the people with whom you choose to associate in college really matter.

Use Campus Resources. Continue using the campus's services and resources that you learned about in this course, such as the learning center or career center. Remember, these services are most heavily used by the best students, and you want to be one of those. Successful students continue to seek help. It's a lifelong behavioral pattern of successful people.

Practice Study Strategies in All Your Courses. It's important to continue practicing the success strategies that were presented in this book. Usually, you don't learn these in just one term or even one year. And if you don't keep practicing them, you'll get rusty. But we also realize that you may not have been ready to attempt some of the strategies we endorsed in this book. The next term or the next year may be a better time to revisit some of these ideas.

Hang on to This Book. There will probably be times ahead when this book will come in handy for dealing with special challenges in some of your future courses. You may need to revisit how to study, take notes, or prepare for different types of exams.

We know that students like to resell their books. If you do resell them, perhaps you could get library copies at some point in the future. But your books could be valuable resources when you might need to revisit course topics.

Consider Maintaining Your Momentum in Summer School. You may have learned in high school that summer school was usually for students who slacked off during the year. In college, nothing could be further from the truth. We now know from national research on college students' progress that continuous enrollment is a good thing; it keeps students in the swing of things, they don't fall out of practice, and they are more likely to graduate on time. If you really need a break from campus, you could shake things up by studying abroad over the summer.

Consider an Internship.   An alternative to summer school is to find work that is connected to your education or sponsored by your college, like an internship or practicum. Continuing your learning by working in the summer maintains your fast pace of uninterrupted development and doesn't allow you to backtrack and get out of practice. Also, students who have held summer jobs or internships are often more attractive to future employers.

Start Planning Your Remaining Time in College.   As you end this course, we suggest that you plan for the rest of your college career. First, think seriously about your major. That decision is important because eventually you have to get a degree in something, and you want to feel confident and comfortable about the major you select. If you're not happy with your choice of major, don't worry. Unlike in the rest of the world, U.S. colleges and universities give students the opportunity to change majors. So this is something we encourage you to revisit now. This course may have given you some new insights into yourself and what might really motivate you now and in the future. Whether you continue with or change your major, you will want to create a tentative plan for the courses you are going to take for the balance of your undergraduate career. If your college has degree-audit software for long-term course planning, use it. You also need a plan for how you are going to finance college. And you need to think about what will be the best living arrangement in the future: on campus, off campus, at home, with old friends, with new friends, and so on.

Reassess Your Relationship with Your Academic Adviser.   Now is also a good time to ask yourself about your academic adviser. Are you getting what you need from this important relationship? If not, don't hesitate to request a change.

Use Your Institution's Career Center.   It's possible that you haven't used the career center yet, even though you learned about it in this course. Now would be a great time to visit the career center to learn about possible internships, summer employment, and additional help with decisions about selecting a major. When you visit the career center, use its career library and career guidance software to give you more insight into your fit for certain occupations.

Reassess Your Most Important Relationships.   Many students come to college with good friends from high school. Some come with a boyfriend or girlfriend. Are these relationships serving you well? Do they still meet your needs, or is it time to move on? College success is achieved in and through relationships with others. They really matter to your sense of well-being and overall success.

Reassess the Merits of Your College Choice.   Now that you have been in college for at least a term, what are your thoughts about the wisdom of your college choice? Does this institution seem to be a good "fit" for your interests, needs, and values? Do you feel at home here yet? If you are getting pressure from family or a significant other to transfer, have you given yourself a chance at the place where you started? Changing colleges is not easy.

Is this the best time to move on? Or do you need to hunker down and make the most of your initial choice?

Take Stock. Ending a course like this is a good time to take stock of your accomplishments this term. By all means, you should pat yourself on the back. But you also may want to take a hard look at those things that didn't go so well. Learn from your mistakes and apply what you learn to future decisions.

Think about Your Purpose and Goals for Being in College. Let's circle back to the concept of purpose. Here at the end of the term, do you feel that this particular institution is helping you find your sense of purpose and meet your goals? Of course, your goals may change during the college years. What may have felt like a good fit when you began college may no longer be appropriate for you. Practice the goal-setting strategies we have tried to teach you in this book.

Think Commitment. When you think about it, nobody can be successful without commitment. Whether we are talking about the president of the United States, a great athlete, or a great musician or actor, anybody who is really good at anything has commitment. You may feel you are not ready for a high level of commitment yet because there are still too many things that are uncertain about your major and your future life. That's perfectly natural. But at the very least, we urge you, we invite you, to make a commitment to returning to college next term and next year to get as much as you can out of this often unpredictable but life-changing experience.

Consider Giving Us Some Feedback. We love to hear from our student readers as well as our teaching colleagues, such as the instructor of this course. You can write Betsy at **barefoot@jngi.org** or John at **gardner@jngi.org**.

In conclusion, we wrote this book to help students like you. Much of what we know about what students need to be successful we learned from our students. Thanks for giving us the chance to help you as you began *Your College Experience*. You've already come a long way from where you started, and there are many great college experiences ahead. So practice the strategies we tried to teach you in this book, and remember, if millions of students before you have made it, you can too. All you have to do is make the necessary commitment and the rest will fall into place.

Sincerely,

John N. Gardner
Betsy O. Barefoot

GLOSSARY

abstract A paragraph-length summary of the methods and major findings of an article in a scholarly journal.

abstract conceptualization A learner's ability to integrate observations into logically sound theories; one of the four stages of the Kolb Inventory of Learning Styles.

academic freedom The virtually unlimited freedom of speech and inquiry granted to professors to further the advancement of knowledge, as long as human lives, rights, and privacy are not violated.

accommodators Individuals who prefer hands-on learning. They are skilled at making things happen, rely on their intuition, and might use trial and error, rather than logic, to solve problems. Accommodators often major in business. One of the learner groups of the Kolb Inventory of Learning Styles.

active experimentation A learner's ability to make decisions, solve problems, and test what he or she has learned in new situations; one of the four stages of the Kolb Inventory of Learning Styles.

active learning Learning by participation, such as listening critically, discussing what you are learning, and writing about it.

adaptability The ability to adjust your thinking and behavior when faced with new or unexpected situations.

annotate To add critical or explanatory margin notes on the page as you read.

argument Reason and evidence brought together in logical support of a claim.

assimilators Individuals who like to develop theories and think about abstract concepts. Assimilators often major in math, physics, or chemistry. One of the learner groups of the Kolb Inventory of Learning Styles.

attention deficit hyperactivity disorder (ADHD) A disorder characterized by difficulty organizing tasks, completing work, and listening to and following directions.

aural learner A person who prefers to learn by listening to information. One of the preferences described by the VARK Learning Styles Inventory.

autonomy Self-direction or independence. College students usually have more autonomy than they did in high school.

behavioral interview An interview in which the interviewer questions the candidate about past experiences and how they helped the candidate learn and grow. This type of interview helps assess your skills and behaviors.

bias A leaning toward a particular point of view. Also, a negative preconceived opinion of certain peoples or value systems that can manifest either in attitude or in acts of discrimination.

biorhythms. The internal mechanisms that drive our daily patterns of physical, emotional, and mental activity.

Boolean operators The words "AND," "OR," and "NOT." They are added to specific terms when searching in databases and search engines to help yield more relevant matches.

budget A spending plan that tracks all sources of income and expenses during a specific period of time.

chunking A previewing method that involves making a list of terms and definitions from the reading and then dividing the terms into smaller clusters of five, seven, or nine to more effectively learn the material.

citation A source or author of certain material. When browsing the Internet for sources, use only material that has citations crediting the author, where it came from, and who posted it.

co-curricular experiences Learning that occurs outside of the classroom, through on-campus clubs and groups, co-op programs, internships, or other means.

cognitive restructuring A technique of applying positive thinking and giving oneself encouraging messages rather than self-defeating negative ones.

concrete experience Abilities that allow learners to be receptive to others and open to their feelings and specific experiences; one of the four stages of the Kolb Inventory of Learning Styles.

content skills Cognitive, intellectual, or "hard" skills, acquired as one gains mastery in an academic field. These include writing proficiency, computer literacy, and foreign language skills.

convergers People who enjoy the world of ideas and theories, and are good at thinking about how to apply those theories to real-world, practical situations. Convergers tend to choose health-related and engineering majors. One of the learner groups of the Kolb Inventory of Learning Styles.

co-op programs Programs offered at many institutions that allow students to work in their field of study while enrolled in college. They offer valuable experience and an excellent preview of what work in the chosen field is actually like. Also called cooperative education.

Cornell format A method for organizing notes in which one side of the notebook page is designated for note taking during class, and the other as a "recall" column where main ideas and important details for tests are jotted down as soon after class as is feasible.

credit score A numerical representation of your level of fiscal responsibility, derived from a credit report that contains information about all accounts in your name. This score can determine your loan qualification, interest rates, insurance rates, and sometimes employability.

critical thinking Thoughtful consideration of the information, ideas, observations, and arguments that you encounter; in essence, a search for truth.

culture The aspects of a group of people that are passed on or learned. Traditions, food, language, clothing styles, artistic expression, and beliefs are all part of culture.

deep learning Understanding the "why" and "how" behind the details.

discipline An area of academic study, such as sociology, anthropology, or engineering.

discrimination The act of treating people differently because of their race, ethnicity, gender, socioeconomic class, or other identifying characteristics, rather than on their merits.

divergers Individuals who are adept at reflecting on situations from many viewpoints. They excel at brainstorming and are imaginative and people-oriented, but sometimes have difficulty making decisions. Divergers tend to major in the humanities or social sciences. One of the learner groups of the Kolb Inventory of Learning Styles.

diversity Variations in social and cultural identities among people living together.

dyslexia A widespread developmental learning disorder that can affect the ability to read, spell, or write.

emotional intelligence (EI) The ability to recognize, understand, use, and manage moods, feelings, and attitudes.

empathy Recognition and understanding of another person's feelings, situation, or point of view.

ethnicity An affiliation assigned to a specific group of people historically connected by a common national heritage or language.

examples Stories, illustrations, hypothetical events, and specific cases that give support to an idea.

explanatory writing Writing that is "published," meaning that others can read it.

exploratory writing Writing that helps you first discover what you want to say. It is private and is used only as a series of steps toward a published work.

extraverts Individuals who are outgoing, gregarious, and talkative. They are good communicators who are quick to act and lead. One of the personality preferences described by the Myers-Briggs Type Indicator.

feeling types Individuals who are warm, empathetic, compassionate, and interested in the happiness of others as well as themselves. They need and value harmony and kindness. One of the personality preferences described by the Myers-Briggs Type Indicator.

financial aid Monetary sources to help pay for college. Financial aid can come in the form of scholarships, grants, loans, work-study, and cooperative education.

freewriting Writing that is temporarily unencumbered by mechanical processes, such as punctuation, grammar, spelling, context, and so forth.

grade point average (GPA) A student's average grade, calculated by dividing the grades received by the number of credits earned. The GPA represents the level of academic success attained while in college.

humanities Branches of knowledge that investigate human beings, their culture, and their self-expression. They include the study of philosophy, religion, literature, music, and art.

idioms Peculiar phrases that cannot be understood from the individual meanings of the words. For example, "costs an arm and a leg" is a familiar American idiom.

inclusive curriculum A curriculum that offers courses that introduce students to diverse people, worldviews, and approaches. Gender studies, religious studies, and ethnic and cultural studies are some areas included in an inclusive curriculum.

Information Age Our current times, characterized by the primary role of information in our economy and our lives, the need for information retrieval and information management skills, and the explosion of available information.

information literacy The ability to find, interpret, and use information to meet your needs.

interdisciplinary Linking two or more academic fields of study, such as history and religion. Encouraging an interdisciplinary approach to teaching can offer a better understanding of modern society.

interpersonal Relating to the interaction between yourself and other individuals. Friendships, professional networks, and family connections are interpersonal relationships that can be mutually beneficial.

intrapersonal Relating to how well you know and like yourself, as well as how effectively you can do the things you need to do to stay happy. Knowing yourself is necessary in order to understand others.

introverts Individuals who like quiet and privacy and who tend to think a lot and reflect carefully about a problem before taking action. One of the personality preferences described by the Myers-Briggs Type Indicator.

intuitive types Individuals who are fascinated by possibilities, the meaning behind the facts, and the connections between concepts. They are often original, creative, and nontraditional. One of the personality preferences described by the Myers-Briggs Type Indicator.

judging types Individuals who approach the world in a planned, orderly, and organized way. They strive for order and control, making decisions relatively quickly and easily so they can create and implement plans. One of the personality preferences described by the Myers-Briggs Type Indicator.

keyword A method of searching a topic by using a word related to the topic.

kinesthetic learner A person who prefers to learn something through experience and practice, rather than by listening or reading about it. One of the preferences described by the VARK Learning Styles Inventory.

learning disabilities Disorders, such as dyslexia, that affect people's ability either to interpret what they see and hear or to connect information across different areas of the brain.

learning styles Particular ways of learning, unique to each individual. For example, one person prefers reading to understand how something works, while another prefers being "hands-on."

long-term memory The type of memory that is used to retain information and can be described in three ways: procedural, semantic, and episodic.

mapping A preview strategy of drawing a wheel or branching structure to show relationships between main ideas and secondary ideas and how different concepts and terms fit together and help you make connections to what you already know about the subject.

marking An active reading strategy of making marks in the text by underlining, highlighting, and writing margin notes or annotations.

mind map A review sheet with words and visual elements that jog the memory to help you recall information more easily.

mnemonics Various methods or tricks to aid memory, including acronyms, acrostics, rhymes or songs, and visualization.

multiculturalism The active process of acknowledging and respecting the diverse social groups, cultures, religions, races, ethnicities, attitudes, and opinions within a community.

multitasking Performing many tasks at the same time, such as eating dinner, typing a paper, and making phone calls.

outsource To contract out jobs to an external organization in order to lower costs.

perceiving types Individuals who are flexible and can comfortably adapt to change. They tend to delay decisions to keep their options open to gather more information. One of the personality preferences described by the Myers-Briggs Type Indicator.

plagiarism The act of taking another person's ideas or work and presenting it as your own. This gross academic misconduct can result in suspension or expulsion, and even the revocation of the violator's college degree.

prejudice A preconceived judgment or opinion of someone based not on facts or knowledge, such as prejudging someone based entirely on his or her skin color.

prewriting The first stage of the writing process. It may include planning, research, and outlining.

primary sources The original research or documentation on a topic, usually referenced at either the end of a chapter or the back of the book.

procrastination Putting off doing a task or an assignment.

race A term that refers to biological characteristics shared by groups of people, including skin tone, hair texture and color, and facial features.

racism Prejudice directed at a racial group, which often stems from one group's fear of losing power and privilege to another.

read/write learner A person who prefers to learn information displayed as words. One of the preferences described by the VARK Learning Styles Inventory.

reflective observation A learner's ability to reflect on his or her experiences from many perspectives; one of the four stages of the Kolb Inventory of Learning Styles.

sensing types Individuals who are practical, factual, realistic, and down-to-earth. Relatively traditional and conventional, they can be very precise, steady, patient, and effective with routine and details. One of the personality preferences described by the Myers-Briggs Type Indicator.

service learning Unpaid volunteer service that is embedded in courses across the curriculum.

short-term memory How many items you are able to perceive at one time. Memory that disappears in less than 30 seconds (sometimes faster) unless the items are moved to long-term memory.

social responsibility The establishment of a personal link with a group or community and cooperation with other members toward shared goals.

sorting The process of sifting through available information and selecting what is most relevant.

statistics Numerical data used to support ideas in a speech or written work.

stereotype An oversimplified set of assumptions about another person or group.

Supplemental Instruction (SI) Classes that provide further opportunity to discuss the information presented in lectures.

syllabus A formal statement of course requirements and procedures or a course outline provided by instructors to all students on the first day of class.

synthesis The process of combining separate information and ideas to formulate a more complete understanding.

testimony Evidence in support of something. Quoting outside experts and paraphrasing credible sources are examples of testimony.

thesis statement A short statement that clearly defines the purpose of the paper.

thinking types Individuals who are logical, rational, and analytical. They reason well and tend to be critical and objective without being swayed by their own or other people's feelings. One of the personality preferences described by the Myers-Briggs Type Indicator.

transferable skills General skills that apply to or transfer to a variety of settings. Examples include solid oral and listening abilities, leadership skills, critical thinking, and problem solving.

visual learner A person who prefers to learn by reading words on a printed page or by looking at pictures, charts, graphs, symbols, video, and other visual means. One of the preferences described by the VARK Learning Styles Inventory.

wellness A catchall term for taking care of your mind, body, and spirit. This includes keeping fit, making healthy choices, achieving balance, and reducing stress in positive ways.

work-study award A form of federal financial aid that covers a portion of college costs in return for on-campus employment.

CREDITS

Data in Did You Know Boxes

Based on data from the Cooperative Institutional Research Program at the Higher Education Research Institute at UCLA *Your First College Year* (YFCY) 2010 survey.

Chapter 1

RH: Photodisc/Punchstock; p. 8: Courtesy of Moodle Pfy Ltd.; p. 12: © Will & Deni McIntyre/Corbis; p. 14: © Kayte Deioma/PhotoEdit

Chapter 2

RH: Rubberball/Punchstock; p. 22: Jonathan Stark; p. 24: Sue McDermott Barlow; p. 34: Jonathan Stark

Chapter 3

RH: © james steidl/istockphoto.com; p. 44: AP Photo/Cathleen Allison; p. 47: www.cartoonstock.com; p. 48: www.cartoonstock.com; p. 49: © Randy Glasbergen; p. 50: © Doug Schneider/istockphoto.com; p. 51: © 2007 Doug Savage from www.savagechickens.com. All rights reserved; p. 52: © Quinn Kirk/Terry Wild Stock

Chapter 4

RH: Digital Vision/Punchstock; p. 68: Jonathan Stark; p. 74: top, PhotoAlto/Getty Images; bottom, Image Source/Getty Images; p. 75: William G. Browning, Minneapolis, Minn.

Chapter 5

RH: © Vincenzo Lombardo/age footstock; p. 89: Jonathan Stark; p. 92: Learn Something New Every Day at LSNED.com; p. 93: Courtesy of RowdyKittens.com; p. 94: The Advertising Archives

Chapter 6

RH: Schulte Productions/istockphoto.com; p. 107: Jonathan Stark; p. 116: Image Source/Jupiter Images; p. 120: Jonathan Stark

Chapter 7

RH: Stockxpert.com; p. 134: Jonathan Stark; p. 136: left, Getty Images; right, Fuse/Getty Images

Chapter 8

RH: Digital Vision/Punchstock; p. 146: Digital Vision/Getty Images; p. 147: © Bloomimage/Corbis; © David Young-Wolff/PhotoEdit, Inc.; p. 151: © Shannon Burns

Chapter 9

p. 169: © fStop/Alamy; p. 172: top, © Fotosearch; bottom, Bigstockphoto.com; p. 177: Jonathan Stark

Chapter 10

p. 188: left, Spectrum Photofile; right, © Pirillo and Fitz; p. 190: David Young-Wolff/PhotoEdit; p. 198: Jonathan Stark

Chapter 11

RH: simple stock shots/Punchstock; p. 213: Jonathan Stark; p. 216: AUTH © 1996 The Philadelphia Inquirer. Reprinted with permission of UNIVERSAL UCLICK. All rights reserved; p. 221: www.cartoonstock.com

Chapter 12

RH: Photodisc/Punchstock; p. 235: Tony Metaxas/Getty Images; p. 244: Jonathan Stark; p. 247: Jonathan Stark; p. 249: © pagadesign/istockphoto.com

Chapter 13

RH: stockxpert.com; p. 262: Jonathan Stark; p. 268: top, bigstockphoto.com; right, Daniel Kaesler/123RF

Chapter 14

RH: stockxpert.com; p. 277: Jonathan Stark; p. 279: top center, Photo by Glenn Grainger/Zebra Studios. Permission granted by Doggles, LLC; top right, Monashee Frantz/Getty Images; bottom right, © Universal Pictures/Courtesy Everett Collection

Chapter 15

RH: stockxpert.com; p. 292: Jonathan Stark; p. 297: Jamie Smith/http://futilephotographer.wordpress.com; p. 301: © Sam Menefee-Libey; p. 302: Al Diaz/Miami Herald/MCT/Getty Images

Chapter 16

RH: © CSLD/Alamy; p. 314: Jonathan Stark; p. 317: www.cartoonstock.com; p. 320: top, istockphoto.com; bottom, Juice Images/Fotosearch

INDEX

Note: Figures and tables are indicated by (*f*) and (*t*) following page numbers.

A

Abbreviations, 118, 193
Abilities. *See also* Aptitudes; Skills
    developing, 66–67
    emotional intelligence and, 43–45
Absences, and note taking, 118–119
Absolute words, 166, 167
Abstract conceptualization, 66, 66(*f*)
Abstracts of journal articles, 137
Academic advisement center, 18
Academic advisers, 3, 4, 14, 15, 40, 138, 254
    emotions and, 58
    procrastination and, 23
    transfer students and, 243
    tutors and, 164
Academic freedom, 277, 278
Academic goals, 7, 13, 23. *See also* Goals
Academic honesty, 173, 176–179, 181. *See also* Plagiarism
    cheating, 176–178, 179, 192, 224
Academic probation, 25
Academic Search Premier, 218
Academic Skills Center, 15, 18, 40
Accommodators, 66, 66(*f*), 67
Acronyms, 151
Acrostics, 151
Active experimentation, 66, 66(*f*)
Active learning, 102, 104, 121. *See also* Engagement in learning
Active reading plan, 126–131, 139
Adaptability, 48, 70, 71, 75
ADD and the College Student (Quinn), 80
ADD (Attention deficit disorder), 60, 76, 80
Addictions, 308, 330, 331–332, 335
Adult students, 183–184, 231–232
    adult reentry center, 18
    relationships and, 12–13, 273–274, 281
    social networks and, 279–280
Advocates for Youth, 323
Aerobic exercise, 312–313
Age, and diversity, 294–295
AIDS (acquired immunodeficiency syndrome), 322(*t*)
Alcohol consumption, 325–329, 338
Ameny-Dixon, Gloria, 296
American College Health Association, 309
American Lung Association, 330
American Psychological Association, 224
Anabolic steroid abuse, 332
Analytical information, 220
Anger management, 44
Annotation, 105, 129, 134
Anorexia, 308, 319
Answer sheet, in tests, 170
Anxiety, test, 42, 173–176, 179, 314
Appeal to false authority, 94, 95
Aptitudes, 240. *See also* Abilities; Skills
Argument courses, 100
Arguments, in reasoning, 90–92, 94–95
Artistic personality type, 238(*t*)

Assertiveness, 47. *See also* Confidence
Assigned reading, 87, 105, 121, 137–138, 146
    See also Reading textbooks
    supplemental, 113, 137, 139
Assignments, 119. *See also* Homework
    group, 114, 147
    time management for, 22, 26, 27(*f*), 28, 33
    written, 187, 189 (*See also* Writing)
Assimilators, 66, 66(*f*), 67
Association of College and Research Libraries, 211
Assumptions, challenging, 90–91, 95, 97
Attention, paying, 102, 105, 144–145. *See also* Listening
Attention deficit disorder (ADD), 60, 76, 80
Attention deficit/hyperactivity disorder (ADHD), 76, 331
Attention disorders, 60, 76, 80, 331
Attention span, 30
Attitudes, 13, 101
Audiences, 184, 193–194, 195, 197, 199. *See also* Speaking; Writing
Aural learners, 61, 65, 74, 103, 117, 150
Authority
    appeal to false, 94, 95
    of sources, 221
Authors, biographical sketches of, 132
Awareness, and diversity, 299–300

B

BAC (blood alcohol content), 325–327, 326(*t*), 328. *See also* Alcohol consumption
Bandwagon, in arguments, 95
Bar-On, Reuven, 46, 49
Begging, in argument, 94
Behavioral interview, 251
Behaviors, 13
    active learning, 102, 104, 121
    emotional intelligence and, 51–52
Behm, Derrick, 289, 290
Beliefs, diversity and, 291–293
Bias
    diversity and, 299
    of information source, 222
Binders, for notes, 105, 113–114
Binge drinking, 328. *See also* Alcohol consumption
Biorhythms, 28, 31
Birth control, 323–325, 324(*t*), 330
Black, Mari, 274
Blogs, 50, 89, 93, 188
Blood alcohol content (BAC), 325–327, 326(*t*), 328. *See also* Alcohol consumption
Bodily/kinesthetic intelligence, 72, 73. *See also* Kinesthetic learners
Body language, 197–198
Bogod, Liz, 80
Boolean operators, 219, 220
Boston University School of Medicine, 330
Boyfriends. *See* Friendships; Relationships
Brainstorming, 89
Branching maps, 127–128, 128(*f*)
Breakups, in relationships, 280–281
Breathing, 176, 314. *See also* Relaxation techniques
Briggs, Katharine Cook, 67

Brown, Lakeishia, 289, 290
Budgeting money, 256–260. *See also* Money management
Budgeting time. *See* Organization, personal; Planning; Time management
Budget Wizard, 272
Bulimia (eating disorder), 308, 319
Bunker Hill Community College, 273–274, 282
Bureau of Labor Statistics, 14
Burka, Jane, 22
Buzan, Tony, 158

C

Caffeine, 163, 312, 312(*t*)
Calculators, used in tests, 169, 170, 176
Calendars, 15, 26, 27(*f*), 35, 42. *See also* Time management
California State University, Chico, 19, 307
Campus organizations, 121, 254
    diversity and, 297–299
    getting involved in, 283–284, 288
    investment group, 268
    sororities and fraternities, 284, 298
Campus resources
    for careers, 254 (*See also* Career center)
    for critical thinking, 100
    for diversity, 306
    on effective communication, 206
    for emotional intelligence, 58
    general information on, 18
    for learning, 80, 124 (*See also* Learning center)
    for memory, 158
    for money management, 272
    for reading strategies, 142
    for relationships, 288
    for research, 228
    student handbook, 225
    for testing, 182
    for time management, 23, 40
    for wellness and health, 338 (*See also* Health center)
Career center, 3–4, 15, 18, 39, 236, 244, 248, 250, 251, 254
Career counselors, 242, 243, 248, 250, 251
Career fairs, 242
Career fields, 241(*t*)–242(*t*)
Careers, 7, 39, 231–246, 264. *See also* Employment
    aligning sense of purpose and, 235–240
    dos and don'ts of, 243
    employment skills, 245–246
    factors that affect choices of, 239–240
    friendships and, 14
    getting experience, 243–245
    major and, 231–232, 236–237, 243, 249, 253, 298
    new economy and, 232–235
    personality and, 237–239, 238(*t*), 240, 251
    planning for, 240–245, 248, 251
    research skills and, 208
    student profile, 231–232
    two-year students and, 242–243
    Web sites for, 249
Carleton University, 23
Catalogs, library, 213, 217
Cell phones, 26, 28, 34, 36, 131, 178
Center for Young Women's Health, 338
Centers for Disease Control and Prevention, 316, 321, 338
Chaplains, 14, 18, 283, 288
Chat rooms, 50

Cheating, 176–178, 179, 192, 224. *See also* Academic honesty; Plagiarism
Chicago Manual of Style, The, 224
Chlamydia, 322(*t*)
ChooseMyPlate.gov (Web site), 318
Chunking, in reading, 128
Citing sources, 223–224
Classes. *See also* Courses; Lectures
    asking questions in, 101
    online registration for, 8
    participation skills, 102, 104–107
    paying attention in, 144–145
    preparation for, 101, 104, 121
    registration for, 30, 31
    speaking up in, 106–107
Class schedules, 28, 29(*f*), 30–31, 33
Cocaine, 334
Co-curricular experiences, 235
Cognitive learning disabilities, 76–77
Cognitive restructuring, 175
Cole, David, 80
Collaboration, 121, 146, 155. *See also* Study groups; Teamwork
    allowed in tests, 172
    critical thinking and, 88–89
    in preparing for exams, 161
College Alcohol Study, Harvard School of Public Health, 329
College Board Profile form, 262, 263
College education
    as investment, 269
    motivation and commitment, 9, 13
    outcomes of, 9–10, 11(*f*)
    paying for (*See* Financial Aid)
College Readjustment Rating Scale, 310, 311
Colleges, 3–18, 15
    and adult and returning students, 12–13
    building your experience, 16–17
    college experience and, 4–7
    first-year experience course, 3, 4, 53, 68
    high school *vs.,* 3, 11, 19, 21, 144, 276, 283
    importance of, 5–7
    making transition to, 11
    purpose of attending, 3, 6–7, 13–14, 23
    setting goals and, 3, 4, 5, 7–9
    social importance of, 5–6
    student profile, 3–4
    Web sites of, 96
College Success courses, 4, 19, 59, 68
Color-coding, 35
Combs, Patrick, 237
Commitments, 28, 246
    motivation and, 13
    procrastination and, 23
Communication skills, 42, 50, 184, 185, 203. *See also* Electronic communication; Language; Speaking; Writing
    audience and, 193–194
    career and, 236, 245
    safer sex and, 321, 323
Community colleges, 242–243, 273–274
Community service, 285
Commuter services, 18
Commuter students, 13, 31, 214, 260
Competencies, 246. *See also* Skills
    in emotional intelligence model, 46–49
Comprehension, 117, 137, 139, 144
Computer center, 8, 18, 35

Computer files, backing up, 26, 35
Computerized tests, 170, 174
Computer literacy, 209
Computers, 8, 245. *See also* Online resources
 calendar on, 26, 35
 as distraction, 36
 note taking and, 117
 organization of, 146
 reading on, 131
 tutorials, 164
 writing and, 191
Concentration, in reading, 127, 129, 131
Concepts. *See* Ideas; *specific concepts*
Conclusions
 in critical thinking, 88, 97
 of speeches, 201–202
Concrete experience, 66, 66(*f*)
Condoms, 323, 324(*t*). *See also* Birth control
Confidence, 10, 175–176, 198
Consequences
 of alcohol and drug use, 327–329, 329(*f*)
 of cheating and plagiarism, 177–178
 of procrastination, 23
 truth and, 86, 87
Content skills, 245
Continuing education, 6. *See also* Adult students
Contraception, 323–325, 324(*t*)
Conventional personality type, 238(*t*), 239
Convergers, 66, 66(*f*), 67
Co-op programs, 244, 262, 284–285
Copyright, 212
Core Institute, Southern Illinois University, 328, 329
Cornell format for note-taking, 108, 109(*f*), 113(*f*)
Cost-benefit analysis, 88, 91
Costs, 258(*t*), 259–260. *See also* Expenses; Money management
 of smoking, 330, 331(*t*)
Council of Science Editors (CSE), 224
Counseling center, 18, 40, 77, 163, 272, 338
 emotional intelligence and, 55, 58
 relationships and, 278, 283, 285, 288
 setting priorities and, 25
 stress management and, 146
 test anxiety and, 174, 175, 179
 unhealthy habits and, 23
Counseling services, 182
Counselors, 15, 40. *See also* Academic advisers; Career counselors
 procrastination and, 23
 relationships and, 278, 281
 tutors and, 164
Course catalog, 9
Course management systems (CMSs), 8, 74
Courses. *See also* Classes; Lectures
 argument, 100
 critical thinking, 100
 discipline-based, 228
 on diversity, 296–297
 emotional intelligence, 58
 foreign language, 171
 humanities and social science, 135
 logic, 100
 math, 115, 133, 164, 169, 170, 174
 online, 147, 172
 science, 115, 133–135, 164, 169
 teaching styles in, 73, 75, 77, 104
Cover letters, 250

Credit, and money management, 265–267, 269
Credit cards, 256, 260, 266–267, 271. *See also* Debit cards
Crime, on campus, 300–301
Criteria-based aid, 264
Critical thinking, 6, 15, 83–100
 arguments considered in, 90–92, 94–95
 asking questions and, 84, 86–87, 90, 97
 building experience and, 98–99
 challenging assumptions and, 90–91, 95, 97
 collaboration and, 88–89
 in college and everyday life, 98
 conclusions in, 88, 97
 courses on, 100
 essay exams and, 160
 evaluating sources and, 220
 examining evidence in, 91–92, 97
 importance of, 85–86
 multiple points of view in, 87–88, 90, 91, 97
 new ideas and, 106
 problem solving and, 84, 88, 246
 research and, 245
 student profile on, 83–84
 tech tips for, 93, 215
Cultural difference, 179. *See also* Diversity; Multiculturalism
Cultural literacy, 210
Culture, 293, 297, 298
Curriculum, diversity in, 296–297

D

Daily planner, 31, 32(*f*)
Daily to-do list, 30(*f*)
Deadlines, 26, 27(*f*), 282
Debating skills, 100. *See also* Argument
Debit cards, 267, 269. *See also* Credit cards
Decision-making skills, 9, 10, 21, 25
 critical thinking and, 6, 86, 87, 88
 parents and, 282
Deep learning, memory and, 148–149
Definitional information, 220
Delayed gratification, 52–53
Department of Agriculture, U.S., 318
Depressants, affect on central nervous system, 331
Depression, 51, 52, 315
Development arithmetic disorder, 77
Dictionaries, 131, 138, 212
Diet. *See* Eating habits (diet)
Disabilities, 60–61, 75–77, 80, 117, 295
Disabled student services, 18
Discipline, 138
Discipline-based courses, 228
Discrimination, 299, 300–301, 303
Discussions, classroom, 87
 note taking in, 114, 115
Dishonesty. *See* Academic honesty
Disorders, 76–77
 attention, 60, 76, 80, 331
 eating, 308, 319, 338
Distractions, 149, 155, 161, 172
 time management and, 33–34, 37
Divergers, 66, 66(*f*), 67
Diversity, 11, 289–306
 age and, 294–295
 challenges of, 301, 303
 discrimination, prejudice, and insensitivity, 299–301

Diversity (*continued*)
   forms of, 293–295
   hate crimes and, 300–301
   multiculturalism and, 291, 296, 297, 300, 303
   source of beliefs and, 291–293
   stereotypes and, 292, 299–300
   student profiles, 289–290
Divorce, parents and, 282. *See also* Marriage
Drafts, in writing, 154, 187, 189
Dress code, for interviews, 251
Drinking, alcohol. *See* Alcohol consumption
Driving, drinking and, 326
Drug usage, 312(*t*), 331–334
Dyslexia, 60, 76

E

Eastern Wyoming College, 231–232
Eating disorders, 308, 319, 338
Eating habits (diet), 307–308, 310, 316–318
   before exams, 162–163
   fast food, 308, 316, 317
E-books, 136, 214
Economy, 4, 5
   careers and, 232–235
Ecstasy (MDMA), 333
Editing, 186. *See also* Rewriting
Editorial reviews, online, 222–223
EI. *See* Emotional intelligence
Eidem, Dalton, 307–308
Elbow, Peter, 186
Elder, Linda, 85–86
Electronic calendar, 26
Electronic communication, 89, 205. *See also* Cell phones; E-mail;
      Internet resources
   blogs, 50, 89, 93, 188
   instant messaging, 36, 50
   social networking, 6, 50 (*See also Facebook.com*)
   text messaging, 36, 50, 193, 194
Electronic documents, 131
   backing up, 116
   E-books, 136, 214
Electronic mail. *See* E-mail
Electronic resources, 225
   authority of, 221
   library research using, 214, 217–220
E-mail, 8, 50, 216
   to fellow students, 118, 121, 141
   informal *vs.* formal, 193
Emotion, 310
   in preparing for exams, 163, 179
Emotional intelligence (EI), 41–58, 55
   academic success and, 51–53
   adaptability and, 46(*f*), 48
   assessing, 45–46
   building experience, 56–57
   competencies in, 46–49
   defined, 43–45
   goal setting for, 43, 54
   how to improve, 54–55
   impulse control and, 49, 52–53
   inter/intrapersonal skills, 46(*f*), 47–48
   mood and performance, 44, 49
   questionnaire on, 45
   stress management and, 46(*f*), 49, 54–55
   student profile, 41–42
   tech tip for, 50

Empathy, 48
Employment, 23, 86, 185, 234, 236. *See also* Careers;
      Working, in college
   on-campus, 244, 284
   skills for, 245–246
Encyclopedia of Stupidity, The, 100
Encyclopedias, 212
Endnotes, 224
Engagement in learning, 101–102, 120–121
Engineering, 262
English as a Second Language (ESL), 138
Enrollment, online, 8
Enterprising personality type, 238(*t*), 239
Entertainment, 260, 298
Episodic memory, 148
ERIC (Education Resources Information Center),
      219
ESL (English as a Second Language), 138
Essay question tests, 154, 160, 165–166, 173
   key task words in, 166, 167(*t*)
Essay writing, 187. *See also* Writing
Ethnicity, 293, 296, 298, 299
Etiquette, online, 50
Evidence
   examining, 91–92, 95
   point of view and, 202
Examinations. *See* Tests and exams
Examples, in speeches, 201, 202
Excel (spreadsheet) software, 8, 17, 39, 116
Exercise, 162, 312–313, 320
Expenses, 258, 259, 262. *See also* Money
      management
Experience
   careers and getting, 243–245
   co-op programs and, 244, 261, 285
   with diversity, 301, 303
   learning styles based on, 78–79
Experts, 8, 84, 87
Explanatory writing, 187–188
Exploratory writing, 187–188, 189
Expressive language disorders, 77
Extracurricular activities, 33, 237, 283–285
Extraverts, 68–69, 71
Eye contact, in speeches, 197, 198

F

Facebook.com, 36, 80, 92, 121, 193, 278–280
Faculty members, 248. *See also* Instructors
   career planning and, 254, 269
FAFSA (Free Application for Federal Student Aid), 262, 263,
      265, 272
Fallacies, logical, 94–95
False claims, identifying, 94, 95, 97
Family relationships, 5, 274, 281–283
   adult students and, 12, 13, 273
   commuter students and, 31
   financial aid and, 262, 265
   marriage and parenting, 281–282
   parents, 13, 265, 282–283
   prioritizing time for, 24, 25
   quiet hours and, 36
   test anxiety and, 173
FAQs link, 219
Fast Company magazine, 234
FastWeb (scholarship service), 272
Faulty reasoning, 94–95

Feedback, 137, 203, 276
    from readers, 190, 191
    as second opinion, 89
Feeling personality type, 69–70, 71
Feelings, 43. *See also* Emotional intelligence
Fehrman, Kameron, 125–126
Fill-in-the-blank question tests, 168
Financial aid, 33, 260–264, 282. *See also*
    Money management
    keeping, 263–264
    loans, 261, 264, 265
    qualifying for, 262–263
    types of, 260–262
Financial Aid Office, 18, 248, 272
Financial aid officer, 263, 264
Financial Basics: A Money Management Guide for Students
    (Knox), 272
First impressions, 251
First-year experience course, 3, 4, 53, 68
First-year students, 25, 84, 256, 281
    bad habits and, 308, 319
    career and, 241(*t*)
    stress and, 41–42, 160, 310
    student profile, 3–4
Fitness center, 18
Fixed expenses, 258
Flash cards, 128, 129, 143–144, 153, 164
Flexibility, 10, 31, 48, 137
    in class scheduling, 31, 161
    personality type and, 70, 71
Florida Atlantic University, 3
Food and Drug Administration (FDA), 332, 338
Footnotes, 192, 215, 224
Foreign language, 171, 294
    English as, 138
Foreword, in textbook, 132
Formal writing, 184, 193–194
Formatting, for research papers, 192
Formulas, in math texts, 133, 164
401(k) savings plan, 268
Fraternities and sororities, 284, 298
Free Application for Federal Student Aid (FAFSA), 262, 263,
    265, 272
Freedom, 11, 12, 13
    academic, 277, 278
Freewriting, 186–188, 189
Freshmen. *See* First-year students
Friedman, Thomas, 232
Friendships, 6, 12, 14, 273–274, 278–280.
    See also Relationships; Social
    networking
    conflicts in, 315
Frontmatter, in textbooks, 132
Frustration, dealing with, 49, 55
Future, planning for, 7, 269
    See also Careers; Goals

G

Gallaudet University, 289–290
Gantt, Denzel, 3–4
Gardner, Howard, 71, 72
Gender, and diversity, 295
General education courses, 297
Generalizations, 95
Girlfriends. *See* Friendships; Relationships
Global economy, career and, 232

Glossary, in textbooks, 131
Goals, 13, 61, 85, 161, 178, 185, 240
    college experience and, 3–4, 7–9
    emotional intelligence and, 43, 54
    in learning process, 103
    long-term *vs.* short-term, 9, 24
    reading assignments, 127, 131
    for study skills, 31, 145
    time management, 21, 22, 23, 24, 25
Gokhale, Anuradha A., 88
Gonorrhea, 322(*t*)
Google searches, 218, 220, 221
Govoni, Paul, 207–208
Grades, 19, 25, 51, 179, 265, 278
    alcohol consumption and, 329, 329(*f*)
    tests and, 163, 166, 176
Graduate Record Exam (GRE), 115
Graduate school, 6, 246
Grammar, 186, 190, 194
Grants, 261, 262, 264. *See also* Financial aid
Greek social organizations, 284, 298
Green, Noelle, 143–144
Group assignment, 114, 147
Group study. *See* Study groups
GUIDE checklist for speaking, 198–202

H

Hallowell, Edward M., 80
Handouts, 105, 114, 115
Hands-on learners, 67, 74
Happiness, 49, 51
Hardtke, Jason, 183–184
Hardy, Jordan, 101–102
Harvard University, 52, 327, 329
Hasty generalizations, 95
Hate crimes, 300–301
Headings and subheadings, 128, 135
Health. *See* Wellness
Health center, 18, 146, 338
Hearing. *See* Aural learners; Listening
Help, from campus resources. *See*
    Campus resources
Help link, in databases, 219
Henley, Megan, 231–232
Hepatitus B, 322(*t*)
Heroin, 333–334
Herpes, 322(*t*)
Higbee, Kenneth, 147, 149, 158
Highlighting, 35
    in note taking, 106, 115, 116, 119
    in textbooks, 129, 130(*f*), 134
High school *vs.* college, 3, 11, 19, 21, 144,
    207, 276, 283
Hill, James, 316
Holland, John L., 237–239
Homework, 22, 119, 133, 164. *See also*
    Assignments
Honesty, 173, 176–179, 181, 279. *See also*
    Plagiarism
    cheating, 176–178, 179, 192, 224
Housing, 18
    on-campus *vs.* off-campus, 259
    roommates and, 25, 36, 54, 55, 259, 278,
    315
Humanities texts, 135
Human papillomavirus (HPV), 321, 322(*t*)

I

Ideas. *See also* Key ideas
    listening for, 105, 106
    in note taking, 110, 111, 114
    in speeches, 200–201
    synthesis of, 223, 225
Idea stage, in writing, 189
Idea-starters, in taking tests, 165
Idioms, 138
Illegal drugs, 332–334
Impulse control, 49, 52–53
Inclusive curriculum, diversity and, 296
Independence, 21, 47
Informal writing, 184, 193–194
Information. *See also* Research; Sources of information
    for budgeting money, 257–258
    on campus (*See* Campus resources)
    evaluating sources, 220–223
    managing, 208, 209
    periodical database, 218
    synthesizing, 223
Information Age, 208
Informational Web sites, 93
Information economy, 4, 5
Information literacy, 208–212, 225
InfoTrac (database), 218
Initiative, showing, 246
Innovation, 246
Instant messaging, 36, 50
Instructors, 4, 105
    absences and, 118–119
    academic code and, 179
    adult students and, 12, 274
    alliances with, 6
    availability of, 11, 34
    cheating in exams and, 178
    critical thinking and, 84
    engaged learning and, 120, 121
    exams and, 160, 161, 163, 165, 166
    expectations of, 28, 36, 275–276, 281
    Facebook profile of, 280
    help from, 119
    interdisciplinary thinking and, 135
    meeting with, 15, 115, 207, 277–278
    multiple points of view and, 87–88
    notes to, 131
    office hours of, 113, 285
    one-on-one attention from, 60
    online courses, 147
    outlines of lectures by, 111
    permission to record lectures of, 102
    plagiarism and, 224–225
    punctuality and, 36
    questions to, 106, 107, 147
    relationships with, 275–278
    research topic and, 228
    study groups and, 164
    supplemental readings and, 137
    teaching style of, 60, 73, 75, 77, 104
    test grading and, 176
    textbooks and, 132, 133
    writing and, 194
Integrity, 246. *See also* Cheating; Plagiarism
Intellectual growth, 10

Intellectual property, 212, 224
Intellectual theft, 177. *See also* Plagiarism
Intelligence. *See also* Emotional intelligence
    learning disabilities and, 77
    multiple, 71–73
Interactive learners, 104, 117, 128
Interdisciplinary study, 135
Interests, and careers, 237, 239–240
Interlibrary loan, 214
International student adviser, 41
International students, 41, 83
International travel, 9, 302
Internet resources, 14, 222–223. *See also* Electronic
    communications; Online resources; Web sites
    googling key words on, 145
    online tests, 172
    outlandish claims on, 92
    research on, 93, 210, 227
    supplemental readings on, 137
    tutorials on, 35
Internships, 244, 248
Interpersonal intelligence, 72, 73
Interpersonal relationships, 48. *See also* Friendships; Parenting;
    Relationships
Interpersonal skills, 46(*f*), 47–48, 246
Interviewing, 236, 250–251
Intrapersonal intelligence, 72, 73
Intrapersonal skills, 46(*f*), 47
Introduction
    in sources, 220
    in speech, 199
    in textbooks, 126, 132
Introverts, 68–69, 71
Intuitive personality type, 69, 71
Inventory of Learning Styles, Kolb, 66–67
Investigative personality type, 238(*t*), 239
IRA (individual retirement account), 268

J

Jargon, 135
Job fairs, 247
Jobs. *See* Careers; Employment; Working, in college
Journal articles, abstracts of, 137
Judging personality type, 70, 71
Jumping on the bandwagon, 95
Jung, Carl Gustav, 67
Junk food, 310

K

Kadison, Richard, 51–52
Kawamata, Ikumi, 289, 290
Kay, Emma, 19–20
Key ideas. *See also* Main points
    in note taking, 110, 111, 114
    in reading, 128, 131
Key words, 116, 152
    in essay questions, 166, 167(*t*)
    online searches, 145, 215, 219
Kinesthetic learners, 59, 61, 65, 104
    bodily intelligence, 72, 73
    memory and, 151
Know How to Go program, 260–261
Knox, Susan, 272
Kolb, David A., 66

Kolb Inventory of Learning Styles, 66–67
Kuriakose, Cindy, 255–256

L

Laboratory tests, 170–171
Labor Department, U.S., 14
Labouré College, 255
Language
    disabilities with, 75, 77
    English as Second, 138
    foreign, 171, 294
Latinos, 294
LD Pride, 80
LDs. *See* Learning disabilities
Leadership, 6, 185, 246
Learners. *See also* Learning; Visual learners
    aural, 61, 65, 74, 103, 117, 150
    hands-on, 67, 74
    interactive, 104, 117, 128
    kinesthetic, 59, 61, 65, 72, 73, 104, 151
    olfactory, 104
    read/write, 59, 61, 65, 150–151
    tactile, 104, 118
Learning, 121. *See also* Learning styles
    building experience in, 122–123
    class participation and, 104–107
    disabilities, 60–61, 75–77, 80, 117, 295
    engagement in, 101–102, 120–121
    idea generation in, 88
    as life skill, 5
    senses used in, 103–104, 121, 131
    setting goals for, 103
Learning center, 102, 119, 124, 142, 182
    learning disabilities and, 77, 295
    memory strategies and, 158
    test preparation and, 163, 164
    tutors and, 164
    writing skills and, 206
Learning community, 118, 163, 173
Learning Outside the Lines (Hallowell, Mooney &
    Cole), 80
Learning relationship, 276–277. *See also* Instructors
Learning styles, 59–80, 103–104
    See also Learners
    building experience, 78–79
    disabilities and, 60–61, 75–77
    Kolb inventory of, 66–67
    memory and, 150–151, 155
    multiple intelligences, 71–73
    Myers-Briggs type indicator, 67–71
    setting goals for, 61
    teaching styles and, 60, 73, 75, 77, 104
    tech tips, 74
    VARK inventory, 59, 61–65
Lecturers. *See* Instructors
Lectures, 11
    See also Classes; Courses
    main points in, 105–106, 110, 118
    recording, 102, 117
    speaking up in, 107
    textbooks and, 129
Legacy students, 6
Legal services, 18
Liberal education, 84

Library, 14, 15, 135, 192
    career center, 254
    digital books from, 136
    quiet study in, 131, 216
    specialized, 228
    supplemental readings at, 137
Library research, 213–220, 228
    choosing and narrowing a topic in, 212–213
    electronic sources, 217–220
    interlibrary loan and, 214
    librarians and, 210, 212, 214, 216–217, 225
    online, 214, 215, 220
    student profile on, 207–208
Life goals, 240. *See also* Goals
Lifelong learning, commitment to, 234
Lifestyle, 284, 314, 328
Listening, 102, 105–106, 117, 323. *See also* Attention, paying;
    Aural learners
List format, in note-taking, 109, 112(*f*)
Lists
    to-do, 23, 24, 28, 30(*f*), 35, 37, 42, 163
    used in reading, 128, 129, 131
Literacy, 209–210. *See also* Reading
    Information, 208–212, 225
Loans, student, 261, 264, 265. *See also* Financial aid
Logical fallacies, 94–95
Logical/mathematical intelligence, 72
Logic courses, 100
Long-term memory, 148, 154. *See also* Memory
Lorayne, Harry, 158

M

Machine-scored tests, 170
Magazines for Libraries, 222
Magazines *vs.* scholarly journals, 221–222
Maharjan, Sabeena, 41–42
Main points, 190. *See also* Key ideas
    in lectures, 105–106, 110, 118
    in speeches, 200–201
Major in Success (Combs), 237
Majors
    careers and, 231–232, 236–237, 243, 249, 253, 298
    discipline-based courses, 228
    knowledge in, 245
    selecting, 7, 22
Mapping, 127–129, 141
    mind, 152–153, 153(*f*)
Mapping Your Future (Web site), 254
Margin notes, 129, 130*f*, 131, 134
Marijuana, 333
Marking textbooks, 129, 130(*f*). *See also* Highlighting
    annotation, 105, 129, 134
Marriage, 280, 281–282. *See also* Relationships
Marshmallow Study, Stanford University, 52–53
Mascots, school, 300
Matching question tests, 168–169
Math center, 18
Math courses
    exams in, 169, 174
    note taking in, 115
    preparing for exams in, 164, 170
Math textbooks, 133
Matrices, 17, 141
MBTI (Myers-Briggs Type Indicator), 67–71, 79

McManus, Kelsey, 83–84
MDMA (ecstasy), 333
Media literacy, 209
Medical College Admission Test (MCAT), 115
Medications, 331–332
Meeting, with instructors, 15, 115, 207, 277–278
Memory, 133, 147–154, 157, 158
    deep learning and, 148–149
    episodic, 148
    improving, 150–154
    long-term *vs.* short-term, 147–148
    mind maps and, 152–153, 153(*f*)
    mnemonics and, 151–152, 157
    myths about, 149–150
    photographic, 149
    procedural, 148
    reviewing notes and, 117
    semantic, 148
    speaking and, 197
    summaries and, 154
    understanding and, 144–145
Mental health, 315–316, 335. *See also* Stress; Test anxiety
    depression, 51, 52, 315
    suicide prevention, 316, 338
Mentor, instructor as, 274
Merit, evaluation by, 6
Merit scholarships, 261
Merriam-Webster Dictionary, 138
Methamphetamine (meth), 334, 338
Michigan State University, 251
Middle Tennessee State University, 142
Mind map, 152–153, 153(*f*)
Missouri Southern State University, 143
MLA Handbook for Writers of Research Papers, 192, 224
Mnemonics, 151–152, 157
Modern Language Association, 192, 224
Money management, 255–272. *See also* Financial aid
    budgeting and, 256–260
    credit, 265–267, 269
    student profile, 255–256
Monitoring the Future study (University of Michigan), 330, 332
Moods, 14, 44, 49
Mooney, Jonathan, 80
Motivation, 9, 13, 14, 22, 276
Multiculturalism, 291, 296, 297, 300, 303. *See also* Diversity
Multiple-choice question tests, 166, 168, 168(*f*), 170
Multiple intelligences, 71–73
Multiple points of view, in critical thinking, 87–88, 90, 91, 97
Multitasking, avoiding, 31, 50, 148
Murray, Donald, 189, 190–191
Musical/rhythmic intelligence, 72, 73
Myers, Isabel Briggs, 67
Myers-Briggs Type Indicator (MBTI), 67–71, 79

N

Nadeau, Kathleen G., 80
National Center for Learning Disabilities, 80
National College Access Network, 260
National Eating Disorders Association, 319, 338
National Institute on Drug Abuse, 330
National Institutes of Mental Health, 76, 315
National Sleep Foundation, 313
Naturalist intelligence, 72, 73
Need-based scholarships, 261
Needs *vs.* wants, in budget, 259

Networking, 236
New York Times Index, 219
Niagara University, Office for Academic Support, 142
Nicotine. *See* Tobacco usage
Northeastern Illinois University, 60
Notebook, 28, 171
Note cards, 59
    for speeches, 197, 201
Note taking, 101, 102
    avoiding plagiarism and, 192
    comparing, 118–119, 121
    effectiveness in, 108–117
    formats for, 108–113
    highlighting in, 106, 115, 116, 119
    in nonlecture classes, 114
    reading and, 129, 139
    reviewing, 26, 31, 117–118, 121, 152
    rewriting, 146
    in science and math courses, 115
    service for, 118
    techniques for, 110–117
    tech tips for, 115, 116–117
    three-ring binder for, 105, 113–114
Nutrition, weight management and, 316–319. *See also* Food (diet)

O

Obama, Barack, 266, 294, 301
Obama, Michelle, 318
Obesity, 316, 319. *See also* Weight management
Observation. *See* Reflective observation
Occupational Information Network, 254
Occupational Outlook Handbook, 253
Oklahoma City Community College, 41
Olfactory learning, 104
Olympic Games, argument about, 90–91
Online calendar, 35
Online catalog, library, 213
Online communications, 205. *See also* Electronic communication
    discussion groups, 89, 147
    with librarian, 214, 217
    social networks, 6, 50, 278–280, 287
Online courses, 147, 172
Online enrollment, 8
Online resources. *See also* Internet
    for careers, 248, 254
    on critical thinking, 100
    on diversity, 306
    for financial aid, 272
    for learning disabilities, 80
    on memorization, 158
    on public speaking, 124
    on reading textbooks, 142
    on relationships, 288
    for research, 213–214, 228
    for test preparation, 182
    trustworthiness of, 222–223
    on wellness, 338
    for writing and speaking, 206
Open-book tests, 171
Open mindedness, 7, 105–106, 303
Open-note tests, 171
Opinions, 160. *See also* Points of view
    defending, 84
    differences of, 10, 87
Opioids, 331, 333–334

Optimism, 42, 49, 51. *See also* Positive thinking
Oral exams, 171
Organization, personal, 42, 126. *See also* Planner; Planning
    daily planner, 31, 32(*f*)
    judging *vs.* perceiving types, 70, 71
    in note taking, 114, 146
    in preparation for class, 105
    in science textbooks, 133–134
    in speeches, 201
    as step in writing, 189–190
    tech tips for, 35
    term assignment preview, 26, 27(*f*)
    time management and, 19–20, 26–30
Outline format, in note taking, 108, 110(*f*), 111, 113(*f*)
Outlines
    in essay tests, 165–166
    in reading, 128, 129, 134, 135
    for speeches, 197, 201
    thesis statement and, 189–190

P

Panic attacks, 51, 149, 165
Paragraph format, in note taking, 108, 111(*f*)
Paraphrasing, 192, 215
Parent Loan for Undergraduate Students (PLUS)
        program, 265
Parents, 13, 282–283. *See also* Family relationships
    financial assistance from, 265
PARK method, for interviews, 251
Participation in class, 102, 104–107. *See also* Active learning;
        Engagement in learning; Listening; Note taking; Questions
Partnership for Service Learning, 9
Paul, Richard, 85–86
Peer review, 190, 191
Perceiving personality type, 70, 71
Periodical databases, 217–218, 222
Personal attacks, 94
Personal finances. *See* Money management
Personality, 20, 246
    career and, 237–239, 238(*t*), 240, 251
    characteristics, 67–71, 79
Personal values. *See* Values, personal
Phone numbers, 118. *See also* Cell phones
Photocopies, 105, 115
Photographic memory, 149
Physical abilities, and diversity, 295. *See also* Disabilities
Physical activity. *See* Exercise
PIN (personal identification number), 269
Pirsig, Robert, 187
Plagiarism, 177–178. *See also* Academic honesty
    Internet and, 215
    research and, 192, 211, 224–225
Plain English Network, 185
Planned Parenthood Federation of America, 324, 338
Planner, 3, 20, 26, 35, 37
    daily planner, 31, 32(*f*)
Planning. *See also* Schedules
    for budgeting money, 258–259
    for careers, 240–245, 248, 251
    emotional intelligence and, 54
    future, 7, 269
    time management and, 24
Points of view, 135, 222
    in critical thinking, 87–88, 90, 91, 97
    speaking skills and, 202

in writing, 193
Politeness, 36, 50
Political/activist organizations, 298
Portfolios, building
    on academic integrity, 181
    on careers and majors, 39, 253
    on credit cards, 271
    on diversity and study abroad, 305
    on emotional intelligence, 57
    on family relationships, 287
    on Internet research, 227
    on MBTI personality test, 79
    on memory, 157
    on personal influences, 99
    on presentation of notes, 123
    on reading strategies, 141
    on skills matrix, 17
    on speaking skills, 205
    on stress and technology, 337
Positive thinking, 42, 51, 163, 175–176
PowerPoint presentations, 8, 60, 116, 184, 205
    good *vs.* bad slides in, 196(*f*)
    for lectures, 111, 195, 197
Practice, memory and, 150
Practice exams, 174
Preface, in textbooks, 132
Pregnancy, protection against, 323–325
Prejudice, diversity and, 299
Preparation
    for class, 101, 104, 121
    for speeches, 194–197, 202
    for tests, 96, 154, 160–164, 179
PREP formula for speaking, 202
Prescription drug abuse, 331–332
Presentations, 246. *See* PowerPoint presentations;
        Speaking
Primary sources, 132
Priorities, setting, 20, 24–25
Privacy, need for, 25
Problem solving, 48, 114
    critical-thinking skills and, 84, 88, 246
Problem-solving tests, 169–170
Procedural memory, 148
Procrastination, 20, 22–23, 37, 70. *See also*
        Time management
    avoiding cheating and, 192, 215
    highlighting as form of, 134
    study time and, 143, 144
    test preparation and, 173
Procrastination: Why You Do It, What to Do About It
        (Burka & Yuen), 22
Professors, 12, 14. *See also* Instructors
    academic freedom and, 277
    paying attention to, 144–145
    setting priorities and, 24
    talking with, 42, 207, 253
    teaching styles of, 77
Pronunciation, in speeches, 198
Proofs of theorems, in math texts, 133
Psychological type, MBTI and, 68
*Publication Manual of the American Psychological
        Association*, 224
Public speaking. *See* Speaking
Punctuality, 36, 37. *See also* Time management
Purdue University, Owl at, 192

Purpose
in attending college, 3, 6–7, 13–14, 23
career and, 235–240
for information searches, 210, 212

Q

Questionnaires
emotional intelligence, 45
VARK, 62–63
Questions, 101
in critical thinking, 84, 86–87, 90, 97
to instructors, 106, 107, 147
tests using, 160, 165–170
Quinn, Patricia, 80

R

Race and racism, 294, 303
Ramos, Kristy, 289–290
Reader's Guide to Periodical Literature, 218
Reading, 87, 125–142
active plan for, 126–131, 139
assigned, 87, 105, 113, 121, 137–138, 139, 146
building experience, 140–141
concentration and, 127, 129, 131
improving, 137–138
mapping and other strategies for, 127–129, 141
marking textbooks, 129, 130(*f*)
monitoring, 137
previewing, 126–129
reviewing and, 128, 131
setting goals for, 127, 131
strategies in, 132–137
student profile, 125–126
tech tip for, 136
Read/write learners, 59, 61, 65, 150–151
Realistic expectations, 15
Realistic personality type, 238(*t*), 239
Reality testing, 48
Reasoning, faulty, 94–95
Recall column, in note taking, 108, 109(*f*)
Reciting, 117, 137
Recording, of lectures, 102, 117
Reference librarians, 192, 215, 216
Reflective observation, 66, 66(*f*)
Registrar, 269
Rehearsal, of speeches, 197, 203
Relationships, 273–288. *See also* Family relationships; Friendships
emotions and, 55
extracurricular involvement and, 283–285
getting serious in, 280–281
with instructors, 275–278
marriage and parenting, 280, 281–282
parents, 13, 282–283
roommates, 36, 54, 55, 278
social networking and, 278–280
student profile, 273–274
Relaxation techniques, 163, 314
Religion, and diversity, 294
Repetition, and memory, 106, 117
Research, 207–228. *See also* Library research
choosing, narrowing topic for, 212–213
critical thinking and, 245
information literacy and, 208–212
Internet, 93, 210, 227

original, 11
plagiarism and, 192, 224–225
retrieval *vs.*, 84
student profile, 207–208
Residence hall advisers, 14, 278
Respect, 36, 50, 295
Responsibility, 21, 48, 149, 259, 278
Résumé, 248, 250
Retrieval, of information, 84, 209, 210, 211, 212.
     See also Memory
Returning students, 12–13, 84. *See also* Adult students
Reviewing, 164
notes, 26, 31, 102, 117–118, 121
reading and, 128, 131
test preparation and, 131, 154
Rewriting and revision, 189, 190
Rhymes, as memory aids, 152
Riley Guide, The, 254
Ritalin, 331–332
Roman numerals, 108
Romantic relationships, 280–281
Roommates, 25, 36, 54, 55, 259, 278, 315
Rose, Reginald, 100

S

Safer sex, 321, 323
Santa Monica City College, 101
SAT scores, 52, 174
Savings accounts, 268, 269
Schedules, 15, 20, 54, 161
class, 28, 29(*f*), 30–31, 33
exam dates on, 160, 162(*f*)
for exercise, 313
term assignment preview, 26, 27(*f*)
Schein, Robert, 59–60
Scholarly journals, 137
     vs. popular magazines, 221–222
Scholarship Office, 18
Scholarships, 255, 261, 262, 263, 272. *See also* Financial aid
Science courses, 115, 133–135, 164, 169
*Scientific Style and Format: The CSE Manual for Authors, Editors,
     and Publishers*, 224
Search guidelines, 219–220. *See also* Research
Second-year students, career and, 241(*t*)
Self-actualization, 47
Self-assessment, in emotional intelligence, 45–46
Self-awareness, 47
Self-confidence, 10, 175–176, 198
Self-esteem, 10, 47
Semantic memory, 148
Sen, Krishneer, 289, 290
Senses, used in learning, 103–104, 121, 131. *See also* Learners
Sensing personality type, 69, 70
Service learning, 9, 244, 285
Services, for students. *See* Campus resources
Sessums, Christopher P., 89
Sewell, Zulma, 289, 290
Sexual health, 319, 321–325, 335
birth control, 323–325, 324(*t*)
Sexually transmitted infections (STIs), 321, 322(*t*), 323, 324(*t*)
Sexual orientation, 280, 295
Short-term memory, 147–148
Sight, learning based on. *See* Visual learners
SI (Supplemental Instruction), 114, 118

Skills, 17, 240. *See also* Abilities; Critical thinking
  debating, 100
  decision-making, 6, 9, 10, 21, 25, 86, 87, 88, 282–283
  in emotional intelligence model, 46(*f*), 47–48
  employment and, 245–246
  information literacy, 209, 211–212
  leadership, 6, 185, 246
  listening, 102, 105–106, 117, 323
  social, 42
Skimming, of textbooks, 127, 134
Sleep needs, 31, 33, 162, 313–314
Slide shows. *See* PowerPoint presentations
SMART (specific, measurable, attainable, relevant, and timely)
    goals, 7
Smiling, in speeches, 198
Smock, Benjamin, 273–274, 282
Smoking. *See* Tobacco usage
Snyderman, Kenzie, 159–160
Socializing, 24, 42. *See also* Friendships
Social networking, 285
  online, 6, 50, 278–280, 287 (*See also Facebook.com*)
Social organizations, 284
Social personality type, 238(*t*)
Social responsibility, 48
Social science texts, 135
Solutions to problems. *See* Problem solving
Songs, as memory aids, 152, 157
Sororities and fraternities, 284, 298
Sources of information, 209. *See also* Research
  bias in, 222
  citing, 223–224
  electronic, 214, 217–220, 221, 225
  evaluation of, 220–223
  primary, 132
Southern Illinois University, Core Institute at, 328, 329
Spanish language, 294
Speaking, 15, 124, 183, 184, 194–206
  building experience, 204–205
  class participation, 106–107
  GUIDE checklist, 198–202
  PREP formula for, 202
  steps in preparing for, 194–197
  voice and body language, 197–198
Special-interest groups, 299
Speeches. *See* Speaking
Spelling, 77, 186, 190
Spending. *See* Money management
Standardized examinations, 174
Stanford University study, 52–53
Statistics, in speeches, 201
Stereotypes, 292, 295, 299–300
Steroid abuse, 332
Stimulants, 331–332
  caffeine, 163, 312, 312(*t*)
STIs (sexually transmitted infections), 321, 322(*t*), 323, 324(*t*)
Stress, 26, 33, 338
  diet, exercise and, 310, 312–313
  emotional intelligence and, 46(*f*), 49, 54–55
  first-year students and, 41–42, 126
  life events scale for, 311(*t*)
  managing, 25, 146, 309–315
  memory and, 149
  sleep needs and, 313–314
  taking control and, 308, 314
  technology and, 337

Student activities, 15
  extracurricular, 33, 237, 283–285
Student Counseling Virtual Pamphlet Collection
    (University of Chicago), 288
Student newspaper, 248
Student organizations. *See* Campus organizations
Student profiles
  adult students, 231–232, 273–274, 281
  critical thinking, 83–84
  diversity, 289–290
  emotional intelligence, 41–42
  engagement in learning, 101–102
  first-year, 3–4
  learning styles, 59–60
  money management, 255–256
  reading skills, 125–126
  research skills, 207–208
  study skills, 143–144
  test taking, 159–160
  time management, 19–20
  wellness and, 307–308
  working in college, 255–256
  writing skills, 183–184
Students, 40, 96, 254. *See also* Adult students;
    First-year students
  help from, 119, 124, 142, 182, 190
  online courses and, 147
  projects/competitions by, 244–245
  second-year, 241(*t*)
  third-year, 241(*t*)–242(*t*)
  transfer, 7, 60, 242–243
Student services. *See* Campus resources
Study abroad, 9, 244, 304
Study groups, 15, 97, 102, 124
  brainstorming and, 89
  collaboration with, 146, 155
  feedback from, 137
  homework and, 119
  preparing for oral exams in, 171
  reviewing with, 129
  take-home tests and, 173
  test preparation and, 163–164, 175–176, 179
Studying, 23, 125, 143–158
  building experience, 156–157
  flash cards and, 128, 129, 143–144, 153, 164
  high school *vs.* college, 3
  learning style and, 77
  library as location for, 131, 216
  memory and, 147–154
  reducing distractions in, 33–34
  routine for, 34
  setting goals for, 31, 145
  student profile, 143–144
  "2-for-1" rule, 28, 37
  understanding and remembering, 144–146
  VARK results and, 65
Substance abuse, 325–334
  alcohol, 325–329, 338
  tobacco, 329–330, 331(*t*)
Suicide prevention, 316, 338
Summaries
  long-term memory and, 154
  in note taking, 108, 118
  in reading, 126–127
  in textbooks, 134

Super Memory, Super Student: How to Raise Your Grades in 30 Days (Lorayne), 158
Supplemental Instruction (SI) classes, 114, 118
Supplemental reading material, 113, 137, 139
Support networks, 47–48. *See also* Study groups
Survival Guide for High School and College Students with ADD or LD (Nadeau), 80
Syllabus, 42, 105
    exam dates on, 160, 162(*f*)
    readings and, 125
Symbols
    in foreign languages, 171
    in math and science texts, 133, 134, 135, 169
Synthesis, in research process, 223, 225
Syphilis, 322(*t*)

T

Tactile learners, 104, 118
Take-home tests, 171, 173
Teaching styles, 60, 73, 75, 77, 104. *See also* Instructors
Teamwork, 147, 246. *See also* Collaboration; Study groups
    critical thinking and, 89, 97
Technology support center, 228
Tech (technology) tips. *See also* Computers; Electronic headings; Internet
    blog writing, 188
    branch out, 74
    computer skills, 8
    e-books, 136
    get organized, 35
    for health, 320
    note taking, 115, 116–117
    online honesty, 279
    online research, 215
    online tests, 172
    research wisely, 93
    stay connected, 50
    stress and, 337
    volunteering, 302
    for wealth and security, 268
Term assignment preview, 26, 27(*f*)
Terminology, in textbooks, 135, 138
Test anxiety, 42, 173–176, 179, 314
Testimony, in speeches, 201
Tests and exams, 6, 11, 26, 159–182
    building experience for, 180–181
    cheating on, 177
    comparing notes for, 118
    computerized, 170, 174
    essay questions, 165–166, 167(*t*)
    fill-in-the-blank questions, 168
    laboratory, 170–171
    machine-scored, 170
    matching questions, 168–169
    multiple-choice questions, 166, 168, 168(*f*)
    online, 172
    open-book and open-note, 171
    practice exams, 59
    preparing for, 96, 154, 160–164, 179
    problem-solving, 169–170
    recall column and, 108
    reviewing for, 131
    student profile, 159–160
    take-home, 171, 173
    taking, 164–169

textbooks as sources for, 132
true/false questions, 168
types of, 169–173
Texas State University, 125
Textbooks, 126, 132–137. *See also* Reading
    e-books, 136
    marking, 129, 130(*f*)
    math and science, 133–135
    referring to visuals in, 115
    social science and humanities, 135
Text messaging, 36, 50, 193, 194
Thesis statement, writing, 189–190, 191(*f*)
Thinking personality type, 69–70, 71. *See also* Critical thinking; Positive thinking
Third-year students, career and, 241(*t*)–242(*t*)
Time management, 11, 19–40, 42, 126, 234. *See also* Procrastination; Schedules; To-do lists
    blocks for reading, 131
    calendars, 15, 26, 27(*f*), 35, 42
    choices and values in, 20, 21–22
    class schedules, 28, 29(*f*), 30–34
    distractions and, 33–34, 37
    family and, 281
    goal setting for, 21
    organizational tools for, 19–20, 26–30
    overextension and, 33
    respecting others' time, 36
    setting priorities and, 20, 24–25
    staying focused and, 25
    student profile, 19–20
    studying, 155
    taking control and, 20–25
    tech tips, 35
    in tests and exams, 160, 165, 171
    weekly timetable, 15, 28, 29(*f*), 37
    writing and, 190–191, 193
Tobacco usage, 308, 329–330, 331(*t*), 335, 338
To-do list, 23, 24, 28, 30(*f*), 35, 37, 42, 163
Tolerance.org, 306
Topic, narrowing, 187, 189, 212–213, 219
Transferable skills, 245. *See also* Skills
Transfer students, 7, 60, 242–243
Transportation costs, 260
Trent University, Ontario, 313
Trichomoniasis, 322(*t*)
TRIO program, 60
True/false question tests, 168
Truman College, 59, 60
Truth, consequences and, 86, 87
Tufts University, 207, 316, 319
Tutors, 102, 119, 124, 138, 155
    exams and, 164, 182
12 Angry Men (Rose), 100
Twitter, 278, 287

U

Underlining, in textbooks, 129, 130(*f*)
Underscoring, of notes, 106
United Way Office, 272
Universities. *See* Colleges
University of Alaska Anchorage, 159
University of Chicago Press, 224, 288
University of Massachusetts, Boston, 274, 282
University of Michigan, study by, 330, 331
University of North Carolina–Wilmington, 83–84

University of Phoenix, 183
University of Texas Counseling Center, 288
Use Your Perfect Memory (Buzan), 158

V

Values, personal, 90, 106, 212, 292
    career choice and, 236, 239, 240
    time management and, 20, 21–22
VARK (Visual, Aural, Read/Write, Kinesthetic) learning styles
    inventory, 59, 61–65, 66
Verbal/linguistic intelligence, 72
Viewpoint. *See* Points of view
Visual aids, 60, 114, 116, 195, 196(*f*). *See also* PowerPoint
    presentations
Visualization, 150, 152–153(*f*), 314
Visual learners, 61, 65, 74, 103, 144
    associations and, 129
    mapping and, 127, 152–153, 153(*f*)
Visual/spatial intelligence, 72, 73
Vocabulary, 135, 138, 139, 171
Voice and body language, 197–198
Volunteering, 244, 285, 302
Volunteer Match, 285

W

Wants *vs.* needs, in budget, 259
Web conference, 50
Web sites
    See also Internet; Online resources
    academic code on, 178
    attention disorders, 76
    blogs, 50, 89, 93, 188
    career, 249, 254
    class materials on, 105, 111, 114, 115
    college, 96
    employment information, 248
    evaluating information on, 91, 93, 100, 222–223
    financial aid, 260
    fitness and health, 320
    healthy eating, 318
    library, 214
    research on, 215, 218, 219–220
    social networking, 6, 278–280
Weekly timetable, 15, 28, 29(*f*), 37
Weight management, 312, 316, 319
Wellness, 10, 15, 307–338. *See also* Stress
    eating habits, 307–308, 310, 316–318
    emotions and, 58, 310
    exercise, 162, 312–313, 320

    mental health, 51, 52, 315–316, 335, 338
    nutrition and weight management, 316–319
    sexual health, 319, 321–325, 335
    sleep needs and, 313–314
    student profile, 307–308
    substance abuse and, 325–334
    unhealthy habits, 23
Wheel maps, 127–128, 128(*f*)
Wikis, 50, 93
Word choices, in speeches, 198
Word processing programs, 8, 39, 116, 141
Working, in college, 12, 24, 247–251, 285
    advantages and disadvantages of, 264–265
    building résumé for, 248, 250
    interviewing, 250–251
    off-campus jobs, 247–248
    on-campus jobs, 15, 232, 244, 247, 264, 284
    student profile, 255–256
Work-life balance, 159
Work-study award, 247, 261
World Is Flat, The (Friedman), 232
World Wide Web, 218. *See also* Internet; Online resources;
    Web sites
Writing, 15, 183–194, 203
    audience and, 184, 193–194
    avoiding plagiarism in, 192
    building experience, 204–205
    citing sources used in, 223–224
    exploratory *vs.* explanatory, 187–188
    formal *vs.* informal, 184, 193–194
    freewriting, 186–188, 189
    narrowing topic in, 187
    process in, 189–191, 193
    read/write learners, 59, 61, 65, 150–151
    student profile, 183–184
    tech tip for, 188
Writing center, 18, 192, 194, 206
Writing disorders, 76–77

Y

*Your Memory: How It Works and How to Improve
    It* (Higbee), 158
Yuen, Lenora, 22

Z

Zen and the Art of Motorcycle Maintenance
    (Pirsig), 187
Zero-tolerance policies, 300
Zinsser, William, 185